AF852770

Data Engineering Crash Course

Learn practical pipeline engineering, from architecture design to cloud analytics

Vipin Naudiyal

www.bpbonline.com

First Edition 2027

ISBN: 978-93-78545-092

LIMITS OF LIABILITY AND DISCLAIMER OF WARRANTY

To View Complete
BPB Publications Catalogue
Scan the QR Code:

www.bpbonline.com

Dedicated to

My beloved Parents

Laxmi Devi and Saklanand Naudiyal

and Inspired by my best friend,

my wife Vaishali, and my daughter Noah

About the Author

Vipin Naudiyal is a seasoned technology leader with over 16 years of experience in software development, automation, and digital transformation. Currently, he is working as the director of digital transformation in one of the leading business process management organizations. He leads GenAI-driven projects and architects enterprise-scale solutions across diverse industries including BFSI, travel, shipping, and logistics.

He has worked with leading organizations like Schneider Electric, General Electric, and Emerson Electric, and has driven the development of several innovative technology solutions.

Vipin holds a postgraduate diploma in data engineering from IIT Jodhpur, and in this book, he shares practical insights to help aspiring data engineers build real-world, job-ready skills.

About the Reviewers

- **Kaushik Ramachandran** is a seasoned technical leader at Amazon, boasting nearly a decade of expertise in architecting high-scale distributed systems and robust data security frameworks. A visionary behind flagship projects like *Buy with Prime* and *Kindle Create*, Kaushik has been at the forefront of innovations in e-commerce platform engineering specializing in **identity and access management** (**IAM**), cybersecurity, and AI automation. He holds two U.S. patents for his groundbreaking work in attribute-based access control and automated digital content processing.

  An entrepreneur at heart, Kaushik successfully launched three startups before the age of 25, earning him titles such as one of India's youngest CEOs and a *child prodigy* in technology. At Amazon, he oversees 2 e-commerce platform teams and has been instrumental in scaling multi-tenant services to handle the high scale of US Merchants and Prime members using the Buy with Prime product. Recognized with the Amazon Inventor Award and granted the EB2-NIW visa for his exceptional contributions to the tech landscape, Kaushik is also a top-tier mentor, ranking in the top 1% of creators on Topmate.

- **Brijraj Limbad** is an AI and data leader with deep experience in designing and delivering next-generation solutions that create measurable business value for CXOs and executive teams. He leads AI, agentic, and data services, helping organizations apply AI in practical, scalable, and outcome-driven ways across industries.

  Brijraj has helped launch AI and data systems for Fortune 500 organizations, co-authored thought leadership on AI innovation, and built strategic partnerships that strengthen market impact. He works closely across data, AI, strategy, product, and business teams to develop solutions that are resilient, scalable, and aligned to long-term growth.

  He is also a frequent speaker at major industry events, where he shares perspectives on AI and data transformation, enterprise adoption, and innovation at scale. At Deloitte Consulting, Brijraj focuses on helping organizations turn emerging AI capabilities into practical results, measurable outcomes, and sustainable growth.

- **Mayuri Dekate** is a Technical Operations Manager at Amazon Web Services with over a decade of experience in cloud support engineering and data operations. She leads a team of engineers supporting AWS data and analytics services including Amazon OpenSearch, Kinesis, MSK, Amazon QuickSight, Kendra, and AppFlow.

Mayuri specializes in cloud support operations, quality frameworks, and data-driven decision making. She is passionate about bridging the gap between technical engineering and business outcomes, and brings a practitioner's perspective to her work as a technical reviewer.

She holds multiple industry certifications and is an active contributor to the broader technology community through speaking engagements, academic publishing, judging industry award programs, and professional mentorship.

Acknowledgement

There are a few people I want to thank for the continued and ongoing support they have given me during the writing of this book. First and foremost, I would like to thank my best friend, who happens to be my wife, for continuously encouraging me to write this book. I could never have completed this book without her support.

I am grateful to the postgraduate diploma in data engineering course that is provided by IIT Jodhpur in collaboration with Futurense Technologies for providing all the logistics support and the course material that contributed to this work. I am especially thankful for the faculty members who put their heart and soul into teaching and invest their valuable time in providing us with assignments and guiding us in the right direction. My gratitude also goes to the team at BPB Publications for being supportive enough to provide me with enough time to finish the book and help me in sorting the challenges that I faced during my book writing journey.

Preface

Since the speed of the adoption of **artificial intelligence** (**AI**) and the innovation around it is increasing at a rapid rate. Each enterprise is trying to figure out technology-led transformation using AI so that the daily operations become efficient, fast, and have as low a cost as possible; because of this, the jobs in AI, **machine learning** (**ML**) domains are increasing day by day. The success of any AI and ML project depends on many factors, such as the right team, the right algorithms, the right tools, and the right infrastructure, but one very important factor is understanding the data and processing it for AI or ML. AI/ML works on the simple phenomenon *garbage in, garbage out*; if the data is good, chances of us getting good results are high and vice versa.

This is why data engineering is a complete field in itself, which guides the engineers to know what the best way is to pick the right data, assess the quality, transform it into the correct format, and create a robust and reliable data pipeline, so that it helps the algorithms to achieve the best results for the organizations and helps them achieve the expected results.

This book is a crash course that covers the fundamental understanding of data engineering and the related concepts. Readers would not only understand the entire data engineering lifecycle in detail but also learn about the building blocks that make it possible. This book also covers the different architectures that are recently used in the industries, various types of tools and services that are available in the market, and frameworks that help in making a robust and reliable data pipeline.

This book covers hands-on examples involving different cloud components, databases, Python, and several industry-standard tools available in the market. These practical exercises help readers become familiar with the technologies and enable them to effectively use these tools to achieve the desired business outcomes.

This book is divided into 16 chapters. They will have a basic knowledge of data engineering, understand the different data source systems, learn the data ingestion process, and know more about different types of storage where the transformed data can be stored. The details are listed in the following:

Chapter 1: Basic Understanding of Data Engineering- This chapter will introduce the readers to the concept of data, data engineering, and a complete understanding of the end-to-end lifecycle of data engineering. In this, readers will learn about data generation, data ingestion, data storage, data transformation, data usage, and data management in the entire lifecycle.

This chapter will also help the readers to understand different job roles that exist today in the data science industry and how they all come together and align on a specific project in an organization.

Chapter 2: Designing a Data Architecture- This chapter will help the readers to understand data architectures and introduce various popular data architecture frameworks. The chapter will guide you in designing an effective data architecture, which is the foundation of any data science project. The reader will understand different data modellings such as the conceptual model, the logical model, and the physical model. The chapter will also cover the different data architectures including data warehouse, data lake, lambda architecture, Kappa architecture, etc., that readers may potentially choose for their business needs.

Chapter 3: Data Generation in Source System- This chapter explains the meaning of data generation, different categories of data, based on different parameters such as structure, nature, source, etc. The readers would also learn about the different types of data sources with examples such as files, APIs, **online transaction processing** (OLTP), **online analytical processing** (OLAP), databases, etc.

Chapter 4: Data Ingestion- This chapter introduces the readers to the fundamental understanding of data ingestion and its complete lifecycle, how the data pipeline works, and how ingestion becomes a part of **extract, transform, and load** (ETL). It also explains the types of data ingestion, such as batch data ingestion and stream data ingestion, and the different aspects that need to be considered while setting up the ingestion process. The chapter will emphasize different ways of data ingestion which are currently done in the industry, some of them mentioned in the chapter are database connection, full or change data capture, APIs, EDIs, webscraping, Webhooks, etc.

Chapter 5: Data Transformation- After understanding the data ingestion in the previous chapter, the reader will be able to learn about the concept of data transformation in this chapter. This chapter covers topics such as data sourcing, **exploratory data analysis** (EDA), **confirmatory data analysis** (CDA), summary statistics, etc. Readers will learn various techniques that are used to analyze the pattern in the data using visualization, and will learn about data cleaning methodologies such as handling missing values, handling outliers, handling inconsistent values, etc. The chapter will also introduce some important aspects of feature engineering, correlation, and regression analysis.

Chapter 6: Statistics in Data Engineering- This chapter covers the statistical analysis techniques that are applied once data is processed, and the decision-making is done based on the statistical outcome. All the important techniques that are currently being used in the industry are covered in this chapter, including inferential analytics, hypothesis testing, and critical value analysis. The chapter also covers the concept of probability and how it is useful in data engineering, along with topics such as normal distribution and the central limit theorem.

Chapter 7: Introduction to Data Storage- This chapter covers the fundamentals of data storage and explains the key factors in choosing the right data storage for the expected business outcome. It covers various types of data storage systems and also introduces readers to the concept of data modelling such as conceptual, logical, and physical data modelling. The chapter also covers the basics of DBMS and big data and explains the architecture of Hadoop in detail.

Chapter 8: Practical Guide to Data Storage- This chapter introduces readers to various modern databases and cloud-based data storage solutions widely used in data engineering and analytics. The chapter covers relational, NoSQL, in-memory, and data warehousing technologies, providing an overview of their architecture, use cases, and key features. Readers will learn the fundamentals of platforms such as Google BigQuery, Google Bigtable, SQLite, MongoDB, Redis, Amazon RDS, and Amazon Redshift.

Chapter 9: Introduction to Machine Learning- The chapter covers the basic understanding of machine learning and explains its applications in the real-world. The readers will learn about different types of machine learning algorithms, such as supervised learning, unsupervised learning, reinforcement learning, and deep learning. This chapter also covers the framework that will help the data scientists select the right algorithm for their business needs. Readers will also learn about MLOps, which explains the different phases of the complete machine learning lifecycle.

Chapter 10: Understanding Cloud Computing- This chapter concentrates on the fundamentals of cloud computing, including the various service models and deployment models used in cloud environments. This chapter will help readers to be able to decide the best components for their requirements that will be in line with the cost vs the outcome. This chapter also covers the current issues that also exist in the real business world, where the limitations of technology and requirements of the customers have to be addressed.

Chapter 11: Mapping Technologies in Data Engineering Lifecycle- This chapter focuses on the key architectural and strategic considerations involved in designing and implementing data engineering solutions. Readers will learn how factors such as team size and capabilities, speed to market, interoperability, cost versus business value, and location of deployment influence technology and design decisions. The chapter also covers important decision points such as build or buy, monolith or modular, serverless or server-based, which will benefit readers in understanding what the key factors are that need to be considered before taking business decisions. In addition, readers will also explore optimization and performance considerations in data engineering as well as the important undercurrents that are unavoidable in any data science project.

Chapter 12: Key Tools Powering Modern Data Engineering- This chapter provides the basic working knowledge of all the useful tools that are mandatory for any data engineer to learn so that they can use them and enhance their knowledge in order to improve the result for themselves or their organizations. These tools include SQL, Python, Hadoop, Apache Spark, Apache Hive, Apache Kafka, Apache Airflow, Databricks, and Docker. This chapter also introduces the readers to the major cloud platforms, including AWS, Azure, and GCP, and their various offerings.

Chapter 13: Understanding Stream Analytics- This is a brief introduction to stream data analytics to make readers understand how a stream is different from static data, what all should be handled differently when we have huge data coming in continuously, and we need to predict the outcome in near real-time. How are the classification or clustering algorithms in the stream data world different from conventional machine learning algorithms? This chapter also covers some challenges that are faced by the data engineers while processing the stream output, how they mitigate these challenges, and various real-world use cases of stream analytics.

Chapter 14: Data Governance and Security- This chapter covers the fundamentals of data governance, a typical data governance organization structure that defines the roles as the user of the data, protector of the data, steering committee etc., all the data governance activities that talk about what are laws that are applicable for keeping the data, how to make data accessible to our applications without compromising on the privacy of the customers or individuals, how the data is stored, in what format, when the data to be washed away permanently. This chapter also covers the understanding of the **General Data Protection Regulation** (**GDPR**) and explains how it works and what the consequences can be if the personal data is compromised. In addition, the chapter covers data protection regulations in the USA and India and provides a detailed comparative analysis of all three regulatory frameworks.

Chapter 15: Core Concepts of Business Analytics- This chapter covers different aspects of business analytics, which is the fundamental step before working on the data. It provides a thought process to get the objective of the business and then align the right methodologies and algorithms so that the results move in the direction of the customer's expectations. Readers will also learn about the various tools that are essential in business analytics, including data visualization, **statistical analysis systems** (**SAS**), and various machine learning tools that can help in building, training, testing, and deploying the ML models. In addition, the chapter also introduces some of the renowned cloud platforms, along with R, Python, and SQL, which are widely used for data analytics. Readers will also be introduced to the maturity stages in analytics, along with some real-life examples.

Chapter 16: Business Analytics Implementation and Problem Solving- This chapter introduces some practical techniques that are used in business analytics and their importance in critical decision-making processes. These techniques involve seasonality analysis, trend analysis, comparative analysis, value-based analysis, correlation analysis, time series analysis, and regression analysis. The chapter also presents a detailed real-world use case demonstrating how the techniques covered in the chapter can be applied effectively in practical business scenarios.

Code Bundle and Coloured Images

Please follow the link to download the
Code Bundle and the ***Coloured Images*** of the book:

https://rebrand.ly/e37g5dn

The code bundle for the book is also hosted on GitHub at
https://github.com/bpbpublications/Data-Engineering-Crash-Course.
In case there's an update to the code, it will be updated on the existing GitHub repository.

We have code bundles from our rich catalogue of books and videos available at https://github.com/bpbpublications. Check them out!

Errata

We take immense pride in our work at BPB Publications and follow best practices to ensure the accuracy of our content to provide an indulging reading experience to our subscribers. Our readers are our mirrors, and we use their inputs to reflect and improve upon human errors, if any, that may have occurred during the publishing processes involved. To let us maintain the quality and help us reach out to any readers who might be having difficulties due to any unforeseen errors, please write to us at: errata@bpbonline.com

Your support, suggestions and feedback are highly appreciated by the BPB Publications' Family.

Piracy

If you come across any illegal copies of our works in any form on the internet, we would be grateful if you would provide us with the location address or website name. Please contact us at business@bpbonline.com with a link to the material.

If you are interested in becoming an author

If there is a topic that you have expertise in, and you are interested in either writing or contributing to a book, please visit www.bpbonline.com. We have worked with thousands of developers and tech professionals, just like you, to help them share their insights with the global tech community. You can make a general application, apply for a specific hot topic that we are recruiting an author for, or submit your own idea.

Reviews

Please leave a review. Once you have read and used this book, why not leave a review on the site that you purchased it from? Potential readers can then see and use your unbiased opinion to make purchase decisions. We at BPB can understand what you think about our products, and our authors can see your feedback on their book. Thank you!

For more information about BPB, please visit www.bpbonline.com.

Join our Discord space

Join our Discord workspace for latest updates, offers, tech happenings around the world, new releases, and sessions with the authors:

https://discord.bpbonline.com

Table of Contents

CHAPTER 1
Basic Understanding of Data Engineering

Introduction

In the current ecosystem, where software has become a commodity, people have started treating software as a tangible thing. They are happily investing a lot of their capital in software solutions that help them optimize their daily tasks, entertain them, and save their time. *MS Word, MS Excel,* and *Netflix* are some of the renowned names. Similarly, organizations have also adopted several tools and utilities that help them in providing operational efficiencies and cost effectiveness.

It has been years now that these software development organizations have collected huge data, and now they are eyeing to leverage this data to serve their existing customers in a better way and market themselves as someone who understands their customers best, to attract potential customers. The objective is to serve the customer before they ask for it, and this can only be possible if they have the right analysis of their past data and choices. Using this analysis, they can offer great products or services to their customers.

The data that is collected must be handled in such a way that the end results will have the right analysis and decisions. So, in this chapter, we will cover the basic understanding of data engineering and its current challenges. It also explains each step of the data engineering lifecycle in detail by providing real-world examples and shows how they fit in the complete data lifecycle.

Since the data goes through multiple phases and each phase requires a unique set of skills, this chapter explains these phases in detail and the boundaries, where one job role finishes and another starts.

Structure

The chapter covers the following topics:

- Data engineering
- End-to-end lifecycle of data

- Data engineering solution architecture
- Data management
- Job roles in the data lifecycle
- Tools and skills required for data engineering

Objectives

By the end of this chapter, you will be able to understand the basic concept of data and the current outlook of organizations on the collected data. You will get clarity about the fundamental reason for data engineering getting so much attention and how it has become one of the critical jobs in the market. By reading this chapter, you will have a fair idea about what is the intention of this book in totality, since each important topic has been touched upon at a very high level. You will also know about the different sources of data, where they can be stored, what the multiple stages of data processing are before actual consumption, what the objective of this whole exercise is, and lastly, what happens to the data when the expected work is completed. By reading this chapter, you will get clarity on the different job roles that are involved in different stages, and what tools you should familiarize yourself with that are important for working in this field.

Data engineering

As we know, engineering is the use of science and logic to make things better. In a similar way, data engineering applies these principles to make raw data usable and valuable. It focuses on building infrastructure and processes to collect, store, transform, and deliver the valuable data. Before diving into its concepts, it is important to first understand what data is and why it plays such a crucial role in organizations.

Data

Data is potential information in raw form. Any text, such as a name, number, date, or an image or a video, will be called data that can be used to get potential information.

The following table has some text; we will try to extract information:

Name	David Wilson
Age	25
City	Phoenix

***Table 1.1**: This table shows the personal information of an employee*

The inference coming out of the data is called **information**. Here, we have an employee, David Wilson, who is 25 years old and lives in Phoenix.

Defining data engineering

Data engineering is the process of setting up the data collection, filtration, transformation, and storage in a format that can be accessed by the downstream processes for further analysis.

These downstream processes can be simply an analysis of data or analytics with some tools, such as visual analysis like dashboards e.g., in a retail store, a store manager can have a daily dashboard for total sales, top-selling products, hourly sales trends, low stock items etc., or it can also be the usage in machine learning algorithms so that some predictions can be made for the future, e.g., rain prediction, stock price prediction, etc.

Data is the new oil. It is valuable, but if unrefined, it cannot really be used. It has to be changed into gas, plastic, chemicals, etc., to create a valuable entity that drives profitable activity; so must data be broken down and analyzed for it to have value.

-Clive Humby, 2006

When the mathematician *Clive Humby* made this statement in 2006, he must have been sure that data was the next big thing, and going forward, organizations would be collecting data from their millions of customers with a limited workforce and optimized techniques.

Organizations currently follow a simple rule: *Collect now and sort later*. Today, organizations may have funds, tools, and technical capability available to them to collect the data, but may not have the right talent, enough experience, or business expertise to think about the usage of this data and process it today. So, they are focusing on utilizing the power of funds and technology to collect it now in any form possible and figure it out later, once they have enough experience and people who will use their experience and brains to figure out a business out of this data. Earlier, social media platforms were collecting the data without any business plans, but later they came up with multiple monetization schemes such as ad targeting, social graph analysis, recommendation systems, etc., which made them one of the richest companies in the world.

The challenge in the current situation is the way the data is being created or the sources of data. As shown in *Figure 1.1*, earlier, the data sources were limited, where it was mainly generated and processed by the experts belonging to a specific field, due to which the source and quality of the data were controlled. E.g., news articles were created by specific companies, blogs were written by some specific set of people, websites were created or curated by mature organizations with multi-level filtering; whereas, nowadays, due to democratization of the technology, tools, or applications, the power is with the common man to create the content and share instantly, such as news, travelogue, political viewpoint and many other niche which different people are working on basis their interests.

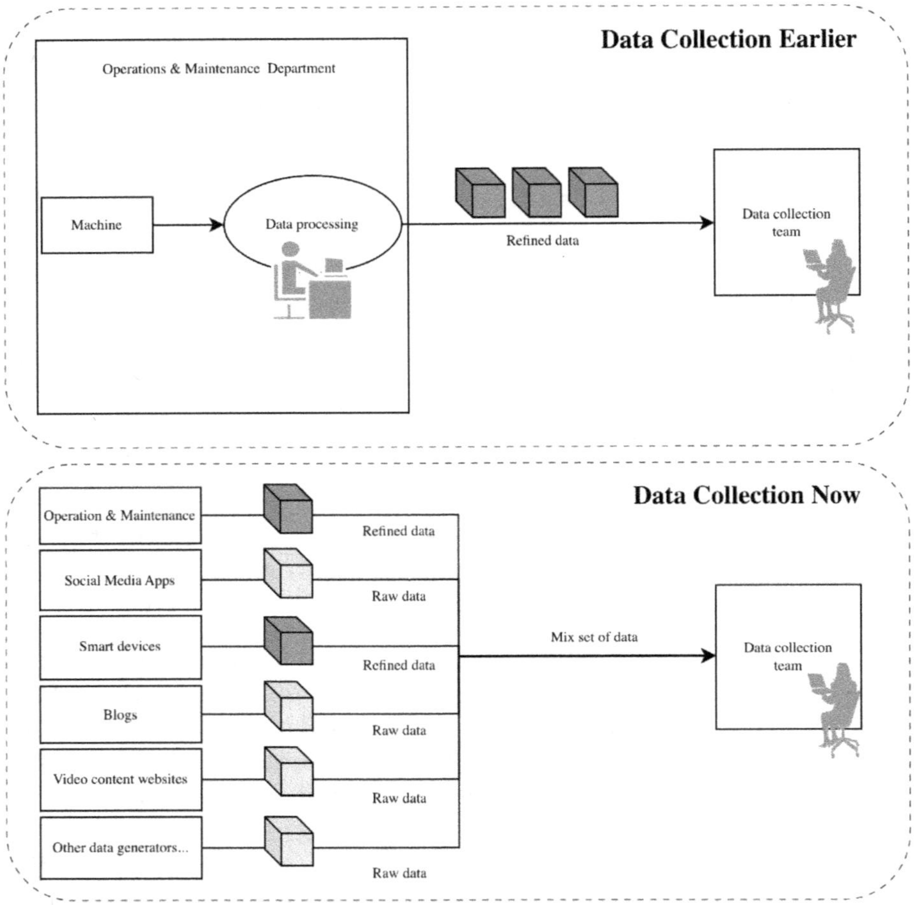

***Figure 1.1**: Difference in data generation and collection, earlier and now*

Apart from an exponential increase in the data creation sources, there has also been a significant surge in data creation platforms. This growth has been driven by the easy availability of interactive devices, such as personal computers, phones, tablets, smart devices, etc., and has been fueled by the low-cost and easy internet availability.

When it is seen individually, it looks to be a powerful ecosystem that many people are creating content on the go and have access to so much information at a given point in time, but if we see that collectively together to do analysis on the data and find the conclusion or information from the collected dataset, it is difficult, since the data may not be curated in the right way or expected way.

So, this gives rise to a data engineering problem, which is significant, looking at it from the broader perspective. It requires us to find the right mechanisms to take this high volume and high-velocity data from its source and convert it into a usable form, like any raw material is processed and transformed into a valuable commodity, as shown in *Figure 1.2*:

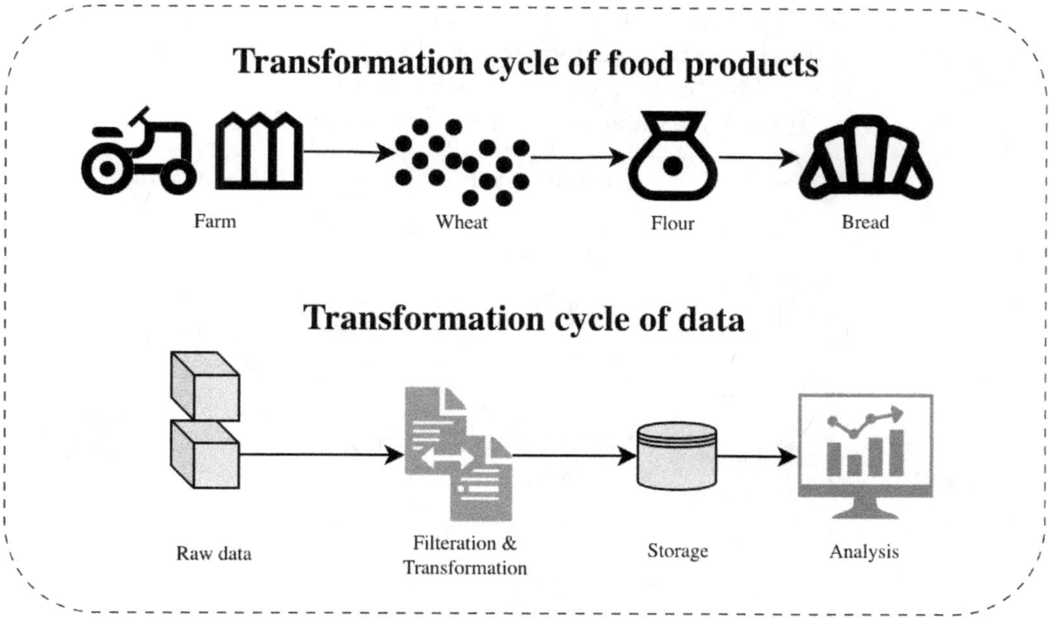

***Figure 1.2**: Showing transformation of data like any commodity, from raw to usable form*

End-to-end lifecycle of data

Every industry has its own set of rules and norms for data handling. So, the end-to-end lifecycle of the data changes based on different industries and their business expectations.

However, ideally, there are eight different stages of data:

- Data generation
- Data ingestion
- Data storage
- Data processing or transformation
- Usage or application
- Data sharing
- Data archival
- Data deletion

Let us understand each stage in detail.

Data generation

Data generation can be defined as the process of getting the data out of any machine in a storable form, as follows:

- **Industry example**: In oil refineries, where the industries need to measure the viscosity of the oil in the pipeline, there are some viscosity sensors that are used to measure the viscosity of the oil every minute or for any duration defined by the company.

This sensor data is connected to a gateway, which converts the data from one protocol to another so that it can be used for further processing. An **Internet of Things (IoT)** device is connected to this gateway that pushes the data to the cloud, where it stores the data every minute in a database, as shown in *Figure 1.3*:

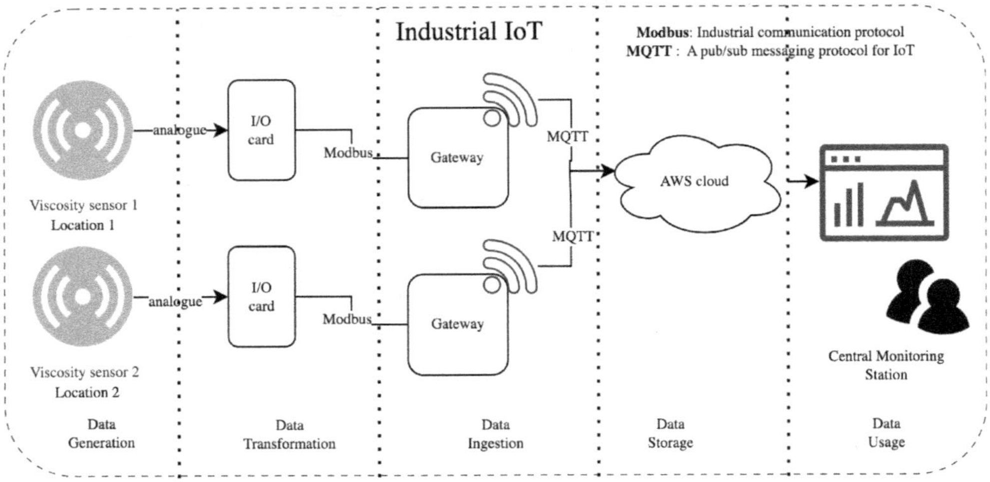

***Figure 1.3**: Showing end-to-end lifecycle of an industrial data analysis process*

The industry gets its oil viscosity data of the pipeline spread across the entire country at a single place, and this data can be used for further processing.

- **Consumer example**: All the wearable devices nowadays, such as smart watches, smart rings, etc., have sensors that continuously take our body data, e.g., temperature, heartbeat, blood pressure, sleep data, etc. This data is received as analogue values and transformed into a human-understandable format, e.g., 37°C for body temperature.

  Since all the smart wearable devices are connected with our smartphones via Bluetooth or wireless technology, which in turn are connected to the internet using 4G/5G or Wi-Fi, these smartphones act as an edge device that does this transformation and pushes the data to the central cloud, where our old data is residing, and that is how we are able to see our bodily trends of our exercise pattern, kilometers walked in a day, or average heartbeat, and so on, as shown in *Figure 1.4:*

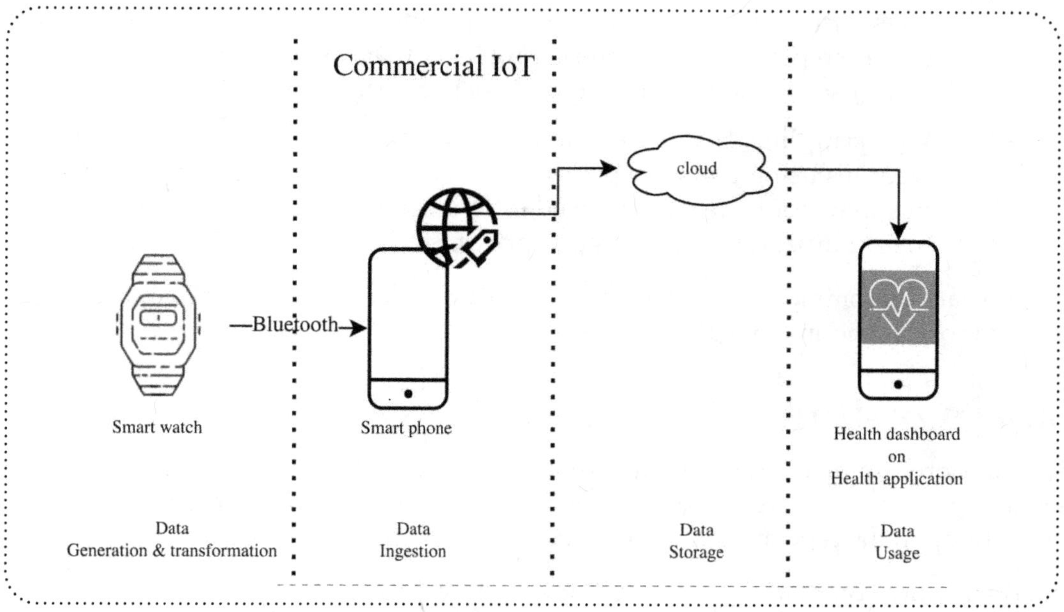

***Figure 1.4**: Showing the end-to-end lifecycle of a consumer data analysis process*

The entities that are generating data can be termed as source devices or data sources.

Both examples stated are for sensor devices with IoT, but in general, data generation can be of the following three categories:

- **Machine-generated data**: Similar to the above example, this type of data is automatically produced by machines, such as data generated from various sensors, GPS devices, mobile devices, etc.
- **Human-generated data**: These are the sources where humans interact and generate the data, such as social media platforms, media content, etc.
    - **User inputs/survey**: There can be some applications where users are required to enter data, which can be used to know the general understanding of the current outlook of people. E.g., date of birth and gender data in a particular sport can be taken from users to analyze the pattern of age and gender-based interest in a particular sport.
- **Business and transactional data**: These may be the activities happening for any particular business that the organization needs to capture in order to serve its customers better. For example, big retail chains store the transactional data of their customers so that they can use internal algorithms to categorize their customers and provide better services and offers to the customers who fall into certain categories. In addition to transactional data, organizations may also collect business-related information from several other sources.

- **Logs**: Some businesses require their systems to generate logs for all transactions, which helps them to diagnose problems that they may encounter and also to make use of historical data to analyze patterns of system behavior.
- **Web scraping**: This is the automated process of extracting data from existing websites using tools, scripts, or bots in order to generate a database. Although this may not be legally allowed, e.g., a company extracting the information of their competitor's products and prices, etc.

These are various common ways of generating data that can be further stored, processed, and utilized for organizational purposes.

Data ingestion

This is the process of taking the data from its source and storing it in a database or any other storage system. There can be various ways of implementing data ingestion, which are dependent upon the type of data availability.

There can be three types of data availability, as follows:

- **One-time**: This can be data that can be transferred only once; this is usually bulk data that may have historical data for many years. This data may be required to make some inferences about the past history.
- **Continuous**: This is real-time or near-real-time data that requires being stored in a continuous fashion. This data may need to be used for continuous monitoring or prediction based on the current flow, e.g., real-time stock price prediction based on current data.
- **Random**: This is a type of data that is not continuous and can be received at any time. The receiving system is nearly active (with some optimization) all the time and waiting for inputs for the next action.

  For example, a failure detection system, when the failure logs are received, triggers the next best action to minimize the loss.

Based on the frequency of data, the ingestion technique is selected. The following factors affect the ways of data ingestion; however, we will cover this in detail in *Chapter 4, Data Ingestion*:

- Frequency of the data.
- Pull versus push mechanism.
- Type of data.
- Sync versus async.
- Data at a fixed interval or at random.
- Future scalability.

Data storage

Data storage is a very crucial step in the data engineering lifecycle, as this is the one that can make or break the entire pipeline. Choosing the right type of storage is important and should be well thought out from a future perspective as well.

Generally, the storage systems are not frequently changed or upgraded, and if required, there may be heavy lifting that may be needed, which may pose risks of data corruption or loss, etc. The storage strategy should emphasize both the direction of storing the data and retrieving the data in an efficient manner. Thus, the decision of the appropriate data storage must involve current and future needs as well.

There are different types of storage architecture, as follows:

- **File storage**: It is simply keeping different files in a folder structure, e.g., the output of an application can be a **text file** (`.txt`) that is stored in a folder location.
- **Block storage**: The data is fixed in blocks of a fixed size and stored in the machines, e.g., databases store data in this format to achieve high performance during data retrieval.
- **Object storage**: In this, data is stored in objects irrespective of their type, e.g., structured, unstructured, pictures, video, etc. The objects are stored with their metadata and a unique ID that makes data access faster. For example, **Amazon Web Services Simple Storage Service** (**AWS S3**), Azure Blob Storage, etc.
- **Relational database**: The data is stored in relations in the form of rows and columns. It follows a fixed schema and has consistency and transactional guarantees, e.g., MySQL, Microsoft SQL (**structured query language**) Server, etc.
- **NoSQL database**: The word NoSQL depicts *not only SQL*, which means that, unlike relational databases, non-relational data can also be stored. These databases have flexible schema, and the data format, such as document, key-value pair, time series data, etc., can be stored as well, e.g., MongoDB, Redis.
- **Data warehouse**: This is a centrally located repository for structured data in huge quantities, and the data that resides here can be used for serving customers using analytics or BI dashboards, etc., e.g., AWS Redshift, Google BigQuery, Snowflake, etc.
- **Data lakes**: These are storage infrastructures for storing structured and unstructured data at a massive scale. The data directly coming from several data sources can be stored in raw format and processed later. E.g., Azure Data Lake, **Hadoop Distributed File System** (**HDFS**), etc.
- **In-memory storage**: This type of storage can typically be used for very high-performance requirements. The data is actually stored in **random access memory** (**RAM**), which gives ultra-fast access with minimum latency, e.g., Redis.

The above data storage concepts are explained in detail in *Chapter 7, Introduction to Data Storage*.

Data processing or transformation

This is the process of transforming the input data that can be used for serving the customer directly or to be given to another downstream process for further analytics.

The process will involve the following techniques:

- **Data cleaning**: This process involves removing duplicates or handling null records.
- **Aggregation**: This may involve combining more than one dataset and combining them to make a more meaningful structure. This case may arise if the data sources have a common identifier.
- **Pre-processing**: This step involves changing the data types into a format that can be used for further processing with ease, e.g., the gender column with values male/female can be converted into 0/1, which can be used in machine learning algorithms. This way, the overall performance gets optimized when we are dealing with huge amounts of data.
- **Standardization**: This is the process of keeping the format of the central repository fixed so that there is no inconsistency seen while taking the data further downstream, e.g., date format can be defined as DD/MM/YYYY or currency to be used in dollars ($) only, i.e., data coming in a different currency will be converted to dollar value.

We will cover this topic in detail in *Chapter 5, Data Transformation.*

Usage or application

Once we have the data ready in the expected format, we may need to use this data to draw an inference from it. These inferences depend upon the type of industry or domain we belong to.

Since data is difficult to understand in its raw form, it must be transformed into a pictorial or graphical format so that it can be easily grasped by the business users and the meaning can be conveyed with minimum mental processing, or in other words, cognitive power.

For example, refer to a fictional company named ABC Corp with the following table:

Month	AR (millions), ABC Corp.
Jan	53.40
Feb	60.02
Mar	51.07
Apr	81.09
May	64.87
Jun	73.99

***Table 1.2**: The monthly accounts receivable of ABC corporations*

Figure 1.5 shows an example of **accounts receivable** (**AR**) for a company, ABC corporations, which is a graphical representation of *Table 1.2*. From the data standpoint, they represent the same information, but from an inference perspective, the graph is more intuitive and shows an increase in AR within the months in an easy way.

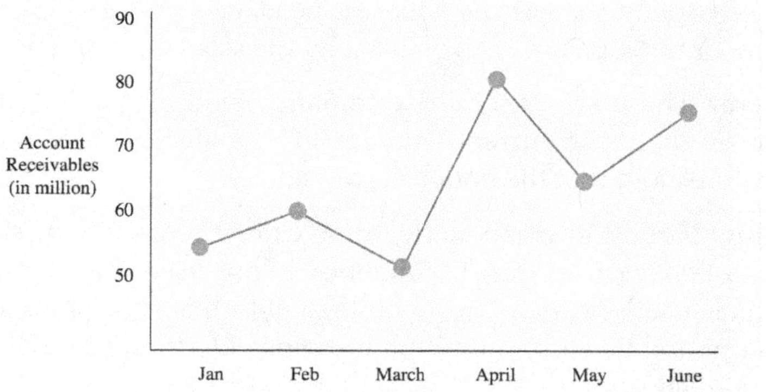

***Figure 1.5**: A graphical representation of the monthly accounts receivable for ABC corporations*

Similarly, when tables get multi-dimensional, it becomes difficult for users to understand the underlying meaning or any hidden important information that may be available in the data. So, graphical depictions come in handy and are very useful.

Nowadays, we have ready-made tools that convert large tables into simple graphs within seconds, like Excel, Power BI, Tableau, etc. These tools can be leveraged for these purposes and help people understand the meaning behind a particular behavior of the data.

Data sharing

This is a phase where readily available data is not directly used for representation but has to be passed to another system, such as an internal application, a third-party application, or for further downstream processing.

There can be various ways of data sharing:

- **Application programming interface (API)**: These are the standard formats, created to be accessed by other or third-party applications, e.g., a third-party app hits a **Representational State Transfer** (**REST**) endpoint of our server, and the server responds with a **JavaScript Object Notation** (**JSON**) file, containing the requested data.

- **OAuth**: OAuth enables third-party applications to access customer data in a secure manner, only after explicit user consent is granted. Instead of sharing credentials, users authorize the applications to access specific data. This ensures controlled and consent-based access to customer information.

- **Report**: These can be meaningful representations that can be generated from the data and shared with customers directly. The frequency of sharing depends upon the business needs, e.g., daily, weekly, monthly report, or incident-triggered report.

- **Data mart**: This is a focused subset of data warehouses for any business department, not the whole company, that serves a specific need, e.g., metrics like lead generation, lead conversion, or revenue data can be used by the sales department of an organization.
- **Email alerts**: These are generally automatic email alerts that are set up to inform the customer about the current situation. These alerts can be regular or based on a particular threshold that the data has crossed.
- **Notification**: Similar to email alerts, these can be sent directly via notification based on the data behavior. In this, the mailbox is not used, but the customer's in-house application is used for this. The advantage with this type of data sharing is that it is more prompt and gets user attention more quickly than an email, which needs to be opened and read through.

Data archival

The process of moving infrequently used data (also termed cold data) out of the active system to long-term storage systems is called data archival. This may be useful data that may not be in use for a very long time and has lost its potential to be used frequently in the future.

Still, this data may be required for any uncertain conditions or historical trend analysis. For example, the police department keeps the very old cases in the archives but does not destroy them, since they were valuable at a particular time but are not now and may be needed in the future. Similarly, the music companies keep old music videos in archives, which the current generation does not take much interest in, but these videos may be helpful for the future or changing trends.

The reason they are not kept in the current systems is that the cost of keeping this old data is higher than the return they bring to the business. Keeping the data in an archive is much cheaper and helps reduce an organization's storage costs.

However, the retrieval time for this data will be higher than that of the active system, which may vary between minutes and hours.

Some of the well-known cloud-based cold/archival storage services are AWS Glacier, Google Cloud Archive Storage, Azure Archive Storage, IBM Cloud Archive, etc., which are designed for long-term archiving and backup.

Data deletion

The process of removing unwanted data from the system is called **data deletion**. This data may have expired or may contain some information that should not be used.

In the current ecosystem, this is done very rarely, since archival is believed to be the right and safe practice, but these actions may also be dependent upon the compliance requirements, such as the **General Data Protection Regulation** (GDPR), the **Health Insurance Portability and Accountability Act** (HIPAA), etc.

The data can be **personally identifiable information** (**PII**) or **sensitive personal information** (**SPI**), which, at the organizational level, does not need to be shared or stored if it is not in use or if the user has explicitly asked for removal (as per GDPR regulations).

Extract, transform, load

Extract, transform, load (**ETL**) is defined as the data pipeline process that is used to transfer the data from one system to another, and is explained as follows:

- **Extract**: Pulling the data from the source system.
- **Transform**: Cleaning, filtering, and aggregating the data.
- **Load**: Storing the transformed data in a storage location. This sits in the middle of the entire data lifecycle; refer to *Figure 1.6*:

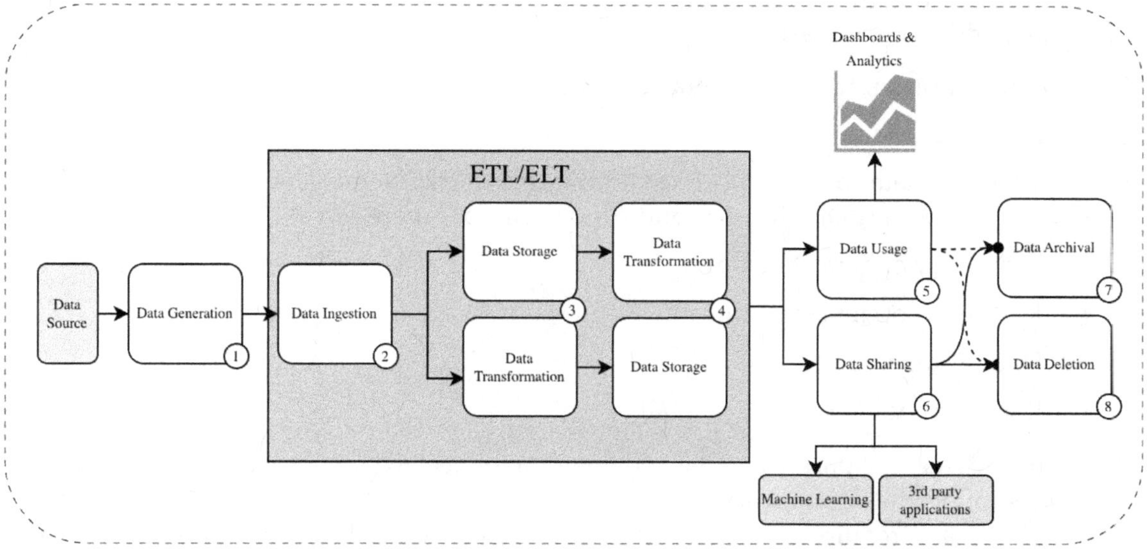

***Figure 1.6**: Showing how ETL fits in between the complete end-to-end data lifecycle*

Usually, ETL is used for more controlled or legacy systems that have defined processes and limited compute requirements. However, there is another process called **extract, load, transform** (**ELT**). In this process, the primary aim is to collect the data first and store it at a storage location, and then apply the transformation techniques, which may be applicable to the type of data received.

This is usually preferred where the data is received from multiple sources or in real-time setups that need quick ingestion. Due to this uncontrolled nature, cloud-based transformation is applied that runs directly on data warehouses or data lakes without any compute limitations.

This brings speed, scalability, and cost-efficiency as native advantages.

Some of the readily available cloud-based services are AWS Glue, Azure Data Factory, and Google Cloud Dataflow, which are fully managed, serverless ETL services that help organizations prepare and move data for analytics or any downstream processing without managing the infrastructure.

Data engineering solution architecture

This implies the design of the complete architecture of the data engineering lifecycle. Since we have already seen the data engineering lifecycle in the previous section, it would be easy to understand how to look at the complete flow from a high level.

The architects typically will understand the business requirements to conclude on the expectations from the whole exercise. The end result that the data collection will serve will have to be defined at the start so that the right tools, technology, and strategies can be applied for secure and optimized results.

Some of the important factors that may be considered include the following:

- Data source
- Type of data output, such as structures (SQL)/semi-structured (JSON, XML)/ unstructured (PDFs, images, audio)/stream (IoT, share price)
- Frequency of data generation
- Frequency of data ingestion
- Data storage
- Usage of data

This is the most crucial part of any data engineering project, where the current state and future state that support the organization's long-term strategy have to be properly considered. Since the organizational requirements change or evolve over the period, new tools arrive in the market on a daily basis, it becomes imperative to understand the architecture well, to serve the best for the current and varying requirements.

Data management

Data management usually refers to practices, processes, and tools to handle data, which also includes the compliance and policies that may be applicable based on the business requirements, location of the customers, etc.

Although we have covered the lifecycle of the data, which clearly articulates the architecture in place, there are three more aspects that need to be understood as well.

Data quality

High-quality data is a foundation of data analytics, **machine learning** (ML), and **artificial intelligence** (AI). Organizations can leverage their data for the right decision making, better services to their customers, and create new revenue streams.

There are four dimensions to the data quality, which are as follows:

- **Accuracy and integrity**: Data should be free from errors and discrepancies and should be able to represent the real-world as closely as possible. Inaccurate data can lead to wrong decisions or outputs.
- **Completeness**: Missing data can lead to voids in decision-making. So, it should be kept in mind that the data selected should contain all the important dimensions.
- **Consistent**: Inconsistencies can arise from duplicate records, conflicting values, or incompatible formats. The chosen dataset should be consistent within the system and across different systems.
- **Timeliness**: It should be noted that the data should not be old or outdated. Relevant data produces correct results or decisions.

Good quality data helps companies do proper analysis that leads to accurate decision making and hence improves their services to their existing and potential customers.

Master data management

Master data refers to the core data entities that are essential for operations and business decision-making.

The following are the six types of data in an organization:

- **Unstructured data**: Emails, white papers, and PDFs.
- **Transactional data**: Financial data such as sales, invoices, and claims.
- **Metadata**: Data about other data, such as reports, logs, and audit trails, etc.
- **Hierarchical data**: Relationships between data, such as organization structure, product lines, etc.
- **Reference data**: The data that is used for classification is called reference data, e.g., country code, currency, etc.
- **Master data**: Business fundamental data describing the key business entities, customers, products, suppliers, and locations.

Master data management (MDM) is the process of consolidating and maintaining a single, high-quality record for customers, products, vendors, research, etc., by taking the data from multiple data sources.

The master data should be consistent, up to date, and accurate. This data becomes the foundation for initial analysis, advanced analytics, and informed decision-making.

Data privacy

Data privacy can be defined as the right of an individual to know and control how their personal information is collected, used, stored, and shared. It is for protecting PII or SPI.

Since the internet has become the core of every business or any transaction between two or more people, it has become imperative to understand how the information that is being entered is used by the application's developers or the application's owners.

The most important aspect of data privacy is to make sure that the way the data is being handled follows regulatory compliance and safeguards data confidentiality. All the data privacy measures are applied with access control, data encryption, and data anonymization.

Data security is to be taken care of at both ends, internally (within the organization) and externally, to make sure only necessary information is shared and should be discarded if not required.

Importance of data privacy

The following is the importance of data privacy:

- **Customer's trust**: Respecting data privacy builds trust with customers. Once they understand and believe that a particular organization follows all the required data privacy aspects, they will be more open to sharing accurate information, and hence, this data may lead to better analytical outcomes and correct decisions.
- **Competitive advantages**: Businesses that prioritize data privacy enjoy a competitive advantage. The customers become inclined towards organizations that value and safeguard their personal data.
- **Responsibility**: This is the company's ethical responsibility to keep the customer's data private.
- **Culture**: Respecting data privacy fosters a positive culture in an organization. Employees also feel safe and trust the organizations they work for. This increases the chances of the employees sticking with these organizations a little longer.

Job roles in the data lifecycle

With the growing demand for AI/ML in the industry and the increasing complexity and scale of projects, the roles and responsibilities have become more specialized. It is no longer a common practice for one person to do everything, from start to end. Only startups or companies having a limited resource budget will get into such a way of working; most of the job roles have been broken into expertise and given specific names based on the type of work they do.

To understand the job roles in the complete data lifecycle, it is important to understand what steps are taken to complete a project, based on which the job roles are defined.

Machine learning lifecycle

In an organization, when an ML project starts, the project goes through different phases, and each phase is very critical and should be executed with utmost care so that the end result is close to the business expectations.

The following are the six phases:

1. **Business understanding**: This role requires understanding the business process and its nuances. It determines the business objective by describing the useful outcome of the project. These outcomes must be quantifiable or measurable, e.g., reduce the time of customer query resolution by 10%.

2. **Data understanding**: This role collects the initial data available in the project resources, followed by understanding the nature of the data. There are some tools and libraries that are used for this purpose, e.g., Pandas in Python.

   The objective of this phase is to describe the data and to understand the high-level properties of the dataset. Explore the data for a much deeper understanding using data visualizations like charts, bar graphs, etc. This may help to understand the behavior of data and hidden patterns. Validate the quality of data by checking the gaps and inconsistencies in the received dataset.

3. **Data preparation**: Once the structure of the data is well understood in the previous step, it is time to make the data ready for further analysis. This may involve the selection of a clean subset of data, insertion of default values, or more ambitious values for the missing data by modeling. Transforming the data into new features (if applicable) and combining the multiple datasets together to create final records.

4. **Modelling**: This phase involves selecting the modelling technique that is to be used. These techniques can be decision tree building, neural network generation, or any other. Before building the model, it is first tested for the quality and validity of results. After testing, the model is built for the prepared dataset. Finally, assess the model and, if needed, tune the model by revising parameter settings.

5. **Evaluation**: In the previous step, the testing factors were accuracy and generality of the model, whereas this step assesses the model against the business expectations and finds the gaps or reasons why the model is not up to the mark. If required, the model is retuned for business outcomes and finally approved.

6. **Deployment**: This step involves the strategy for deploying the model. How the model is to be provided to the end user is defined here, e.g., API access to the model or a direct hardware embodiment.

Some efficient ways of deployment can be through the following:

- **Quantization**: Converting a trained model from 32-bit floats to 8-bit integers, while retaining the original character of the model. This is needed to make models process faster and more efficiently without significantly sacrificing accuracy.
- **Compression**: Shrink the model size by eliminating redundant information.
- **Knowledge distillation**: Training smaller models (child) to mimic the behavior of large models (parent).

These efficient ways reduce the size of the model by a large margin without affecting the accuracy much. This helps them to be easily deployed on the client devices directly and then to run on the servers.

Job roles aligned to each phase

Based on the six phases explained, there are specific job roles, as shown in *Figure 1.7*:

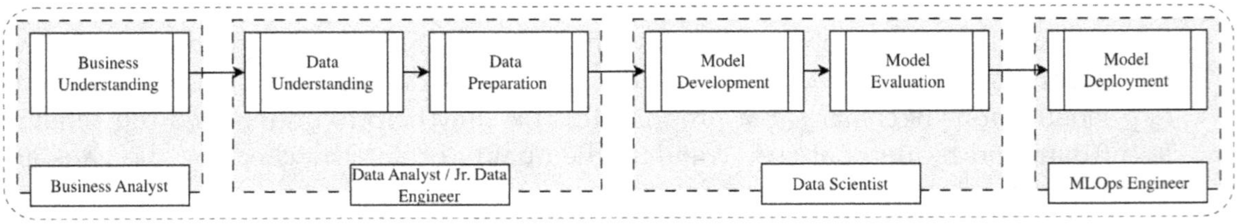

***Figure 1.7**: Job roles aligned to each phase*

The roles are explained as follows:

- **Business analyst (BA)**: Business understanding is done by a BA who makes sure that the business expectation is clear from the start and converts the business problem into a machine learning problem statement. At this stage, because of internal collaboration within the team, the tools and algorithms may also be finalized.
- **Data analyst or junior ML engineer**: This profile works on understanding the data and its underlying hidden behavior and on cleaning and transforming the data. The final dataset is the input for the model creation.
- **Data scientists**: These people actually build the machine learning models, test the models, work on hyperparameter tuning, and finally release the models based on various metrics.
- **ML infrastructure engineer or MLOps engineer**: This role is responsible for architecting the deployment of the model. Their focus is mainly on scaling and serving the model to the end user. They also contribute to handling infrastructure provisioning, model compression, and ensuring the model's availability.

There is one more role that is distinct and complementary to MLOps engineers, that of a data engineer, because this role is responsible for building and managing systems for collecting, storing, and analyzing the data at scale.

Data engineers focus on creating the infrastructure and pipeline to ensure that the data is accessible and usable by data scientists to build the models, whereas MLOps engineers focus on the deployment and management of the model in a production environment.

Apart from the aforementioned, there is a new capability emerging, which is prompt engineering or AI solutioning that enhances the existing roles across the data and AI lifecycle. This proficiency focuses on using readymade generative AI models such as GPT, Gemini, etc. The expertise of these people is in designing applications, building prompts, and orchestrating APIs to solve any customer problem, e.g., chatbots can be created using these generative AI models that answer simple to medium complex queries without human intervention.

Tools and skills required for data engineering

Data engineering as a subject is more about practical implementation than theoretical understanding. If you do not have the required skills already, you may start from here.

This section brings four fundamental knowledge areas that are imperative to learn before proceeding further:

- **Programming knowledge**: This includes the usage of any programming language that will help you to write data engineering-related programs, such as cleaning, transformation, ingestion, and creating an algorithm.
- **Database knowledge**: This includes an understanding of the basics of a **database management system** (**DBMS**) and the programming languages that are used to access the databases.
- **Dataset knowledge**: Before working on the actual data, it is important to know what real data looks like and what the potential challenges are. So, there must be a repository from which the public data or synthesized data can be downloaded and worked upon.
- **Cloud infrastructure knowledge**: Since computing power and unlimited storage space are the fundamental requirements of the data science field, it is impossible to imagine it without a cloud infrastructure. This requires you to understand the fundamental workings of the cloud and have command of any of the available cloud options.

The next few sections discuss the tools that are essential to initiate the practical work for data engineering and data science-related requirements.

Python

Python is a computer programming language that is a perfect combination of performance and features. This makes it suitable for creating simple programs to complex deep learning and AI-based projects. It is used very extensively in the industries for various solutions, quick prototyping, and production-grade implementations.

The reason behind the wide acceptability of Python is the ease of learning and the vast collection of open-source libraries, which are frequently updated by developers around the world, who are contributing to make it better day by day. You may either start by installing Python directly on your system, or refer to the link: **https://www.python.org/**

Also, you may need a user-friendly Python editor that makes it a lot easier to work on such languages and enhances the development experience, such as Visual Studio Code, PyCharm, Jupyter Notebook, etc.

If installing Python and a code editor seems too complex at this stage, Python Notebook can be used as a service provided by Google. This service is known as Google Colaboratory, or Google Colab.

It can be used by following these steps:

1. Create your free Gmail account.
2. Once account creation is successful, refer to **https://drive.google.com/drive/home**
3. Click on **New** (with the + icon).
4. Then, select **Google Collaboratory**, as shown in *Figure 1.8:*

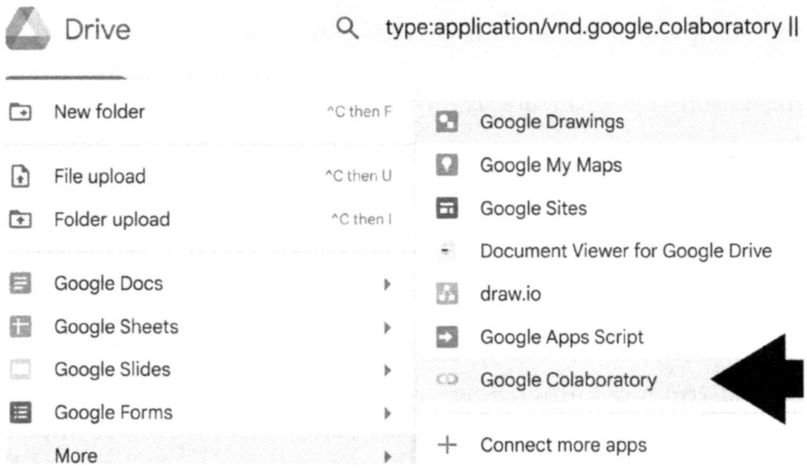

Figure 1.8: *All the free Google applications that can be seen on Google Drive*

SQL

SQL is the standard language that is used for storing, manipulating, and retrieving data from databases. This is a mandatory skill to learn if you want to make your career in data engineering, because there will be requirements to work on multiple databases and create pipelines in the future.

You may start by installing any DBMS on your system and start learning the commands from various online sources, e.g., visit *w3schools* at **https://www.w3schools.com/sql/default.asp**

Dataset repository

As we have covered the programming language to work with and SQL to store the data, the next logical step would be to get the relevant data as we progress. One of the readily available solutions is Kaggle.

This portal has more than 500K public datasets that can be leveraged to learn various machine learning techniques. It is one of the largest AI/ML communities where millions of learners, developers, and researchers have come together to contribute to this valuable source of knowledge. There are readily available models that can be deployed for various purposes.

They also conduct various competitions to motivate people around the world to create amazing algorithms and win prizes.

To visit the website, refer to the link **https://www.kaggle.com/**

Cloud infrastructure

Data science is not a new discipline and has been available since 1962. The reason it was not part of the mainstream was due to the limited data storage capabilities and the lack of sufficient computing power to handle such large volumes of data.

However, now, that has been only possible by cloud computing, which has revolutionized the whole concept of computing, shifting from small, isolated machines to large-scale distributed systems and enabling models such as **infrastructure as a service** (**IaaS**), **platform as a service** (**PaaS**), and **software as a service** (**SaaS**).

Due to this, we have nearly unlimited storage capacity and scalable computing hardware. We can easily balance between the processing power and efficiency based on the needs.

While programming knowledge gives you the ability to create different data science algorithms, and various databases give you the techniques to store and retrieve the data efficiently, cloud technology is the one that has removed all the boundaries and given us the platform where we can deploy our models, which can process gigabytes of data and show the results across the world within seconds.

You may choose to work on any of the cloud providers, such as Amazon AWS, Microsoft Azure, and Google GCP, etc.

Conclusion

This chapter provided a brief introduction to data and its sources, the best practices for storage, followed by the transformation, analysis, and management of data. Also, the readers have learned about the various job roles that exist in this area of work and what tools and skills are an integral part of the data journey.

In the next chapter, we will learn about the data architecture that has to be designed, keeping the efficiency and efficacy of the entire data lifecycle in mind. It will explain the important frameworks that exist in the market today as a reference, and also cover the important principles that need to be followed to achieve the final objectives.

References

1. **https://www.verdanttcs.com/why-data-is-the-new-oil-and-what-that-means-for-your-business/**
2. **https://www.informatica.com/products/master-data-management.html**
3. **https://www.ibm.com/think/topics/master-data-management**

Join our Discord space

CHAPTER 2
Designing a Data Architecture

Introduction

For any data engineering project in its nascent stage, the final objectives are discussed and finalized with the required stakeholders. All the important members come together and ponder upon the requirements and feasibility, which starts with understanding the sources of data, the type of data, the volume, and the variety of the data. Based on this study, appropriate tools are analyzed keeping some metrics in mind, such as data handling capacity, efficiency, optimization possibilities, and most importantly, the return on investment.

Designing the right architecture is considered to be the most important of all the stages, because once components and tools have been fully developed, and at the end, the performance of the overall solution is not up to the mark, then the overall cost of change, i.e., efforts, time, and capital, is very high.

Data architects make sure that they have all the inputs for designing the best architecture, and they keep monitoring the performance of the overall architecture while it is being made. That may help them in making changes while the system is getting built, rather than waiting till the end.

They are not only responsible for orchestrating the data collection, transformation, processing, and storage, but also for providing the data to the end user in such a manner that the internal details are least exposed, with proper abstraction. Since output must be consumed by different types of users, the architectural construct is devised, keeping the balance between standardization of output and ease of use.

This chapter will cover the fundamentals of data architecture, including understanding its components and the need for data architecture. It also explains the principles of designing a good data architecture with some real-life scenarios.

Structure

The chapter covers the following topics:

- Data architecture
- Data architecture modeling
- Examples of data architecture
- Designing effective data architecture
- Understanding the basics of data architecture

Objectives

At the end of this chapter, you will be able to understand the definition of a data architecture and how different organizations define it. You would also learn about the principles that should be followed while designing a data architecture; these principles not only cover the technical aspects of the requirements but also the tactical part of it. You will know how to create different models by analyzing the nature of data and the ways of handling it. You would also get a glimpse of different types of popular data architectures available today, and why they have been introduced, and which problem statements they have solved. You will be able to understand the fundamental differences between these architectures, which will expand your knowledge horizon and help you design the data architecture following the best practices currently available in the industry.

Data architecture

Before we define data architecture, let us understand how organizations perceive its importance:

- **IBM**: A data architecture describes how data is managed, from collection through to transformation, distribution, and consumption. It sets the blueprint for data and the way that it flows through data storage systems. It is foundational to data processing operations and AI applications.

- **Amazon**: Data architecture is the overarching framework that describes and governs an organization's data collection, management, and usage. It defines policies, data models, processes, and technologies that allow organizations to easily move data across departments and ensure it is available whenever needed, including real-time access, while fully supporting regulatory compliance.

- **SAP**: Data architecture is a blueprint for how data is used; it is the high-level structure of data and data-related resources that acts as a framework for data throughout an organization, including models, rules, and standards. With efficient data architecture, organizations track the acquisition, movement, storage, security, and accessibility of data across their IT infrastructure.

Working definition of data architecture

A data architecture is a blueprint that clearly explains how data is collected, stored, processed, and used in an organization. It is a foundation of any small or big data project and a critical component of the company's information technology infrastructure.

This involves documenting the data assets, mapping data flow, and creating an effective blueprint for complete data management to ensure proper data governance and utilization and to meet the business requirements.

To understand the data architecture in detail, let us first understand each component of it.

Refer to *Figure 2.1* to understand each component of any big data architecture:

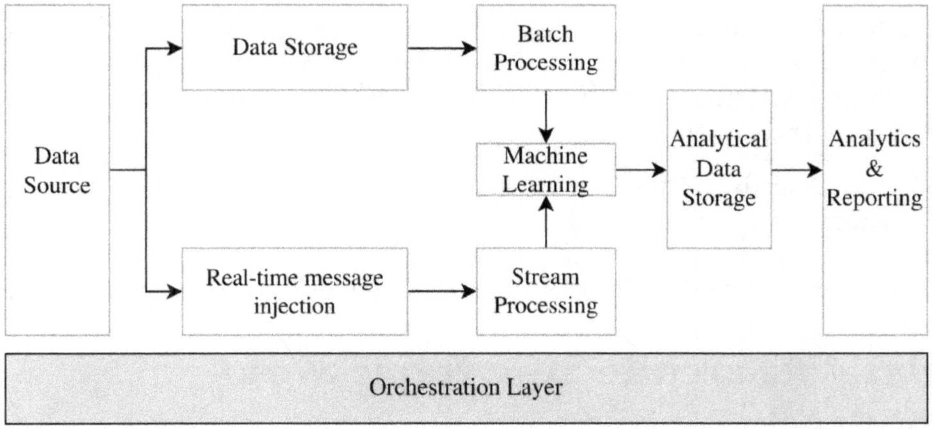

***Figure 2.1**: Components of a big data architecture*

Each component of any big architecture is as follows:

- **Data sources**: These are the sources from which raw data will be collected. These can be databases, files, and sensors. When architecting the solution for any project, the method of data collection should be the top priority.
- **Data storage**: This is the process of storing the retrieved data from the data sources in such a way that it can be made available for further analysis and processing.
- **Orchestration**: This may be defined as the automation of the movement and transformation of data between different systems. This is a very crucial component for any data architecture because it ensures data management is efficient and effective.
- **Real-time message ingestion**: This is defined as the process of capturing and bringing the data in real-time from various sources like sensors, **Internet of Things** (**IoT**) devices, etc. It focuses on the transportation and delivery of data to a system, such as a queue, buffer, or any temporary location. There are multiple tools available for real-time injection, such as Apache Kafka, Azure Event Hubs, Google pub/sub, etc.

- **Batch processing**: This process involves grouping data into sets or batches and processing them together. The processing can be trigger-based or at fixed intervals.
- **Stream processing**: This is real-time processing of data that involves transforming data and generating insights on the go. This also supports real-time decision making, generating alerts, live dashboards, and storage of the analysis to a target system. Tools like Kafka Streams, Azure Stream Analytics, Google Dataflow, etc., are used for these purposes.
- **Analytical data storage**: These are the systems that are used to store the final analysis of the data. These systems ensure the fast and efficient retrieval of the insights for the final reporting. Data warehouses, like AWS Redshift or Snowflake, are renowned tools for this purpose.
- **Analytics and reporting**: These are the tools that are helpful in reporting valuable insights to the customer in graphical formats. These applications are also known as **business intelligence** (**BI**) tools. Tableau and Power BI are some of the big names in the current ecosystem.
- **Machine learning**: These are the algorithms that are executed on historical data to automate the analysis and decision-making. There are different types of machine learning techniques, such as supervised learning, unsupervised learning, etc. We will cover them in detail in *Chapter 9, Introduction to Machine Learning*.

Popular data architecture frameworks

As we already know, the enterprise data architecture is not one-size-fits-all; there are many parameters that are considered before the adoption of any specific method. Some problems are straightforward, but a few of them are new and require an innovative way of finding solutions.

The following are some of the standardized frameworks that exist and may help in deciding the right approach:

- **The Open Group Architecture Framework (TOGAF)**: TOGAF's architectural development method process is specifically designed across four domains of enterprise architecture:
  - **Business architecture**: Keeps the mapping between a business's operational hierarchies, policies, capabilities, and initiatives.
  - **Application architecture**: This takes care of selecting the right applications to handle organizational data so that these applications can be fitted well into the larger existing infrastructure of an organization.
  - **Data architecture**: Responsible for defining the rules and standards for storing and integrating data.

- Technical architecture: Creates a blueprint for development teams by defining platforms, services, and all surrounding technology components.

- **Data Management Association-Data Management Body of Knowledge 2 (DAMA-DMBOK 2)**: It is a globally recognized framework that defines the core principles, best practices, and essential functions of data management. It serves as a universal reference for data professionals, enabling organizations to establish and maintain effective, standardized data management practices across industries.

- **Zachman framework**: It is a schema intersection between two historical classifications that have been in use for thousands of years. The first is the basic foundation of communication, the key questions: what, how, when, who, where, and why. Bringing together the answers to these questions brings clarity to explain the complex idea.

  The second concept comes from reification (in other words, realization), which means turning an abstract idea into something real or concrete. It involves steps like identifying, defining, representing, specifying, configuring, and finally creating the actual form.

  This framework is typically depicted as a bounded *6 x 6 matrix* with the key questions as columns and the reification transformations as rows.

Designing effective data architecture

As we have discussed earlier, the foundation of any solution's efficiency and efficacy is hidden in the construct of how the overall architecture of components is designed. Since there are different solutions to different problem statements, we cannot insist on a particular way of implementation. However, we can focus on some general principles that will help you design a good architecture.

The following are the nine principles that should be followed while designing the data architecture:

- **Consistency**: A well-structured data architecture ensures that the data, tools, and components are uniform across the organization. This involves standardization of data definitions and format so that it is well accepted by different components with minimum changes. Similarly, the components should be selected in such a way that they are commonly used by multiple teams and systems. Relying on common components not only brings the reliability of the overall system but also brings ease across the teams and reduces silos. For example, a well-structured and defined protocol to transform the data helps different teams to follow the common practices that reduce potential integration issues. On similar grounds, leveraging cloud components that can be shared across teams is a good choice to reduce friction within the team. Although there cannot be a one-size-fits-all category here, a judicial decision can be taken keeping consistency as a principle in mind.

- **Adaptability**: The one thing that should be considered while designing the data architecture is that *the current design is not a final design and is subject to change*. Instead of taking time in readjustment and appending a new patch to support a particular ask, the data engineer should be open to using new tools that can solve the problem much faster than a patchwork.

  The advantages of using cloud technology for your deployments give you the flexibility to be updated with new innovations, which the native-cloud system is bringing to the market almost every day. Undoubtedly, this requires constant investment of time and capital, but history tells us that, to grow and evolve, IT systems need to be adaptable to these changing technologies and willing to try new tools.

  Cloud environment does not replace traditional architecture as such, but they are better adapted with minimal issues and rollbacks.

- **Modularity**: This may also be known as plug and play approach. In this, the system is to be designed in small modules that talk to each other via an API. Generally, big-scale systems are developed by multiple teams. Each team has different capabilities and a unique way of implementation. If they have to build a large system that is built by multiple team members, which requires inter-process communication, direct access to data storage, shared memory, etc. This makes the components tightly coupled, which increases the throughput, but maintainability becomes a challenge because fixing one issue leads to a change in the existing code of another component, which may cause regression and other breakages. Thus, the maintainability of such a type of development is expensive. However, when the architecture is designed to be built in small modules, each module is developed by different teams, and all the communication between the modules happens via API calls, then all the communication happens through an abstraction layer. These abstraction layers protect the internal details, such as functions or classes, or database information.

  Another approach is to use **Service Provider Interfaces** (**SPI**), where service owners define extension points in the form of interfaces. Different teams or third-party developers can implement these interfaces to extend functionality. This reduces the direct involvement of the service owner, as the responsibility for building extensions is distributed across teams.

  The overall design becomes loosely coupled, in which internal component-level changes, code updates, and improvements are behind the abstraction layer. This helps the teams to improve and evolve their system independently, and hence, the overall maintainability of the system is easier and less expensive.

- **Security**: In the current ecosystem, when billions of people are on the internet, there have been exchanges of sensitive and personal information. While designing the architecture, it should be noted that we may have to process data that may be sensitive and cannot be shown outside. The requirement can be to show the overall inference of the analysis, but not the specific case. For example, you may work in an organization that conducts research on current health problems and has taken the data from thousands of patients. The overall inference, such as the percentage of people having a particular disease, severity level percentages, and type of symptoms, is fine, but taking the name of a patient having a particular problem is a no.

Since this data is accessible to internal engineers in the company, who are also connected to the outside world via social media or other platforms, some of them become an internal threat to the company.

As we know, most of the development happens on the cloud, and the cloud provider is responsible for the security of the cloud, but you are responsible for the security in the cloud.

Some of the security principles that need to be followed are:

- **Strong identity foundation**: Implement the principle of least privilege and enforce separation of duties with appropriate authorization.
- **Fine-grained authorization**: These access controls are provided at a detailed level based on user, resource, action, and context, rather than broad permissions.
- **Maintain traceability**: Any action done on cloud infrastructure should be traced, monitored, and alerted in real-time, and the necessary action should be taken.
- **Apply security at all layers**: Apply a defense in depth, i.e., security controls should be applicable at the edge of the network, virtual network, load balancer, computing service, operating system, and code level.
- **Protect data in transit and at rest**: The data should be classified based on sensitivity levels, and mechanisms like encryption, tokenization, and access control should be applied.
- **Automate security best practices**: Automation of security mechanisms improves the ability to scale rapidly and cost-effectively. This increases the speed of detection, investigation, and recovery.

However, security is a fundamental right of every human being, and we, as data engineers, should take the responsibility of securing this sensitive information from any unauthorized access.

- **Availability**: While designing the data architecture, we need to make sure that the data is available to the intended recipients at all times for timely and effective decision-making. This may be possible using managed services that are designed to be available all the time, which reduces the headache and concern of managing backend software and infrastructure. There are certain points to be noted, as follows:
    - **Automatic recovery from failure**: This includes monitoring of **key performance indicators (KPIs)** to make sure that the system is behaving in the expected

manner. If there are any faults or changes in the system, then certain automation can be set up that rolls back the system to a stable state or takes actions that may avoid complete system failure.

- **Avoid a single point of failure**: Generally, a large monolith system contains multiple features tightly coupled in one code base. Similarly, there may be a single hardware platform that is scaled vertically for high computing resources. This kind of architecture is prone to failing at a single point, e.g., if the machine fails, the complete system comes to a halt, or if the database connection part breaks due to too many requests at a time, then the entire code stops working.

It is better to design a data architecture that has multiple small resources than a big single resource, to reduce the impact of a single point of failure. Since managed services can be used for this type of implementation, the issue with one service is tackled independently of the other. If there is a scaling requirement for one resource, then that can be scaled without touching other services.

- **Automate changes**: Automation has always been the best practice for software systems. Manual changes or deployment of infrastructure are not only more time-consuming but also error prone. These errors are difficult to debug and frustrating. The best practice is to use automation because, first of all, it standardizes the configuration as much as possible, and second, it makes deployment/changes/repairs much faster than people can. Considering the usage of cloud for data architecture, common areas where automation can help are:

  - **Infrastructure**: The entire infrastructure provisioning can be automated using **infrastructure as code** (**IaC**). Tools like Google Cloud Deployment Manager or Terraform are used for this purpose.

  - **Continuous integration (CI)/continuous delivery (CD)**: This is the automation of build creation, testing, and deployment of the released packages on the infrastructure, which constitutes the whole system. Tools like Jenkins, Azure DevOps, and Google Cloud Build can be leveraged for this action.

  - **Automated scale up and scale down**: Based on the load requirements of the system, the scaling of the system must be controlled. When the load increases, the platform should be scaled up and scaled down as the load returns to the defined limits of normal working. By scaling up, you ensure that your system is up and running and can serve the increased number of users, while scaling down aims at reducing the cost if the number of users becomes low. For example, in mobile banking, where the number of users using the banking application increases during the day for transferring money, checking balances, fetching back statements, applying for a loan, etc., compared to the traffic at night, which has limited people working on the same. So, the servers can automatically scale up as the number of users increases and scale down as the traffic decreases. Also, the automatic scaling not only targets the number of users or load but also the

CPU or memory usage. Whenever the system identifies a shortage of resources, it scales up horizontally to manage the resource requirements and scales down when things go back to normal.

- **Scalability**: Although availability and scalability both go hand in hand, there is a fundamental difference. Availability focuses on keeping the system up at all times, whereas scalability encompasses the ability to handle the increase and decrease in the load (data, users, traffic). Businesses across all industries generate a vast amount of data on a daily basis, which may be consumer data in retail or patient records in healthcare. In today's fast-paced world, the volume is continuously increasing, which needs to be processed within the same or less time than yesterday. A scalable data platform ensures we are able to serve the demands of today and are ready for the challenges of tomorrow.

  Fundamentally, there are two types of scaling:

  - **Vertical scaling**: This is increasing the power of the existing system by upgrading the hardware, such as RAM, CPU, and storage. This may be useful when we have small systems or a monolithic application, but for a system of large scale may find this scaling difficult to handle with a limited scope of upgradation.
  - **Horizontal scaling**: This comprises adding more servers or nodes to the current system, which distributes the increased load across multiple machines. With the growing data, the servers can be added seamlessly to handle the increase in demand. This ensures almost unlimited scaling and reduces the risks of single-point failure.

- **Resiliency**: The degree to which a system can recover from failure and be available for use is called **resiliency**. Apart from other automation aspects that we have discussed above, talk more about preventing the damage from component failures, load spikes, and bugs, but this part covers the minimization of losses when such uncontrollable situations occur, such as natural calamities or war that may destroy the data centers of a particular geography.

  The concept of disaster recovery comes to the aid to ensure the limits of data loss and recovery time in case of such incidents. There are two important concepts to understand:

  - **Recovery time objective (RTO)**: This is the maximum acceptable delay between the interruption of service and the restoration of service. In other words, it is the acceptable time window when the service is unavailable.
  - **Recovery point objective (RPO)**: This is the maximum acceptable amount of time since the last data recovery point. In other words, it is the acceptable loss of data (measured in time) between the last recovery point and the interruption of service. These limits are defined by the organization, based on its business requirements.

For example, for an organization where RTO = 1 hour and RPO = 30 minutes, if a server crashes at 12:00 pm. This means the server should come up by no later than 01:00 pm as per 1-hour RTO, and the data loss should be acceptable after 11:30 pm for 30 minutes, i.e., actual data loss will be between 11:30 and 12:00 pm as per 30-minute RPO.

- **Optimization and distributed data management**: Apart from designing the data architecture, it should also be continuously monitored and optimized for better efficiency. There are three essential ways of handling the huge data:
  - **Data partitioning**: The process of dividing the large dataset into small, manageable chunks is called data partitioning. This is done based on logical grouping, such as time period or region. For example, an SQL partition can be created for monthly data such as January, February, March, and so on, or different partitions can be created for geographical regions like Europe, the Middle East, etc.
  - **Sharding**: This is a technique of distributing the data across multiple servers called Shards. Each shard holds a subset of data, which helps in handling a massive dataset and achieving better performance.
  - **Redundancy and replication**: This technique is implemented to ensure data availability and fault tolerance by replicating data across multiple servers distributed across different locations. If the data server of one location fails, then redundancy ensures that the data is available to the end users without any disruptions. There are different types of redundancy with respect to nodes:
    - **Availability zones**: Data is copied within the same region, usually across different data centers in the same city/area.
    - **Multi-region**: Data is copied across different regions (different cities/countries).

Data architecture modeling

Data architecture design can be defined as a set of rules or a blueprint that shows a neat and clean plan of data collection, data storage, and utilization within the existing/new system and data warehouses for further analysis.

It mainly explains the how part of the whole lifecycle. Since architectural design is done at the very start of the project, it becomes crucial to first understand the source of data.

Based on the expected outcome, the data types of the collected data are analyzed, and the transformation is planned. The entire pipeline has to be designed for seamless connectivity, right from data ingestion to the final outcome.

Any data architecture is incomplete without the following three models:

- **Conceptual model**: This is a high-level business model that depicts relationships between different entities. This is a technology-agnostic, high-level, abstract representation of data that an organization uses for its business operations. These models are usually shown by an **entity relationship** (**ER**) diagram.

  The sole objective of this model is to have a common understanding of a business process by capturing some essential elements. Refer to *Figure 2.2*, showing an e-commerce process where a customer is placing an order and completing their payment:

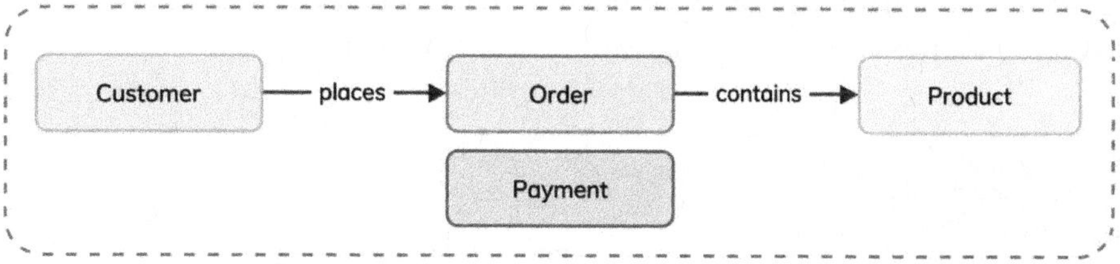

***Figure 2.2**: Representing the entities (boxes) and their relationship*

- **Logical model**: This model represents the data organization in a little more depth than the conceptual model. It includes the information of all the entities and their relationships, along with their attributes, that help stakeholders to understand the business requirements and the quality of the data structure.

  Generally, business analysts and data architects sit together to prepare this model according to the final business objective.

  An example of a logical model can be seen in *Figure 2.3:*

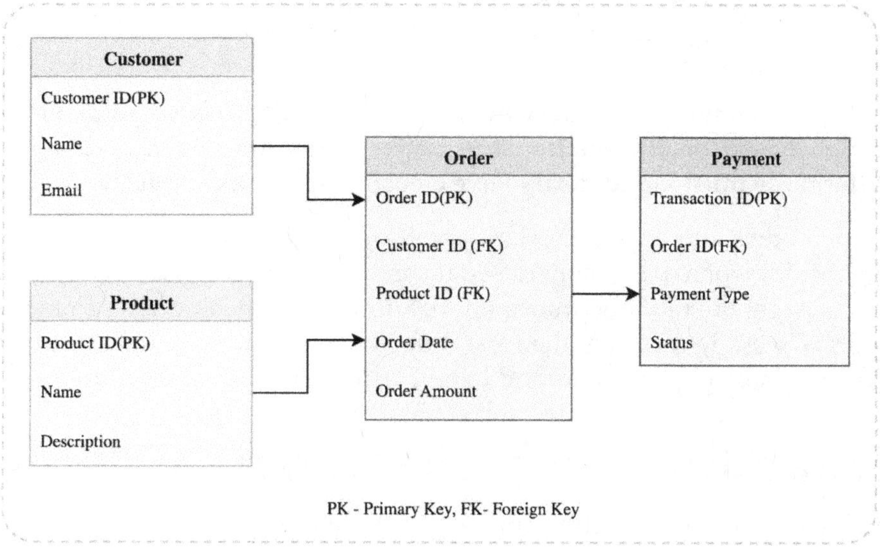

***Figure 2.3**: Representing the logical model of the entities*

- **Physical model**: A physical data model is the actual representation of how the database will be built based on the collected data. It shows additional information in the table, such as column names, data type, primary key, foreign key, etc. It also clearly articulates the relationship between different tables, stored procedures, and views.

  Database administrators, architects, and developers take part in this phase, where they need to have clarity about what tables and other components will be present so that they can start architecting the complete data flow and usage accordingly. *Figure 2.4* clearly shows the detailed version of the physical model:

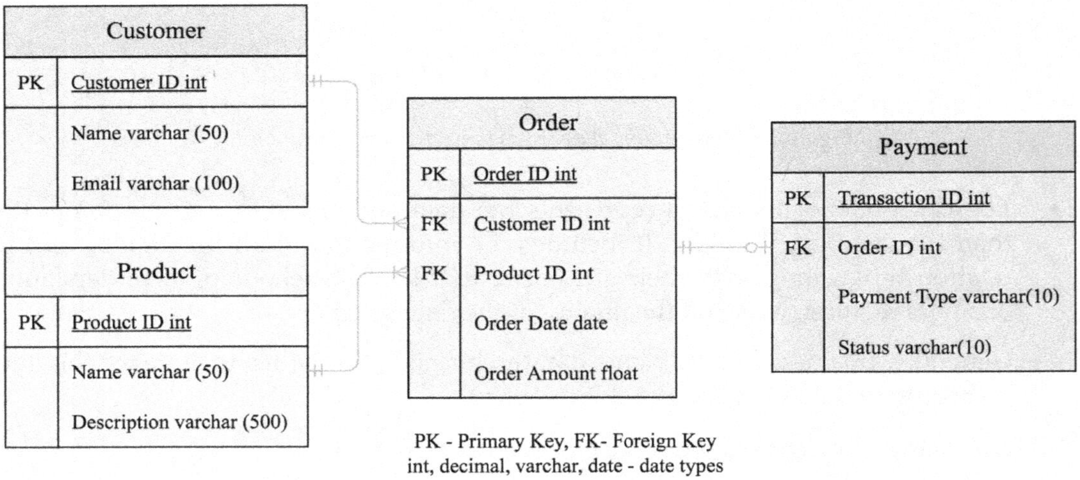

***Figure 2.4**: Representing the physical model of the entities*

> Note: **The connection (lines) between the entities has some symbols; they are created based on the relationship between the entities, e.g., any record in the Order table must mandatorily have a customer and a product.**

Creating these models and providing clarity on the storage, usage, and retrieval of the data is the core responsibility of a data architect. A data architect is an orchestrator who has to involve multiple teams to get the required information, know about the limitations of the system, etc. Once this part is well-deliberated, then the different dimensions of data can be analyzed to align with the business requirements and hence, minimize the risk of failure.

Understanding the basics of data architecture

As discussed earlier, the data architecture is generally designed keeping multiple factors in mind, such as the source and type of data, frequency of data collection, number of users, types of end users, etc.

Generally, any application has three layers:

- **Presentation layer (front end)**: This is the front face of the application where the users or systems interact, e.g., any interactive web page where users can input their queries.
- **Data layer (backend)**: This is the backend layer responsible for the storage and retrieval of critical data; e.g., most databases are present in this layer.
- **Logical calculation (middleware)**: This layer is considered as a middle layer that does all the backend processing for database storage as well as computation for presentation layer, e.g., currency input from the user in euros needs to be converted into dollars before it is stored in the database or any third party data may be collected in this layer which may be an input for calculation with the user's input and the final output will be stored in database.

The following sections explain the different types of architecture.

Single tier

These are the applications where the presentation, logical calculation, and data layer are on the same machine, e.g., the same server or the same virtual machine.

The main advantage of this type of architecture is that the performance is very good due to its tightly coupled nature, but if the system fails, then the entire architecture fails.

These are good architectures for prototyping, but not good for production environments because of the failure risks. Although these risks can be minimized by employing a redundant system, they are only good when the systems are kept isolated from any other extra stress. If there is a requirement to interact with only the database of these systems for any analytics, this may overload the running system and increase the chances of breaking.

Multi-tier

These are the applications where the presentation, logical calculation, and data layer are decoupled. They are also known as n-tier architecture, which is composed of separate layers. These are hierarchical, which means upper layers are dependent upon the lower layers, whereas the lower layers are independent of the upper layers.

For example, if the presentation layer breaks, the logical calculation layer and data layer are still working and can serve other purposes like log analysis, dashboarding, etc. Also, these layers may continue to serve presentation layers of other applications (including third-party) or any downstream process. However, if the data layer breaks, neither user will be able to store any data, nor will the calculation be done if the required data is not available from the data layer.

Monolith

These are like a single program where all the features have been developed, e.g., login, product search, cart product management, and payment, all developed in a single codebase. The extreme version of a monolith can be a single code base on a single machine. This architecture is easy to develop in early stages, but eventually becomes heavy to customize, enhance, and upgrade.

In this architecture, one bug can affect the whole system, and small changes require the entire application to be redeployed.

Microservices

These are separate, decentralized, isolated (sometimes), and loosely coupled services that interact with each other to get the work done.

The microservice can be developed by multiple developers or teams at the same time, where each service can be taken care of independently for maintenance, bug fixing, and upgrading.

This architecture is best suited for scaling, where each component can be configured based on the amount of work it has to do.

Figure 2.5 shows all four different types of architectures. The single tier has both application and database, shown in a single machine or server, whereas in the case of a multi-tier application, the logical calculation and database layers are distributed amongst different servers.

Similarly, monolith architecture is deployed on a single machine, where there is a single codebase with database connectivity, and a complete microservices-based architecture is shown, where services are deployed as independent components that talk to each other. Usually, their interaction happens via an abstraction layer that hides the low-level details.

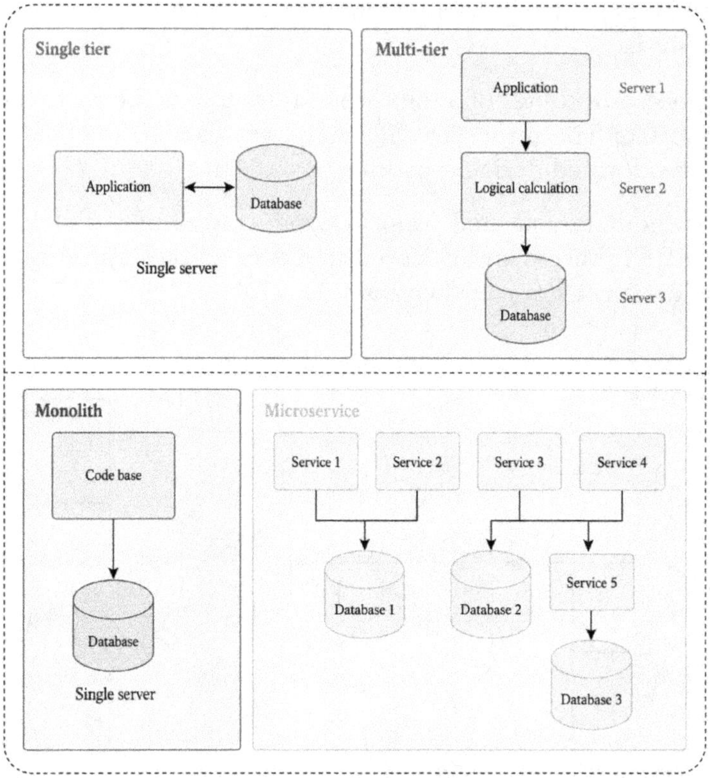

***Figure 2.5**: Explaining the pictorial representation of different architectures*

Examples of data architecture

Since there is no fixed rule for selecting the type of data architecture, the architecture should be designed keeping the final objective in mind. This section will give you an idea about when to select which type of architecture.

Data warehouse

A data warehouse is defined as a central data hub used for storing and managing large volumes of data coming from multiple sources. Since this data is historical, it is used for advanced analytics and informed decision-making by the organizations.

One thing that is very important in the case of a data warehouse is that it is highly structured and well-formatted data, and this data can be direct input for any online analysis utility.

The ingestion of data in a data warehouse follows the ETL process, where the data is extracted from its source and passes through a transformation layer, and then the data is stored in the data warehouse, which has huge amounts of data coming from multiple sources.

Now, this data can be passed to different data marts, which are specific to a department for their respective analysis.

A data mart is defined as a subset of a data warehouse that is meant to have business unit or department-specific data. This improves efficiency, reduces cost, and helps individual sections of the business with informed decision-making.

Figure 2.6 explains the data collected from various sources of a travel organization, which passes through the ETL process and is stored in a data warehouse. After this, business unit-specific data marts are created for further analysis.

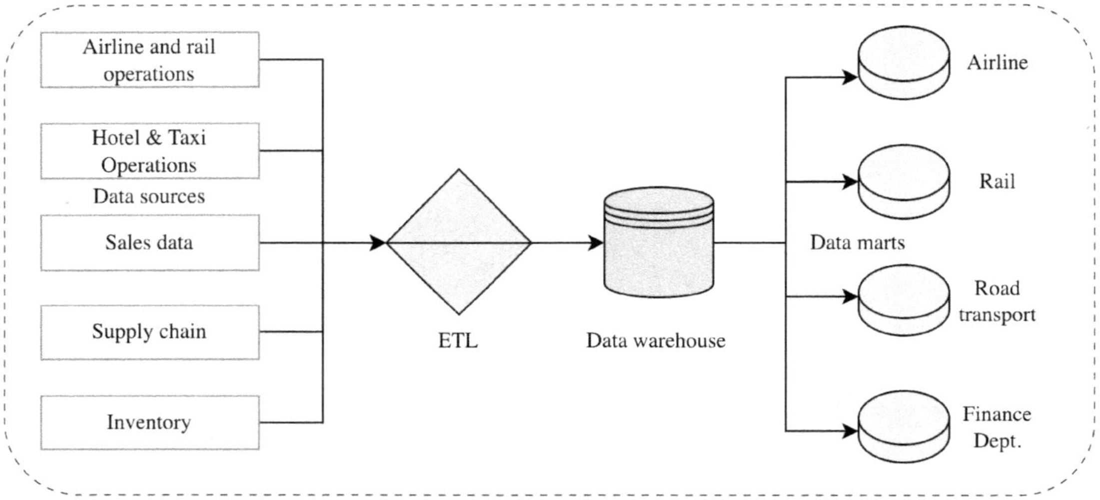

***Figure 2.6**: Example of a data warehouse architecture*

Data lake

A data lake can be described as a central repository that can store big data without questioning its form. That means it can ingest anything, be it structured, unstructured, or semi-structured, from different sources such as sensors, databases, video sources, etc.

Organizations can focus on collecting as much data as possible without caring about the outcome.

By and large, the data is only processed when it is retrieved, not while in storage, and that is the fundamental difference between data warehousing and data lakes. Data warehouses process or transform the data before writing, also known as **transform-on-write**, to make sure well-structured data gets ingested, which can be used for further analysis, whereas a data lake house concentrates on storing the data in whatever form and processing will be done while it is being accessed or read, which can also be called the **transform-on-read** concept. From a cost perspective, data lakes are generally more cost-effective than data warehouses for storage, but total cost depends on processing, governance, and usage patterns. Tools like Apache Spark and Databricks can be used to query or fetch data from a data lake.

Figure 2.7 shows the complete flow of how the data of any type is stored in the data lake in raw format, and then the transformation it goes through when data is required for specific use cases:

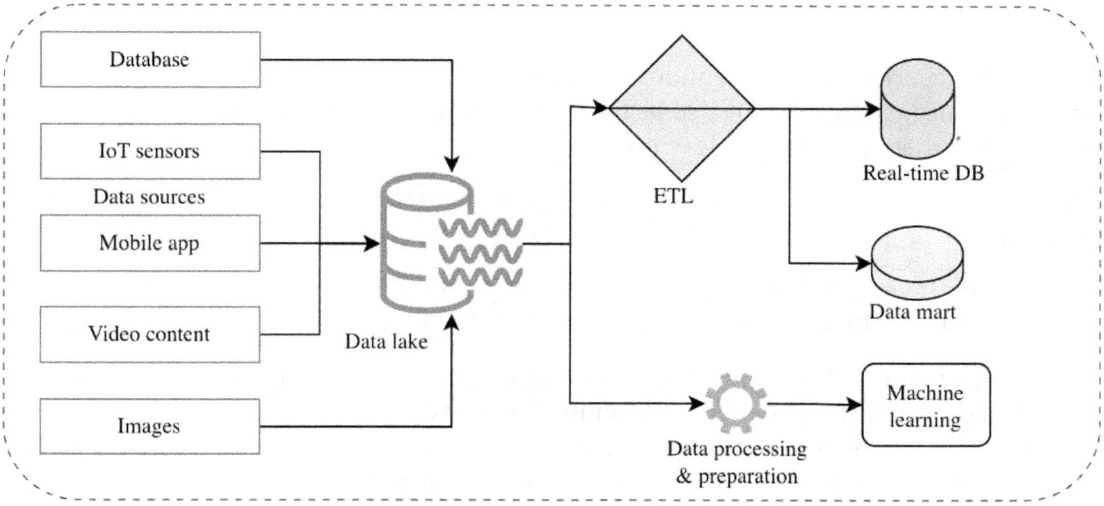

Figure 2.7*: Example of data lake architecture*

Similar to this concept, there is one more way of storing the data in a data warehouse, which is known as ELT, in this, the data coming from various data sources is first staged and then transformed into structured format so that it can be stored into data warehouse, refer to *Figure 2.8*:

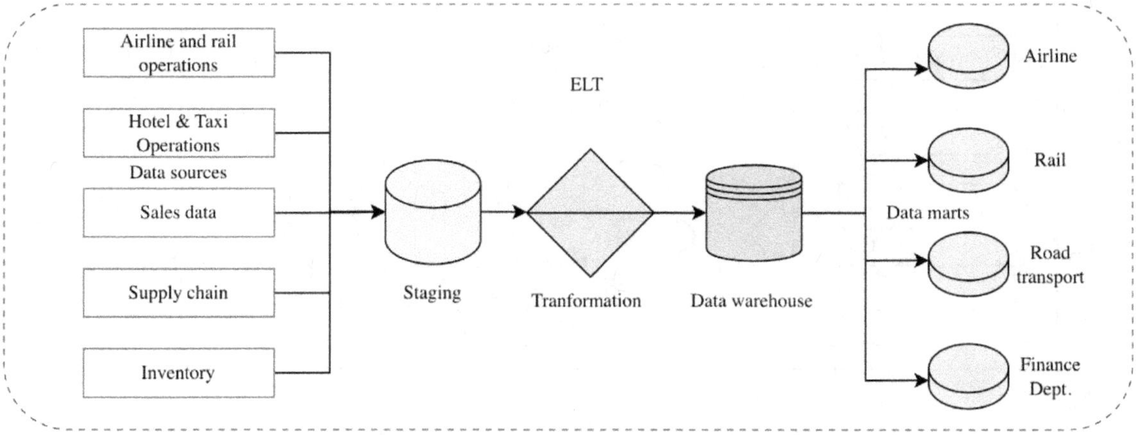

Figure 2.8*: Example of a data warehouse architecture with ELT*

Lambda architecture

When there is a requirement for analysis on a large dataset or big data residing on a data warehouse or a data lake, the challenge is that the query may take time to execute. There may be some methods of processing the requests in parallel for optimized performance, but still, due to the huge size of the data and its ever-increasing nature, querying these systems may take hours.

The main drawback of this conventional approach is that if the query has taken a few hours to execute, the output analysis will also be based on the old data, i.e., the analysis will be without the latest data that may have critical importance.

To solve this, the lambda architecture can be implemented. It has three layers of processing as follows:

- **Speed layer**: This layer operates on stream data that is processed in real-time and is passed directly to the serving layer or to further analysis.
- **Batch layer**: In this layer, all the data is dumped into a staging area or data lake, then it is passed through the transformation layer, and then it is stored in a more structured manner, such as a data warehouse. This processed data can be directly used for analytics purposes or can be used as machine learning input.
- **Serving layer**: As the name implies, this layer acts as a mediator between the analytics application/user and the data processing units. It contains servers that have consolidated processed data coming from both the speed and batch layers.

Refer to the following figure for a representation of the lambda architecture:

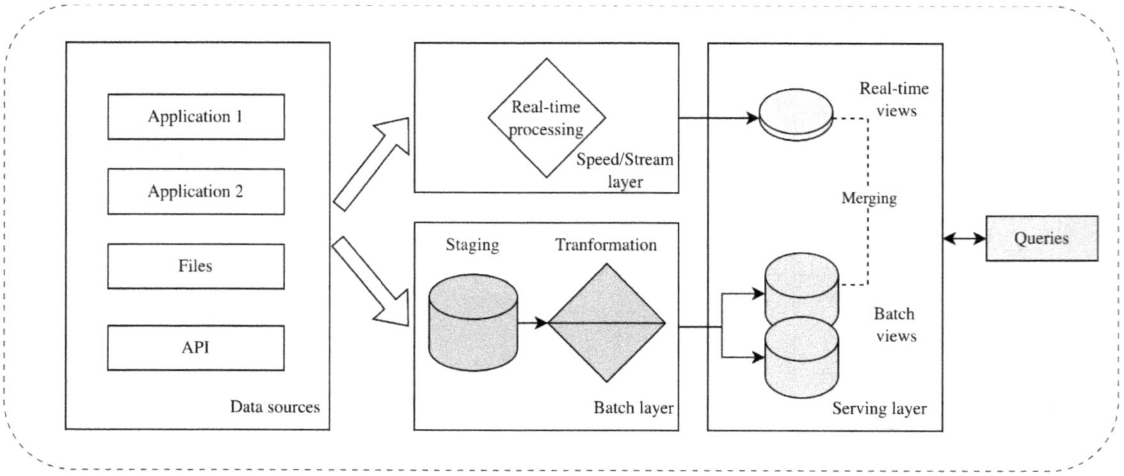

***Figure 2.9**: Representation of lambda architecture*

The advantage of this approach is that when the users want to have a near real-time analysis of the latest or short-duration data, the stream data processing helps, whereas for the requirements of the analysis of longer duration, the batch processing approach comes into play.

Since stream processing is prone to errors compared to batch processing, this becomes a choice of the user, whether they prefer a batch approach for accurate results, versus analysis of data at run-time that may be inaccurate.

Kappa architecture

The major challenge with the lambda architecture was the complexity of managing the two different processing units that are designed as different frameworks and merging them in the serving layer. The batch processing was trusted for its accuracy back then, compared to stream processing, which was meant for low-latency requirements with some acceptable inaccuracies.

However, with time, tools evolved, and the accuracy of processing stream data improved; this gave birth to a new architecture called the Kappa architecture, where there was no requirement for batch processing, and the data stream was being directly fed to the stream processing unit.

In the following figure, the data once received from various data sources is simply taken up by the stream processing unit, which is stored in the serving layer after processing, where users or applications can interact via queries:

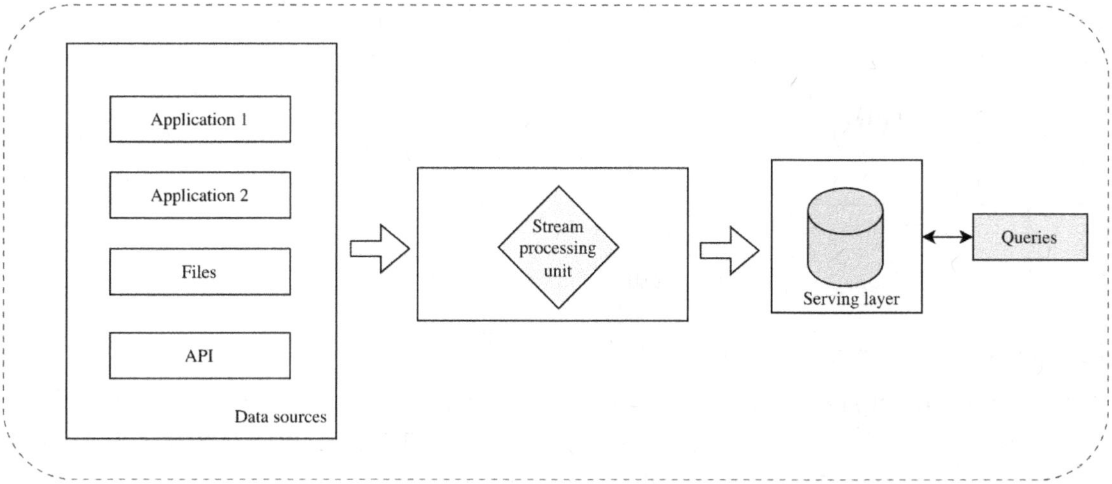

***Figure 2.10**: Representation of Kappa architecture*

All the data is treated as a stream, where data is first stored in a messaging engine, then passed through the stream processing unit, and then stored in an analytics database.

If there were a requirement to go back and analyze the historical data, then the whole stream of that duration could be replayed to re-read old events. This process uses parallelism for the computation of the entire stream, which helps in processing the stream within a reasonable time.

Internet of Things architecture

The IoT is defined as any device that is connected to the Internet to send and receive data. These may be mobile phones, computers, smart automobiles, smart home appliances, etc.

Traditionally, these devices were made for specific work, e.g., air conditioners for cooling the rooms, refrigerators for keeping the food cold for preservation. However, nowadays, due to a reduction in the cost of processing and handling data, internet charges have brought the usage of these devices smartly as an added value. This gives more control to the user. For example, an air conditioner can be switched on with a mobile phone before you reach home on a hot day.

Let us understand the IoT architecture from *Figure 2.11*:

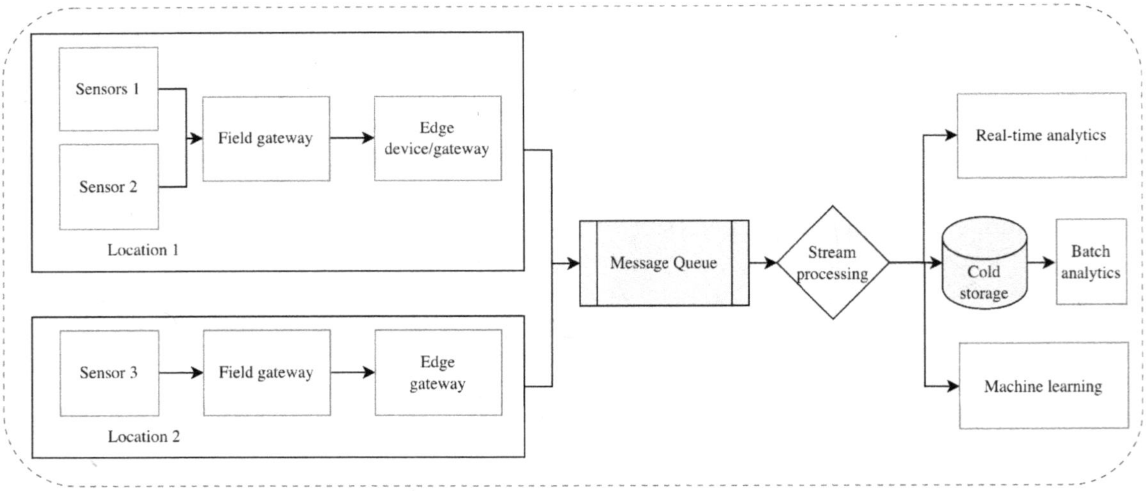

***Figure 2.11**: Logical architecture of IoT*

There are several components to create a complete IoT workflow:

- **Data source**: These are the sensors that are generating the field data, e.g., an air quality sensor is sensing the air quality and generating a small electrical signal, such as 5 mA.
- **Field gateway**: These are the devices that convert the electrical signals to equivalent digital signals using a microcontroller or an **analogue to digital converter** (**ADC**), e.g., taking the above example, the electrical signal of 5mA gets converted into 75 µg/m3 for PM10.

  This data also gets converted into a specific protocol, which becomes an input to the edge gateway, e.g., Modbus/Profibus/**Highway addressable remote transducer** (**HART**), etc.

- **Edge gateway**: These are the devices that take the data from field protocols such as Modbus and convert it into modern IoT protocols like **Message Queuing Telemetry Transport** (**MQTT**). Once this conversion is done, this gateway will push the data to the message queue, which resides on the cloud. The message queue works as a **publish/subscribe** (**pub/sub**) model in which the edge gateway keeps publishing the data on the message queue, and the devices that have subscribed to the data will keep getting the latest messages.
- **Edge device**: These may or may not be a part of the edge gateway, depending on the usage. Since they have a little computational power and memory, they can be used to run a machine learning model to pass the inference to the message queue rather than raw data. Similarly, any other calculation can also be done on this machine that may be fed back to the IoT device for tuning.
- **Message queue**: This is the pub/sub queue containing the stream data.
- **Stream processing**: It is processing the data as soon as it is received for any alert or notification, and decision-making.

  The data, once received, is processed for advanced analytics, depending upon the requirements. The analytics can be shown directly to the visualization dashboards or answer real-time analytics or queries, or it can be transformed into a more structured format and stored in cold storage for any batch or historical analytics for future use and archiving.

  This data can also become input for any machine learning model, where critical decisions or inferences can be made.

Data mesh

Data mesh is a new approach for managing data that takes away the traditional monolith approach of storing big data in a common place like a data lake/warehouse, to build a distributed data architecture. This approach treats data like a product.

It works on four key principles:

- **Domain ownership**: In this approach, there is no single/central team managing the entire big data; rather, it spreads the ownership and responsibility for a specific dataset across the business to the departments that own it and know the best use of it. For example, sales data is owned by the sales team, and operational data is owned by the operations team.
- **Domain data as a product**: This is an essential part of this architecture, in which the domain data owners have to provide the relevant data as a product. Data products need to be discoverable, trustworthy, self-describing, addressable, and interoperable. This should have the important metrics included from the business understanding.

For example, in the customer support department, time to resolve the query, average number of calls to resolve a single query, customer experience, and feedback, etc., are the important metrics that can be shared via an application interface as a product so that it can be used for advanced analytics or machine learning models for decision making.

- **Self-serve data platform**: This includes creating an infrastructure using tools and skills that help the domain team to create, analyze, and publish their data as a product on their own without having a strong dependency on the central team while ensuring security, performance, and scalability.
- **Federated governance**: Since the data mesh encourages decentralized data ownership, there must be some governance that is to be followed for adherence to the organizational rules and to reduce friction amongst the teams. It employs policies for interoperability, documentation, security, privacy, and compliance.

Refer to the following figure:

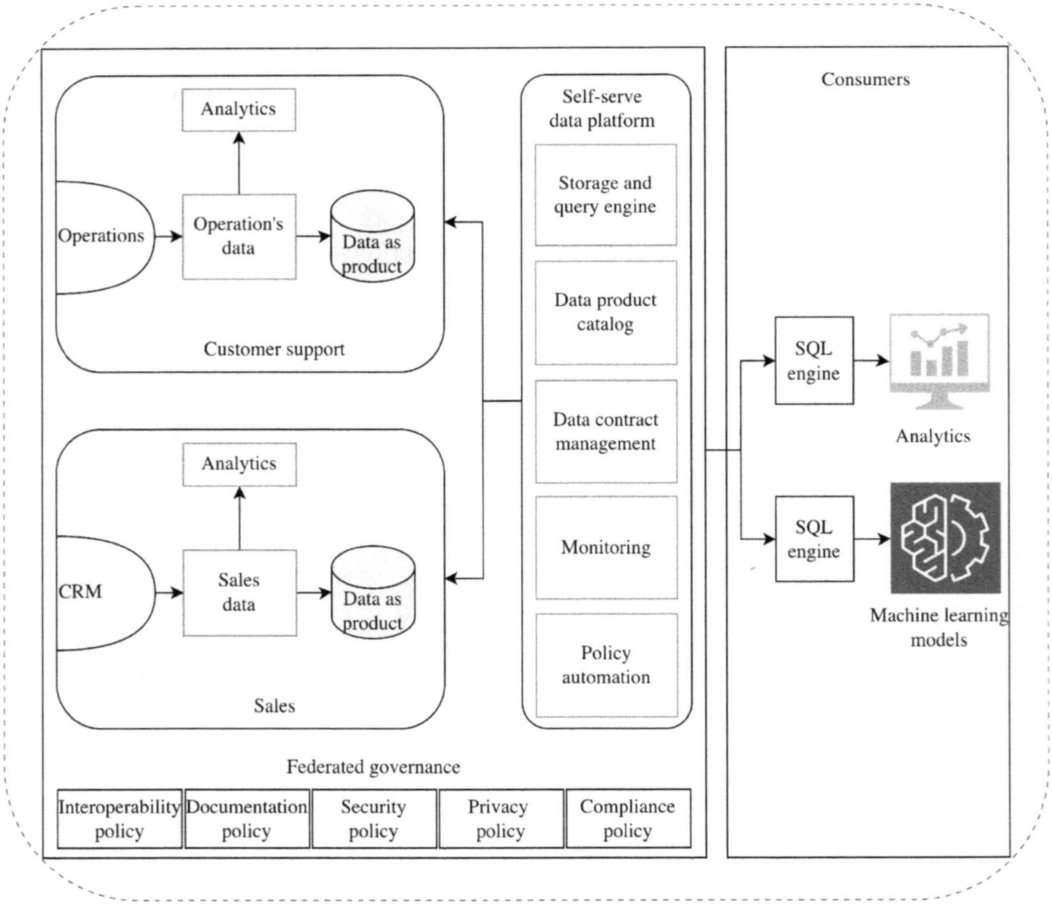

***Figure 2.12**: A high-level architecture of a data mesh*

In the preceding figure, you can see that the two different departments, i.e., sales and operations, are working independently to collect and process their data. They leverage the self-serve platform for tools and skills available for creating a complete architecture.

This complete process is orchestrated, keeping the governance in check, which may come from central teams but is implemented and executed by local teams.

This solution reduces dependencies on the central team since they are responsible for managing their data. Keeping the data closer to the source increases the speed of execution and quality.

Overall, this architecture brings independence and autonomy, which help in faster growth and scalability of an organization.

Conclusion

This chapter discussed the definition of data architecture and its components in detail. Some of the popular data architectures were also covered briefly to give an idea about what best practices are adopted in the industry. It also encompasses the nine important principles that need to be kept in mind before designing any data architecture, and the use of modeling to create a data architecture from scratch. Different types of data architecture and some real-life examples are also covered in the chapter.

The next chapter will cover the data generation section, which explains very clearly how the data is created from new or already existing systems and what can be the source of data exchanges between two or more systems. This chapter will also outline the databases as the data source, where different types of databases available in the market and their applicability will also be discussed.

References

1. **https://www.ibm.com/think/topics/data-architecture**
2. **https://www.leanix.net/en/wiki/ea/togaf**
3. **https://dama.org/learning-resources/dama-data-management-body-of-knowledge-dmbok/**
4. **https://zachman-feac.com/zachman/about-the-zachman-framework**
5. **https://aws.amazon.com/what-is/data-architecture/**
6. **https://docs.aws.amazon.com/waf/latest/developerguide/security.html**
7. **https://docs.aws.amazon.com/wellarchitected/latest/security-pillar/welcome.html**
8. **https://www.ibm.com/think/topics/data-mart**

9. **https://learn.microsoft.com/en-us/azure/architecture/databases/guide/big-data-architectures**
10. **https://martinfowler.com/articles/data-mesh-principles.html**

CHAPTER 3
Data Generation in Source System

Introduction

In any data-related project, after the clarity of data sources, the next important step is to know how the data is generated and what kind of data is available. Since the data engineer knows the objective of the project, they have to look at the data from an angle that makes it available for the downstream system in a readily useful format. This requires them to understand the nature of data, such as whether the data can be quantified for use in mathematical calculations directly. If not, that can be converted into a format using some algorithm that makes it useful. This requires them to deliberate upon it for some time and conclude on the final processing or transformation.

They also have to follow data governance requirements, that is, to know if the data is confidential or public, where it is currently stored, what kind of encryption is in place, and who can access the data. Once this is understood, the next step of data handling needs to be planned; for example, confidential data may not need to be stored as is and may require some conversion or masking, or even deleting it completely after processing.

While planning for a project based on the data sources, the efforts have to be calculated accordingly, as the amount of work done will vary; for example, data collection from an API may be easier and less risky than accessing the data directly from the source database. Similarly, logs generated by multiple sensors may require a different set of tools.

Every use case is different and demands a different set of skills and tools, which becomes evident once we have the clarity of data generation and where it has been captured from.

Structure

The chapter covers the following topics:

- Data generation
- Types of data sources with examples

Objectives

At the end of this chapter, you will be able to understand the definition of data generation and its fundamentals. You would get clarity about the different categories of data, which are defined based on their nature, structure, and sources from which they have been generated. You will also explore different examples of data sources that may be available, such as data received as a file, via an API, or from logs, etc., and their consumption. You will also learn about different types of APIs available in the market that have been derived from one another, based on the problems faced in the past. A brief overview of online transaction processing and online analytical processing has also been covered in this chapter, which will give a concise view of how these are employed in the industry today. This chapter also introduces different types of databases that will help understand the core differences between them and their usage in the current ecosystem.

Data generation

Organizations have been working with their customers or clients for a very long time, and over the period, they have been dealing with the data in some shape or form. Data has been generated for years, but the way of collecting data was not known or was very expensive.

Since we have various advanced tools available today at a lower cost, the ability to collect data has improved. Since we know the data is already there, we are not generating the data; rather, we are finding the mechanisms to collect it.

For example, refrigerators have been keeping our food cold for several years, and have temperature sensors to switch off the compressor when it reaches a cutoff limit, but we, as humans, could not see that. However, now, we have temperature sensors that are **Internet of Things** (**IoT**) enabled and can be connected to our home Wi-Fi and push the data to the cloud. We can open our mobile apps and analyze the temperature patterns of the refrigerator for hours, days, months, and years.

To define, the process of collecting the already available data in any manner is called data generation or data creation.

In *Figure 3.1*, we are focusing on how data is created or generated at its source, before it is ingested, transformed, or stored, or becomes part of the complete ETL pipeline:

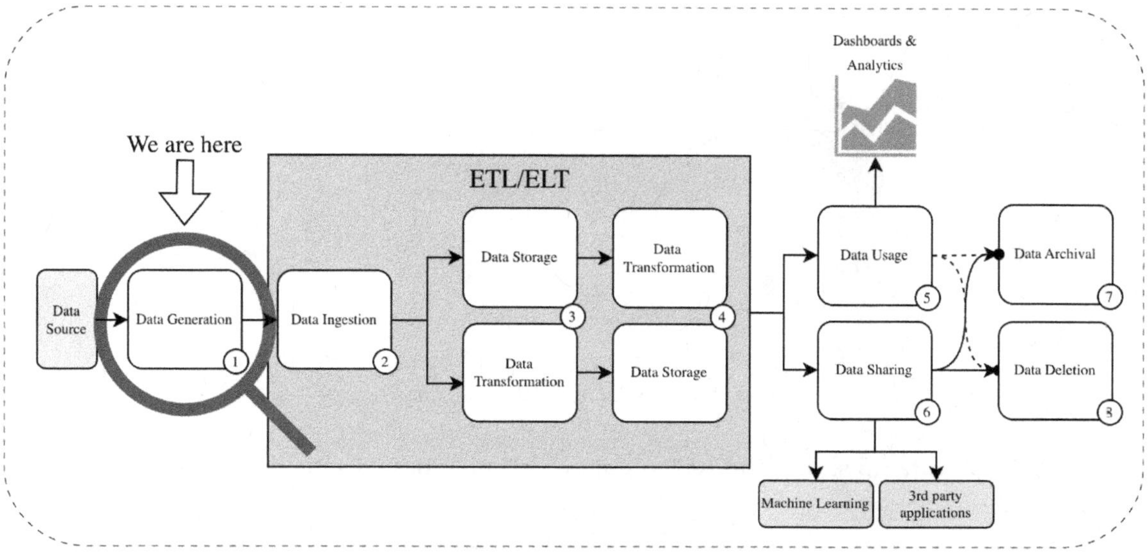

***Figure 3.1**: Showing the current phase covered in the chapter*

Let us understand the data creation or generation process using a real-life example. When humans speak, that is also data, but the only part that we collect comes in the category of data, such as voice recordings, recited poems, songs, etc. Basically, we have two types of data, analogue and digital, and based on that, we have the mechanisms of collecting the same, as follows:

- **Analogue data**: Any data that occurs in the real-world, like speech, music, and writing, is called **analogue data**. Analogue data is continuous and can take infinite values in a given range. When we write something on paper, it is an analogue data storage. Similarly, in earlier times, the music was stored on vinyl records, which was a mechanical way of storing the analogue data.

  Let us see this example in detail:

  - When a singer sings into a microphone, the equivalent analogue electric signal of the sound is generated by the microphone, and this signal is sent to a cutting lathe, which is further connected to a cutting stylus.
  - Based on the frequency and intensity of the analogue signal, this stylus moves and creates grooves on a master disc. This master disc is used to create a master stamper, which is finally used to create a vinyl disc.

    The preceding example shows how the data is created or generated out of a sound, which is coming from an instrument, an animal, a bird, or a singer.

    Figure 3.2 shows the end-to-end process of how music is created, right from a singer singing a song to storing a song on a music disc:

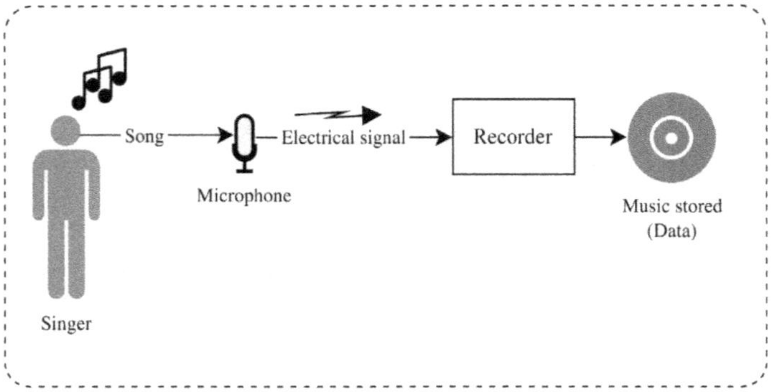

***Figure 3.2**: Songs stored as data*

Figure 3.3 shows the 1000x magnification of how a song is recorded on vinyl:

***Figure 3.3**: Vinyl and stylus at 1000x magnification, showing that the music is stored in the form of grooves*

- To play the recording back, there is a reading head (see *Figure 3.3*) that is connected to the grooves on the vinyl disc and will move according to the engraving. Based on its shape, the head moves and vibrates at a very fast pace, which is connected to a speaker. Since the head vibrates, it makes the coil of the magnet vibrate, which converts the mechanical vibration into an electrical signal, and these signals are passed to an amplifier and speaker, and finally, the sound is produced, and that is how we listen to music.

This is how the giant music industry came into existence, since they now knew how the music could be collected and stored, which could be sold and replayed.

- **Digital data**: When the analogue data is converted into digital form, it is called **digital data**. Some of the examples can be speech-to-text and optical character recognition. Similarly, audio songs played by vinyl discs can be passed to the **analogue-to-digital converter** (**ADC**), which results in a digital audio file such as an MP3.

Categories of data

Although we have already covered the fundamental types of data, there are some categories that can be defined, as discussed:

- **By structure**:
  - **Structured data**: This is the data that is properly organized for easy retrieval, e.g., Excel, SQL.
  - **Unstructured data**: The data that has no defined structure and is difficult to retrieve and analyze, such as the textual content of a paragraph, video, or image.
  - **Semi-structured**: This data is not strictly organized but, in a way, is easily retrievable, e.g., **JavaScript Object Notation** (**JSON**) and **eXtensible Markup Language** (**XML**), which can be extracted using key-value pairs and tags, respectively.
- **By nature**:
  - **Qualitative**: This is the type of data that explains the property of any entity, e.g., gender (male/female), favorite color (red/black/yellow).
    - **Ordinal**: They are qualitative data with an order sequence, e.g., ratings, that vary from worst to excellent, e.g., worst | bad | normal | good | excellent.
    - **Un-ordinal**: These are qualitative data without any order, e.g., gender.
  - **Quantitative**: This is a type of data that is numerical and measurable, e.g., weight, height, air quality:
    - **Discrete**: The data that is countable, e.g., the number of employees.
    - **Continuous**: The data that cannot be counted but can only be measured, e.g., temperature.
- **By source**:
  - **Primary**: The raw data that is collected directly from the source, e.g., sensors, surveys.
  - **Secondary**: The data that is collected/derived from primary data, e.g., a database.
- **By availability**:
  - **Public**: The data that is available on the internet or public forums, e.g., open government data.
  - **Private**: The data that belongs to someone who has no intention to share, for example:
    - **Personal information**: This may be some information that is private and helps in identifying the person, e.g., name, phone number, email address, residential address.
    - **Sensitive information**: This may be confidential information that belongs to a person and is kept within specific members, e.g., salary, medical conditions.

Types of data sources with examples

There are several types of data sources that are possible in client settings, and they may have multiple types of data sources that need to be integrated with the data collection system. Let us look at what kind of data sources are available today.

File and unstructured data

A file is a collection of related data or information, stored under the same name, e.g., a resume is a file in which the career details of a candidate are stored, which can be accessed by a potential employer.

Based on the structure of data, there may be different types of files and their extensions, such as `.txt`, `.docx`, `.mp3`, `.gif`, etc. For example, most `.txt` files have unstructured textual data, stored as plain text, whereas `.mp3` files have compressed binary audio that is represented as hexadecimal data. Depending upon the file extension, the data in a file can be read by the respective applications. For example, only textual reading applications, such as a notepad, can open the content of a `.txt` file, and MP3 players can read the `.mp3` file as sound or music.

In accordance with the above analogy, the data processing approach is selected, developed, or customized based on the nature of the input file.

Looking at a real use case, a `.csv` file about all the listed companies can be downloaded from the **Bombay Stock Exchange** (**BSE**) website, **https://www.bseindia.com/corporates/List_Scrips.html,** and the required information about the status of stocks, face value, etc., can be extracted and utilized in the downstream process.

Refer to *Figure 3.4*, where the data is collected in an Excel file from different portals. This Excel is read and processed by an Excel parser, which extracts the relevant data and passes it to the data processing application. This application cleans, filters, and formats the data based on the requirements from the downstream system and passes it to the downstream world for the next level of processing.

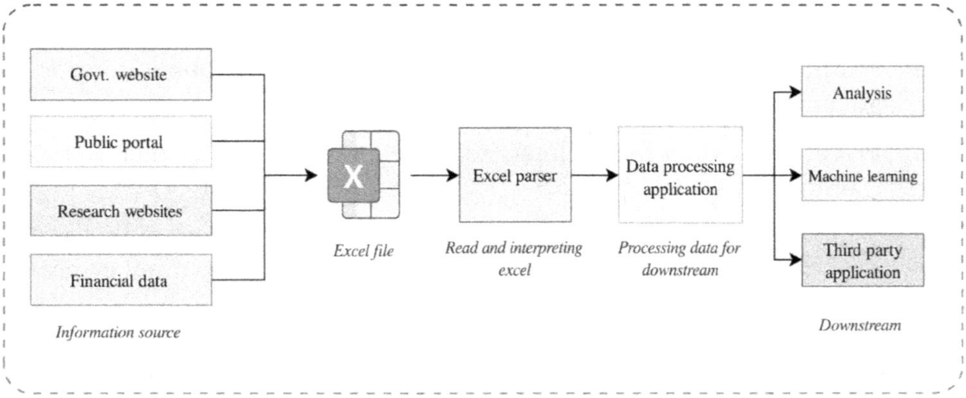

***Figure 3.4**: Example of a cycle of an Excel file for processing*

Similarly, the data received can be in an unstructured format that may need processing in order to extract meaningful information. Nowadays, contextual capability is used in order to understand unstructured information, and the data can be extracted using **natural language processing** (**NLP**). Later, this extracted data can be passed on to the downstream process in a structured format.

Application programming interfaces

APIs can be defined as a set of rules that allow two different systems or services to communicate with each other. For any communication, the API call and response are predefined. This defined structure needs to be followed by the caller (calling system) so that the intended response is received.

The APIs are exposed at the abstraction layer to maintain the flexibility of changes and evolution at lower levels without affecting the upper layer. For example, in *Figure 3.5,* a user is trying to request data of a user with ID=5 from an API server. This server calls an equivalent SQL query to the database and gets the table in response. This table is converted into the predefined format of the response. This response is shared with the user in JSON format.

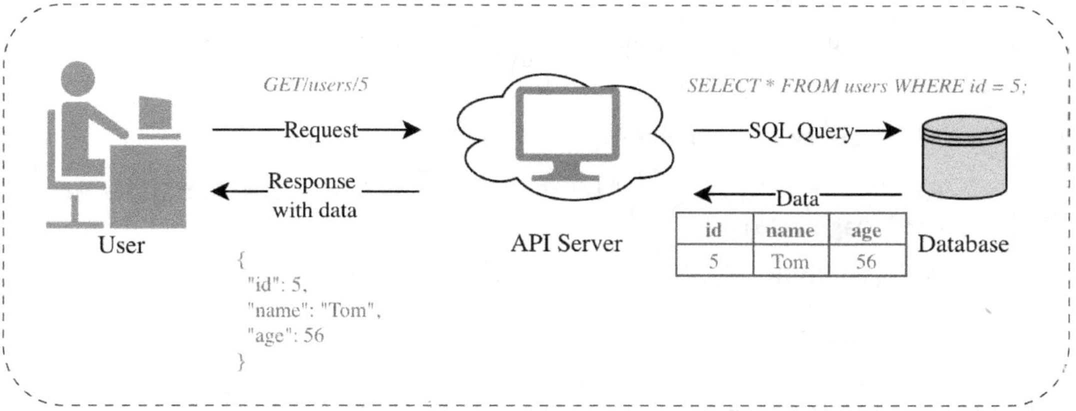

Figure 3.5: *Example of API communication*

If there is a requirement to change the database table structure or the complete **database management system** (**DBMS**) type, then that can be achieved without even making any changes to the API structure; as a result, the user would not know anything about the internal changes.

There are two types of communication mechanisms in data exchanges within the system:

- **Synchronous**: In this mechanism, the client sends a request and waits until the server processes it and returns a response. This means the client cannot proceed until a response is received. For example, REST, SOAP, GraphQL, and gRPC are the APIs that come in this category.

- **Asynchronous**: In this, the client sends a request and does not wait for an immediate response; the server processes it independently and responds later (or via a separate channel/event). This means the client can continue other tasks and work on this task once the response is received via the event. E.g., Webhook.

Let us look at the previously mentioned APIs in detail:

- **Representational state transfer (REST)**: These are hypertext transfer protocol (HTTP/HTTPS) based APIs that are meant to provide server data in a JSON or XML format.
- **Simple Object Access Protocol (SOAP)**: This is a protocol used for the exchange of information in XML format. Unlike REST, it follows a strict structure. This protocol supports multiple protocols like HTTP/HTTPS, **simple mail transfer protocol** (**SMTP**), **Microsoft Messaging Queue** (**MSMQ**), etc.
- **Graph query language (GraphQL)**: This protocol was developed by *Facebook* to overcome the shortcomings of a REST API, which was that every single call had the complete payload as an outcome, even if that much information was not needed. Whereas GraphQL works on an exact request that needs to be asked. In simple words, it asks for specific fields.

  For example, if we need a user's name (only) with `id=5`, then the following query can be added:

  - **REST query**: `GET /users/5`
  - **REST result**: `{"id":5,"name":"Alice","email":"alice@example.com","age":30}`

    Whereas, in the case of GraphQL, we can ask directly for the field as:

    - **GraphQL query**:

      ```
      query{
      user(id: 5){
      name
      }
      }
      ```

    - **GraphQL response**:

      ```
      {
      "data": {
      "user": {
      "name": "Tom"
      }
      }
      ```

As we can see in the above example, GraphQL can be asked for the exact field to be extracted, and it will provide the response accordingly; this saves network flooding with unnecessary data and improves performance.

- **Google remote procedure call (gRPC)**: This is an open source protocol developed by Google that is to be used in microservices architecture applications to talk to each other efficiently. gRPC lets one application call the function of another application as if it were a local function. It uses Protobuf, a compact and binary data format that is more efficient than JSON and XML. In some advanced cases, it may behave asynchronously as well.
- **Webhook**: Unlike APIs, webhooks are event-based data transmission between different applications via HTTP/HTTPS. It eliminates the need for continuous polling to get the data in order to save resources.

  Refer to the following figure:

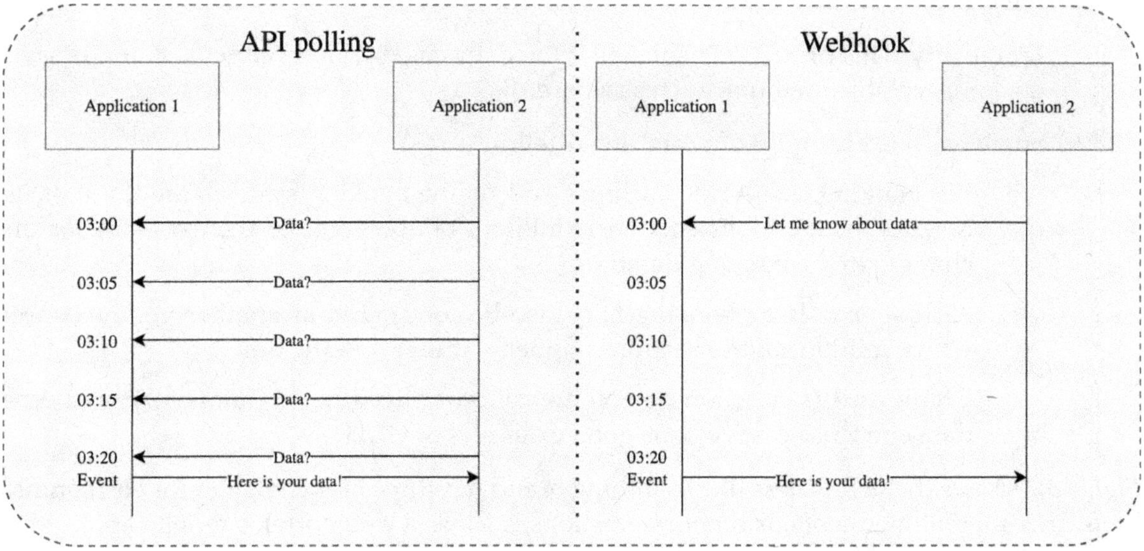

***Figure 3.6**: Example representation of API polling vs. webhook communication*

Online transaction processing

Online transaction processing (OLTP) systems are defined as databases that are designed for executing millions of small, concurrent transactions efficiently. These systems focus on the latency and the accuracy of the transactions and are designed to ensure the **atomicity, consistency, isolation, and durability** (ACID) properties.

These are the systems that are usually designed for write operations rather than read. If any read requirement is needed for analytics, then OLTP systems may not be a suitable choice.

The following explains the ACID properties in detail:

- **Atomicity**: This ensures that a set of transactions is treated as one unit. Either it is wholly completed or none. For example, we have two accounts, A and B. A has $1000 as an account balance, and B has $2000. If we transfer $100 from A to B, the atomic transaction means:
    - Account A will never show a debit of $100 until account B shows a credit of $100.
    - Either the balances will be updated on both accounts A and B, or there will be no change at all.
- **Consistency**: This means that the data access will be on the latest or last written version of the database. It must be consistent across all the read operations.
- **Isolation**: It means multiple transactions are done concurrently without any interference. The final database state will be consistent with a sequential execution of the transactions using locks.
- **Durability**: This property ensures that the data saved will never get lost and is saved on a non-volatile medium, such as a hard disk.

  Some real-life examples of OLTP are as follows:
    - For banking, the ATM machines and online banking systems are the best use cases of the OLTP system, where millions of users around the world are making changes in the banking database.
    - Airline or railway booking may also be considered as another good example, where millions of transactions happen within a specific time.
    - Credit card transactions, e-commerce, centralized health data entry, and other data entry use cases can be good examples of OLTP.

Figure 3.7 shows that a business like a clothing brand has three branches, and for each branch, there are different media of customer interactions, such as a web portal, a mobile application, and physical stores. The customers can shop from any of the existing means, which will eventually update the databases. In the same way, millions of customers do transactions, and hence the OLTP systems are able to efficiently allow these transactions, which are mostly write operations with fewer read operations.

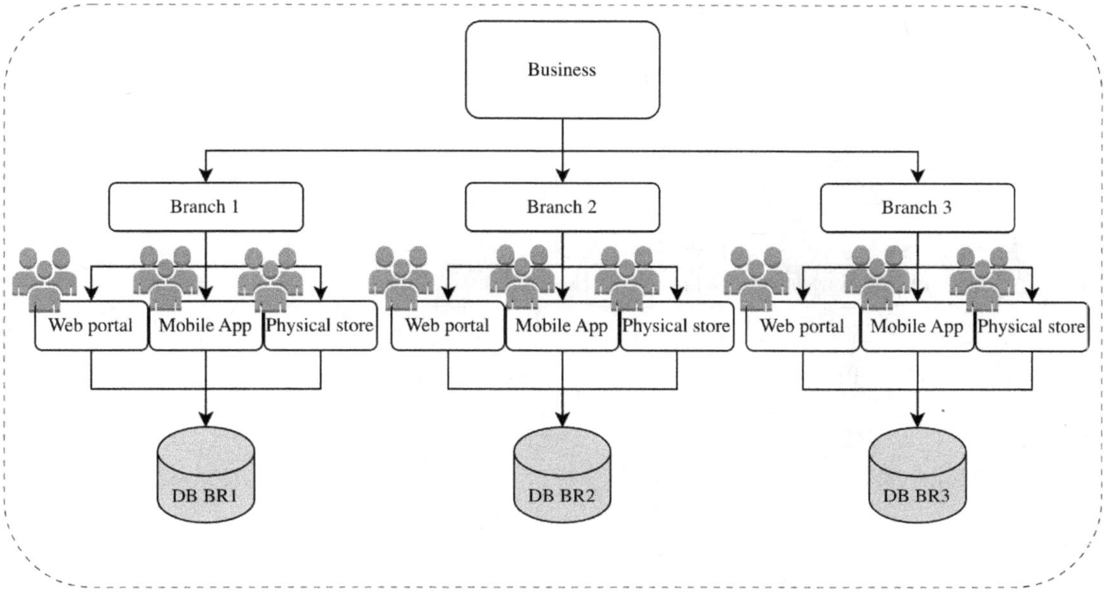

***Figure 3.7**: Example representation of an OLTP system*

Some popular databases that are designed for OLTP are Oracle DB, MS SQL Server, PostgreSQL, etc.

Online analytical processing

An **online analytical processing** (**OLAP**) system, on the other hand, is meant for read operations, and that too for queries that have large results. The size of the result can vary from a few megabytes to gigabytes. These types of systems or databases focus on interactive analytics where users can do multi-dimensional analysis on large data sets, on the go.

This analysis targets business decisions, organizational efficiency, and capacity planning that may help in the improvement of their current services and the betterment of customer experience. It shows the bigger picture and helps in solving many problems that may be ignored when seen from a convergent point of view. On a higher level, it works on **`SELECT`** queries on historical data with **`GROUP BY`**, **`JOIN`**, and aggregations, where the size of the query can vary from gigabytes to terabytes as well.

Figure 3.8 is an extension of *Figure 3.7*, where the database created by millions of operations undergoes a transformation process and is stored in a data warehouse. This data will then be converted to data marts so that it contains the business unit or department-centric information. This data can be further aggregated and precalculated to create OLAP cubes that can be used by the data engineers or analysts for decision-making or further drilldown.

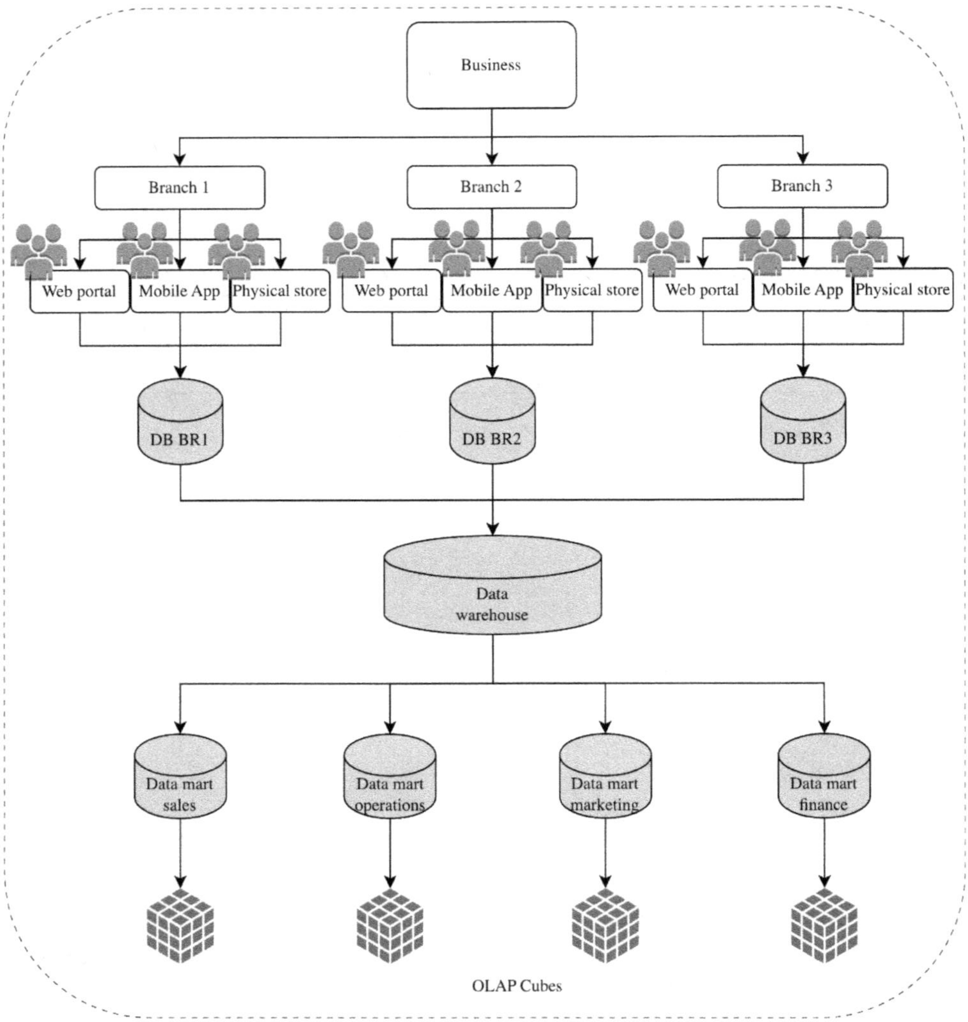

Figure 3.8: *Example representation of an OLAP system*

OLAP cube

It is a multidimensional data structure, characterized by its dimensions. Each dimension is associated with a corresponding attribute, e.g., phones, laptops, tablets, etc.

All the selected dimensions are combined and calculated to derive a certain fact and give a quick multidimensional output.

Take the following table as an example, which shows the sales data of electronic products of a company in different countries:

Country	Product	Year	Sales
India	Laptop	2023	$16000
France	Laptop	2023	$15000
Spain	Laptop	2023	$6700
India	Mobile	2023	$14200

***Table 3.2**: Example of the yearly sales data*

Figure 3.9 shows how the sales of mobiles, laptops, and tablets are mapped across different countries and years in a single cube. Here, it shows three dimensions as countries, products, and years.

The major advantage of this is that, since this is a pre-calculated cube, all the information is quickly available, e.g., India | Laptop | 2023 = $16,000.

An OLAP cube can conceptually have as many dimensions as needed, which are dependent upon business analysis requirements, complexity, and performance of the cube.

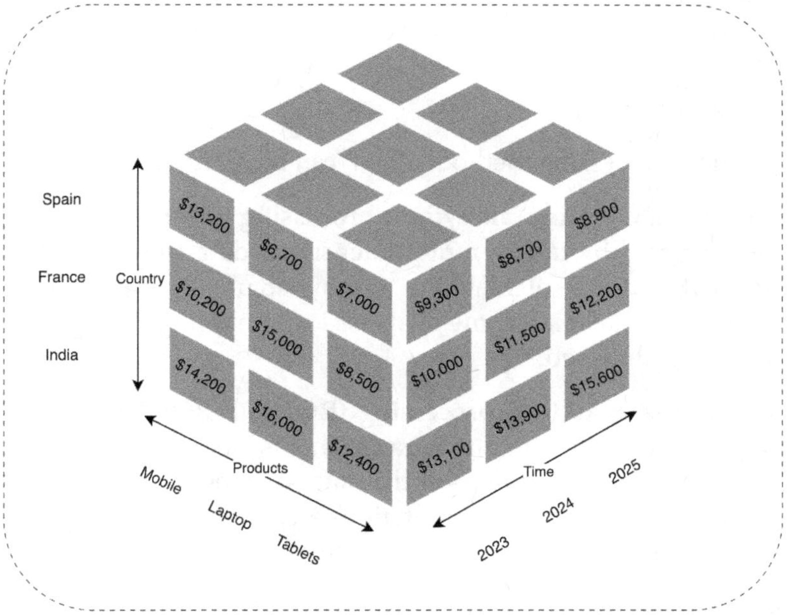

***Figure 3.9**: Example representation of an OLAP cube*

Some of the operations that are possible on OLAP cubes are:

- **Rollup**: Reducing dimensionality by aggregating data along a certain dimension.
- **Drilldown**: Increasing the dimension by splitting the data further for deep analysis, e.g., going from yearly to quarterly/monthly data.

- **Slicing**: Reducing dimensionality by choosing a particular value from a dimension, e.g., all sales in 2024 across countries.
- **Dicing**: Picking up a subset of values from each dimension, e.g., tablets in France for 2024 and 2025.
- **Pivoting**: Rotating the data cube.

Working of OLAP

OLAP works on collecting, organizing, aggregating, and analyzing data as follows:

- The data is collected from various databases or data warehouses by an OLAP server.
- After the data collection, ETL is performed on the data to clean, process, aggregate, calculate, and store it into an OLAP cube with chosen dimensions.
- Now businesses can use OLAP tools to query, analyze, and generate reports from these cubes.

Azure Synapse Analytics, Azure Analysis Services, AWS Redshift, and AWS Athena are some of the managed tools or services available in the market that support OLAP.

Types of OLAP

Based on the analytical processing method, OLAP can be of different types, as follows:

- **Multi-dimensional online analytical processing (MOLAP)**: A MOLAP is a data cube that is created by taking multidimensional data from data warehouses, which is transformed and pre-calculated in the hypercube. Since this is specially curated and pre-calculated, keeping some business logic in mind, it is fast in execution and is widely accepted and used.
- **Relational online analytical processing (ROLAP)**: ROLAP is the method of doing direct analysis on a relational database. This is done using SQL queries to search and analyze different dimensions of the data. It gives the user the flexibility of doing extensive analysis with many permutations and combinations, but due to the varying nature of analysis, it may be slower than the readily available MOLAP.

  For example:

  ```
  SELECT region, YEAR(order_date) AS year, SUM(sales) AS total_sales FROM
  orders GROUP BY region, YEAR(order_date) ORDER BY region, year;
  ```

  This query is trying to read the large data that is being grouped by region and year.
- **Hybrid online analytical processing (HOLAP)**: HOLAP is the combination of MOLAP and ROLAP. The data engineers can start with MOLAP to understand and analyze

the available dimensions of the data, and based on the progress in their approach, they may extend the analysis and move towards ROLAP, where they can add more dimensions and deliberate on the subject.

Logs

Logs can be defined as capturing the events or actions, or messages in the system, with when, what, and who as the basic information, as discussed:

- **When**: When the event occurs, it captures the timestamp of the system, e.g., 2025-07-24T00:02:01.457+05:30, where:
  - **2025**: Year
  - **07**: Month (July)
  - **24**: Date
  - **T**: Time starts
  - **00**: Hour(12)
  - **02**: Minutes
  - **01**: Seconds
  - **457**: Milliseconds
  - +: Addition of time offset
  - **05:30**: Adding time offset of 05:30, i.e., Indian time
- **What**: What the event was, i.e., it may also store the metadata, e.g., **`INFO [auth-service] User login successful`**
- **Who**: This is defined by who was taking the action, a human or a service account; e.g., the user ID of the user can be captured:

  ```
  user_id=78432.
  ```

  As a complete view, it would look something like the following:

  ```
  2025-07-24T00:02:01.457+05:30 | INFO [auth-service] User login successful
  | user_id=78432
  ```

Logs help in monitoring, debugging, auditing, and troubleshooting the system. They are also considered to be rich sources of downstream data analysis, machine learning algorithms, and any other decision-making systems.

Types of logs

Based upon the sources of generation, there are various types of logs as follows:

- **Application**: These are messages generated by any developed application.
- **Operating system**: These are the logs generated by the operating system that may include boot, shutdown, system crash, and any other activities performed by the user.
- **Security**: Logs that have been generated by implemented security controls, such as firewall, login attempts, etc.
- **Access**: Logs that show who accessed the system and web portal and when.

- **Error**: These are the logs that have been configured to be triggered when the system fails or when there is any exception.
- **Transaction**: These are the logs that contain information about all the transactions in the system, such as financial transactions in banking systems.

Levels of logs

Basically, there are levels of logs defined so that the associated action can be taken, as follows:

- **Info**: General event information that does not require any actions.
- **Warning**: These are the potential events that can lead to failure in the long run, but as of now, not creating any issues.
- **Debug**: These are the detailed logs, which are implemented by the developers so that they can go in-depth while debugging a particular issue.
- **Error**: These are the serious issues that are failing some functionalities of an application, but the overall application is running.
- **Critical**: These are the fatal issues that crash the application or system and need prioritized attention.

Database logs

Although it can be covered in the preceding topic, due to its way of working, it can also be categorized as a separate topic.

Generally, logs are post-event activity, but in the case of the database, this is a pre-event one. They are the reason for the reliability and recoverability of the database management system. Whenever there is any **create, read, update, or delete** (**CRUD**) operation that needs to be performed on the database, before the acknowledgment of the operation, the logs are created. These are typically the binary files, stored in a database native format.

Once the acknowledgment of a request is sent, and if the server fails or reboots, it goes through the logs and completes the pending work when it comes back.

This is how logs not only show the operations happening on the database but also play a critical role in database guarantees and recoverability.

Databases

Databases can be referred to as an organized place where data is stored for future retrieval. When we think about the database, data storage is the first thought that comes to our mind without any doubt, but in this section, we are exploring the database as one of the crucial data sources.

These databases can be created from the data collection done by the user's interactive applications or any system that is collecting information from various sources. These databases may also be filled by other databases after data transformation.

There are different types of databases based on the type of data storage and retrieval mechanisms, and they are discussed in the following sections.

Relational databases

The **relational database management system** (**RDBMS**) is the most popularly used application for backend requirements. A relation is a table with tuples (rows) and attributes (columns).

As shown in *Table 3.3*, there is structured data available in relation form with three attributes (ID, Name, Age) and two tuples:

ID	Name	Age
1234	Jane kas	25
5678	Tom Harry	35

***Table 3.3**: Example of a relational database*

They are called relational because they strictly follow the rules of the relational model principles. Examples of some renowned relational databases are Oracle, SQL Server, MySQL, PostgreSQL, SQLite, etc.

Nonrelational databases

On the contrary, nonrelational databases are the ones that do not follow all the principles of the relational model. They do not store data in tabular format; rather, they may store the data in key-value pairs, JSON, graphs, or other flexible ways without strict linking rules.

The following is an example of a JSON format data storage:

```
[
{
"ID": 1234,
"Name": "Jane kas",
"Age": 25
},
{
"ID": 5678,
"Name": "Tom Harry",
"Age": 35
```

```
}
]
```

These types of databases prioritize flexibility, speed, and scalability over a structured way of storing data. In cases where the type of data, attributes, and velocity are not fixed, in these areas, these types of nonrelational data models come in handy to help us achieve the end goal. Some of the well-known names are MongoDB, Redis, and Neo4j.

There are different types of nonrelational databases, as follows:

- **Key-value pairs**: There are databases that store all the data in key-value pair format. For example:

  ```
  "user123": {
  "name": "Tom",
  "age": 30,
  "city": "Delhi"
  }
  ```

  Some popular names are Redis, Amazon DynamoDB, etc.

- **Document stores**: These databases store the data as documents in JSON and **Binary JavaScript Object Notation** (**BSON**) format. The fundamental difference between key-value and document stores is the way data is stored and the search mechanism. In this model, the data is stored as a key and the whole document as a value, which can be queried. Also, document stores support more complex and larger structured payloads compared to key-value stores, as they are designed to store rich, hierarchical data rather than simple key-value pairs.

  E.g., in a key-value-based database, we cannot apply a direct query to find the users where age >25, but a document DB allows us to query the fields directly, by following a certain query format, as follows:

  ```
  e.g.,  db.users.find({ "age": { "$gt": 25 } })
  ```

  The preceding query can be used to find the users having an age > 25, from the document DB, as follows:

  ```
  {
  "_id": "user123",
  "name": "Tom",
  "age": 30,
  "city": "Delhi"
  }
  ```

  MongoDB is the most popular document database.

- **Column-family store**: This type of NoSQL database stores data in a table but in a flexible manner. In this database, the rows are column-agnostic, which means any row can store whatever columns it needs.

  For example:

  - Row1: `user 123 ->{"time": "10am", "device": "Android"}`
  - Row2: `user 456 ->{"device": "Android", "location": "New Delhi"}`
  - Row3: `user 789 ->{"battery": "80%","mode":"airplane"}`

  Databases that support column-family stores are Apache Cassandra, Google Bigtable, etc.

- **Graph database**: This database is meant for use cases where the relationships between the nodes are the primary point of focus, and traversing among the nodes is needed.

  Social media platforms, such as *Facebook*, work on this philosophy.

  For example:

  - **Node**: `Person`:

    ```
    {
    "name": "Tom",
    "age": 30
    }
    ```

  - **Node**: `Company`:

    ```
    {
    "name": "Apple"
    }
    ```

  - **Edge**: `WORKS_AT`:

    ```
    {
    "since": "2007"
    }
    ```

In *Figure 3.10*, it is clearly visible that an entity, Tom, is connected to another entity, Apple, with a relationship as an employee or worker:

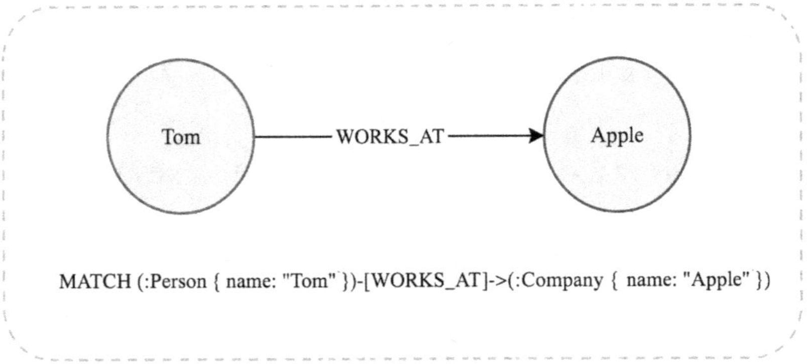

***Figure 3.10**: A visual representation of how the nodes are connected*

Databases like Neo4j and Amazon Neptune are some big names in the industry.

- **Search**: These databases are designed to speed up and optimize text search, filtering, and analytics. These are used in the areas where a quick search is needed from a vast amount of data, e.g., Elastic Search, in which Inverted indexes improve performance by mapping words to documents, enabling direct lookup instead of scanning all data, which makes search operations extremely fast.

  With an inverted index, Elasticsearch stores data in a structure like:

  Apple | doc1, doc3, doc10

  Banana | doc2, doc3

  Phone | doc1, doc5

  When searching for a word like **`Apple`**, instead of scanning every document, the system directly looks up **`Apple`** in the index and retrieves the list of documents where it appears (**`doc1`**, **`doc3`**, **`doc10`**).

- **Time series**: These databases mainly organize the data around timestamps, storing them in a sequence that has been gathered over time. These databases are useful in many industrial applications where the behavior pattern and performance of a particular system or machine over time are to be determined. While a traditional database can use a timestamp as a primary key, it does not achieve the same efficiency as a time series database. This is because time series databases are specifically optimized for time-based queries, high write throughput, and efficient storage mechanisms like compression, partitioning, and time-based indexing, which general-purpose databases are not designed for.

  For example:

```
timestamp = 20250507T00:01:50, temperature =  29.5°C
timestamp = 20250507T00:01:51, temperature =  29.3°C
timestamp = 20250507T00:01:52, temperature =  29.5°C
```

Databases like InfluxDB and Amazon Time Stream are some well-known names.

We will discuss these databases in more detail in *Chapter 7, Introduction to Data Storage*.

Messages and streams

Messages and streams represent the movement of data between the systems, although these two terms are very closely related, they are not the same. Let us understand them in detail.

Messages

A message may be defined as a package that contains data, metadata, and routing information. This is intended for the transportation of data from one system to another only, not for storing; only the data is stored at the final stage, discarding the shell.

For example:

```
data = {"name" : "Tom", "user Id" : "u123"} whereas the
message = {"type":"user generated",
"data":{"name":"Tom","userId":"u123"},
"timestamp":"2025-07-25T10:00:00Z"}
```

Message queue is a mechanism for asynchronous exchange of data between two or more systems. This is like queuing messages one by one on a **first-in, first-out** (**FIFO**) basis. The message will only be removed from the message queue when it has been acknowledged by the receiver.

This usually works on a pub/sub model where the publisher is the source of data generation and the receiving party is the subscriber of that data. There may be multiple subscribers to a single publisher.

Figure 3.11 shows how an individual message is present in the message queue and gets processed in a FIFO manner, and how the respective subscriber takes the messages and acknowledges them:

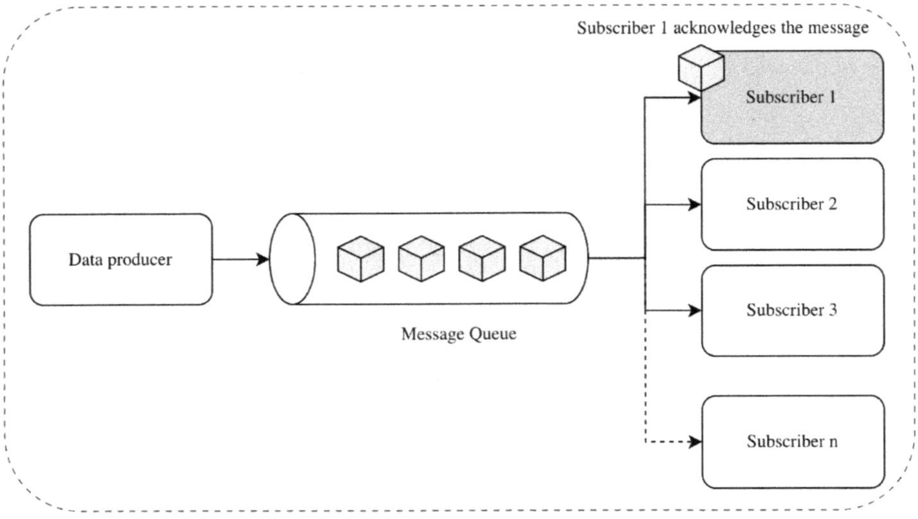

Figure 3.11: *Representation of a message queue*

There are many solutions available in the market that are used for message queues, such as Amazon SQL, RabbitMQ, etc. They are also known as a message broker.

Streams

A continuous flow of messages may be defined as a stream. They are often the ordered pair of messages coming from the source of data, like sensors, logs, etc.

The streams need to be continuously processed and consumed sequentially. On the producer side, there are append-only operations, which means the new records are added continuously, rarely modifying or deleting the old data.

As shown in *Figure 3.12*, many IoT devices are generating a continuous sequence of messages, like a never-ending flow of data; they are ordered, time-based, and can be processed in real-time:

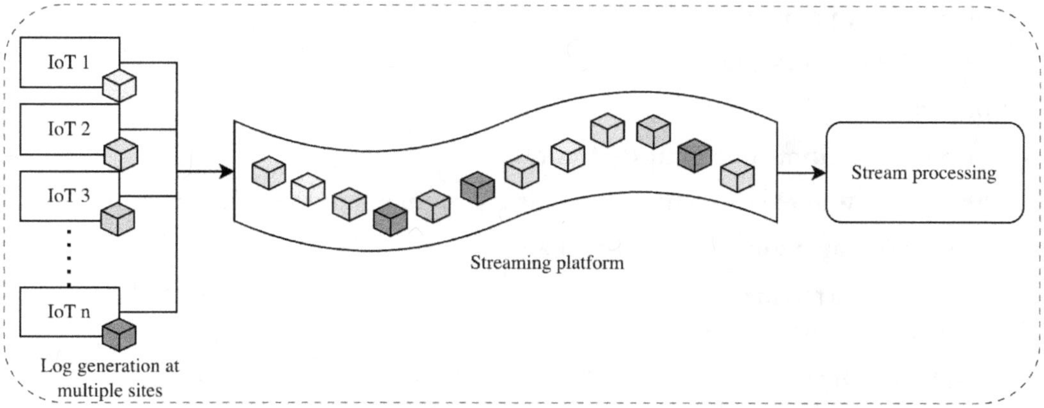

Figure 3.12: *A graphical representation of the stream of data coming from various IoT sensors*

A real-life example can be any video streaming platform like *YouTube* or *Netflix*. Some other examples can be ticker information for any stock when the stock market is live, or the location update of a cab driver every few seconds.

Streaming platforms that are available in the market are Apache Kafka, Amazon Kinesis, etc.

It is important to note that, due to its very nature of high throughput and minimum latency, the processing of any stream, such as a decision on trading based on the current stock price, or the processing of thousands of IoT devices' logs or a real-time auction, is difficult and different from static data analysis and needs specialized types of tools and algorithms. We will cover them in *Chapter 13, Understanding Stream Analytics*.

Conclusion

In this chapter, we covered the basic understanding of data generation, followed by learning the different categories of data. Then we understood the different types of data exchange mechanisms and some of their real-life use cases. We also covered DBMS as a data source and understood the different types of databases available in the market. Lastly, we touched upon the messages and stream types of data sources and how they are handled.

In the next chapter, we will be covering the next step of data generation in the data engineering lifecycle, i.e., data ingestion, and learning about the best practices to follow and different ways of data ingestion depending upon the data source.

References

1. **https://www.zmescience.com/other/great-pics/watch-a-vinyl-and-stylus-at-1000x-magnification/**
2. **https://www.bseindia.com/corporates/List_Scrips.html**

3. **https://blog.postman.com/different-types-of-apis/**
4. **https://graphql.org/learn/queries/**
5. **https://grpc.io/**
6. **https://www.ibm.com/think/topics/oltp**
7. **https://www.geeksforgeeks.org/dbms/difference-between-olap-and-oltp-in-dbms/**
8. **https://aws.amazon.com/what-is/olap/**
9. **https://learn.microsoft.com/en-us/system-center/scsm/olap-cubes-overview?view=sc-sm-2025**
10. **https://neo4j.com/docs/getting-started/graph-database/**

CHAPTER 4
Data Ingestion

Introduction

This book has covered the understanding of various sources of data and how the data can be generated from these data sources. Now, let us try to understand how the data, which is available in various data sources, needs to be handled and ingested in the existing system.

Data ingestion is the entry point to the data pipeline, responsible for bringing data from source systems into the platform in a controlled, reliable, and observable way, often feeding ETL or ELT workflows. This step is crucial for making the decision on the required tools and technologies for data ingestion so that the outcome of the selected approach is as close as possible to the business expectations.

There are many other decisions to be taken at this stage for data movement, whether it is transformation or storage. These decisions include planning the data transformation techniques, applying available tools for it, and finally selecting the right storage medium.

Structure

The chapter covers the following topics:

- Introduction to data ingestion
- Batch data ingestion
- Ways of data ingestion
- Best practices for data ingestion
- Stream data ingestion

Objectives

At the end of this chapter, the reader will be able to understand the basics of data ingestion and what internal processing and validations happen before the data becomes part of the ETL pipeline. This chapter will cover batch and stream data ingestion in detail, and it will also bring up the advantages and disadvantages of both types of ingestion.

The reader would also have a fundamental clarity about how the data ingestion varies depending on the type of data availability at the data source. This will induce a sense of understanding of dependencies and decision-making on infrastructure, which comes only once the type of data, frequency, processing requirement, and criticality of data are clearly assessed.

This chapter will deliberate on the understanding of different ways of data ingestion that will include the connectivity and the ways of receiving the data from the different data sources.

Introduction to data ingestion

Data ingestion may be defined as a process of transferring data from one or more source systems into the platform boundary (such as a storage or streaming layer), ensuring guarantees around reliability, timeliness, and traceability in a complete data engineering lifecycle.

Looking at the complete data engineering lifecycle in *Figure 4.1*, it is clearly visible that it involves collecting, importing, and preparing data from one or more data sources into a system of storage, analysis, or downstream processing.

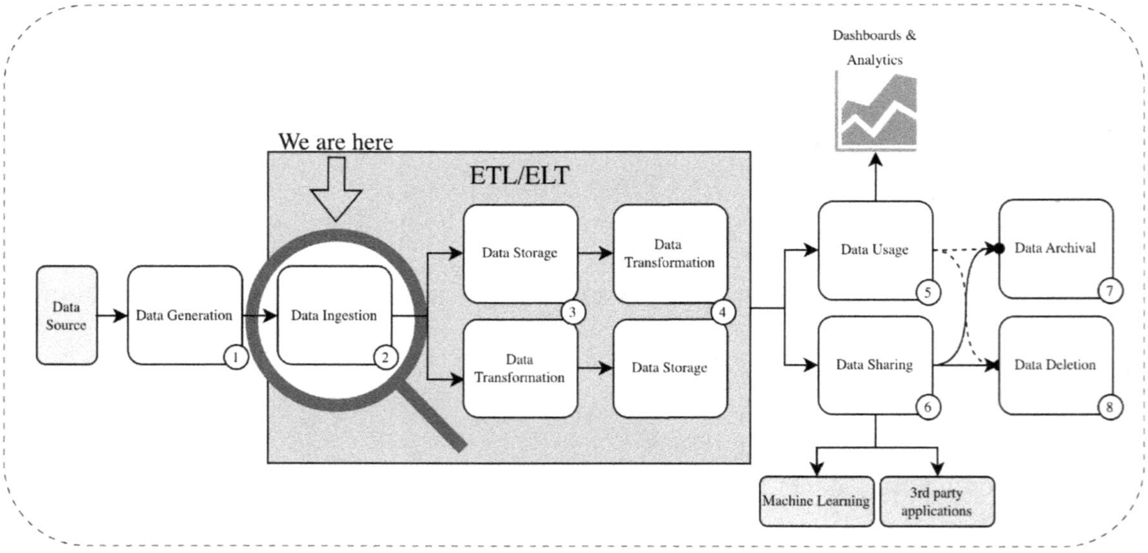

***Figure 4.1**: Showing the current phase covered in the chapter*

As shown in *Figure 4.2*, data ingestion is not limited to collecting the data and storing it in the target storage, but also includes pre-preparation of the data as well, before going into the data transformation pipeline:

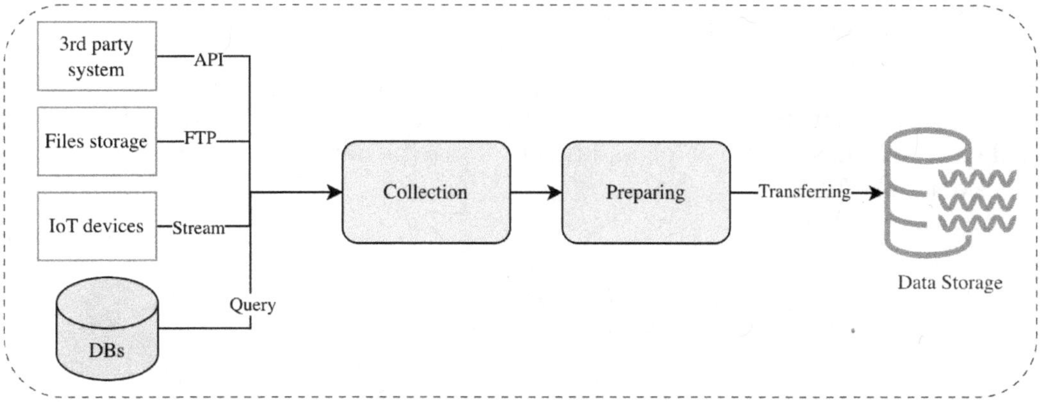

Figure 4.2: *Representation of data ingestion lifecycle*

When the data needs to be gathered from different data sources, the collection process needs to be developed or customized to accommodate different types of data receiving mechanisms. For example, from sources like third-party systems and applications, the API calls need to be developed based on the input structure of the source system to get the appropriate outcome. Similarly, if the data needs to be collected from databases, the right table and its structure need to be known to apply efficient and effective SQL queries, instead of asking for bulk data.

To conclude, the correct method of requesting data is mandatory to make a smooth transaction.

Once the data collection is set up, the raw input data is immediately validated and prepared to ensure that the ingested data is safe to store (without any corruption), consistently formatted (dates, numbers, etc), and clean enough to be stored in the staging environment.

Some of the typical tasks in preparation involve basic cleaning, format standardization, deduplication, and schema validation to ensure the expected consistency; e.g., importing data from Excel may need an initial format validation, which checks if the Excel file has all the required columns. So there must be a program that ensures the availability of these columns and catches this exception beforehand.

Fundamentally, it is making the data clean enough to land on our system safely.

Data pipeline

A data pipeline may be defined as a series of steps that are involved in collecting, processing, transforming, and storing the data into the final destination. As covered in *Chapter 1, Basic Understanding of Data Engineering, Figure 1.6,* it collects data from various data sources, which is ingested into a temporary storage, then transformed, and finally stored in the final storage system, which may be a data warehouse.

It may also follow a straight process, that is, right after the collection, instead of storing it in a temporary storage, it is transformed and stored in the final storage.

Ingestion as a part of ETL

As shown in *Figure 4.3*, ingestion is the starting point of ETL and happens at the extraction layer. It collects the raw data, follows basic cleaning and sanitization, works on the standardization of the data on the go (if applicable), and finally stores the data in the temporary data storage, such as a data lake.

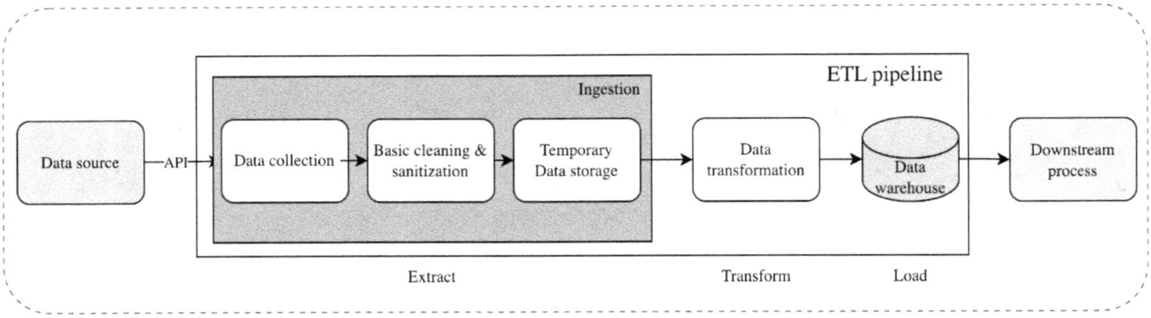

***Figure 4.3**: Representation of an ETL pipeline with ingestion components*

This may also be a part of the ELT pipeline, where it will do the basic checks and sanitization on the data, and then will pass the data onto the transformation layer, where the data will be enriched, aggregated based on certain calculations, different tables are joined together to achieve collective business outcome and after some business logic based transformation, the final outcome will be stored in the data warehouse. Now the data is readily available for any downstream process, whether it is for analytics or feeding into the machine learning models.

Best practices for data ingestion

Data ingestion can be broadly classified into two types, based on the frequency of data arrival and processing:

- Batch data ingestion
- Stream data ingestion

As an architect, there are some considerations that need to be taken care of while setting up the data ingestion. These understandings and practices will cut across both types of processing.

However, before understanding the different ways of ingestion, let us see the important aspects that need to be considered while setting up the whole ingestion process.

Bounded versus unbounded data

Bounded data can be defined as the source data that has a boundary or a limit. They have a clear starting point and a clear end point. Some of the examples can be data present in a **comma separated values** (**CSV**) file, or logs collected from a system overnight, or data accessed from a database for a certain duration.

Unbounded data is continuous and has no boundaries; this may be sensor data, customers' transaction data that is happening 24x7, etc.

Although unbounded data can be given a fictitious boundary, which may be repeated continuously, these boundaries can be of a fixed time interval, count of data packets, or size of a bunch of data packets, etc.

In *Figure 4.4*, the upper figure depicts the bounded data where there is an exchange of data in a CSV file, having fixed data available in the file. Then there is a continuous data flow shown, which has no start or end point. In a real-life analogy, it is just like a river. However, the last one clearly shows the division of continuous data streams in clear hour boundaries. For example, customers' transaction data on an e-commerce company, which is being generated 24x7, can be bound by hours, or, in other words, we may say, hourly sales data.

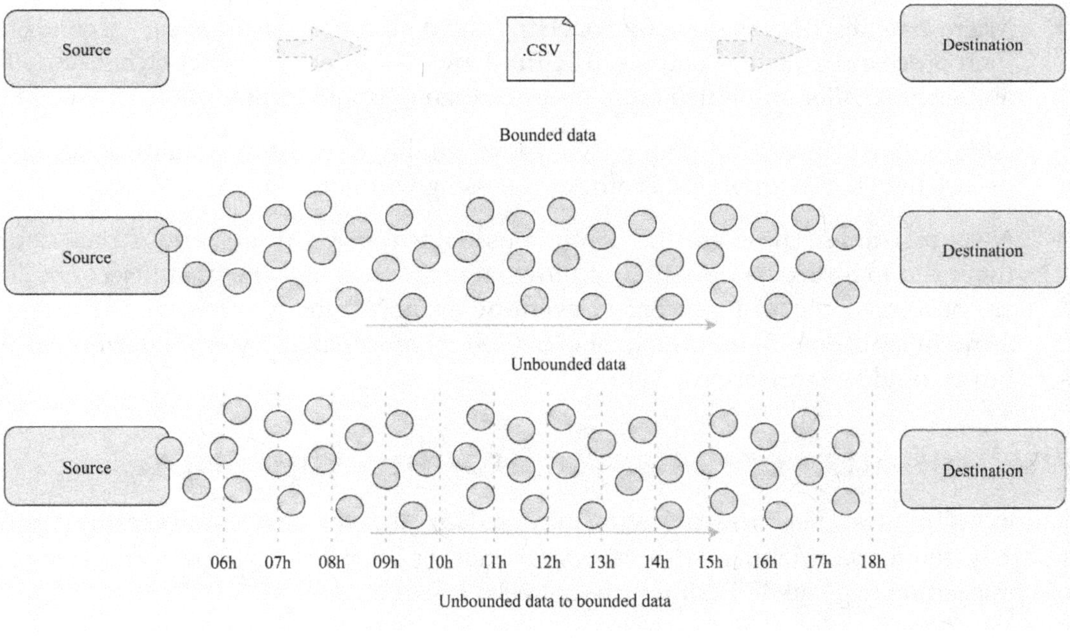

***Figure 4.4**: Illustration of bounded and unbounded processing*

Bounded data generally follows two steps, *store* and *process*, whereas the unbounded data requires to be processed event by event. Analogically, we can say that, as we observe life daily, it is a continuous flow of information that is perceived by our five senses, and our brain is processing it, event by event.

Since the bounded data comes in specific starting and ending points, it must be processed in batches. On the other hand, the unbounded data is continuous and is received as a stream; this means it must be processed as a stream.

Frequency

Frequency of the data may be explained as the rate of receiving the data at a unit time interval, e.g., 25 packets per minute, considering the number of packets as a unit to quantify the data.

While ingesting the data into the destination, the frequency plays an important role, considering the efforts applied in basic quality checks, as part of the ingestion lifecycle.

To process the data based on frequency, there would be different techniques applicable. There is no thumb rule as such, and it solely depends upon the business requirements, but on a higher level, there can be three ways the data can be handled:

- **Batch**: This is taking a big chunk or bulk of data and processing it, chunk by chunk, e.g., processing of logs of an IoT device every five hours.
- **Micro-batches**: This is done by collecting the data for lesser time, e.g., seconds, and then processing them as batches. The fundamental difference is in batch sizes, which are much smaller and much more frequent than normal batches.

  Although the processing frequency is less than that of real-time data processing, it is used where the requirement is quick processing with low latency.
- **Near real-time**: These are the continuous data received from various data sources that need to be processed with ultra-low-latency, which may be in milliseconds. They are processed, record-by-record or event-by-event. Although we strive to process the same in real-time, due to the latency added in processing, using the term near real-time would be more appropriate.

Synchronous versus asynchronous ingestion

Synchronous (request/response) ingestion may be defined as the process of ingesting the data in a strictly sequential manner, with each step waiting for a response or acknowledgment before proceeding (e.g., an API call returns success/failure).

Consider a synchronous ETL workflow orchestration as an example; refer to the first flow in *Figure 4.5*. A pipeline ingests a batch of data, transforms it, and stores it. Since the output of this pipeline is connected to a machine learning model, which takes some time to train, the result or inference finally reaches the destination system. If this whole process takes hours to complete, then in case any process breaks in between due to some issues in the data, the subsequent processes will also go on hold. This makes the complete pipeline vulnerable to issues and complex to diagnose.

On the contrary, an asynchronous ingestion (event/message-driven) is defined as the ingestion process whose intermediate steps have been designed in such a way that each process is handled independently. The data producers do not wait for the data consumer to finish processing. This is typically implemented using message queues or event streaming platforms, where producers and consumers operate independently. Each component in the pipeline is responsible for a specific task and can scale or fail without directly impacting others.

As shown in *Figure 4.5*, the data collection component can take the data and pass it onto the message queue. This message queue will give data to the processing engine, which is responsible for transforming the data. After transforming the data, the data processing engine will put the data back onto another message queue, which will be pushed to the storage medium using a different asynchronous process.

The advantage of this approach is that the message queues act as a cushioning agent, where all the increase in load can be absorbed. This way, any breakage at any step does not affect the whole pipeline, e.g., failure of the processing agent will not stop the data collection process, and this way, the critical data would not be lost in the case of failure.

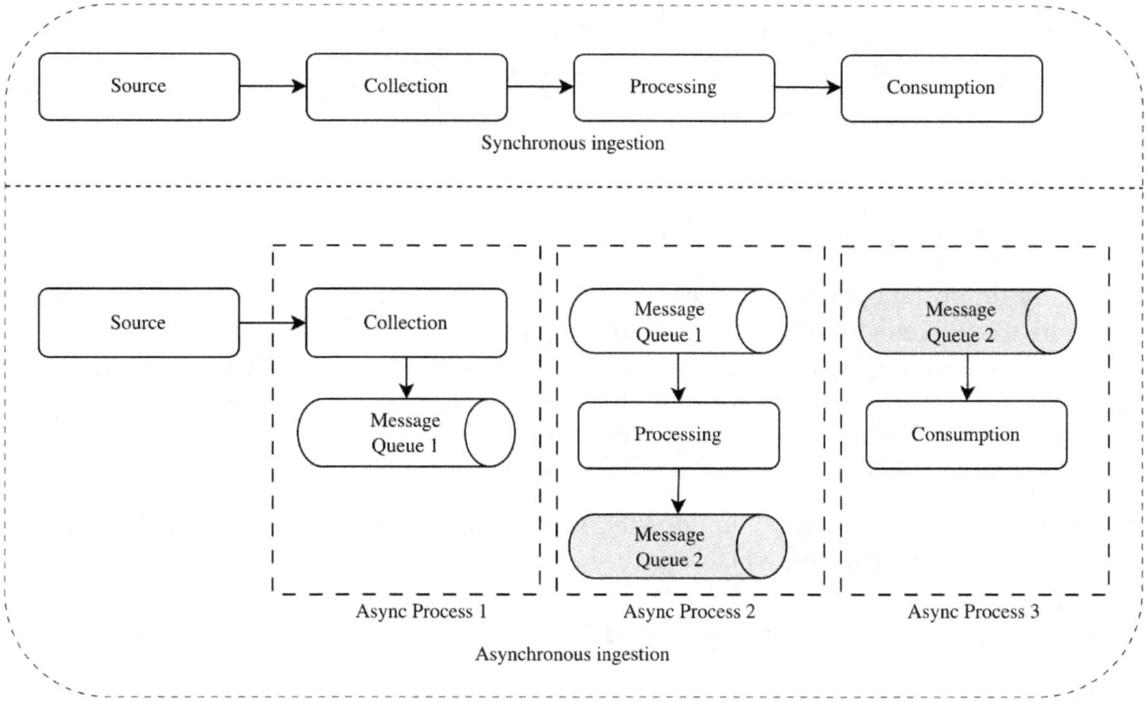

Figure 4.5: *Representation of the synchronous versus asynchronous way of processing*

Serialization and deserialization

Serialization is defined as the process of converting an in-memory data structure or object into a format that can be easily transferred and stored. The result is generally a platform-independent file or a database.

For example, Dictionary in Python | JSON structure

Deserialization is the process of reconstructing a data structure from a serialized form, i.e., a file or a database. It involves interpreting the encoded format and transforming it into an equivalent in-memory representation that the application can use.

For example, JSON structure | Dictionary in Python

By analogy, it is like packing household goods into cartons for transportation so that they can be transferred easily, and unpacking them as they reach the destination.

The API communication commonly uses JSON due to its simple and lightweight structure. However, high-volume data pipelines often rely on binary or columnar formats for better efficiency and performance.

This becomes the prime requirement to convert the in-memory data into these acceptable, platform-independent formats (serialization). Once it reaches the destination, it may be converted back to its original form, if required (deserialization).

This allows the data to be transferred in a standard format for the ingestion process. The efforts for serialization and deserialization need to be considered when setting up the complete ingestion cycle.

Throughput and scalability

This is an important aspect that needs to be worked upon, whether the current ingestion pipeline is capable of handling the high throughput or not. There may be some possibilities that the data source is intermittently generating a huge amount of data, in other words, spikes, for which the ingestion platform should be able to handle these spikes, either by employing the buffering mechanism that will ease the downstream processing, or there may be a usage of scalable components that scale up the processing power to handle an increase in the dataflow.

In general practice, managed components from cloud providers have automatic horizontal and vertical scaling features, which may be helpful in such conditions.

Reliability and durability

Reliability means the uptime of an ingestion system that results in storing data consistently without any data loss. In case of any conditions like network failure or peak load, the loss should be minimal, and also, no data should be duplicated. There should be a mechanism for retries to retrieve data in case of problems.

Durability focuses on the post-ingestion dimension of data, which ensures that the data will not be corrupted or lost in case of any issue, such as a power failure, a hardware failure, or a system crash. It ensures that the system is transferring data to the persistent or storage layer so that when the system comes up after any failure, it has correct and complete data available.

This can be viewed at two levels:

- **Durability of data transfer**: Ensuring that data in transit (e.g., within message queues or logs) is persisted reliably and can be recovered or replayed in case of failure.
- **Durability of the storage layer**: Ensuring that once data is written to the destination (e.g., databases or data lakes), it is safely stored and remains intact over time.

Payload

For any ingestion process, the payload plays a very important role because this is the dataset you are ingesting. The ingestion efficiency depends upon the characteristics of the payload. These characteristics are:

- **Structure**: This is defined as the way the data is arranged. Fundamentally, there are two types of data: *structured and unstructured*. The data that has a well-organized structure and follows a predefined schema is called structured data. Schemas like Excel, .csv, and relational databases fall in this category. On the other side, the data that is not organized in any particular fashion and does not fit in rows and columns format is unstructured data, images, videos, and free text fall in this category. There is a third category, also, which is called semi-structured. This is not rigidly structured like a database or relational tabular structure, but it is not free textual data either; formats like JSON and XML would come in this category.
- **Datatype**: These are the types of data that are being exchanged, e.g., textual, image, video, tabular. According to their type, the file extension also changes. For example, tabular data may come in CSV format, an image file may be available in JPG and PNG formats, etc.
- **Size**: The size may be defined as the number of bytes of a payload. This size can vary, and based on the size, the processing of the payload also varies; some payloads can be consumed as is, and some require chunking into small payloads before actual processing.
- **Metadata**: This is defined as data about data. There may be a possibility that the metadata is also being received from the data source, which has many advantages. For example, it can help as an instruction manual for handling the data.

We may know the definition of each column that has been received so that we can take the right steps, e.g., for **`Column 1`** in a file, we may know the details in metadata, which shows this column is for **`employee_id`**, which is a string type with not more than ten characters.

As a data engineer, it helps us create the required data definition in the database.

Similarly, we have many advantages, like applying validations (Weight < 100 kg), data governance information, and more in-depth information that may help us create a correct data structure, choose the right storage platform, etc.

Ingesting methods

Although we have covered many factors that affect the data ingestion from a throughput and latency standpoint, knowing how the data is being fetched from the source is also critical and affects the overall pipeline.

There are three different ways the data can be fetched:

- **Push (webhook/events/pub-sub)**: This is the simplest method of data ingestion, where the data source simply pushes the data to the receiver as soon as the data is available. This is initiated by the source and has the lowest latency because the data becomes available as soon as it arrives. However, on the other side, the destination should always be ready to receive the data.
- **Pull (on-demand)**: In this approach, the destination system requests data from the source when needed. Here, the destination is the initiator of the request, which means it can control when and how much data is needed. This makes the overall system less compute-intensive, since the call from the destination is generally on a need basis, which may spike very seldom. This approach is preferred where the requirement is to get the latest data without thinking about the missed data. To handle that kind of requirement, it can be configured to pull the entire batch of data at once.
- **Scheduled pull (polling)**: Similar to pull, this approach is initiated by the destination, which checks for data availability at the source, and when the data is available, the data will be pulled on demand. It is like a data pipeline asking for the data every five minutes. This approach is mainly used where the source data availability is unknown or does not have the push method available due to the following:
  - Customer's control over the data, and they do not offer push.
  - Source system lacks push capability, e.g., legacy systems
  - The destination has security restrictions where external pushes are not accepted.

Referring to *Figure 4.6*, it is clearly visible how the data initiation takes place between the source and the destination. In case of push, the source is initiating the communication by directly providing the data, whereas in case of pull and poll, the destination initiates and asks for the data from the source, which responds with the data if it has.

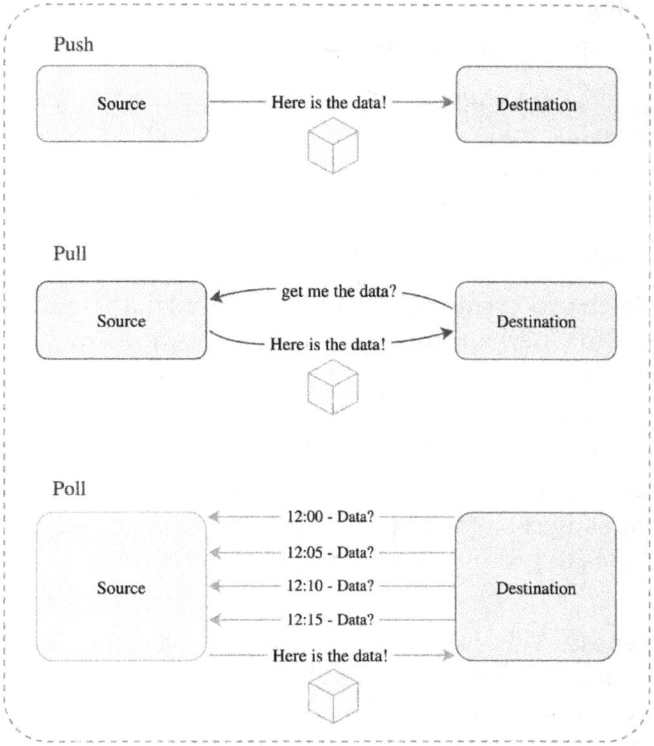

Figure 4.6: *Representation of push, pull, and poll type methods of data ingestion*

As a data engineer or architect, once the ingestion method is clearly defined, the best-suited architecture is chosen for efficient communication, and accordingly, the downstream processes are configured.

Batch data ingestion

Batch data ingestion is defined as the collection and processing of data in predefined, fixed-sized chunks called batches. As discussed earlier, it may also be converting unbounded data into bounded data. These chunks can be created in different ways:

- **Time-based**: It divides the batches based on the time, e.g., hourly, daily, and weekly.
- **Size-based**: It divides the chunks into a fixed size, e.g., the batch file will have a maximum size of 5 MB; if there is more data, a subsequent file will be created.
- **Count-based**: It is defined as the batch created based upon the number of events, and that fixed set of events will be processed in the downstream process, e.g., 100 events per batch will be processed in one go.

The decision on batch processing is highly dependent upon the infrastructure capacity and is usually decided based on the expected business outcomes.

Batch processing is suited for business requirements where real-time or immediate analysis is not required, and the ability to handle huge amounts of data efficiently is the prime objective.

Practically, batch pipelines are often designed using incremental processing patterns such as filtering data based on a last updated timestamp or processing specific partitions so that only new or changed data is handled instead of reprocessing the entire dataset. This improves efficiency and reduces processing time.

The following are the advantages of batch data ingestion:

- **Simplicity**: Batch processing is relatively simple as it does not require a complex real-time data handling mechanism and focuses on the infrastructure that would be able to process the batch efficiently.
- **Scalability**: This type of processing is highly scalable because, as soon as the batch size is defined, based upon the infrastructure and processing capacity, it is just a matter of horizontal alignment of multiple resources together to handle a larger volume, which is also known as horizontal scaling. When the load increases, i.e., when the source has more batches to process, it just adds horizontal components to meet the surge in demand.
- **Cost-effectiveness**: This is because this is a periodic process, which requires the infrastructure and processing to be active at specific times of the hour/minute/day. Due to these computational requirements, the result is a lower processing cost.

The following are the disadvantages of batch data ingestion:

- **Delayed processing**: Since batch processing is designed to execute in fixed intervals, the insights will not be immediately available. This may not be suitable for supercritical requirements, such as analysis of the live data coming from the flight engine.
- **Outdated insights**: Similar to the above point, the batch processing works on relatively old data, potentially making the insights less timely. There may be a case where the latest data has been missed in the last processed batch, due to which the decision taken on the older insight may be far from expectations.

Stream data ingestion

Stream data ingestion is defined as the processing of data as soon as it arrives in the source system. In this approach, the data is collected and analyzed for the correct structure, quality, and other validations in near real-time.

This type of ingestion is ideal for applications that require quick, real-time insights and decision-making. It helps individuals or organizations to respond immediately to critical events, e.g., in the stock trading world, organizations need to make decisions on the current price of a stock in real-time based on the changing price patterns.

Like batch processing, stream data ingestion also has its advantages and disadvantages:

- **Advantages of stream data ingestion**:
    - **Real-time insights**: The major advantage is the rapid response that comes after the real-time processing of data, which helps in quick, critical decision-making.
    - **Low latency**: Based on the nature of stream data processing, the insight is available in an instant, which accelerates decision-making and response to the situation.
    - **Relevant outcome**: The stream data ingestion takes the latest data for processing, so the insights that are generated are appropriate and do not miss out on important latest aspects. This leads to the right decisions that are based upon the correct and up-to-date data.
    - **Scalability**: Managed data streaming services can scale efficiently by automatically handling resource provisioning, load balancing, and fault tolerance.
- **Disadvantages of stream data ingestion**:
    - **Complex**: Stream data ingestion processing is not as simple as batch processing and requires special tools and infrastructure to handle this kind of data.
    - **Resource heavy**: Since the stream data requires the data to be processed continuously, this requires computing power all the time so that, in real time, the insights can be generated and given to the downstream process. This makes the overall system resource heavy.
    - **Costly**: Due to the nature of the requirements of stream data ingestion, the infrastructure needs to be continuously up and running. This results in the high cost of infrastructure and technology.

Ways of data ingestion

Till now, it has been described how the data needs to be ingested based on the business requirements. It is imperative to understand the different ways that the data can be ingested into the destination.

Database connection

When the data source provides direct access to its database, the destination needs to create a connection with the source database using a database driver or connector (e.g., Java Database Connectivity, JDBC, Open Database Connectivity, ODBC, or vendor-specific drivers). Using this, the destination application can use SQL queries to access the data directly from the data source and process it according to the requirements.

Generally, direct database sharing is not considered a good practice because:

- **Schema changes**: Any change in the source database in the later stages may affect the existing ingestion process, e.g., addition or deletion of columns in the source database.
- **Scalability limits**: A database server has limits on concurrent connections. Direct ingestion into the database from multiple connections may exhaust the limits.
- **Security risks**: Direct database access means exposing database credentials. If any ingestion node is compromised, the attackers can get full access to the database, which may affect the organization from a compliance perspective and may incur huge financial losses to the company due to a breach in confidential data.
- **Performance issues**: Connecting directly to the database requires a good amount of resources (CPU, memory, and I/O) from the data source, which may not be available all the time and may result in adverse effects on the final analysis.

The recommended way should be abstracting the access via APIs or putting the data directly into the message queues from which the ingestion system can collect the data.

Full and change data capture

There are two ways of data capture in the context of data ingestion:

- **Full data capture**: In this approach, the complete data is extracted from the data source, despite having information about old data already existing. For example, suppose there are ten sensors in the field; a full data extract means taking all the readings of the sensors at a particular instant.

  This method is usually employed in batch processing, where the complete source table is captured without any logical processing. This leads to resource-heavy transactions and redundant information availability at the destination.

- **Change data capture (CDC)**: This is the technique in which the change in the existing data is detected, and only the changed data is ingested into the destination system. Taking the above example, suppose only three sensors have new readings; then data from only three sensors will be captured at the destination, unlike all ten sensors in the case of full data capture.

  This may be achieved by various means of comparing the old values with the new values, and accordingly, the decision is taken. Typical CDC mechanisms are:

  - **Log-based CDC**: Reads transaction logs to capture changes.
  - **Timestamp-based CDC**: Uses a `last_updated` column to fetch new/changed records.
  - **Trigger-based CDC**: Uses database triggers to record changes.

  This method is very efficient since it involves the movement of changed data only. Due to its very nature of low latency, this can be used in near-real-time data ingestion, which reduces heavy read loads on the source database or system.

Application programming interfaces

As covered in *Chapter 3, Data Generation in Source System,* APIs nowadays are the most popular way of exchanging data between source and destination. In a typical organization, there may be hundreds of source systems that may have exposed their APIs while keeping their internal details hidden, or in other words, abstracted.

These ingestion systems access the APIs, do the basic processing, and store that data for further processing.

An important point to note is that these APIs may be configured or customized based on the business requirements, and how these APIs will provide data (current readings, bulk data, or file, etc.) will be decided based on that.

Electronic data interchange

Electronic data interchange (EDI) is a method of exchanging business documents electronically between the source and the destination. These have been standardized for business documents, e.g., invoices, purchase orders, etc.

In general, without EDI, a PDF invoice is received that needs to be manually entered into an ERP system. This may cause errors and is also time-consuming. However, EDI can be electronically exchanged, and the ERP system can directly consume and store the data without any human intervention. This enables fast and low-error execution. EDI does require validation, data mapping, and coordination with trading partners to ensure data consistency and correct format exchange.

Similarly, in data engineering, if there is a business document that needs to be ingested, a solution like EDI will ease the completed processing, where the EDI messages received will have to be parsed into a structured format like JSON, CSV, or DB, and then will be passed to the downstream processing.

On the downside, there would be some efforts from the data source level or partners for the implementation of EDI. Once successfully set up, EDI processing brings speed, fewer human errors, lower operational costs, and compliance to the overall pipeline.

File export

If the source sends a file as a response to an API call, then the ingestion system may require another layer of processing for the file. The processing also depends upon the type of file received, e.g., the extraction of a response PDF will have a different processing than the extraction of an Excel or a CSV file.

Once the data is extracted from these files, it may be passed to the initial format check and data processing steps, which can then be passed to the next layer of consumption.

Shell

Although the shell is not a data ingestion tool by itself, it is an orchestrator. It is a script where all the commands for calling APIs and processing the response can be written and executed.

The shell script may read the data directly from the database, serialize it into an acceptable file format, trigger the basic processing, and store the data in the database.

Secure Shell

Secure Shell (**SSH**) is a protocol for securely connecting to another computer over the network. SSH is used to securely connect to and access the shell of the remote system.

From a data ingestion perspective, the destination machine can securely log into the source system, transfer the file using **Secure Copy** (**SCP**), or tunnel the data for further processing.

Secure file transfer protocol or Secure Copy

Secure file transfer protocol (**SFTP**) is another way of accessing the file from a source server, where the destination needs to create a connection with the data source machine, and then there would be a command that will be used to download the file directly from the source server.

SCP is a protocol that works in a similar fashion to SFTP; the fundamental difference is that it works in scenarios where the filename and path are exactly known. SCP does not allow file browsing or finding the latest file; it is simply a single-shot transfer when the exact file and path are defined.

Webhooks

As explained in *Chapter 3, Data Generation in Source System*, webhooks are push-based data delivery mechanisms that provide the data when the data is available. This is opposed to a polling system where the destination system is continuously polling for the data. In webhooks, the data source calls the destination endpoint as soon as the data is ready.

This type of communication reduces the load on the system and network by reducing empty polling API calls and reducing processing power.

Web interface

This may not be considered an ideal use case of data ingestion, but it is difficult to ignore as well. In this, the interface is created where the external user data might be collected or analyzed. The collected data is passed through the initial validation so that the consistency of the data is maintained.

Although the percentage of this way of ingestion is very low, there must still be a mention to handle the data of this kind.

Web scraping

Web scraping is the process of extracting meaningful information from the internet. This is generally achieved by accessing the HTML elements of the webpage and then passing them to an HTML parser to get the right information out.

This may have some legal and ethical boundaries, but from the data collection and ingestion point of view, this is another rich source of data.

Open-source data or public data

The data that is available on the public portals for public access falls in the category of open-source data. This data is usually available in the form of downloadable Excel or CSVs. Some advanced portals may provide API-based access as well, but that is not the usual practice.

From the data engineering lifecycle perspective, the issue with this kind of data is that there is no control over the availability of this data, which may be removed or updated at anytime, which may break our working pipeline at anytime.

Figure 4.7 extends *Figure 4.2* and covers all the ways of data ingestion that have been discussed so far, to depict the connectivity and processing requirements for each type of data ingestion:

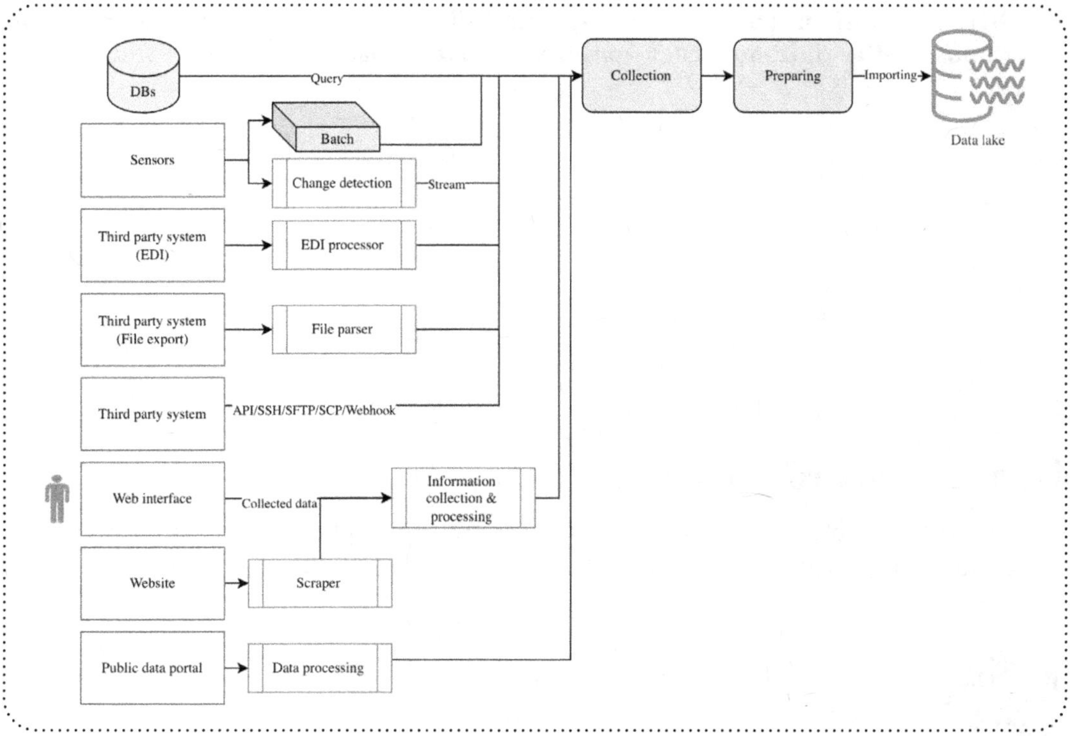

Figure 4.7: *Pictorial representation of different ways of data ingestion*

Conclusion

This chapter explained the definition of data ingestion and the steps involved in it. It also covered the basic concepts of data pipelines and how ingestion fits into the ETL lifecycle. Some of the best practices for data ingestion were explained in detail, such as the type of data flow, frequency of data generation at the data source, synchronous vs. asynchronous data ingestion, etc. This chapter entailed a deep understanding of the differences between batch and stream data ingestion, and finally, it covered thoroughly the different ways of ingestion that may be possible in real-life scenarios.

Since data generation and ingestion have been covered till now, the next logical step is understanding the transformation piece. In the next chapter, we will cover the data transformation techniques that will give a clear idea about how the data is actually transformed so that it can be stored for business insights or passed to any machine learning input.

References

1. **https://atlan.com/know/data-ingestion-vs-etl/**
2. **https://medium.com/@khemanta/data-serialization-and-deserialization-what-is-it-29b5ca7a756f**
3. **https://medium.com/@evertongomede/batch-vs-streaming-data-ingestion-choosing-the-right-approach-for-efficient-data-processing-8fa492299dd4**

Join our Discord space

CHAPTER 5
Data Transformation

Introduction

Till now, we have just touched upon the surface of data engineering, where most of the content covered was related to knowing the data source, finding the right way of collecting the data, and ingesting it into the destination, where the actual work can be started.

Once the data is ingested, it will either follow the ETL path, where the data is transformed right after ingestion, or the ELT path, i.e., it will temporarily store the data in an as-is format in a staging (or bronze) layer within a data lake and then pass it to the transformation cycle. This raw layer is usually immutable and allows replay, auditing, and easy handling of schema changes without affecting downstream systems. In streaming scenarios, transformations may occur continuously as data arrives, and many architectures combine these approaches (e.g., light transformations during ingestion and more complex transformations later).

Data transformation is a very critical step of any data engineering lifecycle, regardless of the domain or business vertical. This is because any mistake at this step will result in a different outcome than expected. This is the step where what data to take forward for business analysis or a machine learning algorithm needs to be finalized. This is the very step that is responsible for creating high-quality data from the raw input, as the consumption of the output of this step should be known and must be aligned to generate the expected business outcome.

Structure

The chapter covers the following topics:

- Data sourcing and profiling for transformation design
- Analyzing summary statistics
- Analyzing patterns
- Data cleaning
- Transformations for analytics/machine learning readiness
- Industrial example

Objectives

By the end of this chapter, the reader will be able to understand data origin and will be able to perform data profiling for transformation, enabling them to support data scientists in analysis and insight generation.

This chapter will cover the techniques to ensure integrity, consistency, and quality for further analysis requirements. It will cover all the important aspects of data transformation, including identifying missing data, implementing strategies to fill them, and maintaining data completeness as much as possible.

The reader should be able to recognize the outliers and calculate the impact on the final results, and if needed, would be able to normalize the data, which would be aligned with the business outcome.

This chapter will also cover the methods of analysis, the relationship between the variables, predicting the outcomes, and interpreting the statistical significance correctly. The reader should be able to understand the trends and structure of the data to facilitate decision-making. While these activities are primarily performed by data scientists, data engineers play a key role in preparing and transforming the data, ensuring its quality, and making it accessible for such analysis.

Data sourcing and profiling for transformation design

The success of any data product or pipeline depends on meeting **service level agreements** (**SLAs**), ensuring data correctness, and maintaining reliable downstream contracts (such as schema and semantics). At the same time, this work must remain aligned with business outcomes, so data engineers design and build systems with the expected results in mind, ensuring that each processing step supports accurate and meaningful insights.

As shown in *Figure 5.1*, once the data is collected, it has to be converted to align it with the business expectations. This way, the data engineers get the direction to shape and prepare the data accordingly.

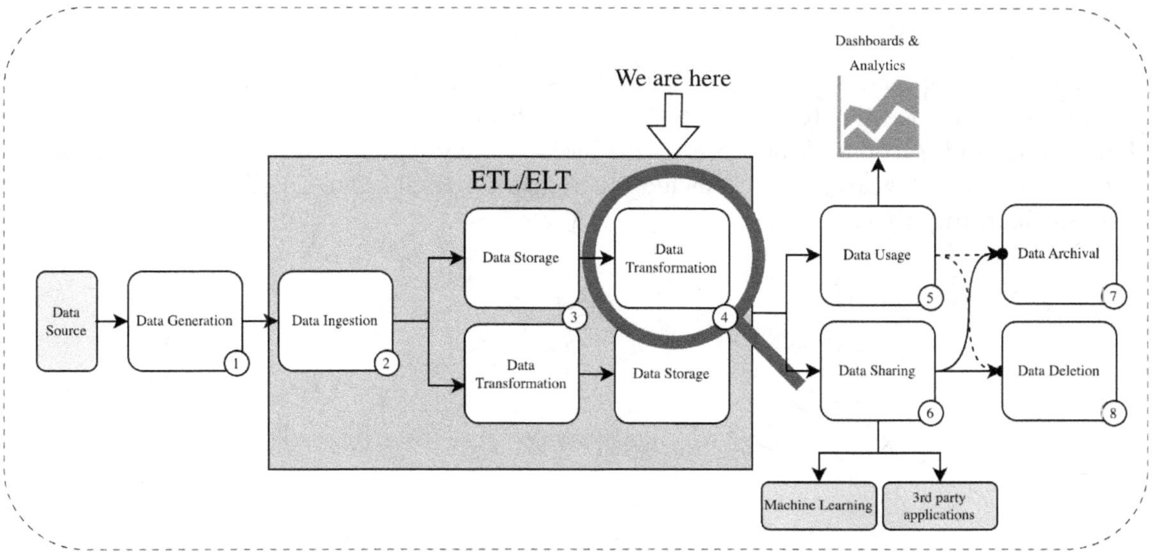

***Figure 5.1**: Showing the current phase covered in the chapter*

Let us see in detail how the process of transformation takes place, starting with data sourcing.

Data sourcing

Data sourcing is the process of identifying and collecting the dataset from the relevant data sources for our analysis, which corresponds to business requirements.

Although the data sources and ingestion have already been covered in the previous chapters, this is the process of identifying the specific dataset out of the entire data that needs to undergo the transformation.

Issues with data sourcing

It is not only about collecting the data from its sources, but also about looking at the other aspects that affect the decision-making. These aspects can be:

- **Data freshness**: This indicates how up-to-date the data is. Fresh data ensures downstream systems use the latest available information.
- **Data quality**: Although the data processing steps take care of the quality of data, as a rule of thumb, we should avoid data that has the potential for inconsistency, duplication, and a breach of data integrity.
- **Data sensitivity**: The data that contains sensitive information must be handled with precautions, and there should be specially curated policies that are applicable to this type of data.

Types of data

In the earlier chapters, different types of data sources and data have already been covered, but it becomes imperative to understand the same from a data engineering perspective, where data is ingested, processed, and made available for downstream systems. *Figure 5.2* shows how the data is categorized and selected for building reliable data pipelines for downstream machine learning use cases:

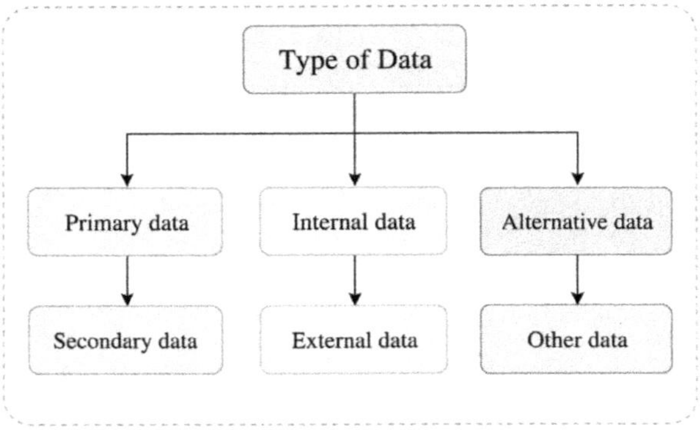

***Figure 5.2**: Shows different types of data used in data science*

Let us understand the different types of data, based on their origin:

- **Primary and secondary data**: The data that is collected by you or your organization for a specific purpose is called Primary data, e.g., survey collection, sensor data, and user feedback. This data has high relevance as it is collected keeping the business expectations in mind. But this data is time-consuming and costly. Contrary to primary data, the data that has already been collected by someone and is reused for our purposes will be called Secondary data, e.g., government reports, research papers, public datasets, etc. This is a quick and cost-effective way to start our analysis, but at times, the data may not completely match our requirements.
- **Internal and external data**: The data coming from internal sources of an organization is called internal data; on the contrary, the data coming from external sources, like the internet or other organizations, will be termed as external data e.g., an analysis of the salary of the employees of an organization will be done on internal data since the data will come from a single source. On the other hand, analysis done on the salaries of different organizations in the same domain will require data from different sources, which will be external data for any organization.
- **Alternative data and other sources**: The data that follows a tree structure of present and future, or past and present, kind of relationship. This follows a left-to-right relationship. For example, for a cancer patient, if the analysis is done on their multiple test reports of different body parts, it will be called an analysis on alternative data since neither of the reports is dependent on nor related to the other, so the relation becomes left-to-right, and the remaining type of data will come under other sources.

Perform data profiling to define transformation rules and quality constraints

This process is meant to analyze the dataset in detail so that we can decide how to clean, standardize, and validate it before using it downstream.

The flow can be:

Raw data | Data profiling | EDA | Transformation rules | Quality constraints | Curated data

Let us look at each of the steps in detail.

Data profiling

Data profiling is the process of examining a dataset to understand its structure, content, and quality before it is used for analysis or processing.

- Identifying data types (numeric, text, date)
- Checking missing values
- Detecting duplicates
- Understanding value distributions
- Finding inconsistencies or anomalies

E.g., 5% of values are missing, values ranging from 500 and above are outliers, etc.

Exploratory data analysis

Exploratory data analysis (**EDA**) is primarily a data science activity that goes a step further by analyzing the statistical and visual characteristics of the data to uncover patterns, distributions, relationships, and anomalies.

While data engineers are responsible for building and maintaining data pipelines, cleaning, and transforming data at scale, data scientists perform EDA to derive insights and guide model development.

The objective of this step is to get insights into the data, understand its flow, and create a hypothesis that will be taken as a base and provide direction for proceeding. It facilitates discovering the unexpected as well as helps conform to the expected.

EDA was developed by *John Tuckey* in the 1960s at *Bell Labs*, US, who had provided essential techniques to visualize and summarize the data. He introduced many basic techniques such as 5-number summary, boxplots, stem and leaf diagram, etc.

The following are the aims for EDA:

- **Maximum insight into the dataset**: This is understanding the data without any bias and trying to get the underlying meaning of it.

- **Uncover underlying structure**: Every piece of data received may follow some patterns or relations, which aim to identify those hidden or visible structures.
- **Extract important variables**: Data may contain too many variables that do not ultimately contribute to the final decision-making. Extracting important variables helps us get the maximum correct insight with a minimum number of columns or variables.
- **Detect outliers and anomalies**: Since data may have some spikes and dips that may be momentarily available. Based on some mathematical readings, these abrupt changes may be categorized as outliers, and they may not be useful for our pattern analysis in the model. Similarly, any anomalies that are seen in the data must be detected and removed for accurate prediction.
- **Test underlying assumption**: Check if the data collected satisfies the requirement of the data collection assumption, e.g., the mathematical model was created by collecting the data only in the morning; when the model is to be tested for accuracy, the data must be collected in the morning only, so that the results are as close to the real-world scenario.
- **Develop valid models**: These models can be mathematical, statistical, machine learning, or deep learning models. It depends on the use cases that are used for future prediction.
- **Determine optimal parameter settings**: Once the model is ready and in use, there are some parameters that are used to fine-tune the model. With time, this model needs to be optimized, and the right parameters need to be kept so that the model can make the right prediction with the changing trend in the real-world.

In simple words, the objective of EDA is:

- To explore the data without any bias.
- As per Tukey, EDA is detective work; unless the detective finds the clues, the judge or jury has nothing to consider. A judge or jury is a confirmatory data analysis.
- To examine the data deliberately and try to understand the deep meaning.

Exploratory vs. confirmatory data analysis: A comparative study

In contrast to EDA, **confirmatory data analysis** (**CDA**) starts with an assumption and tries to see the data from that angle. The objective is to prove the assumption as correct.

The following table lists the EDA versus CDA:

EDA	CDA
No hypothesis to start with	Start with a hypothesis
A hypothesis is generated	Test the null hypothesis
Mostly done using graphical methods	Done using statistical methods
Industrial example : In an e-commerce company, a data scientist uses EDA on data like orders, browsing behavior, and timestamps to identify trends, top products, customer patterns, outliers, and relationships (e.g., discounts vs. sales). The goal is to understand the data and generate hypotheses, such as whether discounts increase weekend sales.	**Industrial example** : In an e-commerce company, CDA is used to validate hypotheses generated during EDA. For example, if the hypothesis is that discounts increase weekend sales, the data scientist may run an A/B test or apply statistical tests to compare results and determine if the observed effect is statistically significant.

***Table 5.1**: Brief difference between EDA and CDA*

The steps to be followed in EDA:

1. Generate good research questions.
2. In data restructuring, the data may be required to be transformed into new ones from the existing ones, such as creating dummy variables from categorical variables by combining two different redundant datasets to make it more meaningful.
3. Based on the research questions, use appropriate graphical tools and obtain the descriptive statistics. This is to understand the data structure, its relationships, anomalies, and behaviors.
4. Identifying the confounding variables, correlated variables, and handling the missing values and outliers.
5. Decide on the need for transformation.
6. Decide on the hypothesis based on the research questions.

Transformation rules

These are some guidelines that define how the data should be transformed and processed to make it usable and consistent. Some of these rules are listed in the following:

- **Clean**: Remove duplicates, handle missing values, treat outliers, etc. This topic is covered in detail later in this chapter, in the *Data cleaning* section.
- **Standardize**: This is the process of bringing data into a consistent format, e.g., date format should be the same across the complete dataset, text casing should be consistent, currency units should be USD, etc.
- **Conform**: Align data across multiple sources, e.g., **`cust_id`** and **`Customer_id`** become **`cust_id`**, for gender **`M`** and **`Male`** become **`Male`**.

The output of this phase is a cleaned, consistent, and structured dataset.

Quality constraints

These are the rules or constraints that define the conditions that data must satisfy to be considered correct and reliable. Some of the constraints can be:

- **Null constraints**: Required fields cannot be empty
- **Range check**: Age must be between 0 and 100
- **Uniqueness**: Employee IDs should not repeat
- **Format checks**: Email must follow a valid pattern
- **Business rules**: Revenue must be greater than 0

The output of this step is a set of rules that would validate and enforce the data quality.

So, the data profiling identifies what is wrong in the data, EDA explains why those issues occur, transformation rules fix them, and quality constraints validate that the data meets the required standards.

From data exploration to production pipelines: An integrated workflow

As seen in the steps of EDA, when the raw data is collected, the statistical structure of the data is understood first, and then a decision on the transformation and processing is taken.

Figure 5.3 explains how the data passes through the different stages after collection. It starts with data processing that may include converting the unstructured data to structured data or reading a JSON structure and deserializing it into in-memory variables. After that, it will move to EDA to understand the basic pattern of data that will give an initial insight into the complete dataset. Then it will move to the cleaning process, where we need to check statistically if there is some problem with the data, detecting outliers or any misinformation that is available. The data is then cleansed by removing outliers and taking care of missing values by either deleting them or adding dummy values instead.

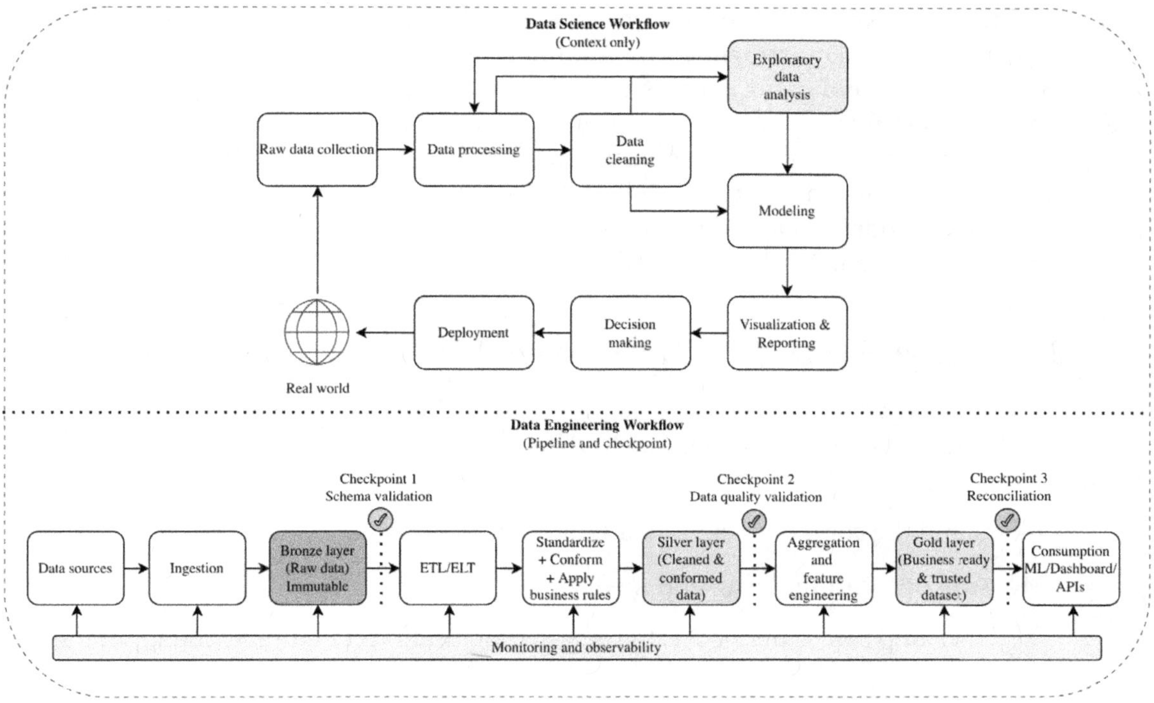

***Figure 5.3:** Data science workflow alongside a production-ready data engineering pipeline*

Post cleaning, it is passed to EDA again, where we may now see the changes in the data patterns. If there is a problem identified in EDA with any data, it will go back to the data processing and cleaning step to resolve the problem, and finally, it will reach the modelling stage.

After selecting the right algorithm or algorithms, the model is created along with the flowchart to explain different parts of the model, and then the final reports are generated, which are usually graphical in nature.

Since the model is ready for testing, which must be done using confirmatory data analysis, the decision is made that it has to be aligned with the business expectations. If all is good, then finally the model is deployed in the real-world, where the new data can be directly fed to the model that will be used for automating the decision-making.

The data engineering flow represents a structured pipeline that transforms raw data into reliable, analysis-ready datasets for downstream consumption. It begins with the data sources, such as databases, APIs, logs, etc., from which the data is ingested into the system either in batch or real-time streaming mode. The data is first stored in the **bronze layer** in its original form to preserve traceability. There is checkpoint 1, which takes care of schema validation and structural correctness. Then, the pipeline moves into the processing and transformation stage, where data is cleaned, filtered, and transformed. This is the stage where key data engineering practices are applied, in which data is standardized into a consistent format, conformed across multiple sources to ensure uniform meaning, and transformed using business rules to align with business requirements. The resulting data is stored in the **silver layer**, where further data quality validations such as null checks, range checks, and duplicate detection are performed. Post this, the data undergoes aggregation and feature engineering to make it suitable for specific analytical and machine learning use cases. This leads to a **gold layer,** which represents a trusted business-ready dataset optimized for reporting, dashboards, or machine learning models. Before the final consumption reconciliation is performed to ensure consistency between source and output data.

Analyzing summary statistics

Summary statistics are the numbers that summarize the properties and attributes of the dataset, e.g., means, standard deviation, etc. This can be calculated in a single pass through the data.

Let us understand the components of a summary:

- **Measure of location**: Mean and median:
  - **Mean**: Mean is defined as the measure of location or central tendency of the data set.

    For example, if we have a dataset with values: $x_1, x_2, x_3, \ldots, x_n,$ then the mean is calculated as:

    Mean = Sum of all the values/number of values:

    $$\bar{x} = \frac{x_1 + x_2 + x_3 + \cdots + x_n}{n}$$

    Since the mean is very sensitive to outliers, the median is used in those cases.
  - **Median**: Median is also a measure of central tendency, but it represents the middle value of an ordered dataset.

    In an ordered data set: $x_1, x_2, x_3, \ldots, x_n$ where $x_1 \leq x_2 \leq x_3 \leq \ldots \leq x_n$

    - **If n is odd**:

      $$Median = x_{\frac{n+1}{2}}$$

    - **If n is even**:

      $$Median = \frac{x_{\frac{n}{2}} + x_{\frac{n}{2}} + 1}{2}$$

- **Measure of spread**: Range and variance:
  - **Range**: It is the difference between max and min, e.g., if we have a data set, 2,3, 5,9,11, the range will be *11-2 = 9*
  - **Variance**: It measures how the data values are spread out from the mean; it is the average of the squared distances from the mean.

    If the variance is small, this means the datapoints are close to the mean; otherwise, they are spread out far from the mean.

$$Variance(x) = s_x^2 = \frac{1}{m-1}\sum_{i=1}^{m}(x_i - \bar{x})^2$$

When the denominator is *(m – 1)*, it represents the **sample variance**, where the data is a subset of the population. To calculate **population variance**, m can be used as the denominator instead of m-1.

Real-life example:

A company has $5000 as a mean monthly salary for a specific job profile. If the variance is low, this means people of that same job profile are earning approximately the same in that company, and a good balance is maintained. On the other hand, if a company has high variance, it clearly says people in the same positions might have very high salary differences, which indicates the high inequality or imbalance in payout for the same role.

  - **Standard deviation**: It is the same as variance, which measures how the data is spread out from the mean, but it is simply the square root of the variance. Unlike variance, which is in spread units, standard deviation brings it back to the same unit as the data.

- **Frequency**: This indicates the percentage of times the value has occurred in the data, e.g., in a survey of a population, the genders male and female occurred 50% of the time.
- **Mode**: This represents the value that appears most frequently in the data, e.g., in the dataset, 1,1,2,3,4,5,16,17,3,4,13,67,5,9,5; the mode is 5
- **Min**: This is the minimum value appearing in the dataset, e.g., in the above dataset, the min is 1.
- **Max**: This is the maximum value appearing in the dataset, e.g., in the above dataset, the max is 67.
- **Percentile**: This tells us about the following value which a given percentage of the data falls. For instance, for a given data x, the 50th percentile is the value of $X_{50\%}$ such that 50% of all the values of x are less than $X_{50\%}$.

For example, the scores for students are 40, 45, 49, 53, 61, 65, 71, 79, 85, 91. Find the percentile value of 71.

Total count (N)= 10, number of values fall under 71, (n) = 6

The 60th percentile is *(n / N) x 100 = 6/10 x100 = 60%.*

- **Quartile**: A quartile is a type of statistical value that divides an ordered dataset into four equal parts, each containing 25% of the data.

As shown in *Figure 5.4*, there is a division of the dataset or observations into four defined intervals. These intervals are based on the values of the data and how they compare to the entire set of observations.

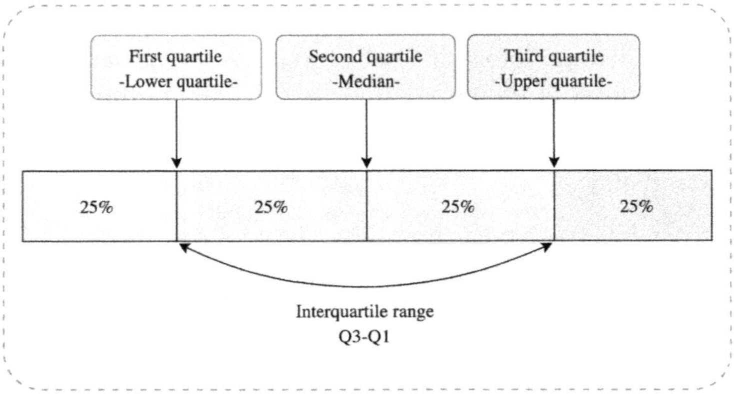

***Figure 5.4**: Showing the quartile mapping of a dataset*

The following formulas show where the quartiles lie in an ordered data set:

$$Firstquartile = \frac{(n+1)}{4} th\ term$$

$$Secondquartile = \frac{(n+1)}{2} th\ term$$

$$Thirdquartile = \frac{3(n+1)}{4} th\ term$$

Interquartile range = Q3-Q1

Where n is the total number of values in the dataset or observations.

For example, for the above scores example, let us find out the quartile division:

- **Dataset**: 40, 45, 49, 53, 61, 65, 71, 79, 85, 91, n =10
- **First quartile**: (10+1)/4 = 2.75, 45(2nd value) + 0.75(49-45) = 48
- **Second quartile**: (10+1)/2 = 5.5, average of 61 and 65 = (61+65)/2 = 63
- **Third quartile**: 3(10+1)/4 = 8.25, 79(8th value) + 0.25 (85–79) = 80.5

- **Interquartile range**: Q3-Q1 = 80.5-48 = 32.5
- **Lower limit**: Q1 - 1.5x IQR = 48 -1.5 x 32.5 = -0.75
- **Upper limit**: Q3 + 1.5 x IQR = 80.5 + 1.5 x 32.5 = 129.25

The following table is an example in Python to see the data summarization:

ID	Birth year	Education	Marital status	Income	Kids home
10001	1988	Graduation	Single	26476	2
10002	1978	Master	Married	71756	0
10003	1964	Master	Together	22382	2
10004	1992	PhD	Single	69683	1
10005	1957	Graduation	Single	65276	2

***Table 5.2**: A sample dataset showing socio-economic information of some individuals*

The following table is a summary of what would look like:

Descriptive statistics	ID	Birth year	Income	Kids home
count	2000	2000	2000	2000
mean	11000.5	1974.76	59441.5615	1.001
std	577.494589	14.270046	23295.15308	0.803319
min	10001	1950	20060	0
25%	10500.75	1962	39578.75	0
50%	11000.5	1975	59118.5	1
75%	11500.25	1987	79682	2
max	12000	1999	99943	2

***Table 5.3**: A summary that is generated using Python*

As shown in *Figure 5.5*, there is a dataset of some individuals that needs to be processed for EDA. As a preliminary step, we can see how the data summary looks, which shows a 5-point summary (min, lower quartile, median, upper quartile, max), along with statistical measures like mean and std deviation.

The command in Python (`pandas` library) for getting the summary is `dt.describe()`, where dt is the name of the dataset and describe is the name of the function that generates the summary of the given dataset.

```
summary_stats = dataset_1.describe()
print(summary_stats)
```

	ID	Birth Year	Income	Kids Home
count	2000.000000	2000.000000	2000.000000	2000.000000
mean	11000.500000	1974.760000	59441.561500	1.001000
std	577.494589	14.270046	23295.153084	0.803319
min	10001.000000	1950.000000	20060.000000	0.000000
25%	10500.750000	1962.000000	39578.750000	0.000000
50%	11000.500000	1975.000000	59118.500000	1.000000
75%	11500.250000	1987.000000	79682.000000	2.000000
max	12000.000000	1999.000000	99943.000000	2.000000

***Figure 5.5**: Showing the output of the Python command in Google Colab*

The above figure clearly shows the command **`dataset_1.describe()`**, which gives the output in the discussed format. It is to be noted that **`dataset_1`** is the name of the dataset on which the **`describe`** function is applied.

Analyzing patterns

After statistical data analysis, it is imperative to understand the underlying message of the data, which can only be done by understanding the patterns that the data generates. For this, we need to do different types of pattern analysis as follows:

- **Univariate analysis**: This is the statistical analysis technique utilized in data science to analyze individual variables only.

  It focuses on examining and summarizing the characteristics of a single variable that include its distribution, central tendency, and variability.

  Measures like mean, mode, median, range, variance, and standard deviation are commonly employed in univariate analysis.

  For example, understanding how the weight of a man varies with time.

- **Bivariate analysis**: This is the analysis that is used to determine the empirical relationship between the two variables.

  Its purpose is to understand the correlation, strength, and direction between the variables. It helps in identifying the patterns, trends, and dependencies between two variables.

  It helps in identifying potential predictors or factors that influence a specific outcome.

  For example, to see the pattern of how the weight varies against height.

- **Multivariate analysis**: This is the analysis that is used to determine the empirical relationship among multiple variables.

  It involves statistical techniques like regression analysis, factor analysis, cluster analysis, principal component analysis, etc.

  Multivariate analysis finds applications in fields such as social sciences, marketing research, finance, and healthcare for data-driven decisions.

  For example, to see the pattern of how the salary varies as per age, gender, experience, knowledge, etc.

Visualization techniques

Visualization may be defined as the process of creating a graphical representation to find any patterns or specific behavior. In production, data engineers rely on sampling, aggregation, and profiling reports instead of plotting entire raw datasets.

It is a very effective technique for finding the inference because:

- It simplifies the complexities
- Pattern recognition is easy
- It enhances the communication, and finding insight is easy
- Anomaly detection, unusual points or outliers can be highlighted easily
- Time efficiency and a rapid overview save time in inspecting data.

Univariate plots

These are the types of plots that are used to analyze the distribution of a single variable. They help us understand the variable's range, central tendency, spread, and frequency without considering their relationships with other variables. Some of these plots are listed in the following:

- **Pie charts**: Pie charts are ideally used for representing the proportions of univariate categorical data.

  As shown in *Figure 5.6*, this pie chart shows the sales data of a company that has three types of sales channels. Based on their current sales, the division is shown in percentages.

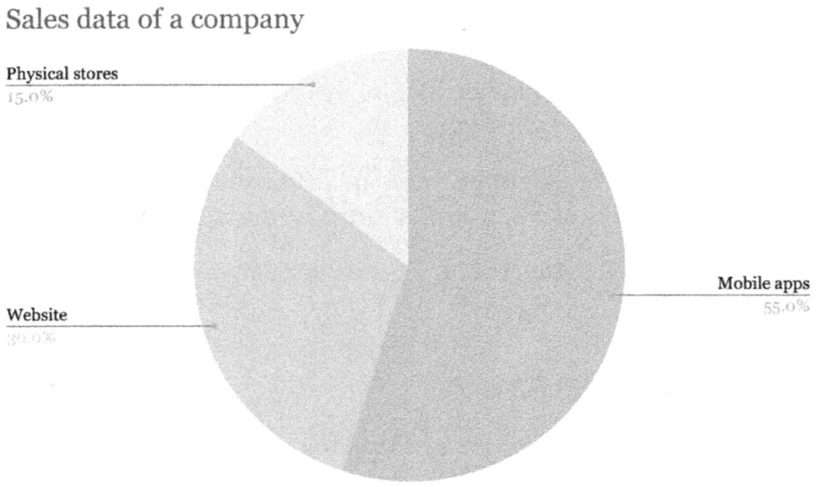

Figure 5.6: A pie chart

- **Histogram**: This is used when data is to be shown over a continuous interval. It helps in understanding the spread of data.

  A histogram is another univariate analysis that uses a single variable plotted against its frequency or any grouped interval. *Figure 5.7* shows the marks of students that have been mapped into frequency and hence plotted over a continuous interval:

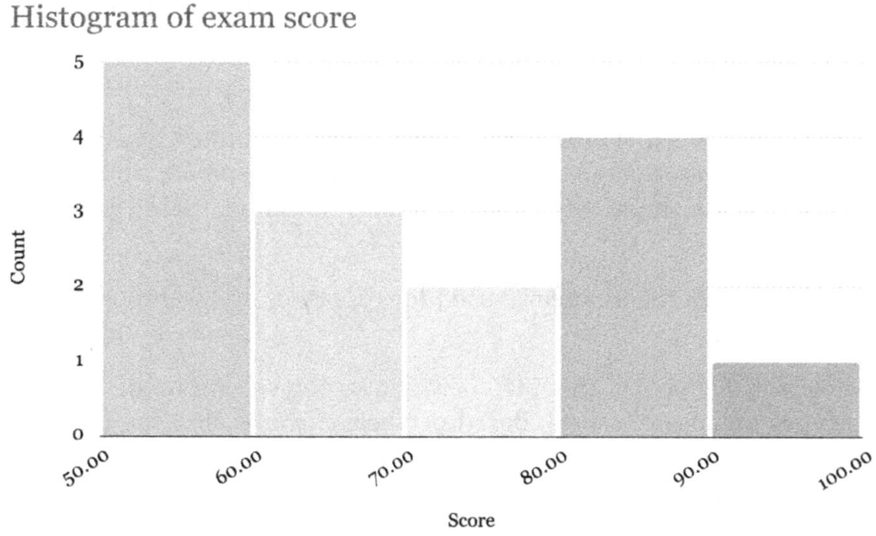

Figure 5.7: A histogram chart

- **Box plot**: The box provides a five-point summary of the data. It is a versatile way of understanding the nature of the data. It not only gives the min, max, interquartile range, and outliers in the data but also provides information on the distribution of the data.

Figure 5.8 clearly shows the box plot summary of the income of different households. This single figure shows the division of data, showing the minimum, maximum, and median, etc.

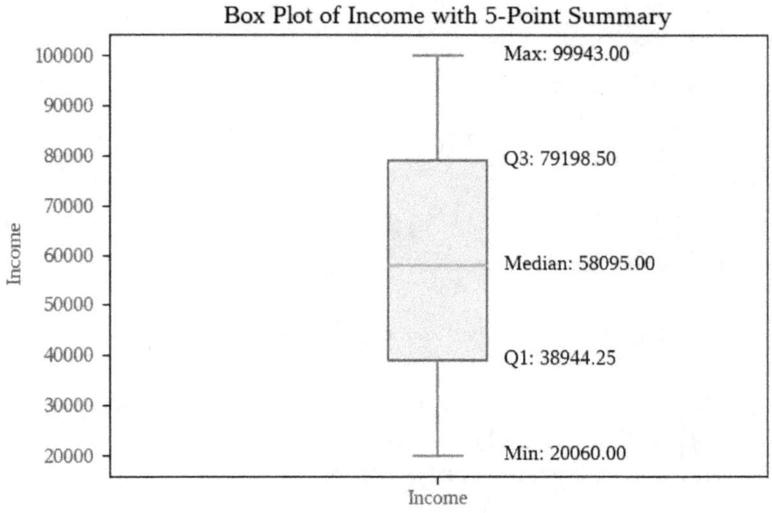

***Figure 5.8**: A box plot*

Bivariate plots

Bivariate analysis examines the relationship between two variables to understand how one variable changes with respect to another. The following are examples of bivariate plots for bivariate analysis:

- **Bar plot**: This graph shows the relationship between a categorical variable and numeric values. Whenever there is a requirement for comparison of numerical vs categorical values, we will always go with the bar plot; on the other hand, if we need to do univariate analysis, we will go with a histogram.

  Figure 5.9 shows a comparative study between categorical values (rent, food, transportation) and numerical values (expenditure amount in INR):

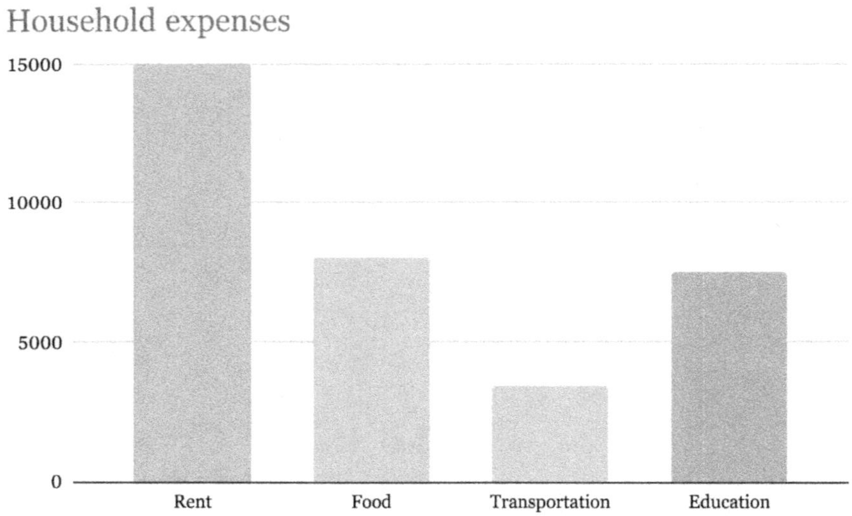

***Figure 5.9**: A bar chart showing the expenses of a household*

- **Scatter plots**: A scatter plot reveals the relationship or association between two variables. In opposition to a bar chart, a scatter plot will be used when the relationship is between numerical variables only.

  As shown in *Figure 5.10*, the data were collected to compare the marks of the students against the hours studied. Since both the variables were numeric, they can be simply drawn onto a scatter plot.

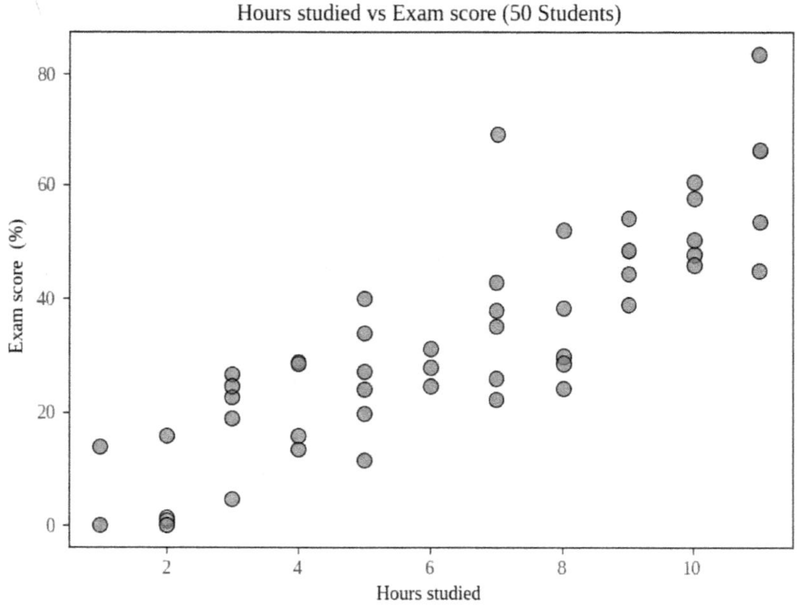

***Figure 5.10**: A representation of a scatter plot*

- **Frequency polygon**: A frequency polygon is another way of displaying the information for an interval. It fundamentally displays the area under the curve. It is identical to a histogram. Any histogram or bar chart can be converted into this kind of polygon.

  By nature, it is a univariate visualization which can be plotted using the midpoint of the class interval on the x-axis and their frequencies on the y-axis, see *Figure 5.11*:

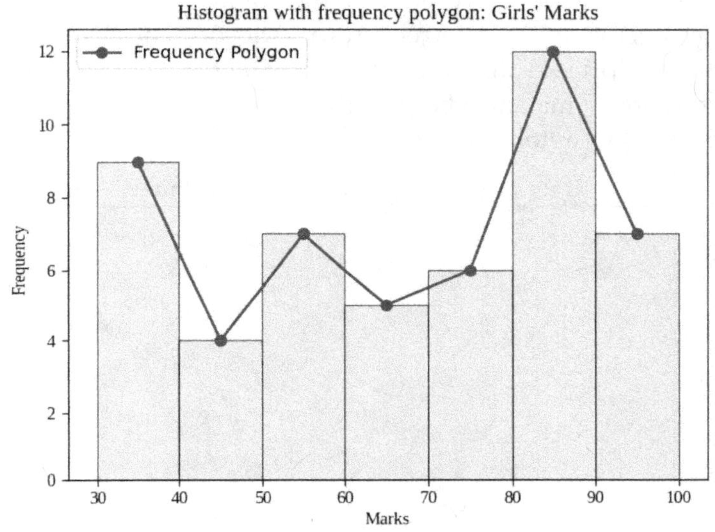

Figure 5.11*: An example of a univariate frequency polygon*

However, this can also be used to compare the frequency of two variables, e.g., marks of girls and boys in the class together, as shown in *Figure 5.12*:

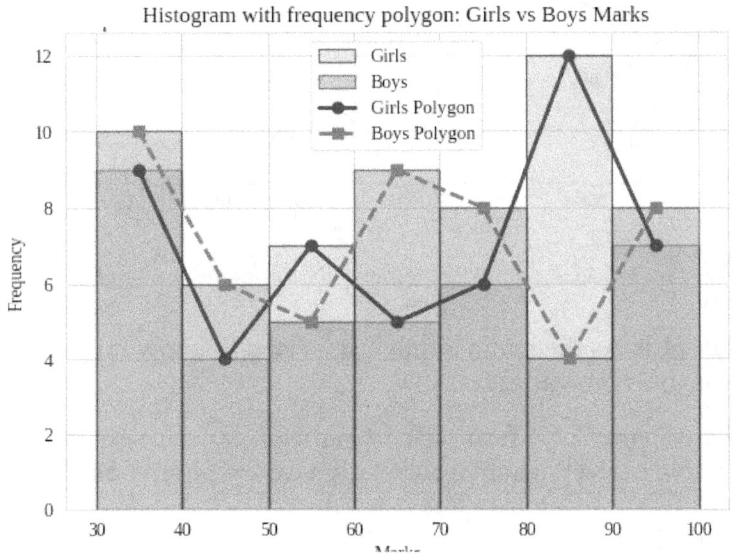

Figure 5.12*: An example of a bivariate frequency polygon*

- **Lag plot**: A lag plot checks whether a dataset is random or not by checking its autocorrelation. Technically, it is a univariate analysis, but since data is compared with its T+1 time or state, it can also be considered as bivariate.

  In the following example, we have taken the daily closing price of Apple (company), starting from 01-Jan-2024 to 01 to Aug-2024, and when these closing prices were compared, they could be seen plotted on the graph as shown in *Figure 5.13*. This shows the closing price of Apple is correlated (or autocorrelated) and not random. In other words, if today's price is high, then tomorrow may also be high, and if today's price is low, then tomorrow may also be low; the price is not jumping randomly day-to-day. This shows positive autocorrelation.

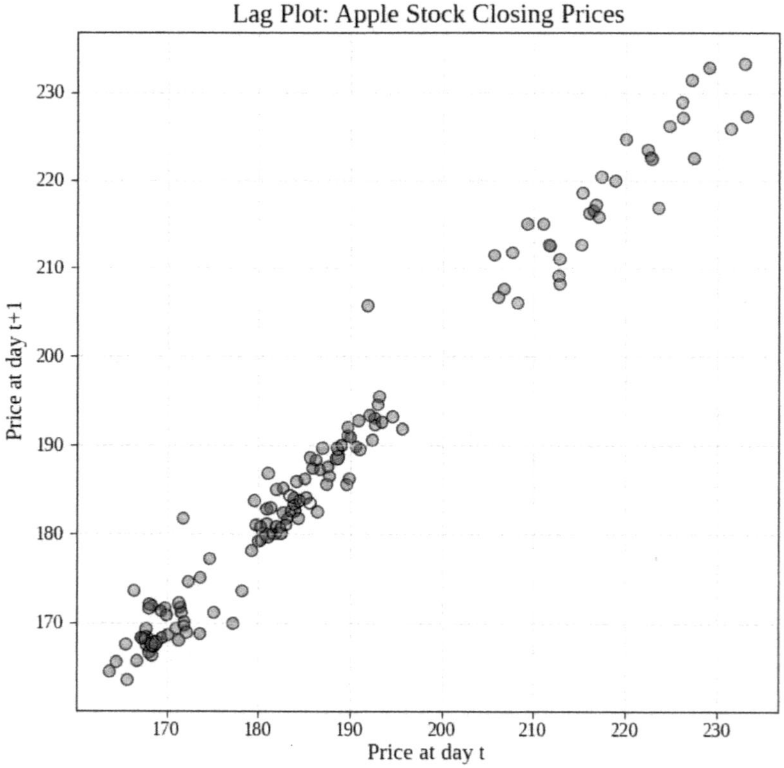

Figure 5.13: *Showing the lag plot of the closing stock price of Apple*

- **Correlation plot**: As the name implies, it is used to know more about the relationship between two or more variables.

  Referring to *Figure 5.14*, from left to right, it can be seen how a perfect positive correlation to a perfect negative correlation can be plotted on the correlation plot:

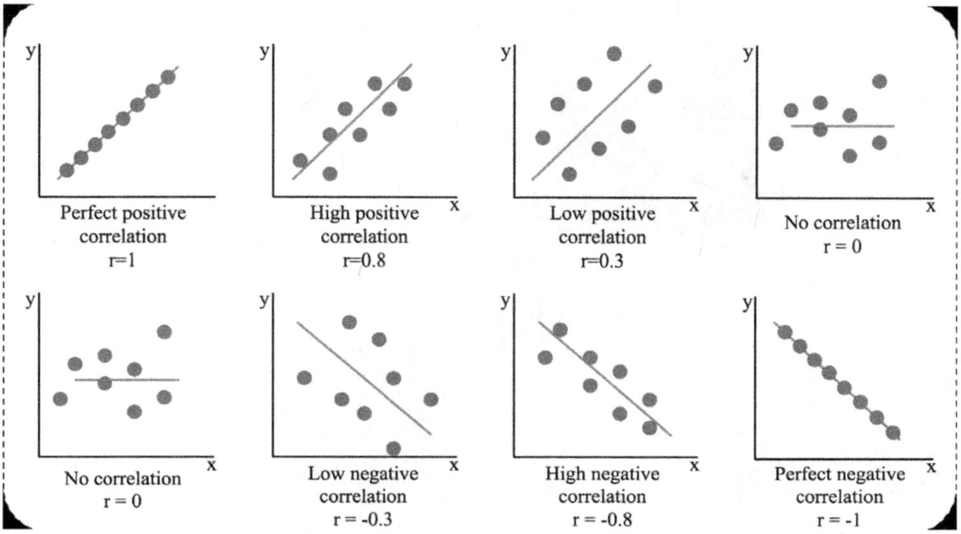

***Figure 5.14**: A representation of different types of correlation*

Multivariate plots

These are the plots that analyze the relationship among three or more variables simultaneously to understand the complex interaction, pattern, and combined effects that are impossible to observe using univariate and bivariate analysis. The following are examples of multivariate plots,

- **Heat map**: This map is created by plotting data points and calculating the correlation coefficients. It helps organizations identify potential dependencies that can inform decision-making and strategy development.

  As shown in *Figure 5.15*, we can see that the scores of students were compared to find the correlation between them on a heat map. This heat map depicts that there is a strong correlation between math and science, which means that students who are good at math also score well in science. On the other hand, there is a strong negative correlation between history and art, which says that students who are good at history are not very good at art, or vice versa.

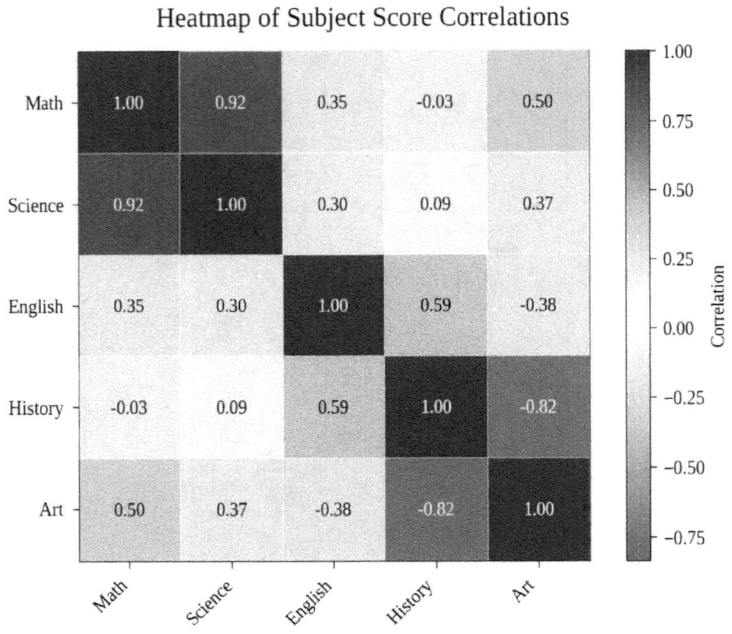

***Figure 5.15**: A visual representation of a heat map*

There can be a heatmap that can be used to find the relation between two variables, which will fall under bivariate analysis.

This helps businesses identify potential dependencies that can be used for informed decision-making and strategy development.

- **Pair plot**: A pair plot is a simple way to visualize relationships between multiple variables. It produces a matrix of relationships between variables in the data for a direct examination of the data. *Figure 5.16* shows what a pair plot looks like:

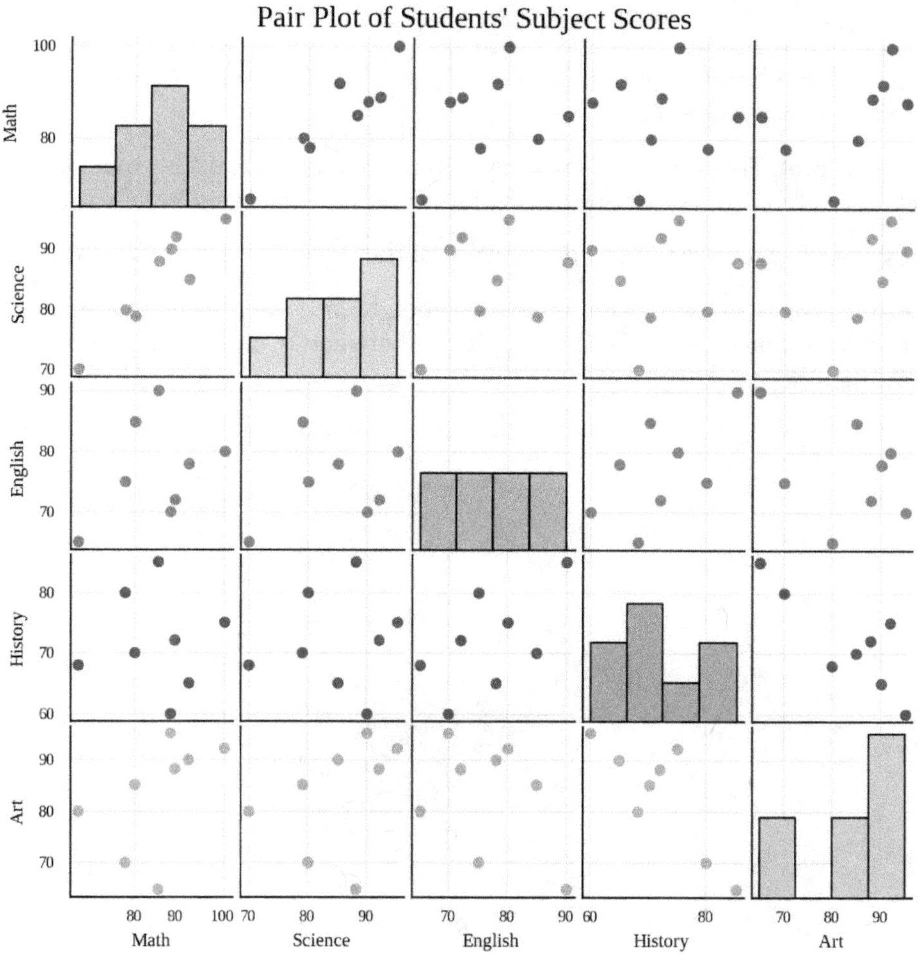

***Figure 5.16**: An example representation of a pair plot for the marks of students*

A pair plot may be called an extension of a heat map.

Taking the same example of a student scoring marks, *Figure 5.16* shows information in two parts:

- **Histogram**: This is the univariate analysis of the data, which shows how the data is distributed, e.g., if we see the first histogram for math, we can see how many students fall in which category and so on.
- **Scatter plot**: This is a bivariate analysis of one datapoint to the other datapoints; here, each subject, in this case, e.g., in the previous example, we can clearly see how art is related to math (consider each dot as one student).

Since it helps us analyze multiple variables at the same time, it comes in the category of multivariate.

Special plots

These plots are called special plots, which are based on **statistical estimation** rather than simple counts. Some of these plots are,

- **Contour plot**: This is a plot that is used to represent a 3D surface in a 2D format. They are generally used for continuous variables rather than categorical variables.

  They are used to understand the density of the data, whether it is high or low.

  Figure 5.17 shows the mapping between height and weight. It can be concluded that in the data sample, most of the people are between 60 and 70 in weight and 160 and 170 in height.

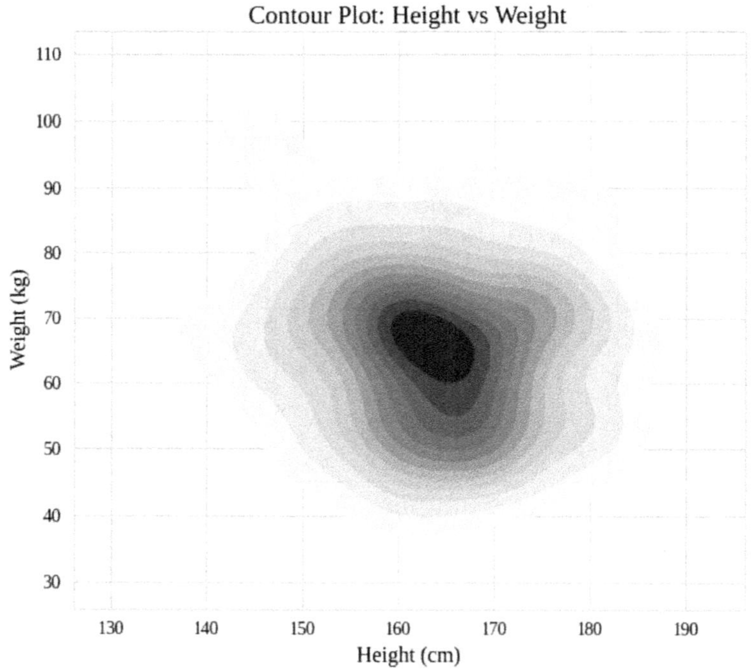

***Figure 5.17**: An example of a contour plot*

- **Density plot**: A density plot is a smoothed, continuous version of a histogram estimated from the data.

  The key difference between a histogram and a density plot is that both are univariate analyses; a histogram divides the data into bins or intervals and counts how many data points fall into them, whereas a density plot estimates a probability distribution instead of fixed bins. Based on *Figure 5.18*, the histogram will tell you that 12 students are between 160 and 165 cm, whereas the density plot will tell you that most likely the height is 167 cm and the distribution is bell-shaped.

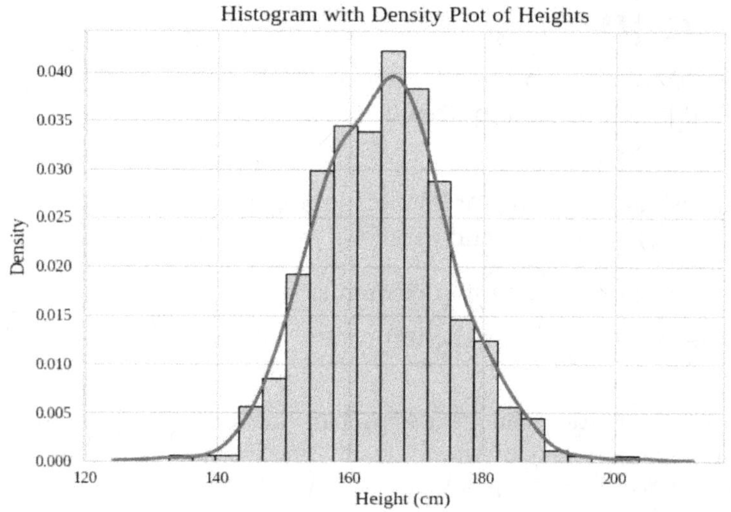

***Figure 5.18**: An example of a view of a density plot for height as a parameter*

- **Radar chart**: A radar or spider chart is a graphical representation of multivariate data of three or more quantitative variables represented on axes starting from the same point. This helps in finding the most dominant variable.

  In *Figure 5.19*, the marks of students are plotted, and now for each student, their dominating subjects can be seen, along with their weakest. This data can be overlapped with other students' data, which helps us to identify the key strengths and weaknesses of each student from a common point. For example, Student A looks dominant in art and math, and Student B does well in science.

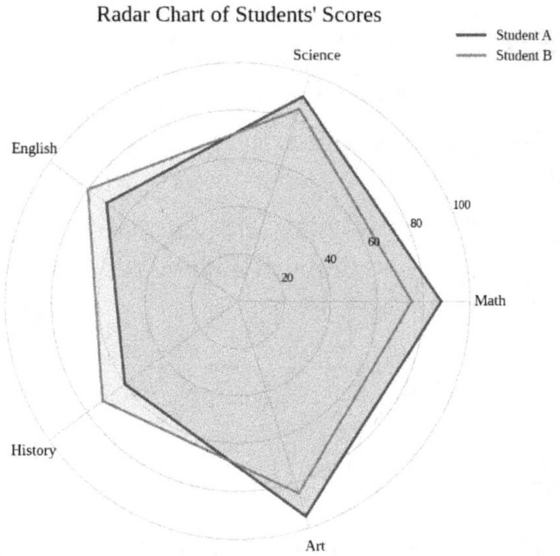

***Figure 5.19**: Represents the radar chart of two students, mapping the marks of all the subjects*

Data cleaning

Data in the real-world is often imperfect, which means there is a very high potential for incorrect data, which may be due to faulty equipment, human or computer errors, and transmission issues.

It is also referred to as data cleansing or data scrubbing, which is the process of identifying and rectifying the issues, discrepancies, and inaccuracies in the dataset.

There are different types of cleaning requirements:

- **Missing values**: This means the important column values or attributes are missing, e.g., `salary = ‘ ’`
- **Outliers**: These values can be defined as the ones that are significantly different from the other observations in a dataset. These may occur due to natural variations, measurement errors, or data entry mistakes, e.g., `salary = -10`
- **Inconsistent values**: These can be defined as discrepancies in values in the related records, where two records of the same entity do not match, e.g., `Date of birth = 05-mar-1988, Age = 70`
- **Duplicate records**: Repetition of the same line of records in a dataset. This may occur due to manual errors or situations where the system inserted the record more than once due to some unexpected condition.
- **Disguised**: Data may appear valid on the surface but is actually incorrect. This can occur due to placeholder values (non-malicious system defaults) or intentional data tampering/fraud (malicious). In both cases, it can mislead analysis and should be handled carefully.

Handling missing values

There are two steps to work on missing values:

1. **Detecting the missing values**: This is the process of finding the missing values in the complete dataset.

   In Python, `isna` and `isnull` are the functions that are used to find the missing values in the dataset. The `sum()` function can then be used to count the number of missing values in each column.

   Python code:

   ```
   dataset.isna().sum()
   ```

   or

   ```
   dataset.isnull().sum()
   ```

   The above command is used to sum all the null values with respect to each column in the dataset named `dataset`, and the output is shown in the following table:

Column name	Missing values
ID	0
Birth Year	100
Education	100
Marital status	0
Income	100
Kids home	100

***Table 5.4**: Shows the output of the above command*

As per *Table 5.4*, it is shown that **`ID`** and **`Marital Status`** columns have no missing values; however, **`Birth Year`**, **`Education`**, **`Income`**, and **`Kids Home`** have **`100`** rows that have null values in the complete dataset.

2. **Fixing the missing values**: Although it is highly subjective to comment on how the missing values should be treated, there may be some thumb rules that may give it a start. Some of the good examples are:

   - If a column has approx. 75% missing values; we can remove the whole column because here we cannot create this many synthetic values, taking the remaining 25% values as reference.

     The following code shows how the missing values percentages can be calculated, and then appropriate action can be taken:

     Python code:

```
# Total rows in dataset
total_rows = dataset.shape[0]
# Missing values in Income column
missing_income = dataset['Income'].isna().sum()
# Percentage of missing values
missing_percent = (missing_income / total_rows) * 100
print(f"Total Rows: {total_rows}")
print(f"Missing 'Income' values: {missing_income}")
print(f"Percentage Missing: {missing_percent:.2f}%")
# Decision
if missing_percent > 75:
    print("More than 75% values missing → Drop the 'Income' column.")
else:
    print("Less than 75% missing → Keep 'Income' and handle imputation.")
```

Output:

```
Total Rows: 2040
Missing 'Income' values: 99
Percentage Missing: 4.85%
Less than 75% missing → Keep 'Income' and handle imputation.
```

- Out of the total dataset, if less than 1% of rows have missing values, then these rows can be deleted. However, deletion should be considered only when the fields are non-critical, missing completely at random, and the impact is acceptable; otherwise, use domain rules, flags, or retain null values.

  The following code shows how the missing values percentages can be calculated, and then the rows will be deleted if they are less than 1%:

  Python code:

```python
# 1. Calculate total rows
total_rows = len(dataset)
# 2. Count rows with any missing values
rows_with_missing = dataset.isnull().any(axis=1).sum()
# 3. Calculate percentage
missing_percentage = (rows_with_missing / total_rows) * 100
print(f"Rows with missing values: {rows_with_missing}")
print(f"Percentage of rows with missing values: {missing_
percentage:.2f}%")
# 4. Condition: If less than 1%, drop them
if missing_percentage < 1:
    dataset = dataset.dropna()
    print("Rows with missing values were less than 1% → Dropped")
else:
    print("Missing rows >= 1% → Consider imputation instead")
```

  Output:

```
Rows with missing values: 462
Percentage of rows with missing values: 22.65%
Missing rows >= 1% → Consider imputation instead
```

- For handling missing numerical values:
  - Missing values can be imputed by the mean or the median of the entire column.

    The following code shows an imputation example using mean and median in Python:

```
print('Missing values in Income column is:', dataset['Income']
.isnull().sum())
# Calculate the mean of the income column
mean_value = dataset['Income'].mean()
print('Mean value:', mean_value)
# Calculate the median of the income column
median_value = dataset['Income'].median()
print('Median value:', median_value)
# Fill the NaN/Null values with mean
dataset['Income'].fillna(mean_value, inplace=True)
print('Missing values in Income column, after replacing by
mean is:',
      dataset['Income'].isnull().sum())
# OR
# Fill the NaN/Null values with median
dataset['Income'].fillna(median_value, inplace=True)
```

Output:

```
Missing values in Income column is: 99
Mean value: 64960.29032511728
Median value: 59019.0
Missing values in Income column, after replacing by mean is: 0
```

- Forward or backward fill, i.e., filling the values based on previous or next rows.

  The following Python code shows how the values are filled using backward and forward fill:

```
# Forward / Backward fill
dataset["Income"].fillna(method="ffill", inplace=True)
print("2. Forward Fill:\n", dataset, "\n")
dataset["Income"].fillna(method="bfill", inplace=True)
print("   Backward Fill:\n", dataset, "\n")
```

- Replace null with 0 (Caution: It may distort the data distribution, especially in financial or transactional datasets where zero has a meaningful interpretation).
- Random sample generation taking the limits of the entire column as reference.
- Predict values using any machine learning model

- For handling missing categorical values:
  - o Replacing missing values with the mode or the most repeated values.
  - o Forward or backward fill.
  - o Pattern recognition, i.e., filling in the values according to the pattern in the completed dataset. For example, suppose 100 missing values are to be filled for gender, suppose the remaining values have male as 80% and female as 20%, then replace 80 values (80%) with male and 20 values (20%) with female.
  - o Using machine learning models.
- Also, the distribution of the graph can be created from the current dataset:
  - o If the graph is normally distributed, then replace the missing values with the mean
  - o If the graph is skewed, then replace the values with the median.

  Figure 5.20 shows that the following Python command can be used to visualize the column values so that the decision on the imputation can be easily taken:

```
import seaborn as sns
import matplotlib.pyplot as plt
sns.histplot(dataset['Income'], kde=True)
plt.title("Income Distribution")
plt.show()
```

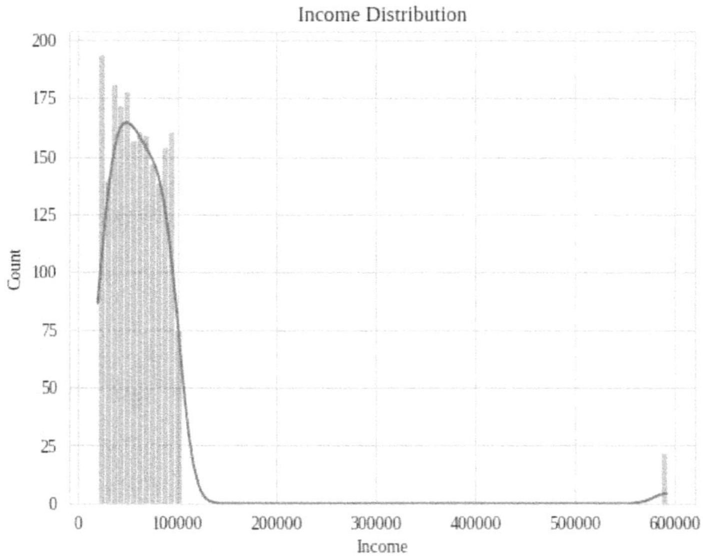

***Figure 5.20**: Example of plotting a graph for the income column*

As mentioned earlier, every use case is different and may have different ways to handle the missing values. This depends upon many known and unknown factors, but the above are some examples that will give the reader an idea of how the decision is taken for handling missing values.

Handling outliers

Addressing outliers is a crucial step in data science to avoid skewed statistical analysis. Detecting outliers using standard deviation for normal data, but let us first understand the normal data. Normal data or normal distribution is defined as data that is symmetric around the mean, just like a bell curve. Since many natural phenomena follow a normal distribution, it becomes imperative to use this for our analysis. Some real-life examples can be marks of students in class, in which some students will be extremely low in marks, some will be extremely high, but the majority will fall in the middle category.

As shown in *Figure 5.21*, there are two extremes that can be seen, one is 30 on the left side, and 90 on the right side. We can see that a limited number of students fall in this category. However, the majority will fall in the middle category.

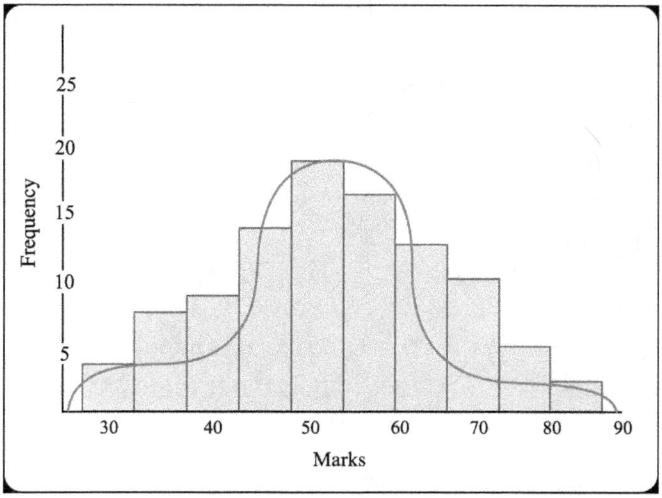

***Figure 5.21**: Showing the normal distribution of marks received by students of a class*

If the data collected for a student has -10 or 1000 as the value of marks, then this will be considered an outlier, which is too far from the other values.

Also, to note, if the data distribution is skewed to a particular direction, left or right, then it is called a skewed distribution.

Let us now look at some ways in which the outliers are managed:

- **Detecting and fixing the outlier values**: This can be done in several ways; it can be done by plotting the graph to see the distribution or checking it statistically.

For normally distributed data (using the 3-sigma method), the mean is calculated along with upper and lower values, and any value falling outside the lower or upper values will be considered an outlier.

Once the outlier values are detected, they must be removed since they may skew our overall results. Or in some cases, they may be given the upper and lower limits if the number of rows is to be kept the same.

The following Python code shows the step-by-step approach to first calculating the mean and its range using the standard deviation. After that, all the values lying beyond this range will be considered as outliers.

Python code:

```
#Calculating the mean
mean_value = dataset['Income'].mean()
#Calculating the upper limit using standard deviation
upperLimit = dataset['Income'].mean()+3*dataset['Income'].std()
#Calculating the lower limit using standard deviation
lowerLimit = dataset['Income'].mean()-3*dataset['Income'].std()
print('Mean value:',mean_value)
print('Upper Limit:',upperLimit)
print('Lower Limit:',lowerLimit)
#-------------------------------
# Records without outliers
final_dataset_without_
outlier = dataset[(dataset['Income'] < upperLimit) & (dataset['Income']
> lowerLimit)]
print("Original dataset size:", dataset.shape[0])
print("After removing outliers:",final_dataset_without_outlier.shape[0])
```

Output:

```
Mean value: 64743.877368421054
Upper Limit: 244133.72468521274
Lower Limit: -114645.96994837062
Original dataset size: 2040
After removing outliers: 2018
```

However, for skewed data, the **interquartile range** (**IQR**) is calculated (refer to the previous section on summary statistics to understand the calculation), and then the lower and upper values are identified.

As shown in *Figure 5.22*, like the normal distribution, any values falling outside the lower and upper limits will fall under the outlier category and hence will be removed:

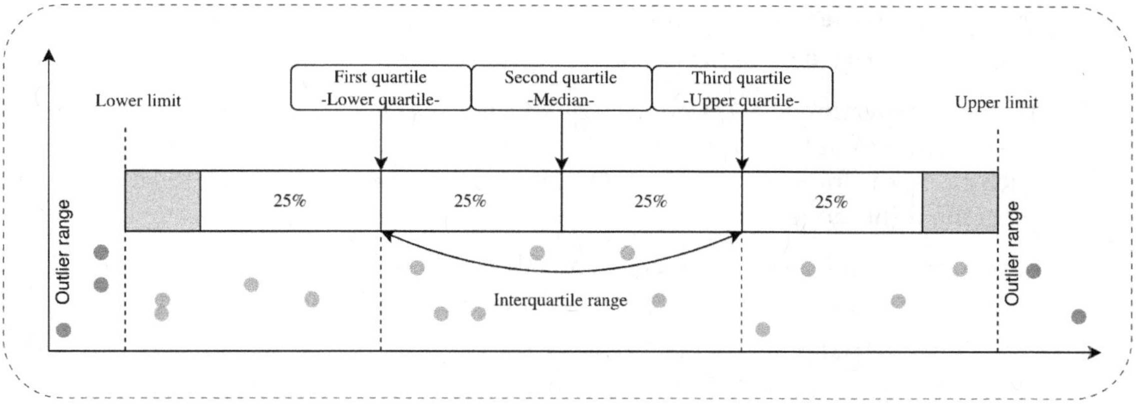

***Figure 5.22**: Graphical representation of quartile mapping of a dataset*

The following Python code shows the step-by-step approach to first calculating the quartile values and their IQR; after that, the upper and lower limits are calculated. All the values lying beyond this range will be considered as outliers and can be replaced by a specific value or removed completely.

```
#Calculate the first quartile
Q1 = dataset['Income'].quantile(0.25)
#Calculate the 3rd quartile
Q3 = dataset['Income'].quantile(0.75)
#Calculate the interquartile range
IQR = Q3-Q1
#Calculate the upper limit
upperLimit = dataset['Income'].quantile(0.75)+1.5*IQR
#Calculate the lower limit
lowerLimit = dataset['Income'].quantile(0.75)-1.5*IQR
print('Upper Limit:',upperLimit)
print('Lower Limit:',lowerLimit)
# Remove outliers
final_dataset_without_
outlier = dataset[(dataset['Income'] <= upperLimit) & (dataset['Income']
>= lowerLimit)]
print("Original dataset size:", dataset.shape[0])
print("After removing outliers:", final_dataset_without_outlier.shape[0])
```

Output:

```
Upper Limit: 141980.75
Lower Limit: 18587.75
```

```
Original dataset size: 2040
After removing outliers: 2018
```

- **Human inspection**: This is not a very efficient way of doing it, but bringing human intervention to detect suspicious values can be a potential solution in some cases. In such cases, the information may look fine at first, but from intuition, the data may not be in the right range.

  Although in some cases, where the removal of outliers is not an option, the smoothening of data can also be done, which is done in various ways, some of which are:

  - **Binning**: Another method to remove outliers is binning, which is done by sorting the data first and partitioning it into equal frequencies called bins. Then one can smooth the data by bin means, bin median, or by bin boundaries, etc.

    For example:

    For a *dataset = 40, 45, 49, 53, 61, 65, 71, 79, 85, 91*

    Min = 40, max = 91

    Range = 91-40 = 51

    Let us say we want the number of bins to be 3, so bin *width = range/3 = 51/3 = 17*

    Bin 1's range = 40 -> 57 (40+17) = [40,57]

    Bin 2's range = 57 -> 74(57+17) = [57,74]

    Bin 3's range = 74 -> 91(74+17) = [74,91]

    Bin 1 = {40, 45, 49, 53}

    Bin 2 = {61, 65, 71}

    Bin 3 = {79, 85, 91}

    Equal frequency binning, say each bin should have 3 to 4 values:

    Bin 1 = {40, 45, 49}

    Bin 2 = {53, 61, 65}

    Bin 3 = {71, 79, 85, 91}

    Smoothing the data by the bin's mean:

    Bin 1 = {40, 45, 49}, mean = 44.67 -> {44.67, 44.67, 44.67}

    Bin 2 = {53, 61, 65}, mean = 59.67 -> {59.67, 59.67, 59.67}

    Bin 3 = {71, 79, 85, 91}, mean = 81.5 -> {81.5, 81.5, 81.5}

    Smoothing the data by bin's median:

    Bin 1 = {40, 45, 49}, median = 45 -> {45, 45, 45}

    Bin 2 = {53, 61, 65}, median = 61 -> {61, 61, 61}

    Bin 3 = {71, 79, 85, 91}, median = (79+85)/2 = 82 -> {82, 82, 82}

Smoothing the data by bin boundaries:

Bin 1 = {40, 45, 49} => {40, 49, 49}

Bin 2 = {53, 61, 65} => {53, 65, 65}

Bin 3 = {71, 79, 85, 91} => {71, 71, 91, 91}

- **Regression**: Another statistical method is regression, where the data can be smoothed by fitting it into a regression function mathematically. This will be covered in the next section in detail.

Handling inconsistent values

There is a possibility that the dataset contains an inconsistent format and values. Taking the above example, date of birth = 05-Mar-1988, age = 70. Since it may not be possible to catch it with the human eye every time, it is imperative to use some ingestion rules, where, when we have two or more columns that are related, we can remove one automatically. Since we can simply calculate the age with the date of birth, we do not need an age-specific column. In other cases, while doing the initial analysis on the project, we, as data engineers, need to decide which is the key attribute that will be considered as a single source of truth and only process the attributes that are necessary.

Also, if it is not possible at an early stage, then we can also use correlation analysis to find the relation between two attributes and decide on which one to go forward with.

Handling duplicate records

Since there may be a possibility of duplicate records due to any unexpected conditions, they can be handled using automation, e.g., a Python script, as shown in the following section, which detects the duplicate records and removes them:

Python code:

```
#Find the duplicate rows from the dataset
duplicate_rows = dataset[dataset.duplicated()]
print("Number of duplicate rows:", duplicate_rows.shape[0],
                            "out of",dataset.shape[0],"rows")
#Removing duplicates
dataset_with_no_duplicates = dataset.drop_duplicates()
print("Number of records after Removing Duplicates:"
                          ,dataset_with_no_duplicates.shape[0])
```

Output:

```
Number of duplicate rows: 40 out of 2040 rows
Number of records after Removing Duplicates: 2000
```

The above code shows that first, the dataset named **dataset** has 2040 records with 40 duplicates; these 40 records were detected using the duplicated function in pandas. Once the existence of a duplicate record is known, the command called **drop_duplicates** can be run, which removes all the duplicate rows in the dataset. Or this **drop_duplicates** can be run directly without even checking, just to make sure the dataset has no duplicates, without the need to look at them.

For duplication removal from a particular column, **dataset_1.drop_duplicates(subset=["CustomerID"], keep="first")** can be used, where **subset = [<column name>]** checks the duplicates in a specific column and **keep ="first"** (or **"last"**) controls which duplicate to keep, the first one or the last one.

In practice, de-duplication is usually based on a **business key** (e.g., **customer_id**, **order_id**) along with a rule such as keeping the latest record based on ingestion/event time. In general, exact duplicates are easy to handle, but real-world data often has near-duplicates that require extra logic, e.g., **"John Smith"** and **"Jon Smith"** in a customer dataset.

Handling disguised values

This is the trickiest part, since disguised values are not obviously null or outliers; they are values that hide in the dataset and may affect the outcome.

For example, we may find 1 Jan as a birthday for most of the records, or 01-01-1900 is shown, which may be a placeholder.

Although there is no strict method that will ensure it will catch the disguised values, it requires common sense to find such data. In practice, data engineering controls such as rule-based checks (valid ranges), uniqueness constraints, referential integrity, and reconciliation with source systems help detect such issues. Some of the following methods may help in finding and correcting these disguised values:

- We may check if any specific value is repeating too many times; this may be the value that has been put to affect the overall analysis.
- We can have a range defined for a value, for example, the birth date should be between 1975 and 2005.
- The reference of the data should be checked, as it should be coming from a trusted source.
- Check the metadata of the data source to find out if the current dataset has been tampered with.

It may not be possible to automate 100% of this, but some level of data validation is needed, which should check the data against predefined rules or criteria. This ensures that inconsistent data does not enter the analysis system, preventing it from jeopardizing the overall outcome.

Transformations for analytics/machine learning readiness

Transformations for analytics/**machine learning** (**ML**) readiness involve converting raw ingested data into a clean, consistent, and structured format suitable for analysis and modeling, including feature engineering, handling missing values, encoding categorical variables, and scaling numerical features.

Sometimes, when the data is being worked upon, some statistical or modeling methods need to be applied to the data so that the dataset can be refined for accurate results.

Also, as a matter of fact, each column in the dataset takes some storage space and may not be contributing to the results, and some of these columns are so related that they carry redundant information, e.g., age and date of birth columns or annual income and monthly income. These columns may be taking substantial computational power while working on a machine learning algorithm.

So, we need to find a way of reducing the dimension of data by removing the correlated columns, which can be automated using a correlation. However, in data engineering layers, such correlated fields are often retained if they represent distinct business concepts, making this more of a machine learning feature-selection step. Also, regression can help us find the hidden pattern in the data, which may not be visible easily by modeling and quantifying relationships between variables for prediction and interpretation.

Correlation

Correlation is a statistical method that is utilized to find the relationship between two or more variables. It basically helps us understand how changing one variable affects changing another. It also provides information about the strength and direction of the relationship between these variables.

Note: **Correlation does not mean one causes the other. It only means they change together.**

It ranges from -1 to +1, with -1 representing a perfect negative correlation, +1 representing a perfect positive correlation, and 0 indicating no relation.

As shown in the following figure, the first graph shows the positive correlation, depicting the value of y increasing along with x; on the contrary, the negative correlation (second graph) shows that the increase in the value of x decreases the value of y. The third graph shows no correlation between x and y.

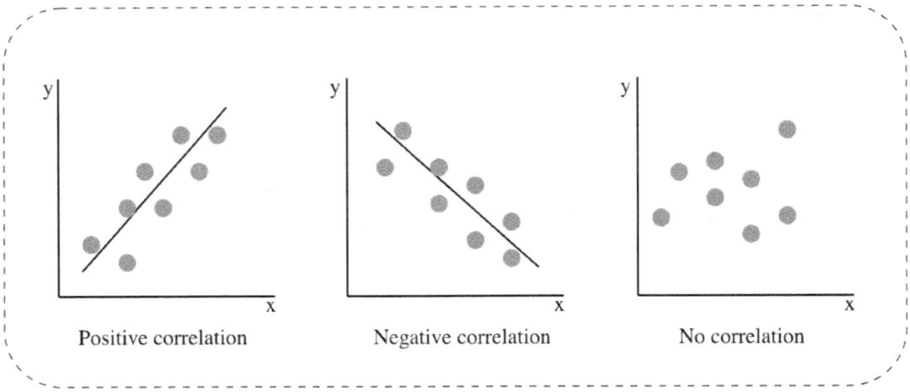

***Figure 5.23:** Graphical representation of correlation*

The mathematical formula to calculate the correlation between X and Y:

$$\rho x, y = \frac{\sum_{i=1}^{n}(X_i - \bar{X})(Y_i - \bar{Y})}{\sqrt{\sum_{i=1}^{n}(X_i - \bar{X})^2}\sqrt{\sum_{i=1}^{n}(Y_i - \bar{Y})^2}}$$

Where:

- X_i, Y_i are individual data points
- n = number of observations
- $\bar{X}, \bar{Y}$ are the means of X and Y

Example:

- **X**: [1,2,3]
- $\bar{X}$: (1+2+3)/3 = 2
- **Y**: [2,4,6]
- $\bar{Y}$: (2+4+6)/3 = 4

Putting it into the formula:

$$\rho x, y = \frac{(1-2)*(2-4)+(2-2)*(4-4)+(3-2)*(6-4)}{\sqrt{(1-2)^2+(2-2)^2+(3-2)^2} * \sqrt{(4-2)^2+(4-4)^2+(6-4)^2}}$$

$$\rho x,y = 1$$

This shows the correlation between x and y is a perfect positive correlation, which means if x increases, then y will also increase, and on the contrary, if x decreases, then y will also decrease.

So, for our data analysis, we do not need both variables as they will not affect the data as such, and a single variable will be enough for the machine learning algorithm.

Similarly, when two columns are highly negatively correlated, then one of them can also be removed as both variables are linearly dependent on each other. Again, they carry the same information, which is just in the opposite direction.

So, to conclude, both columns x and y exist, which are highly correlated (either positively or negatively); one of them can be removed to save the computation cost.

However, this should always be validated against domain knowledge and model requirements, since both variables may still carry distinct business meanings or contribute differently to predictive performance.

Regression

Regression is a statistical method used to evaluate the relationship between a dependent variable and one or more independent variables. For example, exam scores may be the dependent variable, whereas study hours are the independent variable, and we can find the relation: if the study hours increase, then the exam scores will increase.

There is one dependent variable that we are trying to predict using multiple independent variables.

The equation would look like this:

$$Y = \beta_0 + \beta_1 X_1 + \beta_2 X_2 + \cdots + \beta_n X_n + \in$$

Where:

- Y is the variable that can be predicted.
- β_0 is an intercept, a constant, or a base value of y when all the X's are 0.
- $\beta_0, \beta_1, \beta_2, ... \beta_n$ are the coefficients or weights that represent how much the independent variable X influences Y.
- $\in$ is an error value that may be the variable that cannot be explained by independent variables, such as random factors like sudden demand, etc.

This algorithm can also be used to fill the missing data automatically using the other values in the attributes. This approach is generally more accurate than the other methods.

Industrial example

A retail company is facing challenges in effectively segmenting its customers and optimizing marketing strategies. Despite having access to demographic details (age, marital status, education, family structure), financial data (income), and behavioral data (recency, website or social media purchases, total spend), the company struggles to identify profitable customer segments, which means determining which groups contribute the most revenue and how they can be retained.

For the above problem statement, the starting point will be the data, which must be given for the analysis. In this chapter, we will focus on data processing, transformation, and initial analysis only, and see all the steps that need to be taken to generate cleaned and transformed data. From a data engineering perspective, the key deliverable is a curated, analysis-ready dataset that contains the required fields, applies necessary transformations, and passes defined data quality checks and validation rules.

The following Python code explains step by step how a data engineer can proceed towards the expected business outcomes:

1. Create dummy data (optional); since the active dataset is not available, let us create dummy data for ourselves that contains the important columns:

   Note: **We have also introduced the missing values and outliers.**

```
import pandas as pd
import numpy as np
def create_dataset(num_rows=2000, missing_frac=0.05, outlier_
frac=0.01, duplicate_frac=0.02):
    """
    Create synthetic dataset with missing values, outliers, and
duplicate records.
    Keeps all columns in a single dataset (no splitting).

    Parameters:
        num_rows (int): Number of rows in dataset (default = 2000)
        missing_frac (float): Fraction of missing values per selected
column (default = 0.05)
        outlier_frac (float): Fraction of outliers to inject in numeric
columns (default = 0.01)
        duplicate_
frac (float): Fraction of duplicate records to inject (default = 0.02)
    Returns:
        None (saves dataset.csv)
    """
    np.random.seed(42)  # For reproducibility
    # ----- Generate sample data -----
    data = {
        "ID": range(10001, 10001 + num_rows),
        "Birth Year": np.random.randint(1950, 2000, num_rows),
        "Education": np.random.
choice(["Graduation", "PhD", "Master", "2n Cycle"], num_rows),
        "Marital Status": np.random.
choice(["Single", "Married", "Together", "Divorced"], num_rows),
        "Income": np.random.randint(20000, 100000, num_rows),
```

```
        "Kids Home": np.random.randint(0, 3, num_rows),
        "Teens Home": np.random.randint(0, 3, num_rows),
        "Dt_Customer": pd.to_datetime(np.random.choice(pd.date_
range("2012-01-01", "2014-12-31"), num_rows)),
        "Recency": np.random.randint(0, 100, num_rows),
        "Num Own Website Purchases": np.random.randint(0, 10, num_rows),
        "Num Social Media Purchases": np.random.randint(0, 10, num_
rows),
        "Amount": np.random.randint(50, 20000, num_rows)
    }
    df = pd.DataFrame(data)
    # ----- Introduce missing values -----
    for col in ["Birth Year", "Education", "Income", "Kids Home",
"Amount"]:
        df.loc[df.sample(frac=missing_frac, random_state=np.random.
randint(1000)).index, col] = np.nan
    # ----- Inject Outliers -----
    numeric_cols = ["Income", "Amount", "Recency"]
    for col in numeric_cols:
        n_outliers = int(num_rows * outlier_frac)
        outlier_idx = np.random.choice(df.index, n_
outliers, replace=False)
        if col == "Income":
            df.loc[outlier_idx, col] = df[col].mean() * 10
        elif col == "Amount":
            df.loc[outlier_idx, col] = df[col].max() * 20
        elif col == "Recency":
            df.loc[outlier_idx, col] = df[col].max() + 500
    # ----- Inject Duplicate Records -----
    n_duplicates = int(num_rows * duplicate_frac)
    dup_rows = df.sample(n=n_duplicates, random_state=123)
    df = pd.concat([df, dup_rows], ignore_
index=True)  # Append duplicates
    # ----- Save as single dataset -----
    df.to_csv("dataset.csv", index=False)
    print(
        f"""File created: dataset.csv
Rows: {len(df)}, Missing fraction: {missing_frac:.0%}, Outliers
fraction: {outlier_frac:.0%}, Duplicates: {duplicate_frac:.0%}
```

```
Includes missing values + injected outliers + duplicates for testing
data cleaning/imputation."""
    )
# Example usage
create_dataset()
```

Output:

```
Dummy dataset created
```

2. Importing the dataset, which is saved in a **.csv** file, into memory, also known as **deserialization**. The following code shows how a .csv file is read and saved in a dataset in Python:

```
dataset = pd.read_csv("dataset.csv")
print(dataset.columns)
```

Output:

```
Names of columns will be shown as follows:
'ID', 'Birth Year', 'Education', 'Marital Status', 'Income', 'Kids Home',
'Teens Home', 'Dt_Customer', 'Recency', 'Num Own Website Purchases',
'Num Social Media Purchases', 'Amount'
```

3. Check the initial structure of the data using the head function:

```
dataset.head()
```

This command shows the initial structure of the data.

4. Checking summary statistics:

```
summary_stats = dataset.describe()
print(summary_stats)
```

Output:

As covered above, the complete summary of the dataset will be printed for the initial analysis.

5. Data cleaning, i.e., detecting missing values:

```
null_values = dataset.isnull().sum()
print(null_values)
```

Output:

This will list all the columns with the count of missing values, e.g., ID: 0, Birth year: 34

6. Data cleaning, i.e., handling missing values:

```
print ('Missing values in Income column is:',dataset['Income'].isnull().
sum())
```

```
#Calculate the mean of the income column
mean_value = dataset['Income'].mean()
print('Mean value:',mean_value)
#Fill the NaN/Null values with the mean
dataset['Income'].fillna(mean_value, inplace=True)
print ('Missing values in Income column, after replacing by mean is:',
      dataset['Income'].isnull().sum())
```

Output:

```
Missing values in the Income column are: 99
Mean value: 64960.29032511728
Missing values in the Income column, after replacing with the mean, are: 0
```

Note: **This can also be replaced using median or forward-backward imputation**

7. Data cleaning, outlier detection | checking the data distribution.

   Let us see the **Income** column:

```
import seaborn as sns
import matplotlib.pyplot as plt

sns.histplot(dataset['Income'], kde=True)
plt.title("Income Distribution")
plt.show()
```

   Output:

   This will show the histogram that shows data distribution, which will help you visualize the outliers in the distribution in that entire column.

8. Data cleaning, handling outliers | using normalization.

   The following code shows the step-by-step process of detecting and handling outliers using the standard deviation (3-sigma) rule:

```
#Calculating the mean
mean_value = dataset['Income'].mean()
#Calculating the upper limit using standard deviation
upperLimit = dataset['Income'].mean()+3*dataset_1['Income'].std()
#Calculating the lower limit using standard deviation
lowerLimit = dataset['Income'].mean()-3*dataset_1['Income'].std()
print('Mean value:',mean_value)
print('Upper Limit:',upperLimit)
```

```
print('Lower Limit:',lowerLimit)
#--------------------------------
# Records without outliers
final_dataset_without_
outlier = dataset[(dataset['Income'] < upperLimit) &
                  (dataset['Income'] > lowerLimit)]
print("Original dataset size:", dataset.shape[0])
print("After removing outliers:",final_dataset_without_outlier.shape[0])
```

Output:

In this, we calculated the mean, upper limit, and lower limit. Then we used these values to filter out all the values beyond the upper and lower limits.

As discussed earlier in this chapter, in the section *Handling outliers*, based on the data distribution, for normalized data, this method works well, and for skewed data, the IQR makes more sense.

9. Data cleaning handling duplicate records:

```
#Find the duplicate rows from the dataset
duplicate_rows = dataset[dataset.duplicated()]
print("Number of duplicate rows:", duplicate_rows.shape[0],
                        "out of",dataset.shape[0],"rows")
```

Output:

The number of duplicate records will be shown.

10. Data cleaning, removing duplicate records:

```
#Removing duplicates
dataset_with_no_duplicates = dataset.drop_duplicates()
print("Number of records after Removing Duplicates:"
                      ,dataset_with_no_duplicates.shape[0])
```

Output:

The dataset will have no duplicate records.

11. Find the correlation between all the columns and print the highly correlated (80%) columns. The following code shows which Python commands are used to calculate the correlation between the variables/columns and prints only the columns that are highly correlated to each other:

```
import pandas as pd
# Load dataset
df = pd.read_csv("dataset.csv")
```

```
# Compute correlation only for numeric columns
corr_matrix = df.corr(numeric_only=True)
# Find all correlations
corr_unstacked = corr_matrix.unstack().sort_values(ascending=False)
# Remove self correlations (1.0 values)
corr_unstacked = corr_unstacked[corr_unstacked < 0.9999]
# Keep only pairs with correlation > 0.8
high_corr = corr_unstacked[corr_unstacked > 0.8].dropna()
if not high_corr.empty:
    print("Highly correlated column pairs (correlation > 80%):")
    print(high_corr)
else:
    print("No correlation found above 80%.")
```

Output:

This will give the names of the columns that are highly correlated.

Now we can keep only one of two or more highly correlated columns.

Data engineering practices for quality assurance and validation

While the transformation steps discussed so far prepare the data for analysis, real-world data engineering requires an additional layer of rigor to ensure correctness, reliability, and operational stability. The following examples illustrate how these principles can be applied in practice:

- **Standardization (Schema + Format enforcement):**

```
# Standardize column names (lowercase + underscore)
dataset.columns = [col.strip().lower().
replace(" ", "_") for col in dataset.columns]
# Standardize data types
dataset["birth_year"] = dataset["birth_year"].astype("Int64")
dataset["income"] = dataset["income"].astype(float)
dataset["dt_customer"] = pd.to_datetime(dataset["dt_customer"])
# Standardize categorical values
dataset["education"] = dataset["education"].str.lower().str.strip()
dataset["marital_status"] = dataset["marital_status"].str.lower().str.
strip()
print("Schema after standardization:\n", dataset.dtypes)
```

Output:

A schema-consistent dataset with uniform formats, data types, and standardized values.

- **Conforming (Cross-source alignment simulation):**

```
# Example: Map inconsistent categories to standard values
education_mapping = {
    "phd": "postgraduate",
    "master": "postgraduate",
    "graduation": "graduate",
    "2n cycle": "undergraduate"
}
dataset["education"] = dataset["education"].map(education_mapping)
# Example: Create surrogate key
dataset["customer_key"] = range(1, len(dataset) + 1)
```

Output:

A unified dataset where data from different sources is aligned to common definitions and structures.

- **Applying business rules:**

```
# Derive Age
current_year = 2026
dataset["age"] = current_year - dataset["birth_year"]
# Total dependents
dataset["total_dependents"] = dataset["kids_home"] + dataset["teens_
home"]
# Business rule: Customer segmentation
def segment_customer(income):
    if income < 30000:
        return "low"
    elif income < 70000:
        return "medium"
    else:
        return "high"
dataset["income_segment"] = dataset["income"].apply(segment_customer)
```

Output:

An enriched dataset with derived fields and domain-specific logic applied.

- **Validation (quality checks)**

```
# Null checks
null_check = dataset.isnull().sum()
# Range checks
invalid_age = dataset[(dataset["age"] < 0) | (dataset["age"] > 100)]
# Uniqueness check
duplicate_keys = dataset["customer_key"].duplicated().sum()
# Summary
print("Null Check:\n", null_check)
print("Invalid Age Records:", len(invalid_age))
print("Duplicate Keys:", duplicate_keys)
```

Output:

A verified dataset with identified (and optionally corrected) data quality issues.

- **Publishing curated layer**

```
# Select only clean, business-ready columns
curated_dataset = dataset[
    [
        "customer_key",
        "age",
        "education",
        "marital_status",
        "income",
        "income_segment",
        "total_dependents",
        "amount"
    ]
]
# Save curated layer (Gold layer)
curated_dataset.to_csv("curated_dataset.csv", index=False)
print("Curated dataset published successfully")
```

Output:

A clean, trusted, and analysis-ready dataset (curated table) for downstream consumption.

Production-ready data engineering checklist

In production environments, data pipelines must go beyond basic cleaning and transformation to include structured controls and validation mechanisms. The following example of a production data transformation checklist:

- **Schema checks:**

```
expected_columns = {
    "customer_key": "int64",
    "age": "int64",
    "income": "float64"
}
for col, dtype in expected_columns.items():
    if col not in curated_dataset.columns:
        print(f"Missing column: {col}")
```

  Output:

  Confirmation that the dataset adheres to the expected structure and data types.

- **Incremental processing:**

```
# Example: process only new data
last_processed_date = "2014-01-01"
incremental_data = dataset[dataset["dt_customer"] > last_processed_date]
print("Incremental rows:", incremental_data.shape[0])
```

  Output:

  A filtered dataset containing only new or updated records since the last run.

- **Data quality tests:**

```
# % null threshold
null_percent = curated_dataset.isnull().mean() * 100
if (null_percent > 5).any():
    print("Warning: High null values detected")
# Distribution check
print(curated_dataset.describe())
```

  Output:

  A quality report with metrics like null %, distributions, and anomalies.

- **Reconciliation:**

```
# Row count reconciliation
```

```
source_count = len(dataset)
target_count = len(curated_dataset)
print("Source Count:", source_count)
print("Curated Count:", target_count)
# Basic sanity check
if target_count > source_count:
    print("Error: More records in target than source")
```

Output:

A validation report confirming consistency between source and target datasets.

- **Observability**

```
import datetime
log = {
    "timestamp": datetime.datetime.now(),
    "rows_processed": len(dataset),
    "rows_published": len(curated_dataset),
    "null_issues": dataset.isnull().sum().sum()
}
print("Pipeline Log:", log)
```

Output:

Pipeline logs and metrics enable monitoring, debugging, and auditability.

Now, the data is ready to be ingested into any machine learning model or visualization dashboard. The final output of this transformation process is a curated dataset (or feature-ready table), enriched with standardized formats, derived attributes, and cleaned values, along with defined quality checks, validation rules, and data quality reports to ensure reliability and consistency.

In distributed or cloud-based environments, these transformation steps are typically scaled using parallel processing frameworks and managed services to handle large volumes of data efficiently.

Note: **The methods or steps are not limited to the above-listed, but many, and their usage is dependent upon the type of dataset and expected business outcome.**

Also, the code uses a sample correlation threshold; the actual cutoff should be chosen based on the data and use case.

Conclusion

This chapter covered all the essential steps that are required for the transformation of data. It explained the EDA in detail and provided an understanding of the pattern involved in the data. There was detailed information about the graphical representation of data that would help the user identify the inline issues easily. This chapter also explained all the steps required for data cleaning, which involved handling missing values, outliers, inconsistent values, duplicate records, and disguised values.

Post data cleaning, the ways to reduce the dimension of the dataset were covered, which helps in optimizing the computational power of the available hardware.

In addition to these data science aspects, the chapter emphasized key data engineering practices required to make data production-ready. The data is standardized, conformed across multiple sources, and transformed by applying business rules to ensure consistency and usability. It is then validated through defined quality checks and control mechanisms to ensure reliability and accuracy.

In the next chapter, we will go to the next level, where we will see how the data, which has been processed, can be used in many statistical analyses in real-life situations and how critical decisions are taken based on these algorithms.

References

1. **https://www.ibm.com/think/topics/exploratory-data-analysis**
2. **https://consoleflare.com/blog/wp-content/uploads/2022/09/Exploratory-Data-Analysis-1977-John-Tukey.pdf**
3. **https://www.stat.berkeley.edu/~brill/Papers/jwtencyc.pdf**
4. **https://www.geeksforgeeks.org/maths/percentile-formula/**
5. **https://www.geeksforgeeks.org/maths/quartile-formula/**
6. **https://www.investopedia.com/terms/n/normaldistribution.asp**
7. **https://www.geeksforgeeks.org/r-language/handling-inconsistent-data/**
8. **https://www.cuemath.com/correlation-coefficient-formula/**
9. **https://ujangriswanto08.medium.com/feature-engineering-secrets-for-better-multiple-linear-regression-models-6134b129d19c**

CHAPTER 6
Statistics in Data Engineering

Introduction

In the previous chapter, we covered the data transformation that entailed various aspects of data cleaning, manipulation, and logic that are applied to the data to make it useful for our further analysis.

Once appropriate data is available, there can be several steps going further, where the business needs the data for better decision-making and inference. Some businesses want this data to be used in such a way that it can show the productivity, business flaws, and areas of improvement, so that they can think about the next best actions. Some businesses already have advanced analytics with them and want some future predictions for their applications and components, e.g., the **remaining useful life** (**RUL**) of a machine in a manufacturing plant. Some organizations want to use this data for consulting purposes, where they can leverage the power of data to make their statements stronger and fact driven.

There are many statistical methods covered in this chapter that will give an idea about how applying various calculations to the data starts making sense from a business perspective.

Structure

The chapter covers the following topics:

- End-to-end data engineering lifecycle
- Hypothesis testing
- Introduction to probability
- Central limit theorem
- Introduction to inferential statistics
- Industrial example of hypothesis testing
- Normal distribution

Objectives

By the end of this chapter, you will be able to understand the underlying meaning of inferential analysis and its different types. This chapter will also cover hypothesis testing in detail, which gives clarity about how the initial inference from the data can be processed either to confirm or reject the inference. The reader will also get the step-by-step procedure of defining a problem and concluding upon it. There will be some industrial usage of the hypothesis testing that is employed by organizations for critical business decisions. This chapter will also touch upon the concept of probability and its various distributions. This will help the reader to understand the fundamental usage of probability in the data science world. There will be an in-depth understanding of normal distribution and the **central limit theorem** (**CLT**), which is used by most of the research organizations to give an idea of the behavior of the entire population by working on limited samples.

End-to-end data engineering lifecycle

Till now, all the important topics, starting from data generation to data transformation, are already covered. Now it is time to look at the next steps of using the data and making a decision around the direction to take that is in line with the organization's expectations.

As shown in *Figure 6.1*, in this chapter, we are touching upon the data usage part, but it is on the surface level. The major use cases covered in this chapter are inferential analysis, which is used to understand the current sample of data and make an inference for the entire population.

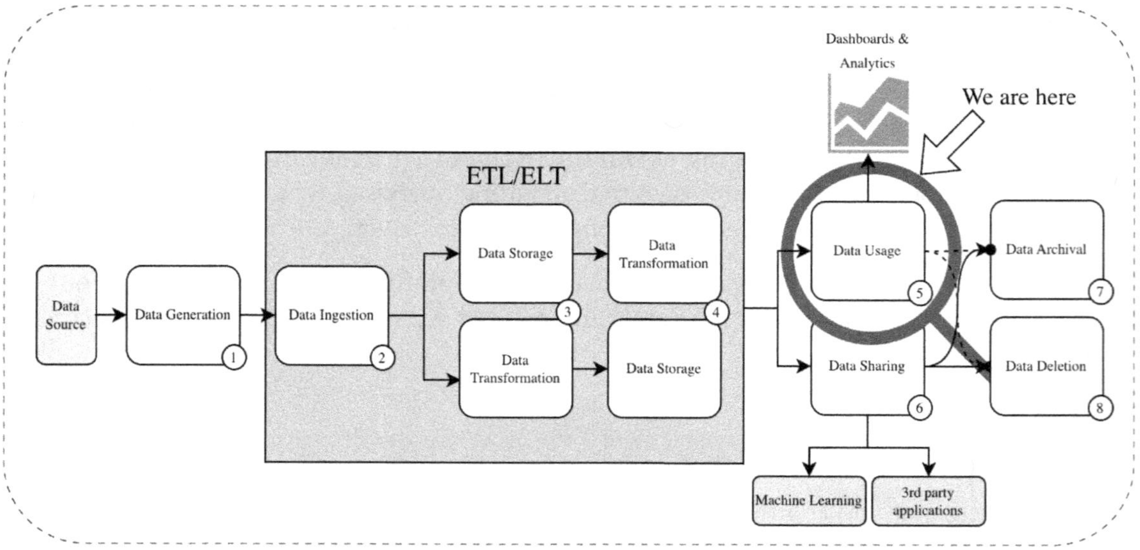

***Figure 6.1**: Showing the current phase covered in the chapter*

Introduction to inferential statistics

This is defined as the statistical branch that involves making inferences about a population based on a sample, with the objective of drawing conclusions about the larger population from a small set of data.

It uses various methods, including hypothesis testing, confidence intervals, and regression testing:

- Hypothesis testing evaluates the strength of evidence against a null hypothesis by comparing sample data.
- Confidence interval provides a range of values that is plausible for the population parameter, e.g., if the mean weight of a sample of 100 people is 70 kg with a 95% confidence interval of 68 to 72, then we can say that we are 95% confident that the true population mean lies between 68 and 72 kg.
- Regression analysis examines the relationship between variables and enables predictions or estimations based on those relationships.

In *Figure 6.2,* since it is nearly impossible to collect the data for the entire population, we derive a sample from it:

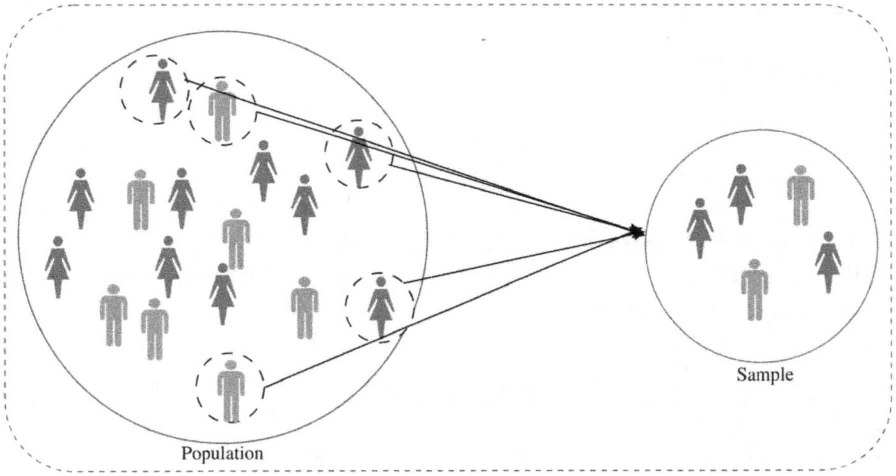

Figure 6.2*: A representation of a sample drawn from a population*

Let us look at the two fundamental terms that are often used in the data science world:

- **Population**: A population is the entire group of individuals or objects that we are interested in studying. The group can be as large as the population of this country or as small as the number of students in a class.
- **Sample**: A sample is a smaller subset of the population that is selected for the study or research. By the rule of thumb, the sample should be selected such that its behavior is as close as possible to the population.

Methods of selecting samples

Based on the ways of selecting samples, there are three ways a sample can be selected:

- **Simple random sampling**: It is simply picking samples randomly from the population.

- **Stratified sampling**: It is a process of dividing the population into certain strata or groups and then selecting the samples randomly from each group.
- **Cluster sampling**: It is the process of dividing the population into clusters based on certain parameters and then selecting an entire cluster, e.g., selecting the working-class females from a city's population.

Statistical inference

Mean:

If x1, x2, …, Xn constitute a random sample, then the sample mean is given by:

$$\bar{x} = \frac{\sum_{i=1}^{n} x_i}{n}$$

Variance:

The sample variance is given by:

$$s^2 = \frac{\sum_{i=1}^{n}(x_i - \bar{x})^2}{n - 1}$$

Note: **We divide by (n – 1) instead of n to correct for bias in the estimation. This adjustment, known as Bessel's correction, ensures that the sample variance provides an unbiased estimate of the population variance.**

Types of inferential statistics

There are different types of inferential statistics that can be applied to sample data:

- Estimation
- Hypothesis testing
- Correlation analysis
- Regression analysis
- ANOVA

Let us cover them in detail in the following sections.

Estimation

Estimation is the process of using sample data to predict the value of unknown population parameters. There are two types of estimations:

- **Point estimation**: A single value that is used to approximate the unknown population parameter, e.g., the sample mean is a point estimate of the population mean.

  A real-life analogy, a company takes a random sample of 100 employees to calculate the mean or average salary as $5000 per month. Now they take this as a point estimate of the average salary of all employees in the company.

- **Interval estimate**: A range of values, derived from sample data, which will be used to predict the unknown parameter. The most common type of interval estimate is a confidence interval, which specifies a range around the point estimates and includes the confidence level that typically ranges between 90-99%. For example, for the same example above, we are 95% confident that the average salary of all the employees lies between $4500 and $5250.

Hypothesis testing

It is a statistical method to make inferences about the population. It compares two opposite ideas about a population and uses a small sample to decide which idea is more likely to be true.

This topic will be covered in detail in the next section.

Correlation analysis

As we studied in the previous chapter, i.e., *Chapter 5, Data Transformation*, correlation measures the strength and direction of two variables that range between +1 and -1. In this analysis, we observe the correlation between the variables in the sample data and infer this as the same relation in the case of the population.

For example, the height and weight of children in one class section have a correlation of 0.85; this means that as the height increases, the weight also increases. Now, the same correlation can be used for all the students in the same class as in other sections.

Regression analysis

This is the process of modelling and predicting the value of dependent variables based on other independent variables. For example, if the sample data has a relationship in which a dependent variable can be derived from the independent variables, then the same equation can be used to predict the value of the dependent variable of the entire population.

Real-life example, if a sample of data shows that the exam scores can be derived from the hours of study with a strong relationship, then we can utilize this regression equation from the sample to estimate or predict exam scores for the entire student population.

Analysis of variance

Analysis of variance (**ANOVA**) is a statistical method of determining whether the means of three or more groups are different. This is done by analyzing the variability within each group and between the groups.

If the difference between the groups is significantly larger than the within-group difference, then ANOVA tells us that one of the groups is truly different; it concludes that the difference is likely due to random chance, but the overall effect is the same.

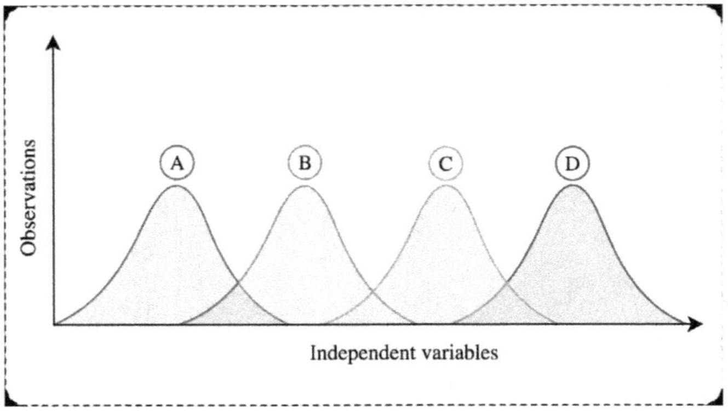

Figure 6.3: A visual representation of the distribution of four different groups

Real-life example, there are three groups of plants, A, B, and C, being given fertilizer. If plants in groups A, B, and C grow very differently on average, such as A = 40, B = 60, C = 91, then ANOVA says fertilizers truly make a difference.

Whereas, if plants within the group vary a lot, e.g., within A, one plant is 30 cm and another 70 cm in height, but the average of A is nearly the same as others, such as A = 49, B = 50, C = 51, then ANOVA says the fertilizers have perhaps the same effect, and the differences are just random.

Hypothesis testing

Before defining hypothesis testing, it is important to understand what a hypothesis is. A hypothesis is a preconceived notion, assumption, guess, or opinion about any field for which we are going to do research.

Hypothesis testing is a statistical method used to determine the validity of a claim or hypothesis about a population. This is mostly employed by data scientists to assess the significance of relationships, with which they compare groups and make predictions with a confidence score.

Hypothesis testing follows a structured approach to determine the right evidence to accept or reject a hypothesis. This follows two categories of hypotheses:

- **Null hypothesis (H_0)**: It is the default state or claim that is first assumed by a data scientist.
- **Alternative hypothesis (H_a)**: It is the other condition as opposed to the null hypothesis

This testing provides data scientists with the power to validate the claim using a data-driven framework.

Real-life example, in a criminal trial:

- **Null hypothesis (H_0 'The accused is not guilty until proven')**: This is the assumption the legal system starts with.

- **Alternative hypothesis (H_a 'The accused is guilty')**: This is what the prosecution is trying to prove with evidence.

The court assumes innocence (H_0) unless enough evidence is shown to reject that assumption. If the evidence is strong enough without any doubt, then we reject the null hypothesis and conclude that the person is guilty. In the case where the evidence is weak, we remain at H_0 To conclude, the person is not guilty.

Note: **Here, we are not accepting the null hypothesis, but due to a lack of strong evidence, we fail to reject it. This does not imply that the person is innocent and accepting the null hypothesis, but we are saying we are not able to prove them guilty.**

As shown in *Figure 6.4*, the middle area is where our null hypothesis lies, and if our statistical calculations lie on the extreme right or extreme left, then we can reject the null hypothesis:

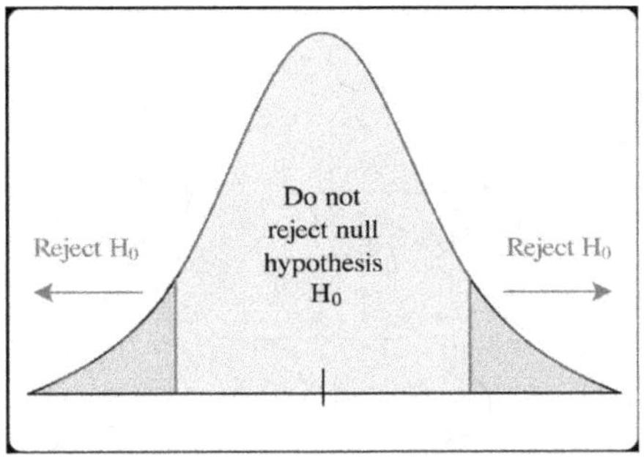

***Figure 6.4**: Showing the area where the rejection of the null hypothesis starts*

The following are types of hypothesis testing:

- **Null hypothesis**: As discussed above, it serves as a baseline against which the alternative hypothesis is tested, e.g., null hypothesis: age has no effect on music ability.
- **Alternate hypothesis**: Opposite of the null hypothesis and suggests that the observed result is not by mere chance or random behavior, e.g., people of older age become more creative in music
- **Non-directional hypothesis**: This is also known as a two-tailed hypothesis, which suggests that there is a relationship or a difference in either direction between the variables. It is applicable where we do not have a predefined direction from the start, e.g., listening to music affects concentration (It may improve concentration or distract; we do not have a direction at the start).
- **Directional hypothesis**: This is a one-tailed hypothesis that suggests a single direction of relationships between the variables. It shows the specific association, positive or negative, in a specific direction, e.g., listening to music while studying maths increases concentration.
- **Statistical hypothesis**: This is a statement or a claim about a population parameter or a relationship between the variables. This is formulated and testable using data and

statistical methods. These hypotheses are specific statistical parameters such as mean, variance, etc. They can be of both directional and non-directional, e.g., the average height of Indian men is 5 ft 7 inches (170 cm).

Making decisions

The ultimate goal of conducting hypothesis testing is decision-making; the calculations are the mathematical or statistical means to give us confidence and strengthen our decision-making.

While doing a hypothesis, we can start with a null hypothesis and try to reject it, but there must be a structured approach to come to a conclusion.

Let us look at the following figure that shows how following the right approach leads us from confusion to clarity:

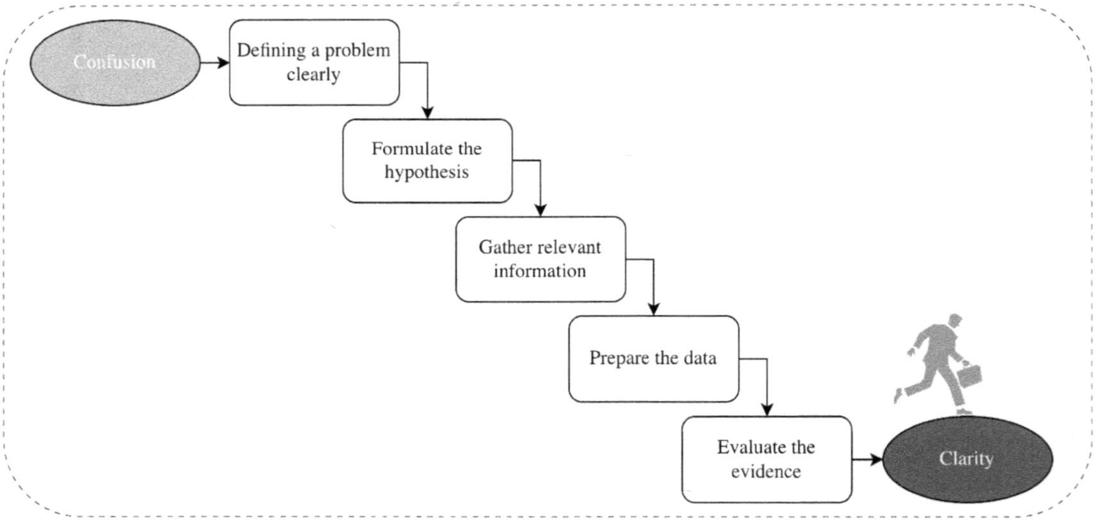

***Figure 6.5**: Steps defined in decision-making*

As shown in *Figure 6.5*, there are some steps that need to be followed for clear decision-making, which are:

1. **Defining a problem clearly**: This is the very first and foremost thing to do, that is, *we must know what we are asking for*, or in other words, the ask should be very clear. Until this is formulated well, the research becomes meaningless. E.g., *does going to the gym make us conscious about health, does eating outside make us unhealthy*, etc.

2. **Formulate the hypothesis**: Once we have clarity in the ask, we will know the direction of research. Now, this is the time to create a null hypothesis. This may be the general belief the population has, and should be testable using some data. For example, null hypothesis: *Eating outside makes us unhealthy*; alternative hypothesis: *Eating outside does not make us unhealthy.*

3. **Gather relevant information**: This process is to collect or prepare relevant data. This data may come from surveys, experiments, past company data, other medical trial results, government public databases, or any other authentic sources.

   Note: **The source of data collection is very important, as the authenticity of data matters a lot. Nowadays, due to the abundance of content creators in the market, it has brought more colorful data that may be based upon the individual choices or preferences, which may be far from reality, e.g., personal blogs, social media information should be avoided if they do not have sufficient citations to strengthen their point.**

4. **Prepare the data**: This is just like the data transformation step, where we are cleaning the data and transforming it in such a way that it can be used for statistical calculations.
5. **Evaluate the evidence**: This is the final step in which we have to apply the statistical methods to analyze the data and find the confidence interval for it. If the evidence is strong enough to reject the null hypothesis, then we conclude the alternative hypothesis as the final decision, or vice versa.

All these steps are to ensure that the decision is logical and evidence-based, and it is not influenced by emotions, bias, or guesswork.

Critical value analysis

A critical value analysis is the decision-making method that is used by defining the rejection region based upon a significance level (α). In this method, the critical value is calculated from the probability distribution, and testing is done against the critical value.

If the test statistic falls into the rejection region, then we will reject the null hypothesis; otherwise, we will fail to reject the null hypothesis.

Figure 6.6 shows the visual representation of critical value analysis in hypothesis testing, where a left-tailed test shows the region of rejection on the left-hand side. That means, if the test statistic is less than the critical value, then the null hypothesis will be rejected; otherwise, we will fail to reject the null hypothesis. Similarly, on the right-tailed test, if the test statistic is greater than the critical value, then the null hypothesis will be rejected in the case of a right-tailed test.

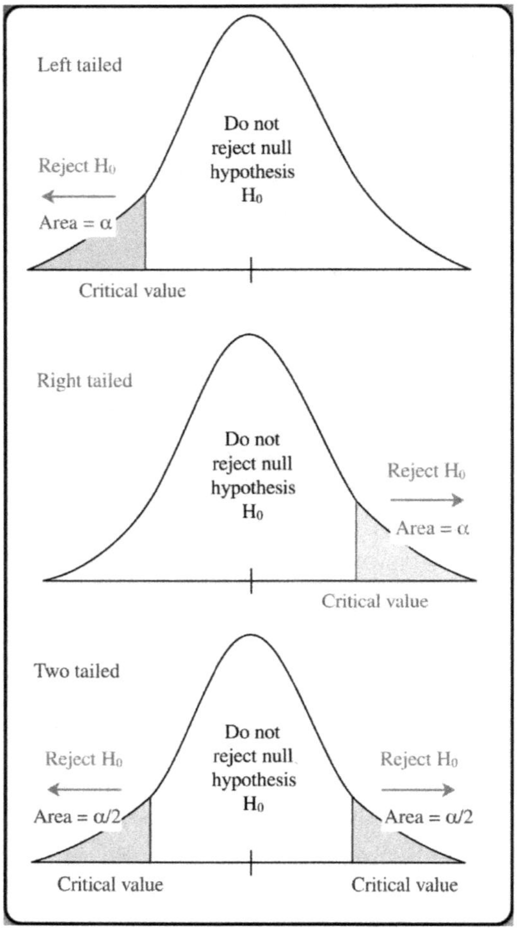

Figure 6.6*: A representation of the critical value in a normal distribution*

For the two-tailed test, if the test statistic is less than the left-critical value or greater than the right-critical value, then the null hypothesis will be rejected; otherwise, it will fail to reject the null hypothesis.

Types of errors

There are two types of errors in hypothesis testing:

- **Type 1 error (False positive)**: This is the case when we reject the null hypothesis even if it is true. This is denoted by alpha (α).

  For example:

  - A medical test says a healthy person has a disease
  - Convicting an innocent person

- **Type 2 error (False negative)**: This is the case where we fail to reject the null hypothesis even though it is false. This is denoted by beta(β).

  For example:

  - A medical test says a sick person is healthy
  - A guilty person is freed

Depending upon the use case, the severity of errors may vary. From the above example, in a medical test, concluding that a sick person is healthy can be extremely dangerous, as it may prevent timely and critical treatment. On the other hand, it is generally considered better to free a guilty person than to wrongly convict an innocent one.

Level of significance

The level of significance is defined as the threshold probability used in hypothesis testing to decide whether to reject the null hypothesis.

Generally is considered 0.05, which means 5%. This means it is acceptable to take 5% risk of making a type 1 error or rejecting the null hypothesis when it is actually true.

If it is less than 0.05, this means it is more strict; if it is more than 0.05, this means it is lenient.

For example:

- H_0: The medicine has no effect.
- H_1: The medicine helps in recovery, α=0.05.

This means we are willing to take a 5% risk in concluding that the drug works when it actually does not.

Note: **The level of significance should be chosen based upon the use cases, for domains like healthcare, aviation, military, etc., should have less tolerance, whereas other general areas that are not mission-critical can have more tolerance.**

P-value

This is the probability of the evidence being strong against the null hypothesis. If the p-value $\leq \alpha$, there is strong evidence against H_0, leading to rejection of the null hypothesis.

On the other hand, if p-value $>\alpha$, there is weak evidence against H_0, the chances of failing to reject H_0 are very high.

For example, suppose we test the average (μ). The score in math is 80.

- $H_0 : \mu = 80$
- $H_1 : \mu \neq 80$
- α: 0.05

We collected the data, and the p-value after calculation is 0.03.

Since p-value $<\alpha$, we will reject the null hypothesis, which means the average score in math is not 80.

A Python example of hypothesis testing:

```
import numpy as np
from scipy import stats
# Example data: marks of 15 students in math
marks = np.array([88, 78, 82, 90, 81, 75, 87, 90, 78, 73, 72, 80, 83, 85, 75])
# Hypothesized population mean
mu = 80
# Perform one-sample t-test
t_stat, p_value = stats.ttest_1samp(marks, mu)
print(f"Sample Mean: {np.mean(marks):.2f}")
print(f"T-statistic: {t_stat:.3f}")
print(f"P-value: {p_value:.3f}")
# Level of significance we are choosing as 0.05, we are taking 5% risk of
stating average being 80 when it is not.
alpha = 0.05
if p_value < alpha:
    print("Reject the null hypothesis: The average is significantly different
from 80.")
else:
    print("Fail to reject the null hypothesis: No significant difference from
80.")
```

Output:

- **`Sample mean: 81.13`**
- **`T-statistic: 0.732`**
- **`P-value: 0.476`**
- **`Fail to reject the null hypothesis: No significant difference from 80.`**

This means the average score is not far from 80.

Industrial examples of hypothesis testing

Hypothesis testing in industry provides a systematic framework for validating insights, optimizing operations, and supporting strategic decision-making instead of intuition-based decision-making.

The tests in the following sections show the different types of hypothesis testing that are done based on the specific use cases.

Two samples means testing

These types of testing come into play where we are comparing the two means of two independent groups, as opposed to the single mean calculation we saw earlier.

These types of tests are often performed when the variable of interest is quantitative and normally distributed in both groups.

This type of testing can be done using a t-test or a z-test:

- **Z-test**: If the standard deviation is known, or the sample size ≥ 30
- **T-test**: If the standard deviation is unknown, or the sample size < 30

Python example

We are trying to check if the two groups (Group A: girls, Group B: boys) in a class have the same mean or same average marks:

```
import numpy as np
from scipy import stats
# Sample data: marks of two groups
group_A = np.array([88, 92, 80, 89, 100, 76, 95, 89])
group_B = np.array([84, 90, 78, 85, 92, 75, 88, 84])
# H₀: Mean of Group A = Mean of Group B
# H₁: Means are different
# If p-value < 0.05, we reject H₀ (there is a significant difference).
# Perform Independent Two-
Sample t-test (Welch's t-test, does not assume equal variance)
t_stat, p_value = stats.ttest_ind(group_A, group_B, equal_var=False)
print("Group A Mean:", np.mean(group_A))
print("Group B Mean:", np.mean(group_B))
print("T-statistic:", t_stat)
print("P-value:", p_value)
# Significance level
alpha = 0.05
if p_value < alpha:
    print("Reject Null Hypothesis → The two group means are significantly
different.")
else:
    print("Fail to Reject Null Hypothesis → No significant difference between
group means.")
```

Output:

- `Group A mean: 88.625`
- `Group B mean: 84.5`
- `T-statistic: 1.2127529939876498`
- `P-value: 0.2468737647779963`
- `Fail to Reject Null Hypothesis: No significant difference between group means.`

Other use cases can be testing of medicine results in two different groups of people, comparing the salaries of different corporations in order to conclude upon market standards, etc.

Proportion testing

This is another type of testing that is used in the industry, which is to compare the percentages of two categorical data variables. This type of testing is used to determine if there is a significant difference in the proportion of two different groups.

This type of testing can be done using the chi-square test or the z-test:

- **Z-test**: If comparing proportions across one or two groups only, or sample size ≥ 30, e.g., out of 100 voters, 55 say they *support*.
- **Chi-square test**: If comparing proportions across multiple categories or sample sizes < 30, e.g.

  In the following table, we have added the complexity of two groups with *support* and *oppose* information as well:

Gender	Support	Oppose	Total
Male	60	40	100
Female	72	48	120

***Table 6.1**: Gender wise distribution of support and opposition*

A Python example:

```
import numpy as np
import statsmodels.api as sm
from scipy.stats import chi2_contingency
import matplotlib.pyplot as plt
# ------------------------------
# Data
# ------------------------------
successes = [60, 72]    # supporters
```

```
samples = [100, 120]    # total voters
alpha = 0.05  # significance level
# ------------------------------
# 1Two-Sample Proportion Z-Test
# ------------------------------
z_stat, p_value_z = sm.stats.proportions_ztest(successes, samples)
print("Two-Sample Proportion Z-Test")
print("Z-statistic:", round(z_stat, 3))
print("P-value:", round(p_value_z, 4))
if p_value_z < alpha:
    print("Reject Null Hypothesis: Proportions are significantly different.\n")
else:
    print("Fail to Reject Null Hypothesis: No significant difference in 
proportions.\n")
# ------------------------------
# 2Chi-Square Test of Independence
# ------------------------------
# Contingency table
table = np.array([[60, 40],    # Male
                  [72, 48]])  # Female
chi2, p_value_chi, dof, expected = chi2_contingency(table)
print("Chi-Square Test of Independence")
print("Chi2 statistic:", round(chi2, 3))
print("P-value:", round(p_value_chi, 4))
print("Degrees of freedom:", dof)
if p_value_chi < alpha:
    print("Reject Null Hypothesis: Gender and preference are associated.\n")
else:
    print("Fail to Reject Null Hypothesis: Gender and preference are 
independent.\n")
print("Expected frequencies under H0:\n", expected)
```

A and B testing

This is also called split testing, where the two versions (A and B) of anything are compared to find which one performs better:

- **Version A**: Current version (also called control).
- **Version B**: New version or target version to test (also called a variation).

Both versions are shown to two different groups of users randomly, and their responses are measured.

The data is then recorded and analyzed to see which one works better.

For example, on an e-commerce website, testing the product with images generates more user engagement than the product with videos.

Otherwise, a structural change in a website that has product photos on the front with a small font of price is more likely to be liked by customers, or the product photos on the side panel with bigger font of price.

As shown in *Figure 6.7*, it is clearly visible that the variation is created, which is significantly different than the current version. Both versions will be compared based on the user engagement, and the output of the experimentation will be analyzed to conclude which version is most liked by the readers.

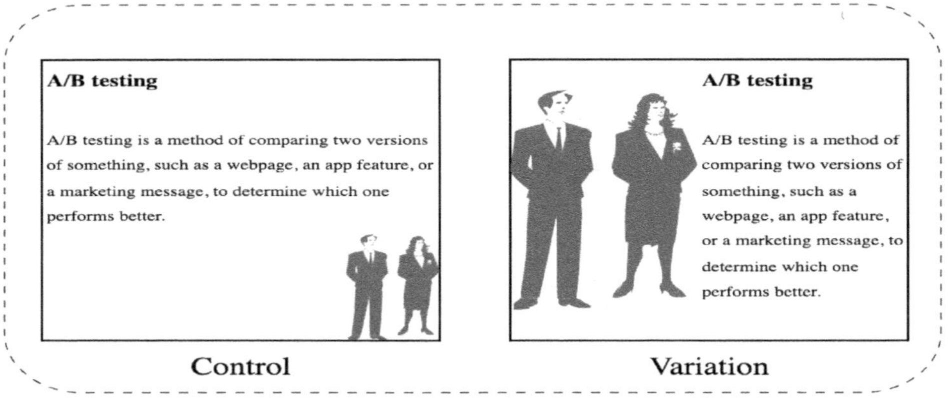

***Figure 6.7**: Shows an example of A/B testing done for a technical blog*

The following are the steps for A / B testing:

1. **Collect data**: For any website, mobile app, or target product, find ways to generate the data. This may be capturing the clicks of the users on a particular link, or time spent on a particular page, or adding the products into the cart. Use analytics tools like Google Analytics to identify the opportunities.

2. **Set goals**: To measure the target, it is imperative to know what should be measured. The metric should be clearly defined, and measurement criteria should be established.

3. **Create a test hypothesis**: This is the step where the clear predictions should be formed based on a universal truth or strong belief with respect to the business outcome.

4. **Design the variation**: Make specific and visible changes to the target system so that proper tracking can be done.

5. **Run the experiment**: Make both systems live, split the traffic randomly without any bias, and collect the data systematically. The current system should be monitored for any issues.
6. **Analyze the results**: Review all the metrics, compare them against each other, and find the statistical significance.
7. **Document the experiment**: Once analysis is completed and the results are identified, it is crucial to document them, as this is critical data that can be used in the future for any reference or retrospection.

A Python example of A/B testing:

```
import numpy as np
import statsmodels.api as sm
# Example data
# Group A (control)
visitors_A = 1000
conversions_A = 120   # 12% conversion
# Group B (variation)
visitors_B = 980
conversions_B = 150   # 15.3% conversion
# Conversion rates
rate_A = conversions_A / visitors_A
rate_B = conversions_B / visitors_B
print(f"Conversion Rate A: {rate_A:.3f}")
print(f"Conversion Rate B: {rate_B:.3f}")
# Prepare data for z-test
count = np.array([conversions_A, conversions_B])      # successes
nobs = np.array([visitors_A, visitors_B])             # trials
# Perform two-proportion z-test
z_stat, p_value = sm.stats.proportions_ztest(count, nobs)
print(f"\nZ-statistic: {z_stat:.3f}")
print(f"P-value: {p_value:.3f}")
# Interpret result at 5% significance level
alpha = 0.05
if p_value < alpha:
    print("Significant difference: Version B outperforms A.")
else:
    print("No significant difference: Keep testing.")
```

Output:

```
Conversion Rate A: 0.120
Conversion Rate B: 0.153
Z-statistic: -2.143
P-value: 0.032
Significant difference: Version B outperforms A.
```

Although it was easy to recognize the differences in the conversion percentages, using statistical methods, we can clearly conclude the significant differences. For example, in critical systems like an Airplane engine's operational behavior, even decimal-level differences can be considered significant.

Introduction to probability

Ideally, probability is a statistical subject and sounds like it must be used in various algorithms in data science, but probability is also useful for the work related to data engineering, which we will be covering soon. Let us understand probability.

Probability is defined as the quantification of the likelihood of an event. The value of probability lies between 0 and 1, where 0 means the unlikelihood of an event and 1 means the likelihood of the event.

Real-life examples, rain prediction, sunrise or sunset predictions, snow prediction, etc. These all predictions work by collecting the historical data and applying some statistical techniques to predict these conditions.

A simple illustration of how to use probability:

Suppose there is a bag with 3 red balls, 4 blue balls, and 3 green balls. If we need to take out one ball from this bag without replacing it, *what is the probability of selecting a blue ball?*

Solution:

1. Find the total number of favorable outcomes, i.e., *balls in the bag = 3 red + 4 blue + 3 green = 10 balls*
2. Find the number of favorable outcomes, *blue ball in this case = 4*
3. Divide the total number of favorable outcomes by the total number of outcomes, *4/10 = 0.4*

In other words, there are 40% chances that if one ball is taken out, it will be a blue ball.

Use of probability in data engineering

It is time to look at the scenarios where the probability can help data engineers while they process the data:

- **Data quality and missing data**: As data engineers often deal with quality issues with data. Sometimes, probability-based data imputation helps them improve the quality of data. e.g., imputing gender values when 70% males and 30% females based upon the likelihood estimation using probability.
- **Anomaly detection**: In the dataset, the outliers or anomalies can be detected using a probability distribution. E.g., if the daily user count follows a Poisson distribution, then sudden spikes in user count can be considered as outliers.
- **Data sampling**: Sometimes big data is difficult to process; in such cases, probability-based sampling helps create samples that are as close to the population as possible.

In many other areas, like data compression, stream processing, and feature engineering, the use of probability is required.

The following are the real-life examples:

- **Automatic log monitoring**: Probability can be used to detect unusual server activity, which will help the system identify potential attacks.
- **Fraud detection**: There are some probabilistic models that are used to detect suspicious transactions.
- **A/B testing**: using the data collected from previous A/B testing, the engineers predict the probability of conversions.

Probability distributions

In the above section, probability is introduced, but it covers the chances of a single event happening at an instant, e.g., the probability of getting 6 when a die is rolled. These are single or simple events. However, in real life, we deal with infinite random variables, and those may have different possible outcomes. When a random experiment is performed, we are often interested in the complete outcome rather than individual probabilities.

For example, suppose there are 2 dice rolled, we may be interested in the final outcome rather than the individual probabilities. For instance, we are interested in 7 as an outcome, which is the sum of the individual dice's outputs. The combinations of output of dice may be (1,6), (2,5), (3,4), (4,3), (5,2), or (6,1), all summing up to 7.

Similarly, we may be interested in looking at the number of cars on the road on a festival day, but not interested in studying the probability of each car.

If the variable X is the random variable that is defined as the sum of two fair dice, then the probability of $X = 2$ means that the sum of the dice outcomes is 2.

P{X=2}: (probability of 1 in dice 1 AND probability of 1 in dice 2) => P{(1,1)} = $\frac{1}{6} * \frac{1}{6} = \frac{1}{36}$

Similarly, the probability of a sum of 7 means:

P{X=7} = P{(1,6) OR (2,5) OR (3,4) OR (4,3) OR P(5,2) OR P{(6,1)} =

$$\frac{1}{36} + \frac{1}{36} + \frac{1}{36} + \frac{1}{36} + \frac{1}{36} + \frac{1}{36} = \frac{6}{36}$$

So, a random variable is a number that connects theoretical probability with real-life data.

A random variable X represents a numerical value associated with each outcome of a probability distribution.

Probability distribution is defined as the spread of probability across all the possible values of a random variable. As an example, for the probability of getting 7 when 2 dice are rolled, $\frac{1}{36} + \frac{1}{36} + \frac{1}{36} + \frac{1}{36} + \frac{1}{36} + \frac{1}{36} = \frac{6}{36}$ is the probability distribution.

Types of probability distribution are:

- **Discrete probability distribution**: This works on a finite sample space, such as the number of students in a mathematics class.
    - **Bernoulli distribution**: One trial and two outcomes (success/failure), e.g., tossing a coin.
    - **Binomial distribution**: Where for a fixed number of trials, which are independent of each other. There are only two possible outcomes that are classified as success (S) or failure (F), and the probability of success is the same in each trial. E.g., tossing a fair coin 10 times.
    - **Geometric distribution**: Count of independent trials until first success, e.g., number of coin flips until first head.
    - **Poisson distribution**: Counting the number of events in a fixed interval of time/space at a given constant average. The probability of each event is the same in each interval. For example, a website gets 50 clicks in a minute.
    - **Uniform distribution**: Number of outcomes are equally likely, i.e., they have equal probability, e.g., the probability of getting any number on a dice is the same as $\frac{1}{6}$.
- **Continuous probability distribution**: This works on an infinite sample space, like the distance travelled by a car on a full tank. This happens when the random variable takes real values.

- **Normal or Gaussian distribution**: When the distribution becomes a bell curve plotted across the mean and standard deviation, e.g., marks of students in a class

  This is covered in detail in the following section.
- **Exponential distribution**: It describes the time taken to complete a task, e.g., time until the next customer enters the store.
- **Uniform or continuous distribution**: All values in an interval are equally likely, e.g., picking a random number between 0 and 1.

Normal distribution

Normal distribution is defined as the probability distribution that becomes normalized and symmetrical as the number of random experiments increases.

It is defined by two parameters:

- **Mean (μ)**: It is the center of the distribution
- **Standard deviation (σ)**: It shows how the data is spread across both sides of the mean.

For example, the marks of the students in the class, $\mu = 75$, $\sigma = 5$

As shown in the following figure, it is clearly seen that the density of students around 75 marks is the highest, and that becomes the mean, and then it can be seen how the distribution of marks varies with the standard deviation:

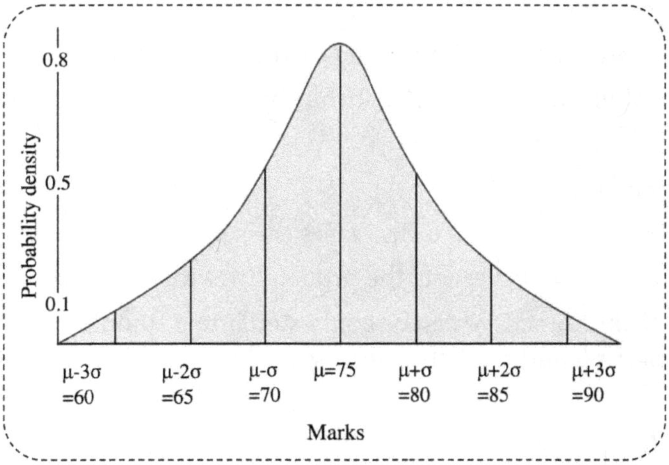

***Figure 6.8**: A normally distributed graph for marks distribution*

Standard normal distribution

This is the special case where the normally distributed curve can be converted to the standard normal distribution by bringing the mean to 0 and the standard deviation to 1.

The mathematical equation to do that is:

$$Z = \frac{X - \mu}{\sigma}$$

So taking X = 75 will make Z as $\frac{75-75}{5} = 0$

Similarly, 80 as 1, 85 as 2, 90 as 3, and so on.

If we try to plot the same in the graph, see *Figure 6.9*

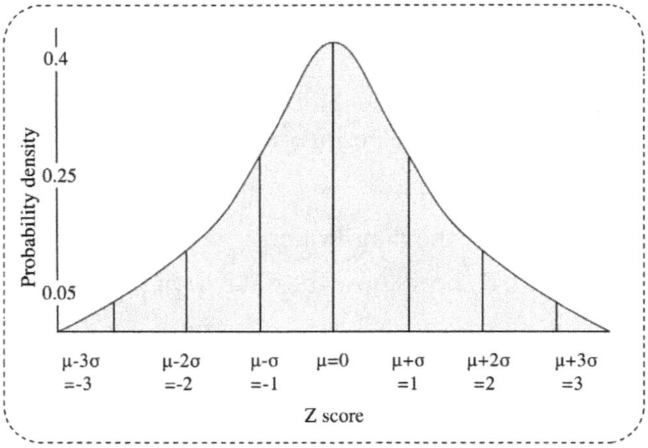

***Figure 6.9**: A standard normally distributed graph for marks distribution*

The following are the properties of the normal distribution curve:

- Most of the values in the normal distribution lie around the centre (μ).
- The median and mean are equal.
- It has only one mode.
- It is symmetric, which means it decreases the same amount on both sides.
- Area under the curve represents the probabilities for the data.
- A normal distribution curve can be converted into a standard normal curve to plot the graph against $\mu = 0$ and $\sigma = 1$ this process is also called the Z-transformation.

Empirical rule

This rule is also called 68-95-99.7 rule. It is a statistical guideline that states that in a bell curve shape, 68.3% of data falls within one standard deviation from the mean, around 95.5% within two standard deviations from the mean, and 99.7% of data lies within three standard deviations from the mean.

- **68.3%**: From μ-1σ to μ+1σ
- **95.5%**: From μ-2σ to μ+2σ
- **99.7%**: From μ-3σ to μ+3σ

Figure 6.10 represents how this rule can be visualized on a bell curve:

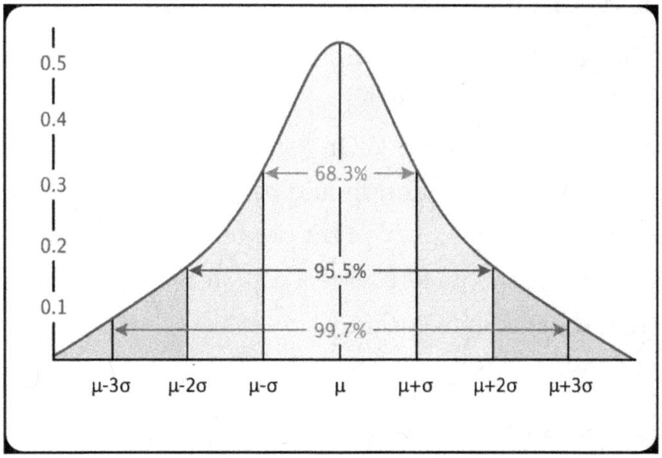

***Figure 6.10**: Representing the probability distribution*

In a real-life example, if the average score of a class in a test is 70 with a standard deviation of 5, then:

- 68.3% of scores lie between 65 (*70-5*) and 75 (*70+5*)
- 95.5% of scores lie in between 60 (*70-2*5*) and 80 (*70+2*5*)
- 99.7% of scores lie between 55 (*70-3*5*) and 85 (*70+3*5*)

Real-world examples of normal distribution

The normal distribution looks magical, but in reality, it is the way natural distribution also occurs. For example, the height of men or women in the population follows the bell curve, as most of the people are average in height, and very few people are very tall or very short.

Similarly, if the IQ tests are conducted, then they will follow the same bell curve.

In fact, analysis of Nobel prize winners shows that the age distribution also follows the bell curve, where the majority of Nobel prizes are received by people between 50 and 60 years of age. The details are available in the following links:

1. **https://backend.orbit.dtu.dk/ws/portalfiles/portal/215281397/NP_article.pdf**
2. **https://lav30.github.io/nobelprizes/**

Central limit theorem

This is the basic theory in statistics where the central limit states that when the sample taken out of the population is sufficiently large, then the sample mean distribution will have a normal distribution, regardless of the underlying population distribution, whether it is normal or skewed.

The number of samples is generally recommended to be 30 or more, though not a strict rule, as the applicability of the CLT also depends on the underlying distribution.

This is crucial, since the population distribution is unknown, statisticians will be easily able to draw a conclusion based on the sample data.

The following are the assumptions of the CLT:

- Samples drawn from a population should be random and independent of each other.
- Sample size should not exceed 10% of the population when done without replacement.
- Sample size should be adequately large, i.e., ≥30.
- Population should have finite variance.

The following are the practical uses of the CLT:

- **Opinion and poll surveys**: News channels predict the election results by taking limited samples (a few thousand out of millions) from the entire population.
- **Quality control**: A company that manufactures any machine wants to test the working life of the machine; they cannot test all the machines, so they take samples and test their life. The sample mean of the machine's life will be normally distributed.
- **Stock market**: Daily return of any stock changes up and down and may not be normal, but the distribution of the averages of return checked over a particular duration follows a normal distribution.
- **Medical trials**: When drugs are tested on a limited number of individuals, the average effect of their behavior is used to predict the behavior of the entire population.
- **Agriculture**: A farmer measures the yield of a crop on a few samples; the average yield per acre can follow a normal distribution. This can be used to predict the yield of the whole farm.

Similarly, this can be applicable to many areas where a sample can be collected from a limited set, and the requirement is to understand the behavior of the complete population.

The following is a Python example of how a stock return data (population) of 2 million can be used for sampling:

1. Import required libraries:

```
import numpy as np
import matplotlib.pyplot as plt
from scipy.stats import norm
```

2. Setting fonts (Optional):

```
plt.rcParams['font.family'] = 'Liberation Serif'
```

3. Fix randomness to get the same results every time:

```
np.random.seed(42)
```

4. Generating a large population of stock returns using a **normal distribution,** mean = 0.001, standard deviation = 0.02, size = 2 millions:

```
population_size = 2000000
population_returns = np.random.
normal(loc=0.001, scale=0.02, size=population_size)
```

5. Add skewness, exponential distribution adds large positive values, final data becomes skewed. This is done intentionally to make the data not perfectly normal and demonstrate the importance of the CLT:

```
population_returns += np.random.exponential(scale=1, size=population_
size) - 0.01
```

6. Function to compute sample means, number of default samples 5000. Randomly picks n values from the population, compute their mean, repeat this 5000 times, and store all the resulting means in a list:

```
def get_sample_means(pop, n, sims=5000):
    return [np.mean(np.random.
choice(pop, n, replace=True)) for _ in range(sims)]
```

7. Computing sample means (for n =1, 30, and 500):

```
sample_sizes = [1,30,500]
sample_means_dict = {n: get_sample_means(population_
returns, n) for n in sample_sizes}
```

Output:

```
n = 1: picked 1 number each time → mean is the same number → very random
results
n = 30: picked 30 numbers → average them → results become more stable
n = 500: picked 500 numbers → average them → results are very stable
and close to the true mean
```

8. Plot population distribution:

```
plt.figure(figsize=(12,6))
plt.hist(population_returns, bins=100, color='grey', edgecolor='black',
alpha=0.7, density=True)
plt.title("Population: Simulated Stock Daily Returns (Skewed)",
fontsize=18)
plt.xlabel("Daily Return", fontsize=14)
plt.ylabel("Density", fontsize=14)
plt.xticks(fontsize=12)
```

```
plt.yticks(fontsize=12)
plt.show()
```

9. Sampling distribution:

   Calculates true population mean and standard deviation

```
pop_mean = np.mean(population_returns)
pop_std = np.std(population_returns)
```

10. Creates 3 plots (for n = 1, 30, and 500):

```
fig, axes = plt.subplots(1, 3, figsize=(18,5))
for ax, n in zip(axes, sample_sizes):
    # Histogram of sample means
    data = sample_means_dict[n]
    ax.hist(data, bins=40, density=True, alpha=0.6, color='grey',
edgecolor='black')
    # Overlay normal curve
    se = pop_std / np.sqrt(n)
    x = np.linspace(min(data), max(data), 200)
    ax.plot(x, norm.pdf(x, loc=pop_mean, scale=se), 'k-
', lw=2, label="Normal Curve")
    # Bigger fonts for labels and title
    ax.set_title(f"Sampling Distribution (n={n})", fontsize=20)
    ax.set_xlabel("Sample Mean Return", fontsize=16)
    ax.set_ylabel("Density", fontsize=16)
    ax.tick_params(axis='both', labelsize=16)
    ax.legend(fontsize=12)
plt.tight_layout()
plt.show()
```

11. Printing population results

```
print("Population mean (approx):", pop_mean, "\
nPopulation std (approx):», pop_std)
for n in sample_sizes:
    print(f"Sample means (n={n}) -> mean: {np.mean(sample_means_
dict[n]):.5f}, std: {np.std(sample_means_dict[n]):.5f}")
```

Output:

As shown in *Figure 6.11*, the graph clearly shows a skewed curve where the X-axis shows the values of daily stock return from the simulated values, and the Y-axis shows the probability density of these returns:

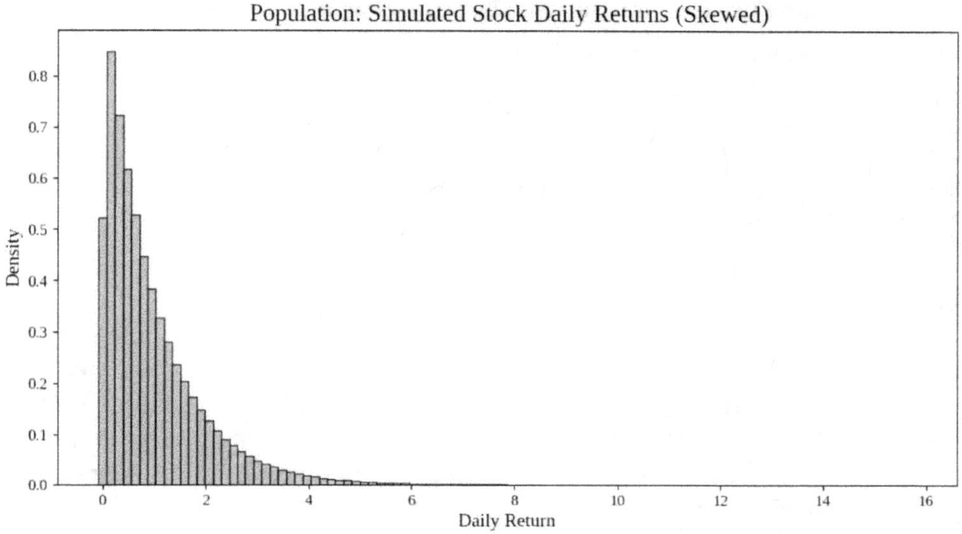

***Figure 6.11**: A population distribution plot of the return of a stock on 2 million data points in 100 bars*

The following observation shows the true mean and standard deviation of a population:

- **Population mean (approx.)**: 0.990758626294031
- **Population std (approx.)**: 0.999440589650185

As shown in *Figure 6.12*, on the X-axis, we see the sample mean return, e.g., if n=30, each point on the X-axis is the average of 30 randomly selected daily returns, whereas on the Y-axis, we can see the probability density. If we see from left to right, as n increases, the curve becomes more normalized.

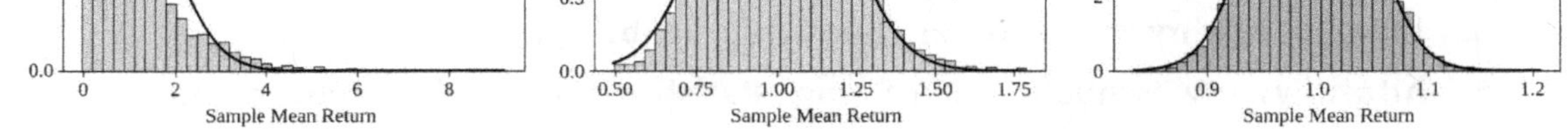

***Figure 6.12**: Histogram created with 40 bars after taking different sample sizes*

From the above figure, it is clearly seen that the mean remains approximately the same, but the variability (standard deviation) decreases as the sample size increases, see the following observations:

- **Sample means (n=1) -> mean**: 1.00620, std: 1.00660
- **Sample means (n=30) -> mean**: 0.99284, std: 0.18146
- **Sample means (n=500) -> mean**: 0.99040, std: 0.04461

Conclusion: Although the population is skewed but the distribution of sample mean becomes more and more normal as the sample size increases and the spread decreases. This clearly demonstrates CLT.

Conclusion

This chapter covered the aspects of looking at the data from an angle of data science, where the important statistical calculations can give an inference of the entire population from a relatively small subset of data. It covered the key concept of population and sample. It covered the various techniques of inferential analysis, such as estimation, hypothesis testing, regression analysis, and correlation analysis. This chapter covered some of the topics in depth, like hypothesis testing, which helps data scientists in making critical decisions and understanding important factors they should be looking at. Some of the industrial use cases were also covered in this chapter, which gave clarity on how inferential statistics is used in real life. The understanding of important concepts like probability and their distribution provides data scientists with an edge to understand the data in depth and generate facts around it.

In the next chapter, fundamentals of data storage will be covered, which will give an idea about the different types of storage mechanisms that exist in the market and what the deciding factors are, or the use cases where specific types of data storage are chosen.

References

1. **https://decodingdatascience.com/sample-population-statistics-understanding-the-basics/**
2. **https://www.geeksforgeeks.org/maths/difference-between-point-and-interval-estimate/**
3. **https://www.geeksforgeeks.org/maths/anova-formula/**
4. **https://www.optimizely.com/optimization-glossary/ab-testing/**
5. **https://www.investopedia.com/terms/p/probabilitydistribution.asp**
6. **https://www.w3schools.com/statistics/statistics_normal_distribution.php**
7. **https://www.geeksforgeeks.org/maths/empirical-rule/**
8. **https://www.sciencedirect.com/topics/mathematics/central-limit-theorem**
9. **https://www.geeksforgeeks.org/maths/central-limit-theorem/**

CHAPTER 7
Introduction to Data Storage

Introduction

Till now, this book has explored the different stages in the journey of data, which include data collection from various sources, processing, and finally storing in the memory. Based on the business expectations, the storage sources are identified, keeping the efficiency and efficacy of data reading and writing in mind.

Based on the types of storage sources, the data access mechanisms are defined or developed so that a data pipeline can be created from data generation to data usage. The final usage of the processed data can be a visualization dashboard of various business metrics with some statistical inferences, or feeding the data to a machine learning model for predictive and prescriptive analysis of the data.

Structure

The chapter covers the following topics:

- Requirement for data storage
- Different types of data storage systems
- Introduction of data modelling
- Understanding the relational data model in DBMS
- Introduction to data operations
- Introduction to big data
- Understanding the architecture of Hadoop

Objectives

By the end of this chapter, the readers will have clarity about the need for data storage and the different types of data storage systems available in the market. This chapter will touch upon the high-level concepts of data modelling and **data operations** (**DataOps**). There will be a deep dive into concepts of **database management system** (**DBMS**) and its important properties and principles. Additionally, readers will learn how modern architectures decouple storage from compute, allowing each to scale independently, marking a significant shift from the tightly coupled designs seen in traditional Hadoop-based systems.

At last, the readers will be able to clearly understand the fundamental difference between data and big data, and how big data is processed in the current enterprise world.

Requirement for data storage

In the data engineering field, everything revolves around data availability. Making data available does not only mean storing the data anywhere, but it also includes data reliability, organization, and managing the huge volume of data across different distributed systems.

Since it is about the data storage, we are in the phase of **extract, transform, and load** (**ETL**), where the data storage part will be discussed, as shown in *Figure 7.1*:

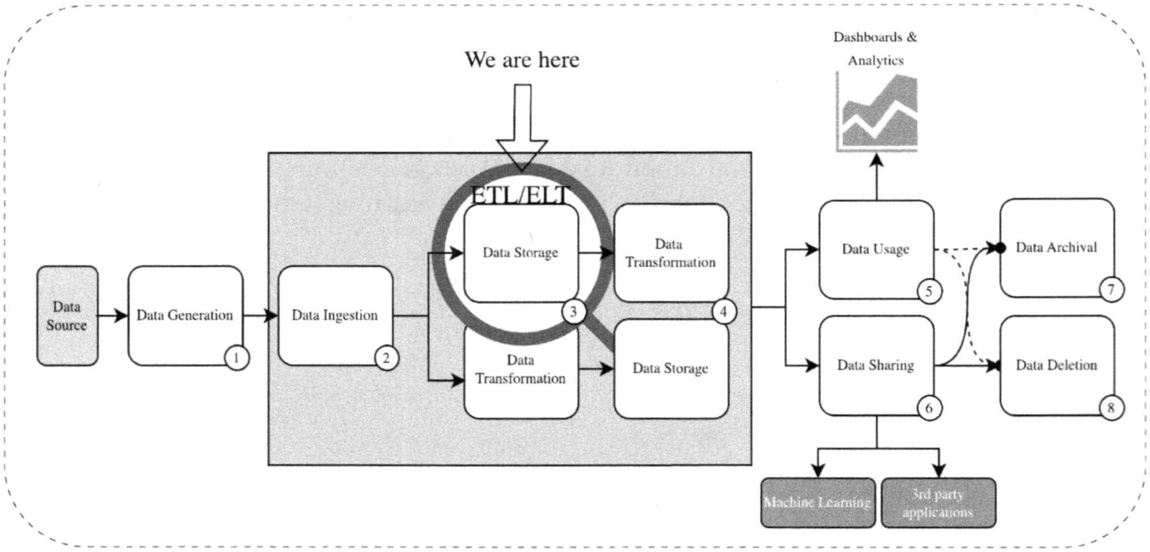

***Figure 7.1**: Showing the current phase covered in the chapter*

Key requirements

Since the requirement is to select the right database management system for our business, there are some key factors that should be considered:

- **Persistence and reliability**: This implies that the data is stored in such a format that it does not get corrupted or lost over time.

- **Scalability**: The data storage system should be able to handle an increasing amount of data, traffic, and users. And it should have the same performance, even if the data accumulates over time.
- **Accessibility**: The data should be accessible at all times, as per different requirements such as real-time dashboarding, batch processing, and inputs to various machine learning algorithms.
- **Performance optimization**: Based on the use cases, the data storage should have optimized performance; some systems may allow fast writing of data, whereas some systems may allow fast reading or access of data.
- **Cost efficiency**: For businesses, the use of technology is beneficial when they have costs under control. Data engineering requires a huge amount of data for better decision-making, but the cost becomes the deciding factor on how much to spend on keeping what volume of data. The ideal storage system should have costs under control, which is well accepted by different businesses or organizations.
- **Governance**: The good data storage system should have all the required compliance for regulations like **General Data Protection Regulation** (**GDPR**), **Health Insurance Portability and Accountability Act** (**HIPAA**), and it should ensure that it has access control, encryption, and auditing in place.
- **Integration**: Another important property of an ideal data storage system is that it should easily be integrated with the outer world, so that pipelines for data storage and access can be created easily, or any other upstream and downstream systems can make use of data without any challenges.

Different types of data storage systems

Over the course of time, there has been an evolution of technology for each of the problems faced by humans. Some businesses required humongous data to be stored at a lower cost, some were asking for speed of data processing at the cost of less data storage, and some of the big giants of the industry were ready to spend the money on technologies that would allow big data chunks to be processed in seconds. It is because of this that today we are equipped with more powerful technological tools that help us achieve those tasks.

Let us understand this, based on the layers that are available in the database storage ecosystem.

Physical storage layer

This is the section that discusses the storage system that actually stores the data and provides the mechanisms for storing data in physical form. There are two types of physical storage:

- **Disk drive storage**: This is the place where the data is stored physically. It is also known as a persistent layer of data storage. There are two types of disk drives:

- **Hard disk drive (HDD)**: This is a combination of one or more magnetized spinning disks or platters, which have tiny magnetized regions. Each platter can have billions of magnetized regions that can be magnetized separately. The hard disk stores data by changing the magnetic direction of these billions of tiny regions. The data is stored and retrieved by a magnetic coil, which finds the location of the data, i.e., tracks and segments, using disk firmware.
- **Solid state drive (SSD)**: In contrast to HDD, which uses rotating magnetic disks to save data, SSD stores data in **Not AND** (**NAND**) flash, which is a non-volatile storage technology and does not require power to store the data. The way NAND stores data is by using a sophisticated arrangement of memory that consists of transistors. Since these transistors can trap electrons, which can be considered as data available or unavailable (1s or 0s, respectively), that is the foundation of digital storage. Modern SSDs often use **Non-Volatile Memory Express** (**NVMe**), a high-speed interface that allows faster communication between the storage and CPU, significantly improving performance compared to older interfaces like **Serial Advanced Technology Attachment** (**SATA**) that would connect HDDs and older SSDs to the motherboard for data transfer.

- **In-memory storage (RAM)**: This may also be called **random access memory** (**RAM**). It is made of millions of tiny memory cells that store data as 0s and 1s. It is a volatile memory that disappears when the power is off. It is mainly used by the **central processing unit** (**CPU**) of a computer, which uses RAM to temporarily copy data from the hard disk so that it can work at extremely fast rates. For example, if we want to work on any application, like a notepad, then it will be temporarily loaded into the RAM, where the CPU can access it for its desired operations. The larger the RAM size, the higher the ability of the system to work on multiple files at the same time.

Architecture layer

This layer takes care of the arrangements and set of rules of how the data has been stored and organized in the memory. There are three types of storage architecture:

- **File-based storage**: It is an architecture that uses files and folders to organize data. The complete data hierarchy is arranged in directories and subdirectories. The file storage takes the file names, their extension, and location as a unique identifier to search the data. *Figure 7.2* represents the hierarchy in the file-based storage:

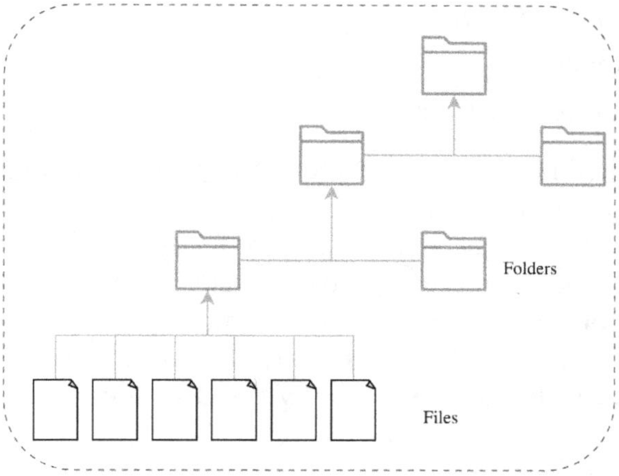

Figure 7.2: *Visual representation of a file hierarchy system*

Use cases are as follows:

- o It can be used for document management systems.
- o Disaster recovery and backup retrieval.
- o Data analytics and machine learning.

- **Block storage**: It is a data storage system that stores the data in fixed-sized blocks, e.g., 4 KB or 8 KB, depending on the operating system. Each block is given a unique identifier and can be stored in any location. With the help of this unique identifier, the search in block storage is fast and efficient, instead of searching for the data in hierarchies. See *Figure 7.3* to visualize how the data is stored in the fixed-sized blocks:

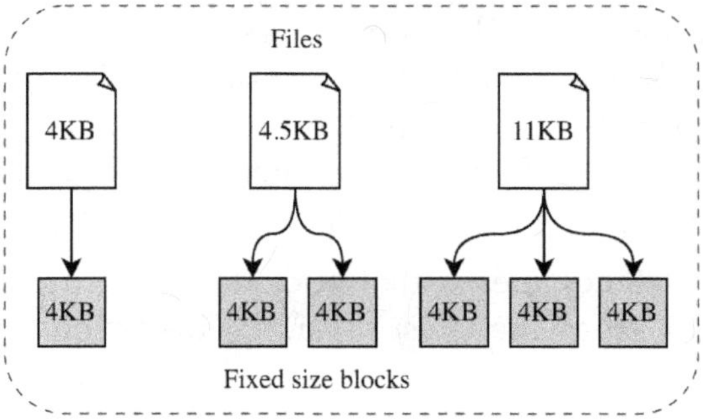

Figure 7.3: *Visual representation of a block storage*

For example, a file name **`test.txt`** with exactly 4096 characters will be stored in one block of size 4096 bytes or 4 KB. If the size is increased by one byte, i.e., 4097 characters, then it will be given two blocks.

$$Block\ A + Block\ B = test.txt$$

The use cases are as follows:

- o Large database
- o Virtual machines
- o **Content delivery networks** (CDNs)

- **Object-based**: In this type of architecture, the data is stored as objects that have unique identifiers, data, and metadata. It is optimized for massive unstructured datasets. In comparison to file storage, there is no hierarchy, and everything is stored as a flat structure. This type of storage is mostly used by the cloud. The flat memory model makes it ideal for handling unstructured data, such as social media content (textual, videos, photos, etc.), as well as time series data coming from sensors, which are often difficult to store in hierarchies. *Figure 7.4* shows the visual representation of object storage:

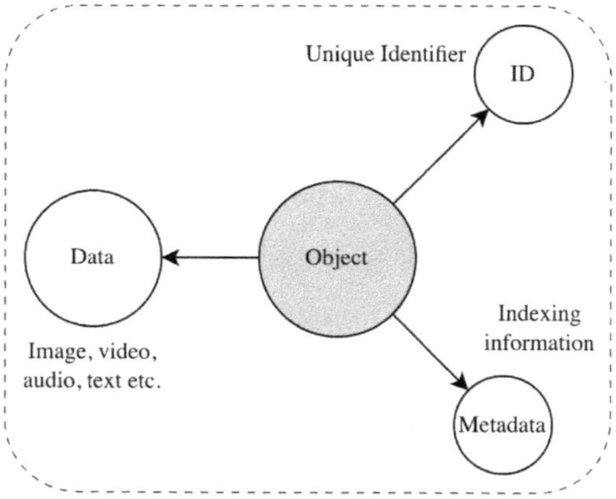

***Figure 7.4**: Visual representation of an object storage*

The advantage of this type of data storage is that it can spread across different systems and geographies as distributed storage system, which makes it infinitely scalable. However, one important trade-off in distributed storage is between strong consistency and eventual consistency which data engineers should consider while designing data pipelines.

- o **Strong consistency** means that once data is written, its subsequent read will immediately return the latest version. This is found in file storage and block storage.
- o **Eventual consistency** means that after write operation, it may take some time before all the nodes reflect the latest data in the next read operation. During this period, some nodes may return old records, but eventually system will become consistent. Object storage traditionally followed eventual consistency, but many modern systems now provide strong consistency.

Internally, it also divides data into variable chunks, not as fixed blocks, but bigger in size with unique identifiers. These chunks can be stored in different nodes or locations and are accessed by the unique IDs or REST APIs, unlike block storage, which can only be read or written in fixed blocks, that too managed at the OS level.

The use cases are as follows:

- o Cloud system storage
- o Storage of large multimedia files
- o Cloud recovery and backup management

Data management and processing layer

This layer is a software layer for storing and analysing data. On this layer, an end user may interact directly via the user interface or connect their application via the application programming interface.

Some of the main data management solutions are:

- **DBMS**: These are the software that are responsible for storing, managing, and retrieving structured data in tables (rows and columns).

  They have the following properties:

  - o It is responsible for **create, read, update, delete** (**CRUD**) operations on the data.
  - o It ensures **atomicity, consistency, isolation, durability** (**ACID**)
  - o They are of two types: relational and non-relational.
  - o Support a query language to retrieve the data.

  Use case:

  - o DBMSs are used in sophisticated requirements that are critical, such as banking systems(transactions), inventory management, etc.

  This topic has been covered in detail in *Chapter 3, Data Generation in Source System,* in the section *Database*.

- **Streaming data processing system**: These are the systems specially designed for capturing, managing, and analyzing the real-time data or data in motion. It has to process the data as soon as it arrives.

  Some of the properties of streaming systems are:

  - o **Low latency**: The expectation of data processing time from these systems is very low.
  - o **Event-driven**: As soon as the event appears, it needs to be processed.
  - o **High capability**: It is able to handle high-volume and high-velocity data.

  Use cases:

  - o IoT sensors monitor and take critical actions if anything goes wrong.

    - Fraud detection in banking for real-time alerts
    - Stock market real-time price feeds

  This topic has been covered in detail in *Chapter 3, Data Generation in Source System*, in the *Messages and streams* section.

- **Data warehouse**: These are the large-scale central repositories, designed to store structured and processed data. The data is cleaned and transformed before being stored in the data warehouse.

  Some properties of data warehousing are:

    - It aggregates the data into a structured format after **extracting, transforming, and loading** (**ETL**).
    - It is optimized for read operations and analysis on data.

  Use cases:

    - It may be used for the sales dashboard of a company around the world.
    - Financial data analysis.

  This topic has been covered in detail in *Chapter 2, Designing a Data Architecture*, in the *Data Warehouse* section.

- **Data lake**: These are the large-scale storage systems designed to store the data in a raw format (structured, unstructured, and semi-structured). Unlike a data warehouse, the schema is applied while retrieving data rather than while storing the data.

  Some of the properties of a data lake are:

    - Stores any type of data
    - Built for scalability
    - Very low cost
    - No fixed schema for storing data

  Use cases:

    - Processing of IoT data analysis
    - Storing unstructured media data such as photos, audio, and videos.
    - ML model training

  This topic has been covered in detail in *Chapter 2, Designing a Data Architecture*, in the *Data Lake* section.

- **Data lakehouse**: A data lakehouse is a modern data architecture that combines the best features of data lake and data warehouse by adding structure, governance, and transactional reliability, making it suitable for both analytics and machine learning. Some properties of data lakehouse are:

    - Stores structured, semi-structured and unstructured data at one place just like data lake.

- o ACID transactions that ensure reliable read and write operations with no partial corrupted data.
- o Supports validation, access control and data consistency for data governance and quality.
- o Faster query execution using indexing, caching and optimized storage formats.
- o Decoupled storage and compute which helps them scale independently.

Use cases:

- o Business intelligent dashboards and reporting on large datasets.
- o Training machine learning models on large and diverse datasets.
- o Near real-time analytics on streaming data e.g., user activity or IoT sensors etc.

Special storage systems

These are the storage mechanisms that inherit the characteristics of the above-defined categories, but they are the application of those in some specific conditions:

- **In-memory storage**: In some of the use cases where the data read/write operations have to be extremely fast, in-memory operations make this possible. In this case, the data is stored in the RAM rather than secondary storage.

  Some of the important characteristics are:

  - o Ultra-low latency
  - o Data disappears when the power is off

  Use cases:

  - o These types of storage are used to cache the web session.
  - o Real-time recommendation engines.
  - o Live feed videos such as cricket telecast on OTT devices.

- **Cloud storage**: These are storage as a service, provided by cloud providers. Users do not need to manage the hardware and just need to pay for the usage. Fundamentally, at the hardware level, they follow the same file-based, block-based, and object-based storage. For example, some available tools in the market are:

  - o **File storage**: Azure files, Amazon **Elastic File System** (**EFS**)
  - o **Object storage**: Azure blob storage, Amazon **Simple Storage Service** (**S3**)
  - o **Block storage**: Azure managed disks, Amazon **Elastic Block Store** (**EBS**)

  Some of the important characteristics are:

  - o Highly scalable
  - o Pay per use pricing
  - o High availability

Use case:

- o Storing enterprise data for geographical level availability.
- o Enterprise backup and disaster recovery.
- o Part of the application that requires collaboration between the team spread globally and working simultaneously.

- **Hybrid storage**: The above-discussed storage systems have specific characteristics for which they have been developed and introduced to the market. Based on the use cases, they are used; either they solve the latency problem at a higher cost, or they solve the cost problem at the expense of performance. In practical scenarios, enterprises need a balance between the two, and this type of storage makes it possible to use different types of storage in order to balance between the two.

  As shown in *Figure 7.5*, the data that is needed for instant decision-making or information can be kept in memory (RAM), whereas the data that is huge and does not need to be accessed for any critical requirement can be stored in HDD or cloud storage. Backups are typically maintained in the cloud for disaster recovery. Additionally, rarely accessed data can be moved to colder tiers such as cloud cold storage or archival solutions (e.g., Amazon S3 Glacier Deep Archive), completing the full data lifecycle from high-speed access to long-term, low-cost retention.

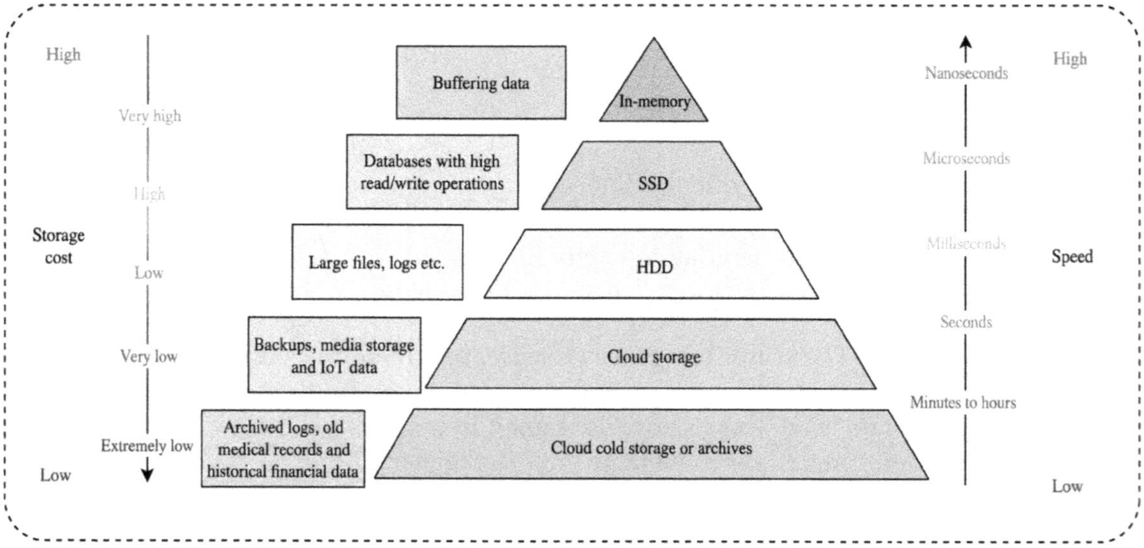

***Figure 7.5**: Representation of memory hierarchy in terms of speed and cost*

Introduction to data modelling

Although this topic has also been covered in *Chapter 2, Designing a Data Architecture*, in the section *Data architecture design (modelling)*, where we discussed the preliminary steps required to design the architecture, here this topic covers the nuances from the data engineering standpoint.

Data modelling is the process of creating the visual representation of the information structure that supports business processes. It explains about the data storage, how it is organized in the database, and how any manipulation of data takes place.

Analogically, it may be considered as a blueprint or foundational framework, based on which the selection of databases, data warehouses, and other analytical systems is designed.

Since any enterprise-level project requires multiple people and multiple teams to work in a collaborative fashion, it becomes imperative to have something systematic or standardized that brings everyone on the same page and reduces conflicts around business understanding and project execution.

In technical terms, it is about defining the data entities, attributes, relationships, and constraints in a structured format. This is usually created with the help of diagrams.

Benefits

Although it requires huge effort in creating these initial blueprints, it also brings the following benefits:

- **Clarity**: Creating a data model helps in making a clear representation of the data attributes and their relationships, which brings coherence to the knowledge source and reduces miscommunications.
- **Quality**: When the blueprints are created, they bring a lot of feedback about the quality aspects of the data, which helps in finding inconsistencies, duplication, and errors in the data that might have been missed in the data cleansing process. This process improves the overall quality of data and helps catch the big errors before they occur to reduce the chances of project failure.
- **Decisioning**: Creating a blueprint means bringing the future to the current; this helps the organization to visualize the critical relationships before even realizing the actual output. This helps them to make critical decisions that may support the expected business outcome.

Types of data models

Similar to any design process, database and information system design starts with the high-level details and gets deeper over time. Analogous to the same concept, the data models are also divided into three different levels, which are based on their abstraction level.

The process will start with the conceptual model, get deeper using the logical model, and finally conclude with the detailed findings in the physical model.

Conceptual data model

As the name implies, these models are created at the requirement gathering phase, where all the entities will have to be thought through and defined. After all the entities are listed, the relationships between all the entities are understood and drawn on a whiteboard. This gives a high-level view of the business entities and their relationships without considering implementation details.

As shown in *Figure 7.6*, while studying at the university, there are three entities that can be initially thought of: student, course, and professor. They are clearly related to each other, with some cardinality. Sometimes cardinalities may or may not be available at the requirement phase, but it is very important to know at the start.

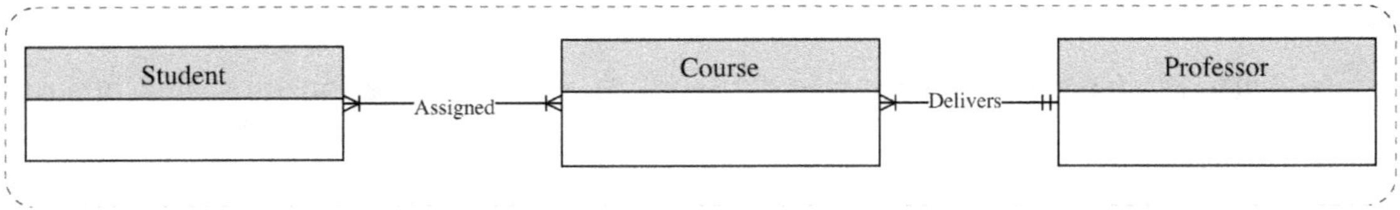

***Figure 7.6**: An example representation of entities in a university*

Here, the figure says that a student and a course have many-to-many cardinality, which means a student can select many courses and a course can have many students. Whereas in the case of a professor, it is one-to-many, that means a course can be taken by a single professor only, but a professor can teach many courses.

Logical data model

This data model is less abstract and gives a detailed description of the entity and their attributes. This model does not specify the technical system requirements but gives the right information from a data-oriented approach.

As clearly shown in *Figure 7.7*, all the attributes of each entity can be seen clearly, and this representation gives more in-depth information about the relationships amongst them:

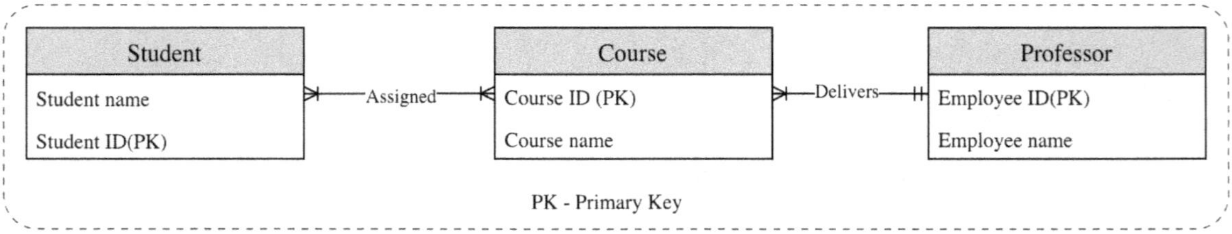

***Figure 7.7**: A logical model showing relationships between student, course, and professors*

Physical data model

This is the model that gets into the nuts and bolts of the schema to show how exactly the data will be stored in the database. The abstraction is minimal here, and the final design of a relational schema can be created after this step.

As shown in the following figure, the datatypes are clearly shown in this model, which a database administrator can take as input and start creating the required schema and tables with minimal need for communication, and hence reduce the confusion and communication gaps:

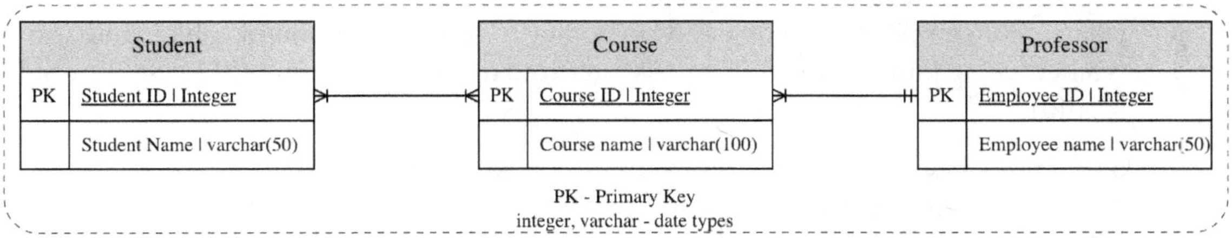

***Figure 7.8**: A representation of a physical model for student, course, and professor entities*

Data modelling process

It is now clearly understood that data modelling is a crucial step because all the concepts that are in the team's mind come on a whiteboard, and minute details around that can be pondered upon. The following are the steps that need to be taken to create a good data model:

1. **Identify the entities**: This is the first and foremost step, which involves cognitive thinking about identifying the entities without any overlap.

2. **Identify the attributes**: Once entities are identified, the associated attributes around them should be clearly jotted down. Attributes help in identifying the overlaps between two or more entities. For example, professors and accounting staff look to be different entities but if the objective is to look at them from the university's employees perspective then their attributes will be same such as employee id, joining date, data of birth, salary etc. and the entity will be *employee*, whereas if the business objective is about the analysis about their work then these two will be different entities with different attributes, e.g., for *professor*, entity, the attributes can be employee id, employee name, department, courses and *accountant* entity will have employee id, employee name, office location, reports to etc.

3. **Identify the relationships amongst entities**: While creating a data model, a relationship plays a very important role in connecting the tables of different entities to each other. Here, the concept of foreign keys comes into the picture, e.g., a professor entity may have a *course id* as one of the key attributes (as a foreign key), which tells about the course taken by the professor.

4. **Mapping of attributes**: The next step is to map all the attributes and relationships into each entity to ensure all the required details about the entity have been captured completely.

5. **Map the cardinality**: This defines the number of instances of one entity that can be associated with instances of another entity, e.g., one course will be taught by only one professor, or one student should have at least one course. This makes sure the attribute value can be null (empty) or strictly one, or at least one or more.

6. **Decide the degree of normalization**: Normalization is the process of structurally organizing the data to reduce redundancy and improve data integrity. It is like a clear architecture of a database where data is stored in different tables and can be fetched using join commands in the **structured query language** (**SQL**) by their unique identifiers.

   Sometimes decisions on normalization are also taken, thinking around the business objectives, e.g., read-heavy operations should have minimal normalization because for every read operation, it will require a join operation, which increases unnecessary computation cost. In such cases, denormalization is commonly used, especially in analytical workloads and data warehouses (e.g., star or snowflake schemas) to optimize query performance by reducing the need for complex joins.

7. **Validation**: This is the final step where the entire model is validated and released. However, this has to be a continuous process that requires repeated views and refinement for any business requirement changes or updates.

Understanding the relational data model in DBMS

The relational data model was proposed by **International Business Machines** (**IBM**) researcher *Dr. Edgar F. Codd* in 1970, and it is still being used today. These rules are made to ensure data integrity, consistency, and usability.

The relational model organizes data into tables (relations), which consist of rows(tuples) and columns (attributes). The relational model transforms conceptual design from **entity relationship** (**ER**) diagrams into implementable structures.

See *Table 7.1* for professors' details, with attributes **`PROF_ID`**, **`NAME`**, **`DEPARTMENT`**, **`DEPT_ID`**, **`EMAIL`**, **`SALARY`**:

PROF_ID	NAME	DEPARTMENT	DEPT_ID	EMAIL	SALARY
101	Dr. Alan Brooks	Computer Science	1001	abrooks@univ.edu	$85000
102	Dr. Emily Carter	Mathematics	1003	ecarter@univ.edu	$90000

103	Dr. James Wilson	Physics	1097	jwilson@univ.edu	$88000
104	Dr. Gupta	Chemistry	1023	NULL	$87000

***Table 7.1**: A relation showing the details of professors of a university*

Key elements in the relational model

The relational model is built on a set of fundamental elements that define how data is organized and managed. To understand the relational model, it is important to look at the following key elements :

- **Attributes**: Attributes are the properties that define an entity, e.g., **PROD_ID**, **NAME**, which define the **PROFESSOR** entity.
- **Tuple**: A tuple represents a row in a relation. Each tuple shows the attributes of a particular entity, e.g., Dr. Alan Brooks has an ID of 1001, belongs to the computer science department, and earns around $85000 as salary.
- **Relational schema**: This defines the structure of a relation, e.g., **PROFESSOR(PROF_ID, NAME, DEPARTMENT, DEPT_ID, EMAIL, SALARY)** is the relationship schema of a relation **PROFESSOR**.
- **Relation instance**: The set of tuples at a particular instance of time is known as a relation instance. This changes every time there is an insertion, deletion, or any update in the table or relation.
- **Degree**: The number of attributes in a relation is known as the degree of the relation, e.g., the **PROFESSOR** relation has a degree of six because it has six attributes.
- **Cardinality**: The number of tuples in a relation is called cardinality, e.g., the **PROFESSOR** relation has cardinality four in *Table 7.1*.

Types of keys in the relational model

In the relational model, different types of keys are used to ensure data integrity and proper linkage between the tables. Let us look at the following keys:

- **Primary key**: It is the attribute in a relation that uniquely identifies each tuple. It must contain unique values and cannot be empty or **NULL**, e.g., in *Table 7.1*, the **PROFESSOR** relation has **PROF_ID** as the primary key, in which each tuple has a unique value that identifies the professors uniquely.
- **Candidate key**: It is the attribute or attributes that are good candidates to become a primary key or can uniquely identify a tuple in a relation. They are not a primary key because a primary key already exists. For example, in *Table 7.1*, the email id also uniquely identifies professors; since there cannot be the same email id given to more than one employee.

- **Super key**: It is a set of one or more attributes that uniquely identifies the tuple, e.g., combining `PROF_ID`, `NAME`, `DEPARTMENT`, and `SALARY` uniquely identifies the tuple in the above example. The following are examples of other super keys in the same table:
    - `{PROF_ID}` -> primary key
    - `{PROF_ID, NAME}`
    - `{PROF_ID, DEPARTMENT}`
    - `{PROF_ID, DEPT_ID}`
    - `{PROF_ID, EMAIL}`
    - `{PROF_ID, SALARY}`
    - `{PROF_ID, NAME, DEPARTMENT, DEPT_ID, EMAIL, SALARY}`
- **Composite key**: It is a type of super key that is made up of two or more attributes, and all the attributes are needed to uniquely identify the record or tuple. It is generally employed in cases where there is no primary key available, and it requires combining multiple attributes to make the complete tuple uniquely identifiable.
- **Foreign key**: It is an attribute in one relation that refers to the primary key of another relation. It is used to create a link between the data in the two tables or relations. For example, the `DEPARTMENT` relation can have `DEPT_ID` as the primary key, which is being used in the `PROFESSOR` relation to ensure every professor is assigned to a valid department.

Codd's rules in DBMS

Codd has listed twelve rules that signify the characteristics and requirements of a **relational database management system (RDBMS)**, which are as follows:

- **Rule 1**: The information rule:

  All the data should be presented to the user in a table form.

- **Rule 2**: Guaranteed access rule:

  All the data should be accessible without ambiguity using a combination of table name, primary key, and column (attribute) name.

- **Rule 3**: Systematic treatment of `NULL` values:

  This means a cell with a `NULL` value should be treated differently from an empty string or a 0 value for a numeric field. This is to make sure `NULL` should not be interpreted as missing data, unknown data, or not applicable, and it is not applicable for a primary key, since it cannot be `NULL`.

- **Rule 4**: Active online catalog:

This means that the database catalog, which contains metadata about the database, must be stored in the RDBMS known as the data dictionary. Users can access the catalog using the same query language that is used to access the database itself.

- **Rule 5**: Comprehensive data sublanguage rule:

  A database must support at least one clearly defined **data manipulation language** (**DML**) that can be used for querying and modifying information within the database.

- **Rule 6**: The view updating rule:

  All the views that are theoretically updatable must also be updatable by the system. This means that the data that is presented to the user in logical combinations called views should also allow for updating the data in the view directly without touching the main table.

- **Rule 7**: High-level insert, update, and delete:

  This rule states that the insert, update, and delete operations should also be supported for any retrievable set of rows instead of any single row in a table.

- **Rule 8**: Physical data independence:

  The user should be isolated from the method of physically storing and retrieving the information from the database. If required, changes can be made to the underlying architecture (physical storage structure or methods) without affecting the method of access to the database for any user or application.

- **Rule 9**: Logical data independence:

  Any change in the logical structure of the tables should not affect the user's view of the data, e.g., if the two tables are merged or one table is split into two different tables, there should not be any impact or change on the user application. Fundamentally, it is the most difficult rule to apply.

- **Rule 10**: Integrity independence:

  The database must be independent of the application that uses it. All the integrity constraints or rules about the data should be stored in the database, not in the application or program accessing it. This is to ensure that the front end is isolated from the backend. For example, a rule that age must be greater than five is a constraint; this must be implemented in the database, not in the application code. This way, it will be independent of applications, and this rule will always be enforced.

- **Rule 11**: Distribution independence:

  This rule states that the end-user must not be able to see that the data is transparently distributed over various locations, and should get the impression that it is located at one site only.

- **Rule 12**: Non-subversion rule:

There should not be anyway to modify the database structure, other than the database language (such as SQL) to break the rules or bypass the constraints, e.g., if the constraint is applied as salary cannot be less than 0, then if someone uses SQL to enter the value less than 0, this rule will be enforced but even if someone writes a low-level script or uses backdoor method to insert data manually, then also this rule should be enforced.

Introduction to data operations

DataOps is defined as a set of practices, tools, and philosophies that target the speed, quality, and reliability of the data workflows. This ensures end-to-end coverage right from data collection to analysis and delivery.

It helps the data team, which involves data engineers, data analysts, and data scientists, to work in tandem to automate data processing, data quality checks, and deliver data quickly and accurately to the target audience. It has inherited the DevOps practices, ensuring the previously siloed development functions are automated and agile.

The reason this topic brings seriousness at this point is that once the data pipelines are set up from source to destination, the work is not finished. It is the starting point of continuous monitoring of data. There have been some cases in the real-world where the changes in the flow of data or the unavailability of data went unnoticed for months, due to which the machine learning algorithms were using stale data and giving outputs, and these outputs were being used in critical business decision-making.

DataOps provides the mechanism to have continuous monitoring of the dataflow by creating **continuous integration/continuous deployment** (**CI/CD**) pipelines that ensure the data is well version-controlled, properly validated, and then only deployed to the target system.

Benefits of data operations

Let us look at the benefits of the data operations:

- Faster time with predictable delivery and data observability.
- Productivity improvements and reduced error frequencies.
- Improved data quality and more trusted business data available for analytics.
- High collaboration between teams (development, operations, data, and business teams).
- Reduced cost and improved operational efficiencies across all the data management workflows.

Introduction to big data

In today's world, we are surrounded by machines, be it a simple machine like a spoon or a complex machine like a car. The machines, too, have become smart, due to which each operation is being captured every now and then. For example, now cars have internet connectivity in them, which helps to store all the critical information like location, fuel efficiency, number of clutch presses or brake presses, distance traveled, etc., and share it with the user's handheld devices. This helps the organizations to cater to their existing users with better services, or this data can be collected to make their product better, more informed, and smarter, such as driverless cars, an automatic service scheduler, and so on.

Similarly, many enterprises are collecting tons of users' data every minute and are analyzing the customer behavior, and therefore improving their overall customer service. This improves the customers' satisfaction score as well.

Billions of smart devices in existence have led to an increase in large volumes of complex data, especially when it comes to heterogeneous data, such as structured (e.g., tables, spreadsheets), semi-structured (e.g., JSON, XML), and unstructured data (e.g., text, images, audio, and videos). Due to this, it becomes essential for organizations to adopt advanced tools and technologies to capture, store, analyze, and utilize data properly, which may not be possible using conventional tools.

When big data is thought about, there are three V's that are majorly discussed:

- **Volume**: This means terabytes or petabytes of data generated every minute.
- **Velocity**: This implies the speed at which the data is being generated. The evolution of social media and democratization of content creation have led to real-time data generation from billions of devices, sensors, and transactions at the same time.
- **Variety**: Data that is being generated is not in a fixed format but in all sorts of structured, semi-structured, and unstructured types.

Above are the general properties that are discussed when big data is looked at. However, in simple terms, the data that cannot fit in the main memory for processing can also be considered as big data. This is a subjective definition because it becomes dependent upon the chosen size of main memory; e.g., smartphones can have limited memory compared to heavy-duty servers. So the definition changes with respect to memory. Fundamentally, it is about handling the data, and the data that cannot be handled by main memory needs different mechanisms to process it.

For the argument's sake, consider a movie of high-definition quality with a size of 6 GB, while the system has only 4GB as main memory (RAM). In that case, the entire movie cannot fit in the memory. This situation cannot be considered as big data.

Firstly, it does not fit into the three fundamental V's, especially velocity and variety. In addition, movies can be processed by using a paging mechanism that is employed by the

operating system (**OS**) to process large pieces of information. In which the OS divides the main memory into small fixed-size parts called pages, where the parts of the programs are stored and processed. In the case of a movie, it will be a sequential operation, where the requirement is to get frame-by-frame processing, but imagine an operation that requires us to sort a dataset in petabytes. This cannot have a sequential or linear operation and requires all the data to be present in memory to sort (because the next sequence of data may be the last member of the file), and using a conventional mechanism will take a very long time, which may not be a viable business solution.

The challenge here is not the complexity of processing, as the processing requirements are mostly simple and straightforward, such as searching, sorting, finding maximum, minimum, average, or any other statistical calculation; e.g., just think about calculating the mean on a dataset with a hundred billion rows. The operation is simple, but the volume is humongous.

A practical use case can be an e-commerce website like Amazon. Understanding how they use this much data processing to provide near real-time recommendations using machine learning, that too when the data is still being continuously generated every second.

So, the challenge with big data is not about the complexity of processing, but taking it all together and processing it for better decision making, and helping organizations to serve their customers in a better way.

There are some ways the problem can be sorted from a conventional viewpoint:

- Improve the algorithms to perform in an efficient manner or choose the better ones, e.g., quick sort is supposedly the most efficient and fastest algorithm theoretically for sorting, but this will not be efficient when it is applied to work on petabytes of data.

  The alternative solution can be using randomization and approximation methods for the same operation. The solution may not be 100% correct, but 90% of the time it works well. Now, if the end user is satisfied with 90% of accuracy, then opting for faster approximation solutions has a better business case than spending excessive time to compute the results with precision.

- Use the right programming languages that may have better memory management in allocating memory for variable definition, allocation of data, updating the data, and clearing of memory. It is not a simple task to change the entire programming stack, and that too may not guarantee the expected results.

- Hardware architecture changes, changing the hardware architecture completely, may allow us to mold things based on our requirements, but this is also a very difficult way to progress since billions of devices are already running on the current hardware architecture, and changing the architecture will affect the underlying drivers and programs running on them. However, introducing the **graphics processing unit** (**GPU**) was an example of innovative thinking from the hardware architecture perspective, done by *NVIDIA* in the early 2000s.

So this requires a completely new way of working, which will keep the conventional way of processing the data, but in different arrangements. This new way of processing has been brought by some open-source tools like Hadoop that use a distributed computing approach.

The big data is stored across many machines, which are connected to each other with a very high-speed network connectivity (such as a LAN with a speed of several gigabytes per second). The data is then processed in parallel on different nodes, and the partial results are combined to produce the final outcome.

Understanding the architecture of Hadoop

Hadoop is an open-source software framework in Java that is used for storing and processing large amounts of data in a distributed computing environment. Big companies like *Meta* and *Netflix* use the Hadoop framework to handle large data efficiently.

Components of Hadoop

Hadoop is a framework designed on four pillars:

- **Hadoop Distributed File System** (**HDFS**)
- MapReduce
- **Yet Another Resource Negotiator** (**YARN**)
- Common utilities or Hadoop common

Hadoop Distributed File System

HDFS is a distributed file system that is designed to run on commodity hardware, similar to any existing distributed file system. But the differences from the other file systems are significant, such as HDFS is highly fault-tolerant and is designed to be deployed on low-cost hardware. It provides high-throughput access to large datasets by storing data in large blocks (128 MB) to optimize performance.

Keeping the hardware failure as a norm, HDFS has been designed to detect the fault quickly and automatically recover from it.

With a belief that *Moving Computation is Cheaper than Moving Data,* HDFS aims to process the data where it is located and run the application at the location, which improves the throughput and reduces the congestion due to the transfer of huge amounts of data.

As shown in *Figure 7.9,* HDFS has been built on a master/slave architecture, where it consists of a single node called **Namenode**, a master server that is responsible for managing the file system namespace and regulating the access to files for clients, and there are slave nodes called **Datanode**, which are responsible for storing the data in blocks.

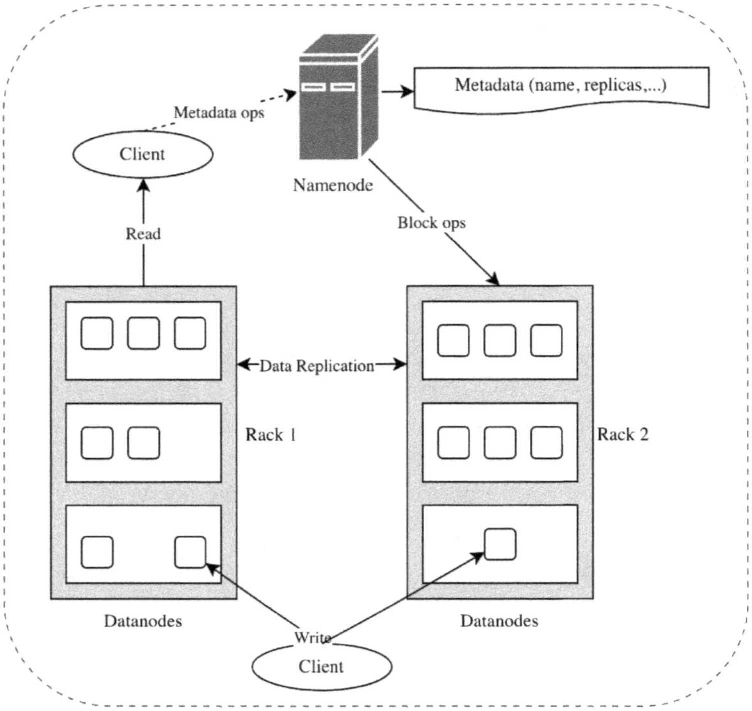

Figure 7.9: Architecture of HDFS

The Namenode executes the file system namespace operations like opening, closing, and renaming files and directories, and also keeps the information of the mapping of blocks in Datanodes.

The Datanodes, on the other hand, are responsible for serving, i.e., read/write requests from clients. Along with this, Datanodes perform block creation, deletion, and replication based on the instructions from the Namenode.

The following is an example that shows how the file replication works:

- **File name**: `/users/analysis/data/mydatafile.csv`
- **File size**: 500 MB

Assume the size of the HDFS block is 128MB (this is configurable), which means this file has to be divided into four blocks:

- **Part-0**: First 128MB
- **Part-1**: Next 128MB
- **Part-2**: Next 128MB
- **Part-3**: Last 116MB

For high availability or fault-tolerance, each part will also be replicated to three nodes (this is also configurable). See *Table 7.2* for more details:

Block name	Replication factor	Stored on nodes	Description
Part-0	r:3	{1,3,5}	Three copies on Datanodes 1,3,5
Part-1	r:3	{1,4,6}	Three copies on Datanodes 1,4,6
Part-2	r:3	{1,5,6}	Three copies on Datanodes 1,5,6
Part-3	r:3	{1,2,3}	Three copies on Datanodes 1,2,3

***Table 7.2**: Showing how the data has been replicated in different Datanodes*

The above information is stored in **Namenode** as metadata:

```
Namenode(Filename, numReplicas, block-ids,…)
/users/analysis/data/mydatafile/part-0,r:3,{1,3,5},…
/users/analysis/data/mydatafile/part-1,r:3,{1,4,6},…
/users/analysis/data/mydatafile/part-2,r:3,{1,5,6},…
/users/analysis/data/mydatafile/part-3,r:3,{1,2,3},…
```

This is how the HDFS stores the data, ensuring the correctly mapped blocks and availability of data whenever needed.

MapReduce

Hadoop MapReduce is a software framework that processes large amounts of data in parallel or large clusters of commodity hardware in an efficient, reliable, and fault-tolerant manner. It is a data processing layer that allows the data to be processed near the location of the data and combines the outcomes to finalize the results.

Let us understand how MapReduce works by considering a word count example on a log file of 10 TB in size:

1. **Input phase**: HDFS divides the file into blocks of 128 MB each and stores them in the respective nodes (as explained in the last section). Now these blocks become the input split for MapReduce.
2. **Map phase**: Each node runs a mapper program on its data block and produces key-value pairs as output.

   For example:

   Input line: **`Hadoop is good Hadoop is fast`**

   The output of the mapper will be:

   ```
   (Hadoop, 1)
   (is, 1)
   (good,1)
   (Hadoop, 1)
   ```

```
(is, 1)
(fast, 1)
```

3. **Shuffle and sort phase**: All the same key-values will be sent to the same reducer for processing, e.g., *Hadoop,1* will reach a reducer that is processing the **Hadoop** keyword for word count. Then the output of a mapper is grouped and sorted.

   The output looks like this:

```
(Hadoop, [1,1])
(is, [1,1])
(good,1)
(fast, 1)
```

4. **Reduce phase**: Reducer takes one key and all its values, then combines them to produce the final result.

```
(Hadoop, [1,1])     ->     (Hadoop, 2)
(is, [1,1])         ->     (is,2)
(good,1)            ->     (good,1)
(fast, 1)                  ->     (fast,1)
```

5. **Output phase**: Reducers write back to HDFS for output.

   Figure 7.10 shows how the mapper and reducer steps work together on big data to generate the output:

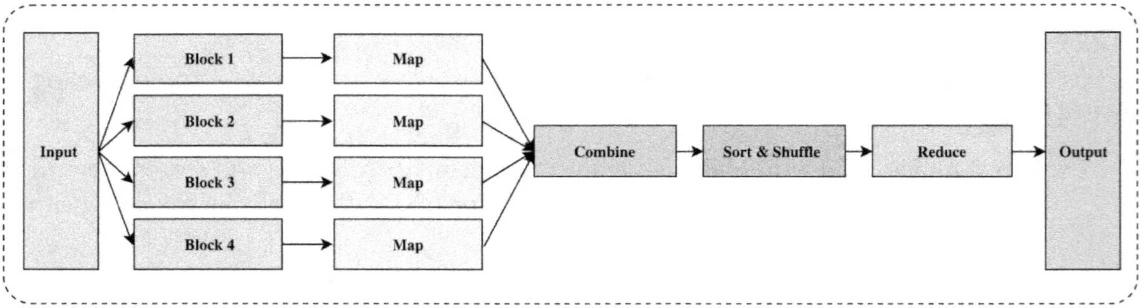

***Figure 7.10**: Representation of the MapReduce workflow*

If any node fails during execution, MapReduce automatically re-runs the task on another node to ensure the complete system is fault-tolerant.

Yet Another Resource Negotiator

YARN is a resource management layer in the Hadoop system, where it focuses on splitting up the functionalities of resource management and job scheduling into separate daemons or entities.

Components of YARN are as follows:

- **Resource Manager (RM)**: It is the boss who manages all the cluster resources like CPU, memory, disk, and network, and decides which job gets which resources.

  It has two parts:

  - **Scheduler**: Allocates resources to jobs.
  - **Application manager**: Manages job submission and starts the application master, also restarts if it fails to execute.

- **Node Manager (NM)**: It is the worker that is situated at each cluster node, manages containers on that node, and monitors the resources CPU, memory, disk, and network for each container.

- **Application Master (AM)**: It is a job manager (one for each application), which negotiates resources with the resource manager and confirms if it has all the required resources to start the job. It also tells the NM where and how to run the tasks, and monitors the progress of the tasks and the application.

- **Container**: It is the virtual space for a particular job, which has resources like CPU, memory, and disk on which the tasks run.

Let us look at the following example for YARN workflow:

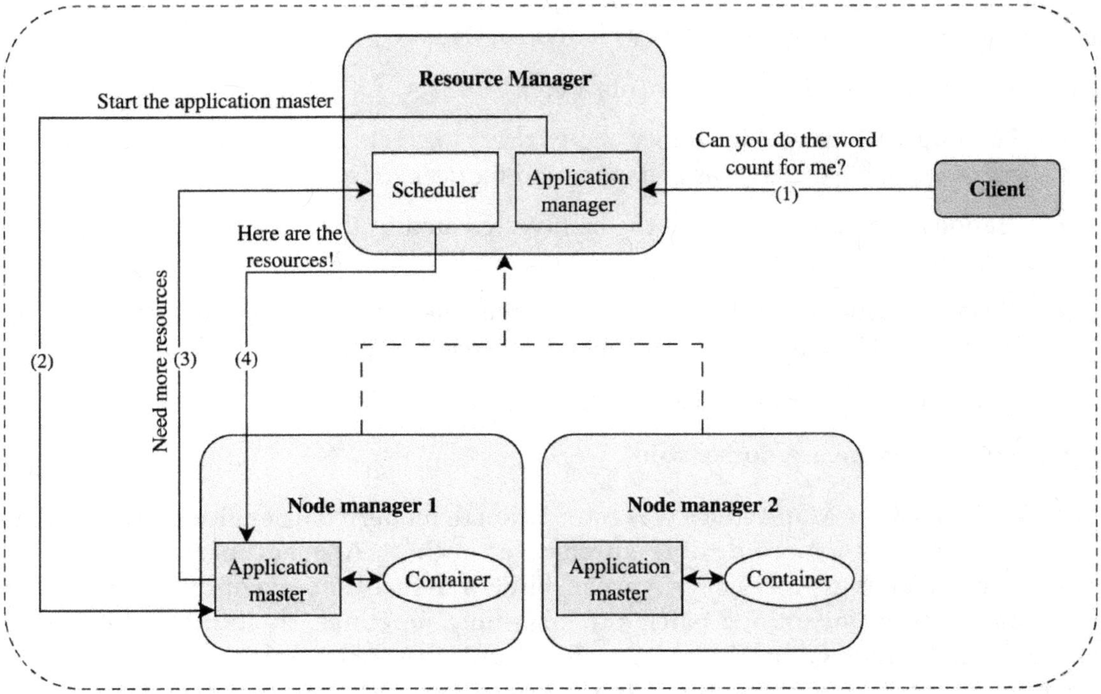

Figure 7.11: Representation of the YARN workflow

As shown in *Figure 7.11*, let us understand how it works. Taking the same example of word count and the workflow:

- Client submits word count job to the RM or AM.
- The resource manager allocates containers to the required node and starts the Application master that is situated at the respective nodes.
- Application master is registered with the RM.
- Application master requests more containers to run mapper and reducer tasks at the nodes.
- Application master asks the node managers to launch the containers.
- Mapper and reducer tasks run inside the containers.
- After the job finishes, the application masters get deregistered, and containers are released.

Hadoop common

Apart from the major components of Hadoop, there are other essential components and scripts without which the Hadoop ecosystem will not function. They are the common libraries that help all the Hadoop components to work together. It handles hardware failure automatically and logs all the critical actions taken by Hadoop systems.

To name them, some of these components are:

- **Hadoop streaming**: This utility allows users to create and run map/reduce jobs with any executable or script as a mapper and reducer script.
- **Hadoop archives**: These are the archives created in the Hadoop ecosystem for data and metadata.
- **Resource estimator service**: This is an intelligent system that automatically predicts how much CPU, memory, and containers a recurring job will require.

More information about Hadoop can be found in the following link:

https://hadoop.apache.org/docs/stable/

Note: **While Hadoop MapReduce was foundational, modern data engineering has largely moved to faster and more flexible alternatives such as Apache Spark for in-memory batch and streaming processing, Apache Flink for real-time event-driven workloads, and Apache Beam for unified batch and streaming pipelines. In addition, cloud-native platforms like AWS Glue, Google Dataflow, and Azure Databricks provide managed, scalable processing, making them the preferred choice over traditional MapReduce systems.**

Conclusion

Till now, this chapter has covered the understanding of the requirements of data storage and explained the different types of data storage systems in detail. This topic has also entailed an in-depth understanding of how data is stored physically and how it is shown by the management layer or the presentation layer.

This chapter also touched upon the data modelling that will help a reader to clearly structure the data model and its relationships. The fundamentals of database management systems were also covered, which explained the key elements of the database management system and the twelve principles that were introduced by *Dr. E.F. Codd*. Lastly, this chapter also introduced an understanding of some concepts like DataOps, big data, and ended with a deep understanding of one of the renowned architectures in the industry, i.e., Hadoop, to handle big data.

In the next chapter, the practical aspects of different advanced databases will be covered, which will focus more on their practical implementation with a brief theoretical introduction of the topic.

References

1. **https://www.ibm.com/think/topics/data-storage**
2. **https://www.seagate.com/in/en/blog/how-do-hdds-and-ssds-store-data/**
3. **https://www.ibm.com/think/topics/object-vs-file-vs-block-storage**
4. **https://cloud.google.com/discover/object-vs-block-vs-file-storage**
5. **https://www.stackscale.com/blog/types-of-storage/**
6. **https://www.geeksforgeeks.org/data-engineering/data-modeling-in-data-engineering/**
7. **https://www.ibm.com/think/topics/data-modeling**
8. **https://www.geeksforgeeks.org/dbms/codds-rules-in-dbms/**
9. **https://www.tutorialspoint.com/dbms/dbms_codds_rules.htm**
10. **https://www.scribd.com/doc/271898782/Codd-s-12-Rules**
11. **https://www.informatica.com/resources/articles/dataops-and-data-management.html**
12. **https://www.geeksforgeeks.org/data-engineering/what-is-big-data/**
13. **https://hadoop.apache.org/docs/stable/index.html**
14. **https://www.geeksforgeeks.org/data-engineering/hadoop-architecture/**
15. **https://www.geeksforgeeks.org/data-science/mapreduce-understanding-with-real-life-example/**

CHAPTER 8
Practical Guide to Data Storage

Introduction

This book has covered the key important aspects of data engineering that require us to understand the type of data sources, working on the data transformation, storing them in the database, and then utilizing the processed data directly for plain dashboarding, advanced analytics, critical decision-making, or input to further processing using machine learning, etc. The final application of data may have a business outcome, but some of the factors, like how frequently they are being used by the end application or users, what size of data is processed, whether it is near real-time processing or batch processing, etc., some of these factors also matter.

Customers may be happy with the output and are able to take an informed decision with that, but they may need it instantly or may need it to be accessed by another hundred people in the company. To tackle these situations, it is important to understand how the data is stored and the underlying storage technology. This is because there are dozens of database technologies available in the market, and they cater to a specific problem statement. It is imperative to understand the fundamental difference between them from a technical standpoint, and some proof of concepts need to be done before finalizing a particular database engine.

Structure

The chapter covers the following topics:

- Introduction to Google BigQuery
- Introduction to SQLite
- Introduction to Redis
- Introduction to Amazon Redshift
- Introduction to Google Bigtable
- Introduction to MongoDB
- Introduction to Amazon RDS

Objectives

At the end of this chapter, the reader will be familiar with some of the most widely used database engines in the market. This chapter provides a basic understanding of different types of databases including both on-premises and cloud-managed ones. Additionally, it also provides a technical understanding of some of these databases so that readers would learn the common commands that are used to create basic database schema for each type, serving as a starting step for practicing each of the databases in detail.

Finally, the readers will be competent enough to try some of these databases on their own and check the suitability based on their current business requirements.

Introduction to Google BigQuery

BigQuery is a serverless data warehouse from tech giant Google, which is used for analyzing large amounts of structured data using SQL. It is a managed service that can also be used to analyze data or to apply a machine learning algorithm and business intelligence.

Architecture

BigQuery's architecture consists of two parts:

- **Storage layer**: This layer ingests, stores, and optimizes data.
- **Compute layer**: This layer provides the data analysis capabilities.

  As shown in *Figure 8.1*, these two layers operate independently of each other and communicate with Google's petabit network:

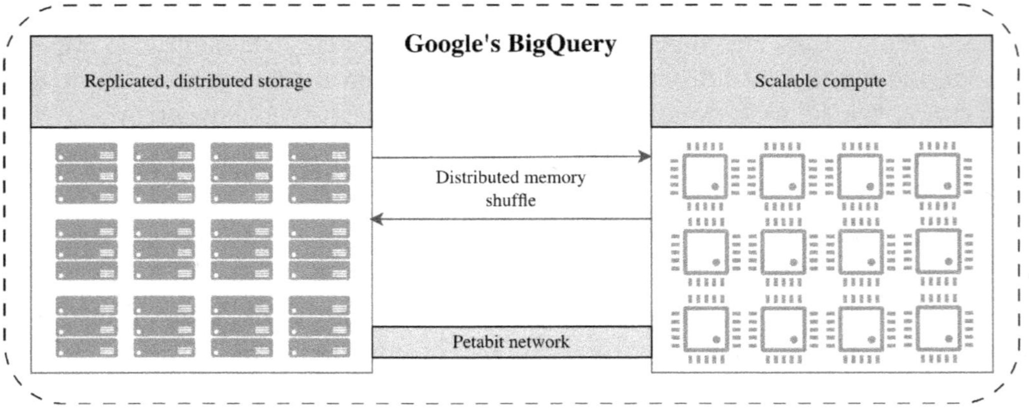

Figure 8.1: *A visual representation of Google BigQuery high level architecture*

For executing a query, the query engine distributes the work in parallel (into multiple stages) across multiple workers or compute nodes, which scan the relevant tables in distributed storage, process the query, and then gather the result.

Each stage processes its portion of data independently, and intermediate results (especially for operations like **`JOIN`**, **`GROUP BY`**, **`ORDER BY`**, and aggregations) are shuffled across nodes using this in-memory distributed shuffle mechanism.

This distributed memory shuffle is a high-speed in-memory distributed buffer that avoids writing intermediate data to disk, significantly improving performance and scalability.

Working with BigQuery

This can be accessed by visiting the **Google Cloud Platform** (**GCP**) console.

Let us look at the steps to create a new project and a table:

1. Visit **https://console.cloud.google.com**
2. Create your first project. You will see the page, as shown in the following figure:

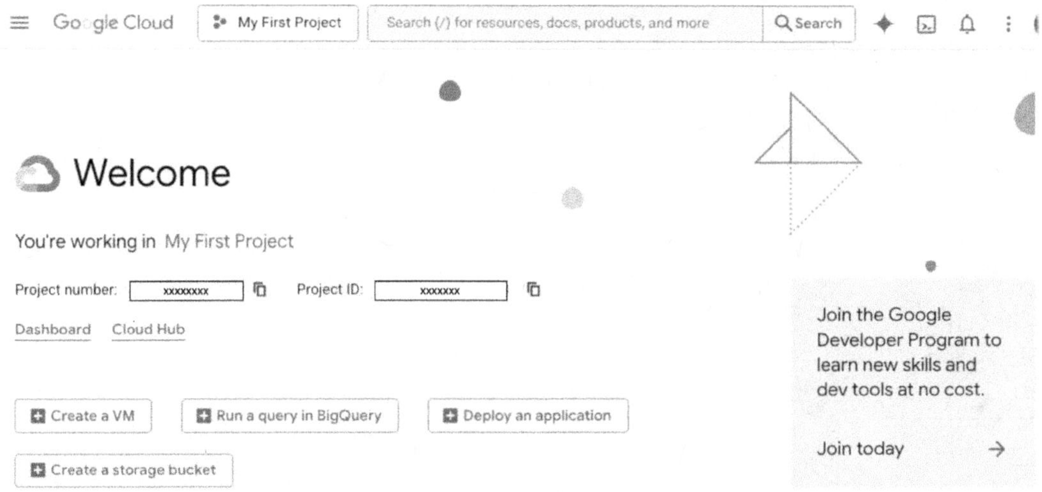

***Figure 8.2**: The home screen of GCP after login*

3. In the search bar above, write **`bigquery`**. This will open a sandbox environment for BigQuery. See the following figure to see how it appears on the GCP console.

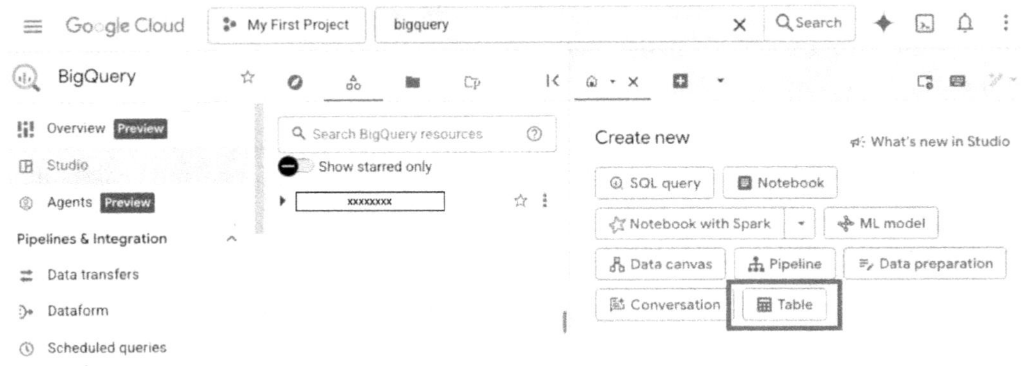

Figure 8.3: A view after search query

There are several ways to work on this, as this is visible in the above figure, we can create a new table, notebook, or a new pipeline, etc., to take it forward. We will cover two ways for now.

4. Creating a new table, as shown in the figure, click on the table and fill in the required fields:

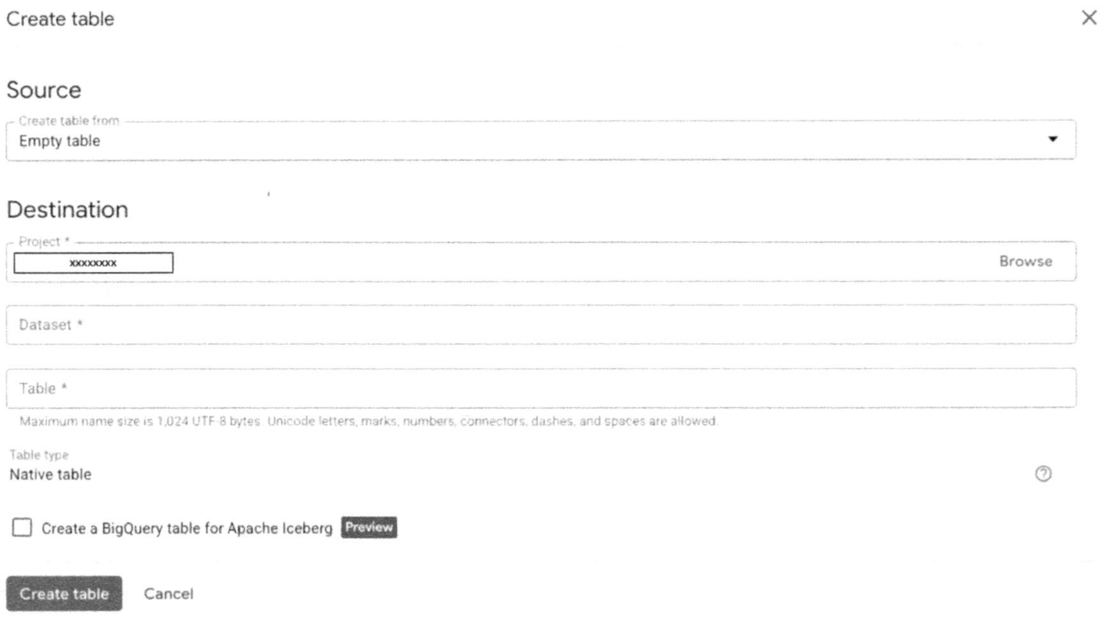

Figure 8.4: A view of a Create table form

5. Once the table is created, create the required fields by clicking on **Edit schema**, see the following figure to see how it appears on the GCP console:

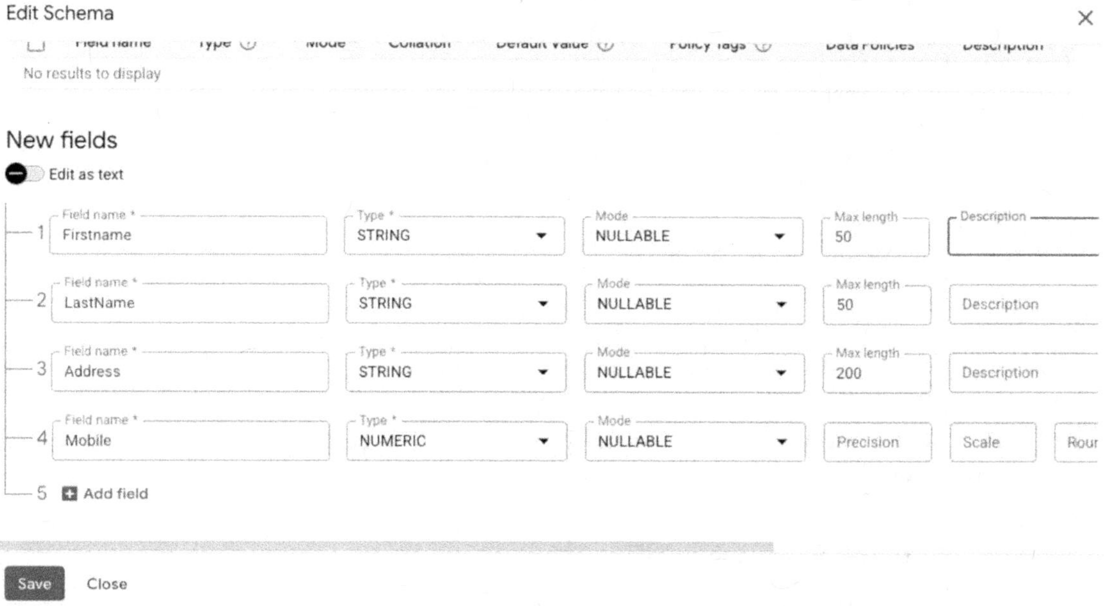

Figure 8.5: Table schema edit window in GCP console

6. Save and close, then we can see our table as shown in the following figure:

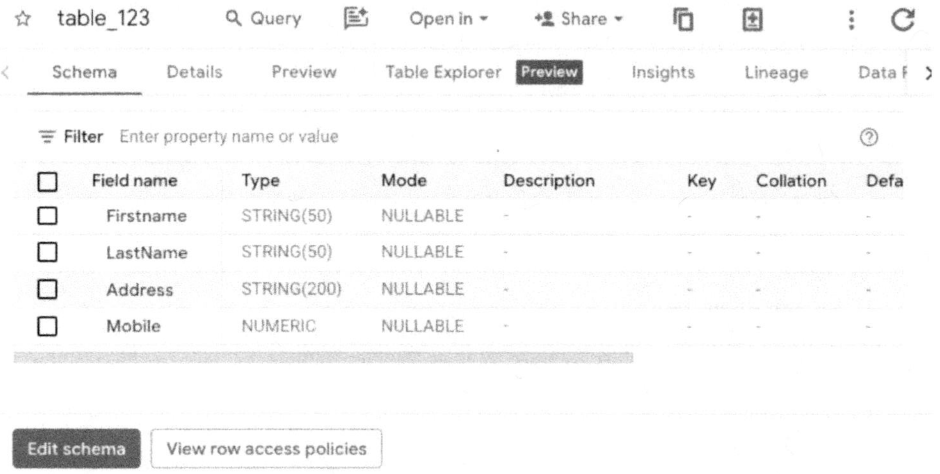

Figure 8.6: A schema view of a table named table_123

7. Now the table can be filled using the **INSERT** command, the following figure shows the command:

Figure 8.7: A view of insert command in BigQuery

8. Once the table is set up, it can be used by different applications using API or any other connectivity.

Use the existing database

To gain experience, the existing public dataset can also be worked on. This can be done following the steps:

1. Click on **Explorer**, then click on **Add data** and click on **Public Datasets**, then we can see a list of datasets available, see the following figure:

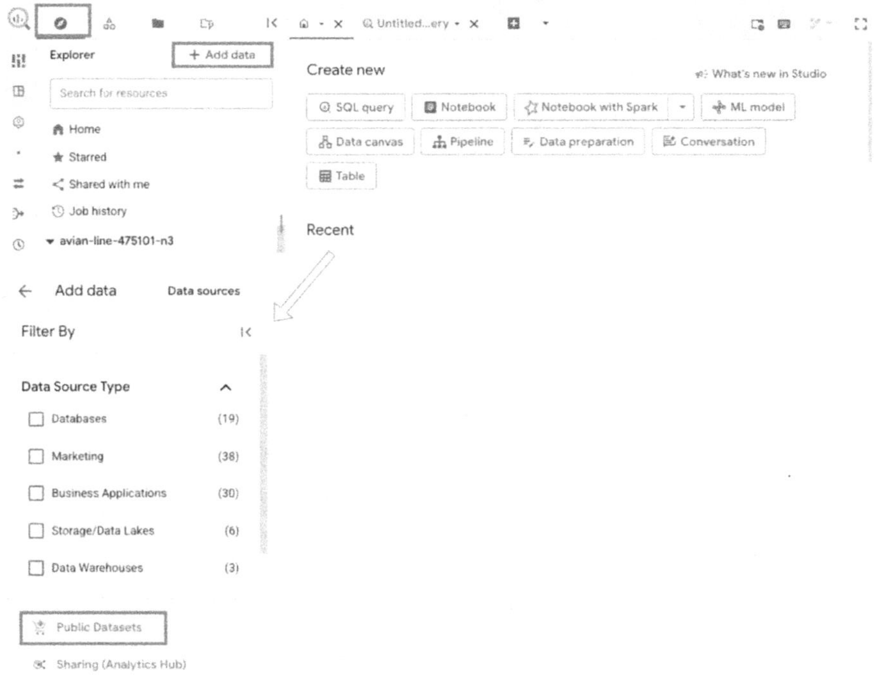

Figure 8.8: Explorer view to select the public datasets

2. For now, let us find the dataset that shows how many solar panels have been installed in the United States and select the **Project Sunroof**, and click on **View datasets**. See the following figure for reference:

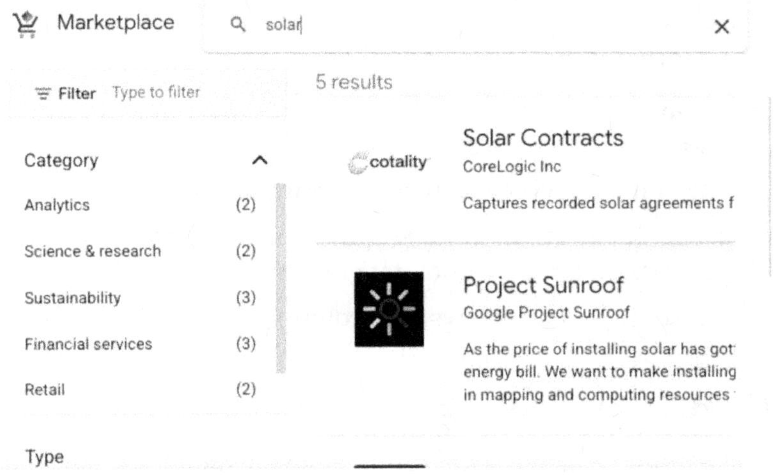

Figure 8.9*: Search result for solar dataset*

3. We can try to use SQL commands to see the data or do some calculations based on the requirements, as shown in the following figure:

Figure 8.10*: Output of SELECT query of public dataset*

Similarly, other existing datasets can be explored, and hands-on work can be done on them.

Details around all the commands and features of BigQuery can be found in the following link:

https://cloud.google.com/bigquery/docs/introduction

Key features of BigQuery

Here are some important key features of BigQuery:

- Despite the complex architecture in the backend, BigQuery allows users to interact with native scripting languages like SQL and Python to answer most of the business queries.
- A uniform way to work with both structured and semi-structured databases (e.g., JSON, Array etc.).
- Supports streaming data ingestion with continuous analysis.
- Highly scalable due to its distributed infrastructure that allows querying of terabytes of data in seconds and petabytes of data in minutes.
- It presents the data in tables, rows, and columns that follow the ACID property.

Introduction to Google Bigtable

Google Bigtable is a fully managed, wide column NoSQL database developed by Google that offers low latency and high availability. It is designed to handle thousands of columns with billions of rows. This means that terabytes to petabytes of data can be stored in it.

Architecture

Bigtable stores data in scalable tables, each of which is a sorted key-value map. Each row is indexed by a single row key, and the columns are related to a single column family.

Each intersection of row and column may contain multiple cells, which are timestamped versions of that row and column that have changed over time. The following table shows the visual representation of the Bigtable:

	Profile (Column family 1)		**Stats (Column family 2)**	
User ID	Name (Column Qualifier)	Age (Column Qualifier)	Visits (Column Qualifier)	Purchases (Column Qualifier)
User1 (row key)	Tom	26	100	23
User2 (row key)	Harry	35	129	12
User3 (row key)	Peter	17	1	-

***Table 8.1**: Example visualization of data stored in Bigtable*

Although in *Table 8.1*, the structure looks like any ordinary table, the data is internally stored in a simple key-value pair format:

```
(row_key, column_family: column_qualifier, timestamp) -> value
```

See the following table for reference:

Row_key	Column_family: Column_qualifier	Timestamp	Value
User 1	Profile: Name	2025-10-27T05:00	Tom
User 1	Profile: Age	2025-10-27T05:00	26
User1	Stats: Visits	2025-10-27T05:00	100
User1	Stats: Purchases	2025-10-27T05:00	23
User2	Profile: Name	2025-10-28T03:01	Harry
User2	Profile: Age	2025-10-28T03:01	35

***Table 8.2**: Logical representation of how the data is stored in Bigtable SSTables*

It may be called a table, but it is just a logical grouping with no fixed schema. Here, column families need to be defined at the time of table creation, but not the individual columns or column qualifiers inside them.

As shown in *Figure 8.11*, all the client queries are handled through the front-end server pool before being processed by the Google Cloud Bigtable nodes. These nodes are arranged into a Bigtable cluster that belongs to a Bigtable instance, which is a container for clusters. We may have multiple clusters in an instance for data replication to improve data availability and durability.

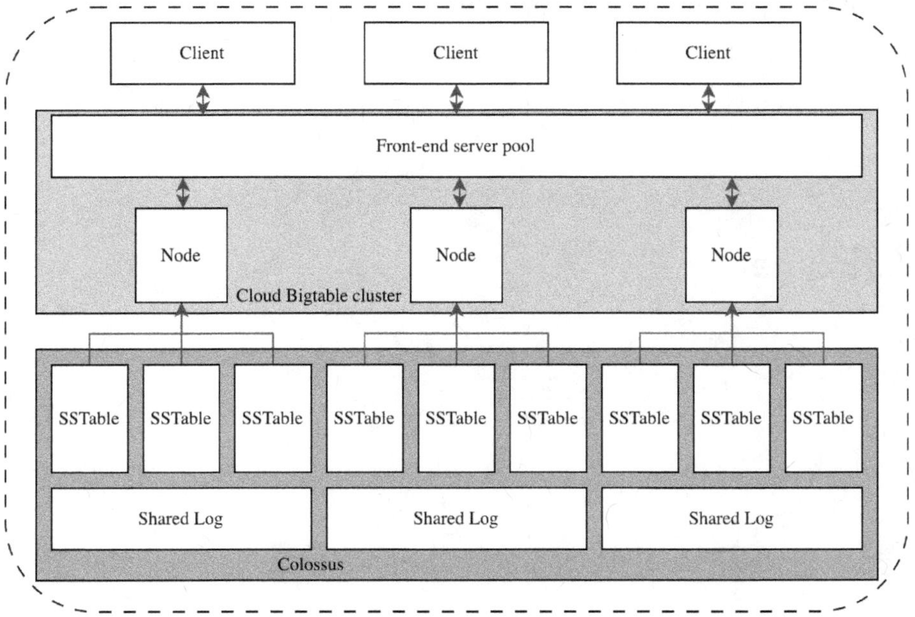

***Figure 8.11**: Architecture of Google Bigtable*

Each node in the Bigtable cluster handles a subset of the requests. The number of simultaneous requests that a cluster can handle can be increased by adding more nodes.

These clusters can also be replicated to handle different types of traffic, and if one cluster is unavailable, then a failover to another cluster can be done.

A Bigtable is sharded into blocks of contiguous rows called tablets to balance the workload of queries. These tablets are stored in Colossus (Google's file system) in **Sorted Strings Tables** (**SSTable**) format, where the actual data is stored. This data is saved as an ordered, unchangeable key-value pair. So, each SSTable is like a neatly sorted, read-only dictionary saved on disk.

An important point to note is that the nodes do not store the actual data but hold pointers that tell them where on Colossus the tablets are stored. This design makes Bigtable very flexible and fault-tolerant.

For writing, all the writes are stored in Colossus's shared log. Once the write is safely recorded there, Bigtable acknowledges the write operations to ensure the data is safe in Colossus, even if the node crashes.

Working with Bigtable

This can be accessed by going to the Google Cloud console. Refer to the following steps:

1. Visit: **https://console.cloud.google.com**
2. Create your first project. You will see the page, as shown in the following figure:

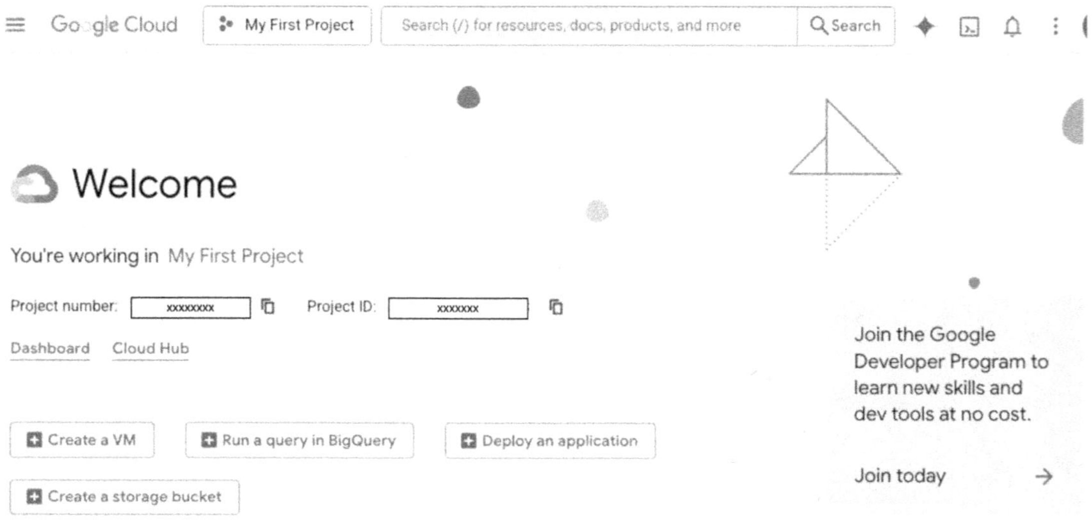

***Figure 8.12**: The home screen of GCP after login*

3. In the search bar above, write **bigtable**. This will open a sandbox environment for Bigtable where the new instance can be created, as shown in the following figure:

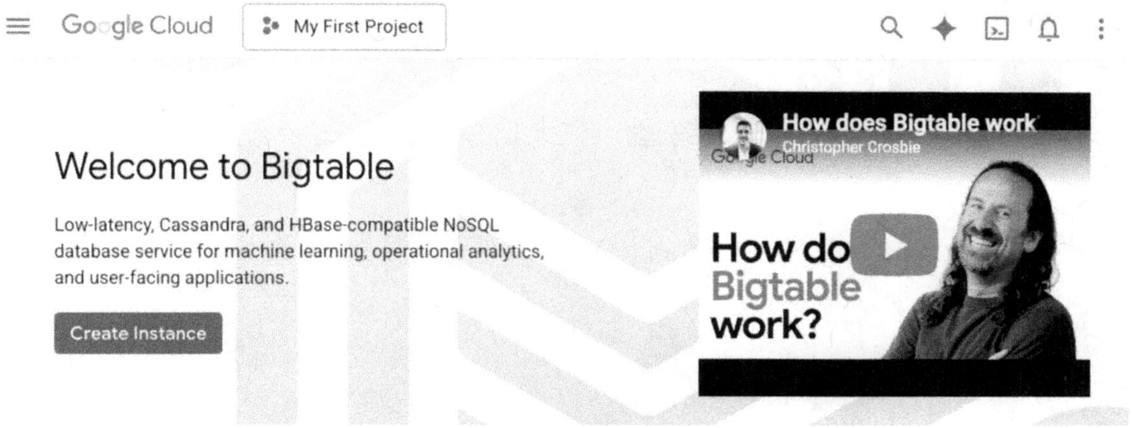

Figure 8.13: A Bigtable homepage in GCP

4. Fill in the required details and create the instance, as shown in the following figure:

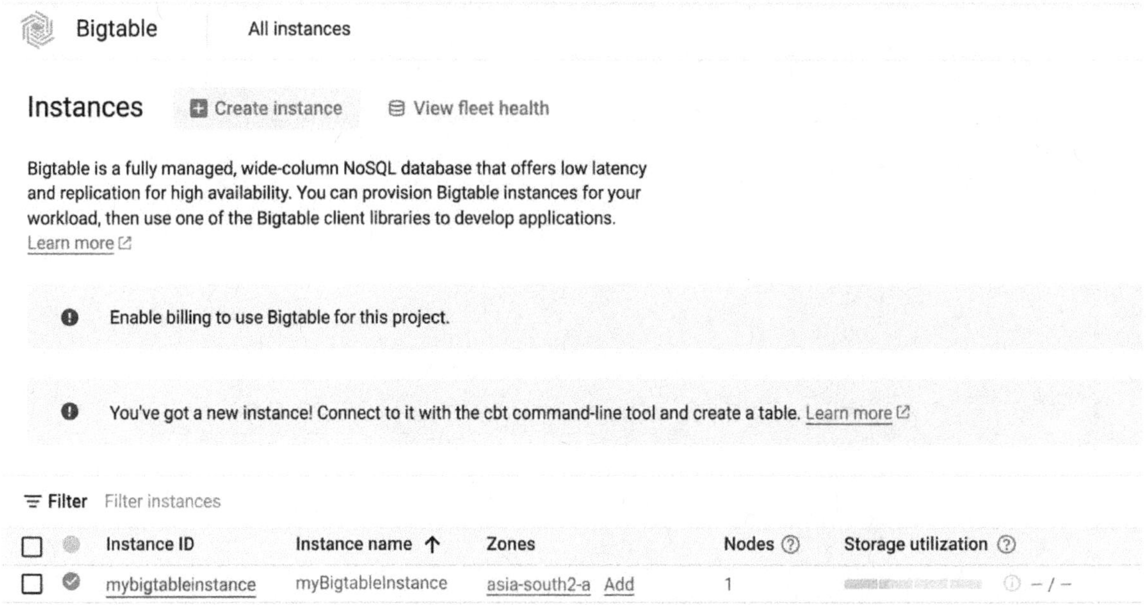

Figure 8.14: GCP page showing created Bigtable instance

5. Click on the **Instance ID** as shown in the figure above and click on the **Tables** tab. See the following figure for reference:

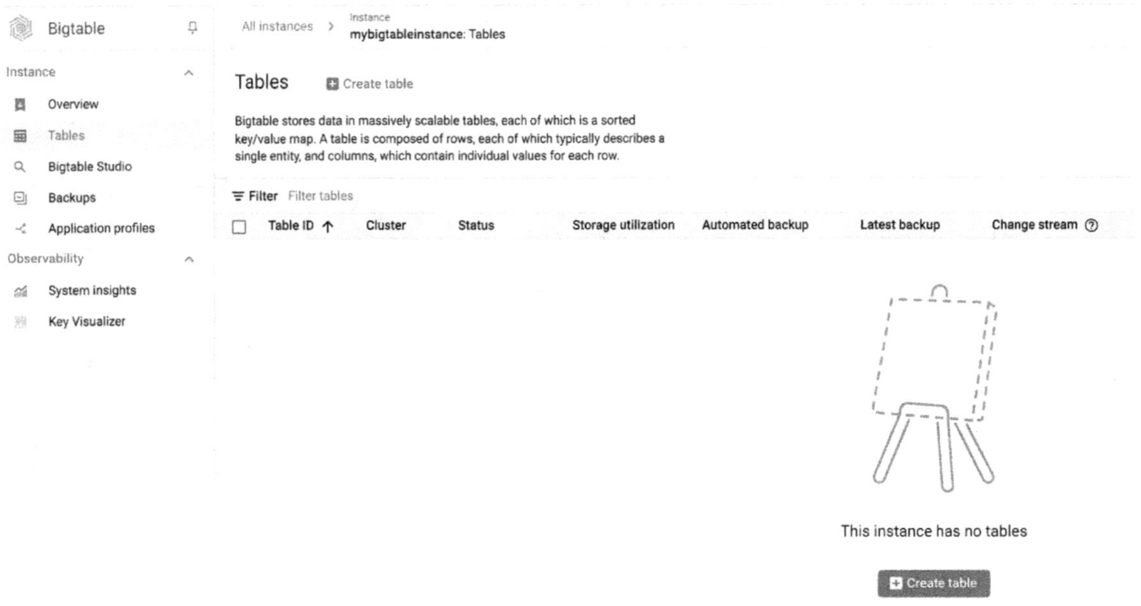

Figure 8.15: An instance view in GCP

6. Click on **Create Table** and fill in the required details, including column families. Click on the **Create**. This will create a table. See the following figure:

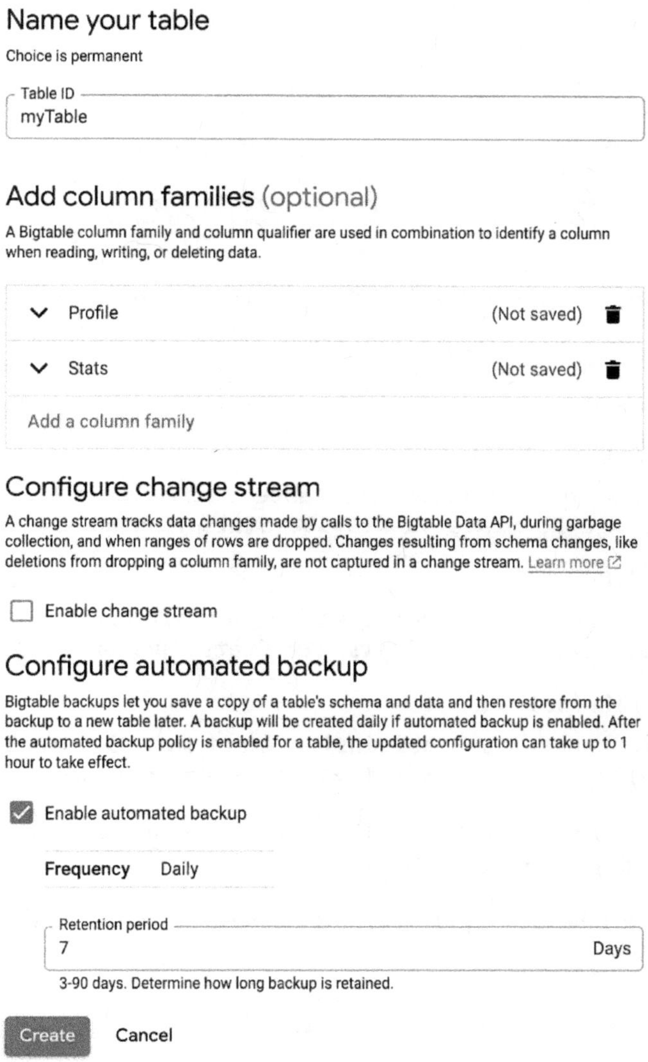

Figure 8.16: *A view of table configuration for Bigtable in GCP*

7. The data can be inserted using **Cloud BigTable** (**CBT**), which is Google's command-line tool used to interact with and manage Bigtable instances, rather than through Bigtable Studio using SQL commands.

   Note: **SQL commands are not fully supported by Bigtable. It can have limited operations to view the table using `SELECT` queries, but not `INSERT`, `UPDATE`, or `DELETE`.**

   To open CBT, go to the top and click on the **Activate Cloud Shell** and complete the authorization:

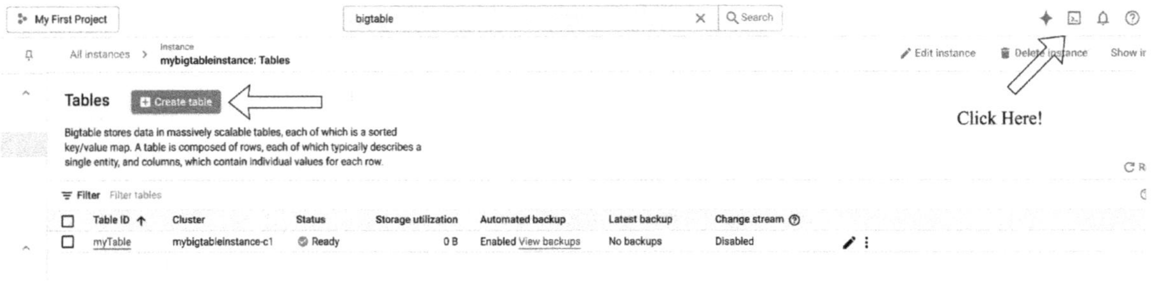

Figure 8.17: *A picture of the GCP view showing the cloud shell activation process*

8. Use the following commands to enter the key-value pairs we used in previous examples:

    - **Insert data for User1:**

      ```
      cbt -instance=mybigtableinstance set myTable User1 Profile:Name=Tom
      Profile:Age=26 Stats:Visits=100 Stats:Purchases=23
      ```

    - **Insert data for User2:**

      ```
      cbt -instance=mybigtableinstance set myTable User2 Profile:Name=Harry
      Profile:Age=35 Stats:Visits=129 Stats:Purchases=12
      ```

    - **Insert data for User3:**

      ```
      cbt -instance=mybigtableinstance set myTable User3 Profile:Name=Peter
      Profile:Age=17 Stats:Visits=1 Stats:Purchases=0
      ```

9. All the values that have been added to the database can be seen by going to the Bigtable Studio and using a simple **`SELECT`** statement.

    Use command | **`Select * from myTable`**, (see the following figure):

Figure 8.18: *Figure showing the output of the SELECT command on the bottom (right)*

All the values that have been added to the database can be seen on the bottom right panel of the Google Bigtable Studio, or the same can be seen using CBT, where it shows the timestamped values as well, using the command: **`cbt -instance=mybigtableinstance read myTable`**. Refer to the following figure:

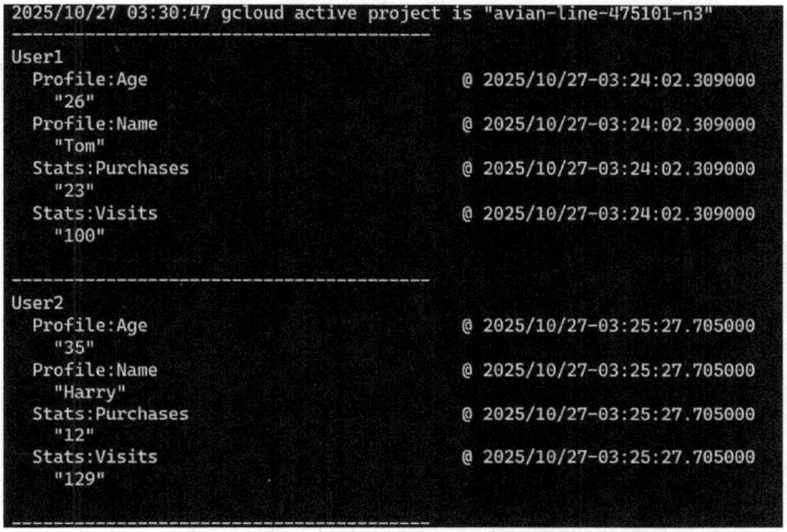

***Figure 8.19**: CBT view of the table content*

Apart from Google's CBT, Bigtable can be accessed via client libraries developed in the renowned programming languages such as Python, Java, Node.js, Go, etc. Also, it can be accessed via REST APIs or by setting up pipelines using Apache Beam or Google Cloud Dataflow, etc.

Key features of Bigtable

Some of the important key features that should be looked at for Bigtable are:

1. **Massive scalability**: Due to its flexible architecture, it can handle thousands of columns with billions of rows.
2. **High performance**: It is designed for very fast reads and writes even on huge datasets, where query scans are efficient.
3. **Automatic sharding and load balancing**: Bigtable automatically splits the data into tablets (small data chunks) that are spread across multiple nodes for even workload distribution. If one table gets too big or busy, it is automatically split and rebalanced.

Introduction to SQLite

SQLite is a free, lightweight, serverless, self-contained SQL database engine, which is the most widely used database engine in the world. SQLite requires no installation or setting up a separate server. It is a widely used database with around one trillion footprints. This is used in most mobile devices and most available operating systems.

SQLite is great for prototyping and developing small applications. It is compatible with most of the SQL commands. The complete SQLite is compiled into a single C library file (**`sqlite3.c`** and **`sqlite3.h`**) for high performance and portability.

Although SQLite's core is in C, it provides official interfaces for many programming languages such as Python, C++, Java, PHP, C#, Go, etc.

Architecture

From a high-level understanding, SQLite works by compiling SQL text into bytecode, then running that bytecode using the virtual machine. Let us look at the architecture of SQLite (refer to the following):

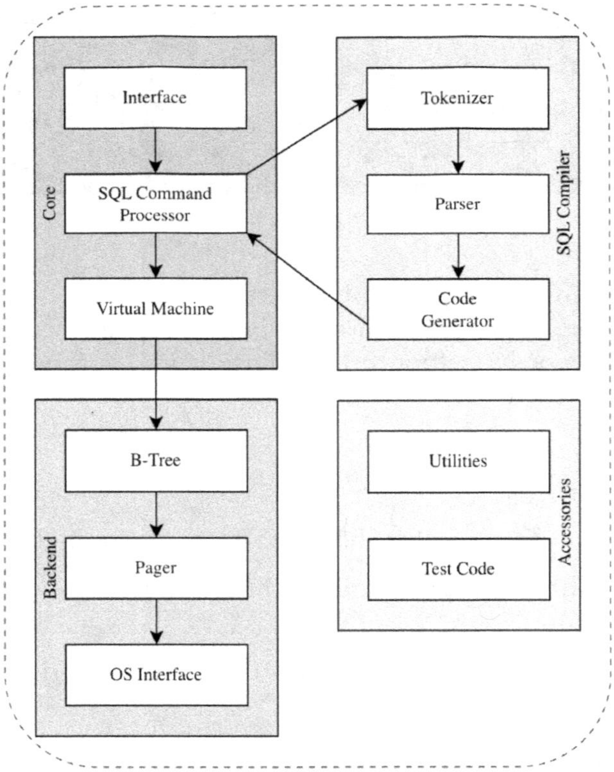

***Figure 8.20**: Architecture of SQLite*

Figure 8.20 shows the major components of SQLite, and the following are the components that work with each other to process any query received from an application or a user:

- **Interface**: This is the entry point for all the SQL commands.
- **SQL command processor or SQL compiler**: This is the section where the SQL command is converted into bytecode. It further has three components:

  - **Tokenizer**: This breaks SQL strings into tokens, which are keywords, operators, and identifiers, and hands these tokens to the parser for processing.
  - **Parser**: The parser assigns meaning to the token based on its context and builds a parse tree.
  - **Code generator**: This analyzes the parse tree and generates the byte code that performs the work of the SQL statement.
- **Virtual machine or byte code engine**: The bytecode generated by the code generator is executed by a virtual machine. This virtual machine itself is entirely contained in a single source file.
- **B-tree**: The database in SQLite is maintained using a B-tree implementation to optimize data access, which is used for each table and index in the database.
- **Pager or page cache**: A B-tree module requires information from the disk in the fixed-size pages (default 4096 bytes). The page cache is responsible for reading, writing, and caching these pages.
- **OS interface**: This is the lowest layer of SQLite, which is used for all the file operations such as reading, writing, locking, and deleting database files. Since SQLite works on different types of operating systems, and each operating system operates differently, SQLite has created this layer that works with all operating systems
- **Utilities**: These are the supporting modules that make the SQLite core cleaner and more modular. Tasks like memory management, configuration, debugging, and string handling are handled by this module.
- **Test code**: This module is designed for testing to verify SQL parsing correctness, transaction atomicity, concurrent operations, locking mechanisms, boundary conditions, etc. These files are not included in a standard build of the library.

Hands-on with SQLite using Python

Since SQLite is written in C, Python interacts with it using a built-in sqlite3 module, which wraps a C library underneath. The code listed in the following steps shows how to work with SQLite for general database operations:

1. **Importing SQLite, creating and connecting to the school database**:

```
# Import sqlite module
import sqlite3
# Connect to a database (creates file if not exists)
conn = sqlite3.connect("school.db")
# Create a cursor to execute SQL commands
cursor = conn.cursor()
print("Connected to SQLite successfully!")
```

Result: A file named **`school.db`** is created in your current directory.

2. **Create a student's table**:

```
cursor.execute("""
CREATE TABLE IF NOT EXISTS students (
    rollnumber INTEGER PRIMARY KEY AUTOINCREMENT,
    firstname TEXT NOT NULL,
    lastname TEXT NOT NULL,
    age INTEGER,
    grade TEXT
);
""")
conn.commit()
print("Table created successfully!")
```

Result: A table gets created with this command with the name **`Students`**, having fields **`rollnumber`**, **`firstname`**, **`lastname`**, **`age`**, and **`grade`**.

3. **Insert values in the table**:

```
cursor.execute("INSERT INTO students (firstname,lastname, age, grade)
VALUES (?, ?, ?, ?)", ("Leonardo","DiCaprio", 7, "2nd"))
cursor.execute("INSERT INTO students (firstname,lastname, age, grade)
VALUES (?, ?, ?, ?)", ("Tom","Cruise", 10, "5th"))
cursor.execute("INSERT INTO students (firstname,lastname, age, grade)
VALUES (?, ?, ?, ?)", ("Harry","Potter", 12, "7th"))
conn.commit()
print("Data inserted successfully!")
```

Result: **`Students`** table will be inserted with three records

4. **Querying the data**: See the complete table:

```
cursor.execute("SELECT * FROM students")
rows = cursor.fetchall()
for row in rows:
    print(row)
```

Result:

```
(1, 'Leonardo', 'DiCaprio', 7, '2nd')
(2, 'Tom', 'Cruise', 10, '5th')
(3, 'Harry', 'Potter', 12, '7th')
```

5. **Querying the data**: See the table with a conditional statement (getting the results of students older than 8 years of age):

```
cursor.execute("SELECT * FROM students WHERE age > 8")
rows = cursor.fetchall()
for row in rows:
    print(row)
```

Result:

```
(2, 'Tom', 'Cruise', 10, '5th')
(3, 'Harry', 'Potter', 12, '7th')
```

6. **Querying the data**: See specific columns of the table (only first name and age):

```
cursor.execute("SELECT firstname,age FROM students")
rows = cursor.fetchall()
for row in rows:
    print(row)
```

Result:

```
('Leonardo', 7)
('Tom', 10)
('Harry', 12)
```

7. **Updating the data**: Modify a specific record (Change the grade of Leonardo to 3rd):

```
cursor.execute("UPDATE students SET grade = ? WHERE firstname = ?",
("3rd", "Leonardo"))
conn.commit()
cursor.execute("SELECT * FROM students")
rows = cursor.fetchall()
for row in rows:
    print(row)
```

Result:

```
(1, 'Leonardo', 'DiCaprio', 7, '3rd')
(2, 'Tom', 'Cruise', 10, '5th')
(3, 'Harry', 'Potter', 12, '7th')
```

8. **Updating the data**: Delete a specific record based on a condition (Remove the students younger than 8 years of age):

```
cursor.execute("DELETE FROM students WHERE age < 8")
conn.commit()
cursor.execute("SELECT * FROM students")
rows = cursor.fetchall()
for row in rows:
    print(row)
```

Result:

```
(2, 'Tom', 'Cruise', 10, '5th')
(3, 'Harry', 'Potter', 12, '7th')
```

9. **Delete a table**:

   ```
   cursor.execute("Drop table students")
   conn.commit()
   ```

   Result: `Students` table is deleted.

10. **Close the connection**:

    ```
    conn.close()
    ```

    Result: The connection we had created at the first step will be closed.

Similarly, many other SQL queries can be used to work on a SQLite database with various programming languages on different operating systems.

Key features of SQLite

Let us look at the following important key features of SQLite:

- **Self-contained**: It is a standalone system that has very few dependencies. It is platform independent, which means it can run on any operating system. The complete SQLite library has been encapsulated in a single source file, which does not require special tools to build.
- **Serverless**: Unlike other SQL database engines that require a program or a client to connect to a server to get the data, SQLite allows the client or any process to read and write the data directly from the database files on disk. This saves the complexity of installing, configuring, and maintaining a separate server.
- **Zero-configuration**: SQLite does not need to be installed before it is used; there is no setup procedure, no need to start or stop the server, and no configuration to be done on the server. There is no need for an administrator to create a new database instance or manage the users.
- **Transactional**: All the changes within a transaction in SQLite are either complete or not at all, even if the current transaction has been interrupted by a program crash, server failure, or power failure. In other words, it follows the ACID property.
- **Write-ahead logging (WAL)**: SQLite supports WAL mode, which helps multiple users read the data at the same time while one user is writing to it. This makes it faster and better when many operations are happening together.

Introduction to MongoDB

MongoDB is a NoSQL or non-relational database that stores data in a flexible JSON-like format called **Binary JSON** (**BSON**). It is designed for large-scale data storage, high performance, and easy scalability.

In MongoDB, collections are used instead of tables, which are groups of related documents. A document is used instead of rows, which is a single record stored in JSON-like format. A column is replaced by a field, which is a key-value pair inside a document.

For example, an SQL table would show a record of a person as listed in the following table:

Id	Name	Age	Hobbies	City	Zip
1001	Tom	45	Reading, traveling	New York	10001

Table 8.3: *A relational view of a SQL table*

The same record in MongoDB would look like:

```
{
  "_id": 1001,
  "name": "Tom",
  "age": 45,
  "hobbies": ["reading", "traveling"],
  "address": {
    "city": "New York",
    "zip": "10001"
  }
}
```

Architecture

MongoDB has three major layers, which are responsible for the interaction with the external world, routing the queries, and finally processing the queries and giving the result back to the external world. Let us understand the architecture of MongoDB in the following figure:

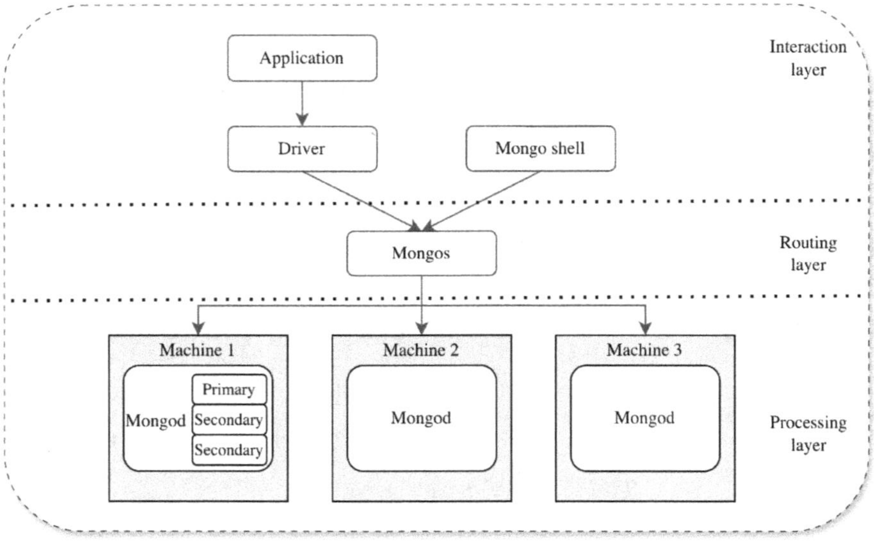

***Figure 8.21**: Architecture of MongoDB*

As per *Figure 8.21*, there are three layers:

- **Interaction layer**: This layer is meant for interaction between the user or any application and MongoDB.
    - **Drivers**: These are client libraries that let any application communicate with MongoDB. These drivers include Java, .Net, JavaScript, Node.js, and Python.
    - **Shell**: This is an interactive JavaScript-based interface that lets developers run commands, examine the results of queries, and check the test cases.
- **Routing layer**: This is the layer that contains Mongos, which routes client requests to the correct shard.
- **Processing layer**: This is a core component of MongoDB, which is responsible for managing the data, handling client requests, and performing database operations. Multiple MongoDB instances can work together to form a cluster in a typical setup. There can be many MongoDB daemons running as primary and secondary instances, where primary instances handle writes and change operations, and secondary instances copy the data from the primary and help distribute read workloads for load balancing.

In MongoDB, the data is made available and reliable by maintaining multiple copies across different nodes.

Hands-on with MongoDB using Python

The following steps show the stepwise configuration in MongoDB:

1. Visit **https://account.mongodb.com/account/login** and sign up with any email account.
2. Fill in the required details and create a cluster, as shown in the following figure:

Figure 8.22*: Home page of MongoDB view*

3. Select the **Free** tier, fill in the required details, and click on create deployment. See the following figure showing the selection:

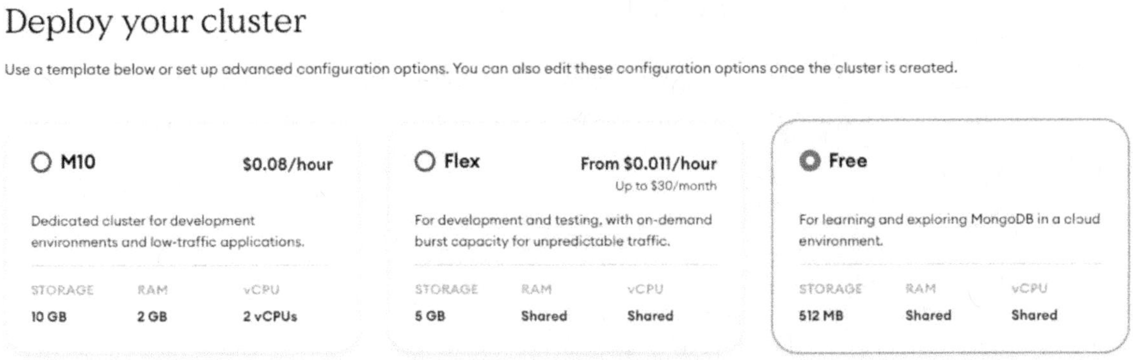

Figure 8.23*: Cluster selector in MongoDB*

4. The required action needs to be taken. See the following figure for the required configuration:

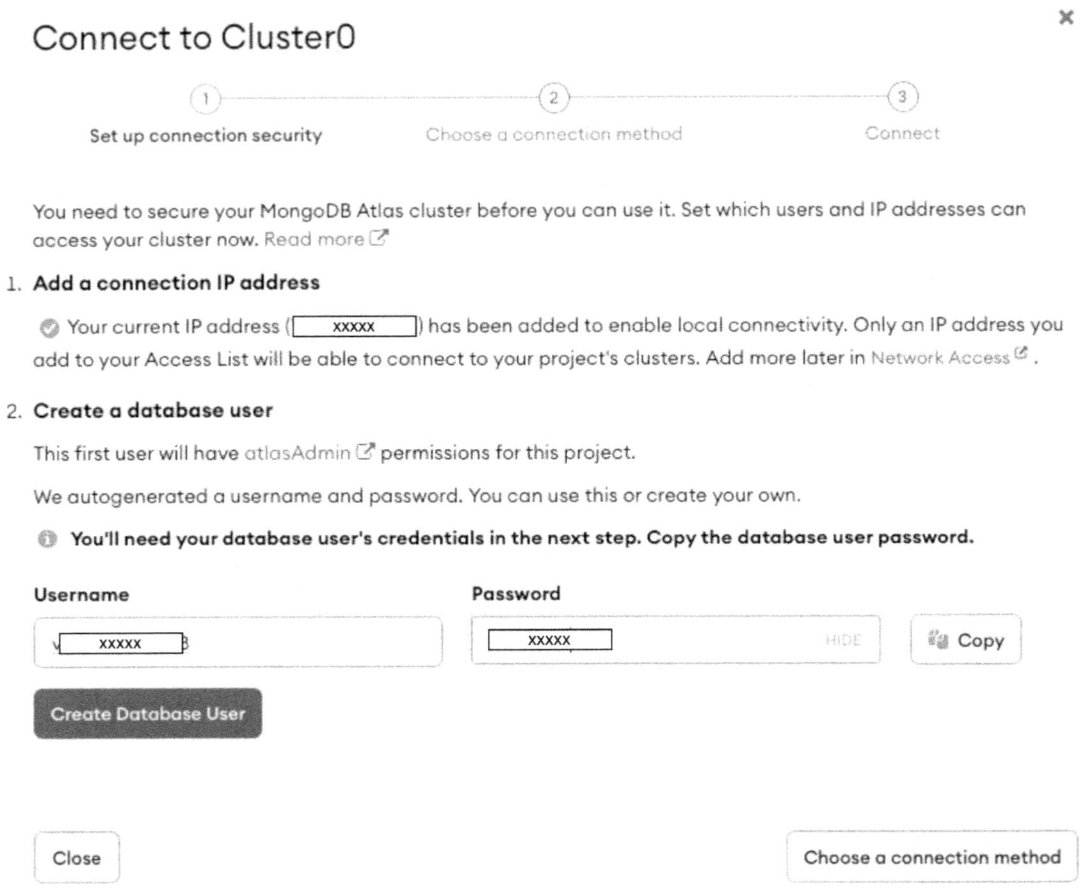

Figure 8.24: *Configuration page for cluster*

5. Select the preferred way of interacting with MongoDB; we will stick to Python. Select **Python**, check the required details, and click on **Done**. See the following figures for the steps:

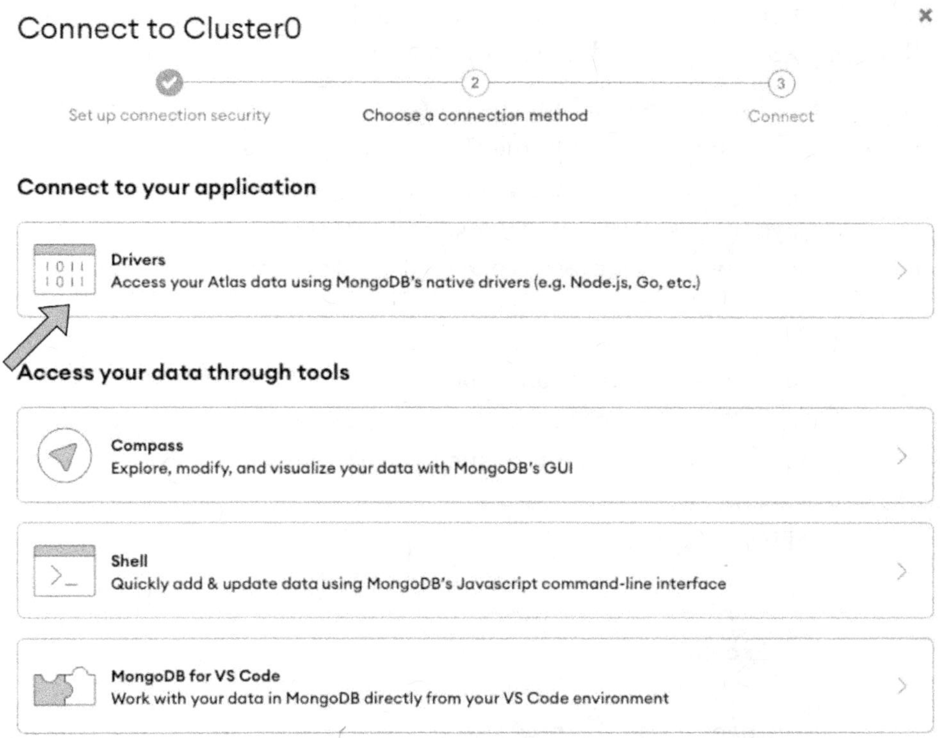

***Figure 8.25**: Driver selection for the cluster to connect an application to the MongoDB Atlas cluster*

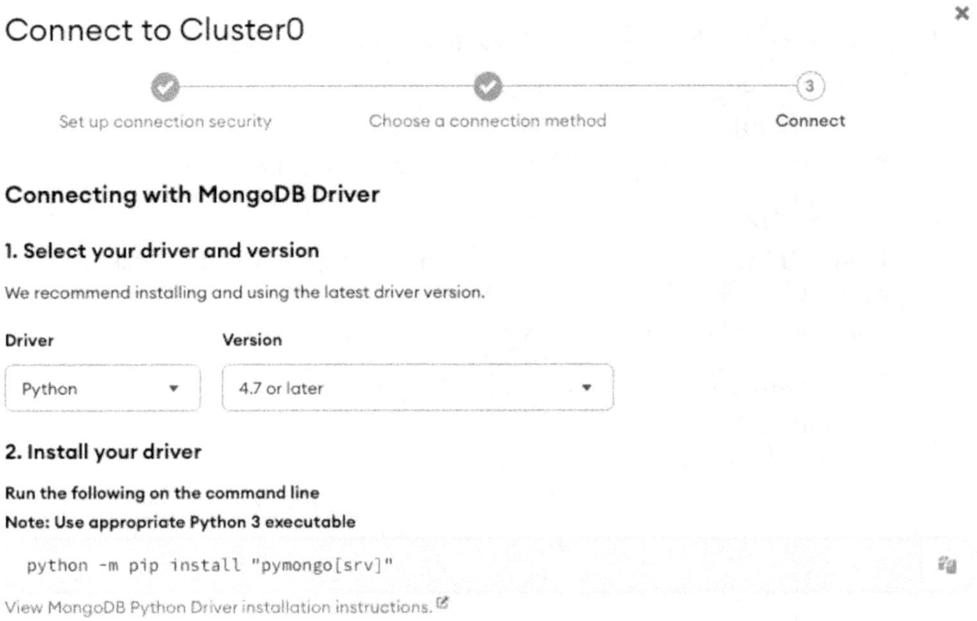

***Figure 8.26**: Showing Python selected as the connecting driver*

6. Go to the Python development interface and write the commands given in the following steps for general database operations:

   a. **Connecting to MongoDB**:

```
# Import the necessary modules from pymongo
from pymongo.mongo_client import MongoClient
from pymongo.server_api import ServerApi
# Define the connection string (URI) for MongoDB
uri = "mongodb+srv://<username>:<password>@cluster0.uqmarno.
mongodb.net/?appName=Cluster0"
# Create a new client and connect to the server
client = MongoClient(uri, server_api=ServerApi('1'))
# Send a ping to confirm a successful connection
try:
    client.admin.command('ping')
    print("Pinged your deployment. You successfully connected to
MongoDB!")
except Exception as e:
    print(e)
# The MongoClient is now set up and connected to the MongoDB
server
```

   Result: A connection to MongoDB is successful.

   b. **Create a school database and create a students table**:

```
# Create or use database 'school'
db = client["school"]
# Create (or use) a collection (table equivalent) 'students'
students = db["students"]
```

   Result: References for the database named **`school`** and a table **`students`** are created, but actually, the DB and table will be created when the tables are actually populated with values.

   c. **Insert values in the table**:

```
students.insert_many([
    {"firstname": "Leonardo", "lastname": "DiCaprio", "age": 7,
"grade": "2nd"},
    {"firstname": "Tom", "lastname": "Cruise", "age": 10, "grade":
"5th"},
    {"firstname": "Harry", "lastname": "Potter", "age": 12, "grade":
"7th"}
```

```
])
print("Data inserted successfully!")
```

Result: DB created, **`Students`** table will be created and inserted with three records.

d. **Querying the data**: See complete records:

```
for student in students.find():
    print(student)
```

Result:

```
{'_id': ObjectId('6905622042c967e5e062b6fc'), 'firstname': 'Leonardo', 'lastname': 'DiCaprio', 'age': 7, 'grade': '2nd'}
{'_id': ObjectId('6905622042c967e5e062b6fd'), 'firstname': 'Tom', 'lastname': 'Cruise', 'age': 10, 'grade': '5th'}
{'_id': ObjectId('6905622042c967e5e062b6fe'), 'firstname': 'Harry', 'lastname': 'Potter', 'age': 12, 'grade': '7th'}
```

e. **Querying the data**: See records with a conditional statement (getting the results of students older than 8 years of age):

```
for student in students.find({"age": {"$gt": 8}}):
    print(student)
```

Result:

```
{'_id': ObjectId('6905622042c967e5e062b6fd'), 'firstname': 'Tom', 'lastname': 'Cruise', 'age': 10, 'grade': '5th'}
{'_id': ObjectId('6905622042c967e5e062b6fe'), 'firstname': 'Harry', 'lastname': 'Potter', 'age': 12, 'grade': '7th'}
```

f. **Querying the data**: See specific fields of the records (see only first name and age):

```
for student in students.find({}, {"firstname": 1, "age": 1, "_
id": 0}):
    print(student)
```

Result:

```
{'firstname': 'Leonardo', 'age': 7}
{'firstname': 'Tom', 'age': 10}
{'firstname': 'Harry', 'age': 12}
```

g. **Updating the data**: Modify a specific record (change the grade of Leonardo to 3rd):

```
students.update_one(
    {"firstname": "Leonardo"},
```

```
    {"$set": {"grade": "3rd"}}
)
print("\nAfter updating Leonardo's grade:")
for student in students.find():
    print(student)
```

Result:

```
{'_id': ObjectId('6905622042c967e5e062b6fc'), 'firstname': 'Leonardo', 'lastname': 'DiCaprio', 'age': 7, 'grade': '3rd'}
{'_id': ObjectId('6905622042c967e5e062b6fd'), 'firstname': 'Tom', 'lastname': 'Cruise', 'age': 10, 'grade': '5th'}
{'_id': ObjectId('6905622042c967e5e062b6fe'), 'firstname': 'Harry', 'lastname': 'Potter', 'age': 12, 'grade': '7th'}
```

h. **Updating the data**: Delete a specific record based on a condition (remove the students younger than 8 years of age):

```
students.delete_many({"age": {"$lt": 8}})
# Updating the data: delete a specific record based on a condition
print("\nAfter deleting students with age < 8:")
for student in students.find():
    print(student)
```

Result:

```
After deleting students with age < 8:
{'_id': ObjectId('6905622042c967e5e062b6fd'), 'firstname': 'Tom', 'lastname': 'Cruise', 'age': 10, 'grade': '5th'}
{'_id': ObjectId('6905622042c967e5e062b6fe'), 'firstname': 'Harry', 'lastname': 'Potter', 'age': 12, 'grade': '7th'}
```

i. **Delete the table and database**:

```
students.drop()
print("\nCollection 'students' dropped.")
client.drop_database("school")
print("Database 'school' dropped.")
```

Result: The `students` table and the entire database (this may have several tables) are deleted.

j. **Close the connection**:

```
client.close()
```

Result: The connection we had created in the first step will be closed.

Key features of MongoDB

MongoDB has the following essential key technical features:

- **Document model**: It is a document-oriented data model, which means data is stored as documents. These documents are a flexible schema, unlike other databases, where data must be spread across specific columns in a table. This flexibility helps developers to iterate faster.
- **Faster processing**: Since the data is stored in BSON, which is binary-encoded JSON, it is much faster than JSON for processing.
- **Sharding**: MongoDB is designed to be distributed across multiple instances called shards, which allows horizontal scalability. This way of implementation is better suited for handling multiple requests on a huge database.
- **Replication**: If data resides on a single server, it becomes a single point of failure that may be due to a system crash, a power failure, or other unknown factors. In MongoDB, there are replicas that are created, where all the write operations are done on primary servers, which are then replicated on secondary servers. When the primary server goes down due to any failure, any one of the secondary servers will assume the responsibility of the primary server.
- **Load balancing**: For any enterprise-level database, load balancing is the key to handling millions of client requests at a time. With the existing replication and sharding architectural construct, MongoDB is designed to handle multiple concurrent read and write requests with best-in-class concurrency control and locking mechanisms that ensure data consistency without the need for an external load balancer.

Introduction to Redis

REmote DIctionary Server (**Redis**) is an in-memory NoSQL database that works on the philosophy of key-value pairs. These keys can support various types of data, such as strings, lists, sets, sorted sets, and hashes.

Due to its very nature of keeping the entire key space in memory during operation, it is very fast and reduces the overhead of accessing the non-volatile memory. It also optionally saves the data to disk for recovery.

Architecture

To achieve top performance, Redis works with an in-memory dataset; however, depending upon the use case, it can persist the data either by periodically dumping the dataset to the disk or by appending each command to a disk-based log. This feature can be enabled and disabled as well. Let us understand the Redis architecture using the following figure:

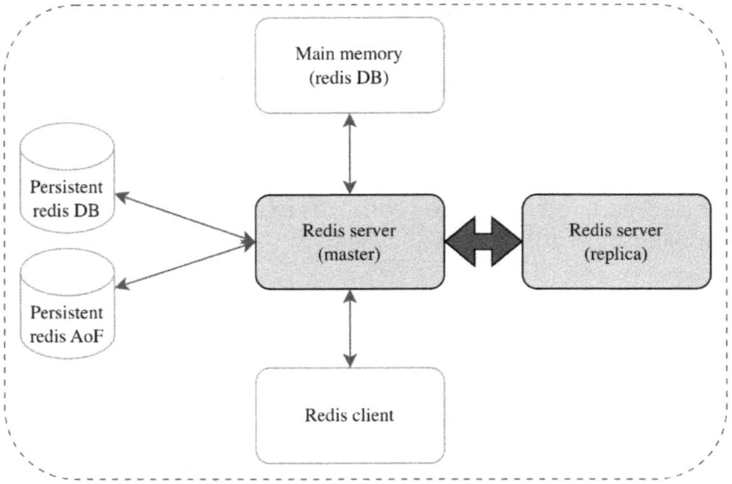

***Figure 8.27**: Architecture of Redis*

As shown in *Figure 8.27*, Redis is based on the client or server architecture that consists of the following components:

- **Redis server**: It is the central node that handles all read/write operations from clients. It keeps active datasets in the main memory for high-speed access. Client applications communicate directly with this server (master) via Redis client.
- **Redis server replica**: It is a replica of the master server, which gets the data from the master server using asynchronous replication. It helps in load balancing for high read requests, failover support, and data redundancies (backup copies).
- **Redis client**: This is an interface through which the different applications interact with Redis in various languages. Internally, Redis has different client interfaces for each language, e.g., Redis-cli for a C-based command line interface, Redis-java for a Java client library.
- **Main memory**: Redis stores all the data in memory for ultra-fast operations, which support various data structures such as strings, lists, sets, hashes, etc. It also periodically persists this in-memory data to disk (if configured).
- **Persistence options**: There are two ways Redis persists the data:
    - **Redis database backup**: The snapshot of the dataset can be stored at a predefined interval. Though this is fast and lightweight, data between the snapshots may be lost.
    - **Append only file (AoF)**: This logs every write operation received by the server. This is near real-time persistence but is slightly slower.

Redis Enterprise architecture

The above architecture is for Redis, an open-source project by *Redis Limited*, which shows a single master and its replica without mentioning clustering, multi-tenancy, and replication, which are available in the Redis Enterprise edition.

Redis Enterprise can be either a single Redis server database or a cluster. This allows the database to scale horizontally across many servers through sharding, which ensures high availability.

Sharding is a type of database partitioning that breaks large databases into smaller, faster, and more easily manageable pieces, which are called shards. Shards remove the limitation of storing the data in the memory of a single computer, and the computational power of multiple cores can also be utilized.

In Redis Enterprise, a cluster is a set of cloud instances, virtual machines, or containers that help us create Redis databases that are shared across the set of machines. This provides horizontal scalability, and the increasing data and traffic can be handled by simply adding more nodes. The following figure explains the Redis Enterprise architecture:

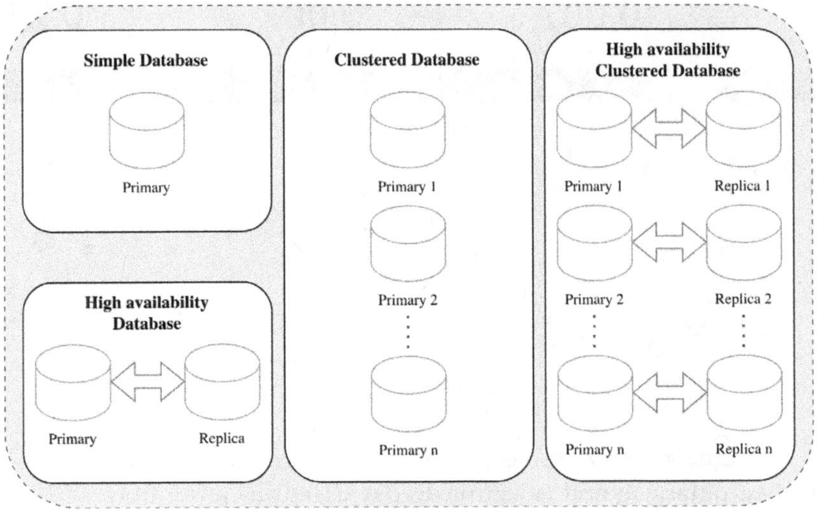

***Figure 8.28**: Architecture of Redis Enterprise*

As shown in *Figure 8.28*, there are four different types of configurations:

- On the left top, a simple database or single shard.
- On the bottom left, a **highly available** (**HA**) database, where the backup of the primary database is created to ensure the database is always available in case of primary node failure, ensuring fault-tolerance and uptime.
- In the middle, a clustered database that has divided the database into small, manageable shards, managing a subset of the dataset.

- On the right, a highly available clustered database that ensures that the data is divided into small, manageable chunks for faster execution, and they are always available in case any node goes down.

Hands-on with Redis using Python

The following are the steps showing how to use Redis with Python:

1. Visit **https://cloud.redis.io/** and create your account using your email id.
2. Click on new database, select the free plan or paid plan based on the requirements, fill in the required details, and click on create database. The following figure shows the plan selector:

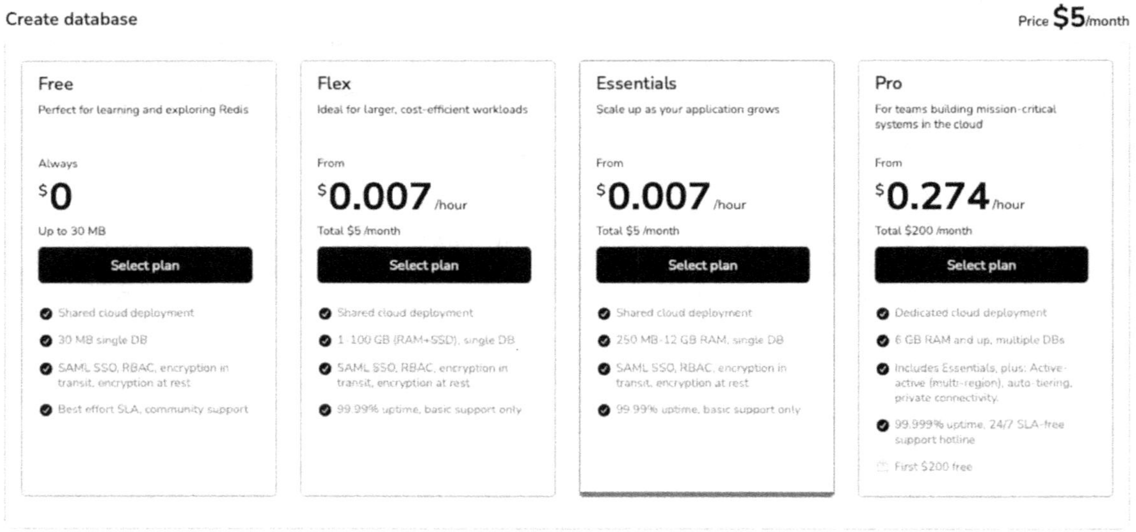

Figure 8.29: Plan selection view for creating the Redis database

3. When the database is created successfully, create the connection by clicking on **Connect to database** and selecting **Redis Client** as an option, and thereby selecting **Python** as the client from the dropdown. Refer to the following figure to see how to create a client:

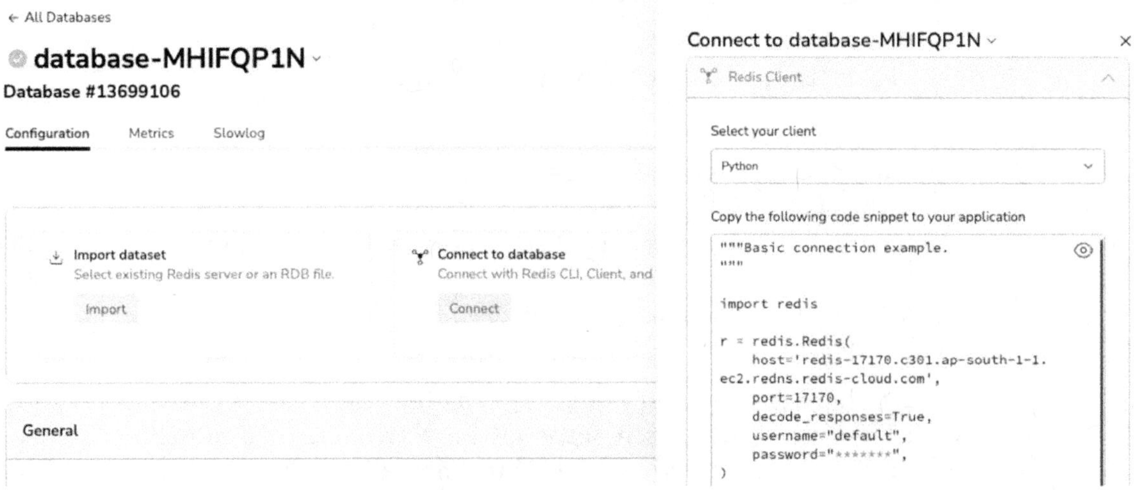

Figure 8.30*: Connect to database configuration view*

4. Copy the code and go to the Python development interface, where this code can be executed. Let us see the following operations on the Redis database using Python:

   a. **Connect with Redis and create a Python client:**

```
import redis
client = redis.Redis(
    host='redis-17170.c301.ap-south-1-1.ec2.redns.redis-cloud.com',
    port=17170,
    decode_responses=True,
    username="default",
    password="******",
)
```

   Result: The client creation is successful.

   b. **Create a school database equivalent and students table equivalent hash and insert the data**:

```
client.hset("school:student:1", mapping={"firstname": "Leonardo",
"lastname": "DiCaprio", "age": 7, "grade": "2nd"})
client.hset("school:student:2", mapping={"firstname": "Tom",
"lastname": "Cruise", "age": 10, "grade": "5th"})
client.hset("school:student:3", mapping={"firstname": "Harry",
"lastname": "Potter", "age": 12, "grade": "7th"})
```

   Result: Data will be inserted successfully

c. **Querying the data**: See the complete table

```
for key in client.keys("school:student:*"):
    print(key, "=>", client.hgetall(key))
```

Result:

student:1 => {'firstname': 'Leonardo', 'lastname': 'DiCaprio', 'age': '7', 'grade': '2nd'}

student:2 => {'firstname': 'Tom', 'lastname': 'Cruise', 'age': '10', 'grade': '5th'}

student:3 => {'firstname': 'Harry', 'lastname': 'Potter', 'age': '12', 'grade': '7th'}

Note: **Using `client.keys()` in a loop can block the Redis server when working with large keyspaces, as it scans all keys at once. In production, SCAN is preferred because it retrieves keys incrementally without blocking the server.**

d. **Querying the data**: See the data with a conditional statement (getting the results of students older than 8 years of age):

```
for key in client.keys("school:student:*"):
    student = client.hgetall(key)
    if int(student['age']) > 8:
        print(key,"=>", student)
```

Result:

student:2 => {'firstname': 'Tom', 'lastname': 'Cruise', 'age': '10', 'grade': '5th'}

student:3 => {'firstname': 'Harry', 'lastname': 'Potter', 'age': '12', 'grade': '7th'}

e. **Querying the data**: See specific fields (only first name and age):

```
for key in client.keys("school:student:*"):
    student = client.hgetall(key)
    print({
        "firstname": student['firstname'],
        "age": int(student['age'])
    })
```

Result:

{'firstname': 'Leonardo', 'age': 7}

{'firstname': 'Tom', 'age': 10}

{'firstname': 'Harry', 'age': 12}

f. **Updating the data**: Modify a specific record (change the grade of Leonardo to

3rd):

```
client.hset("school:student:1", "grade", "3rd")
print("\nAfter updating Leonardo's grade:")
for key in client.keys("school:student:*"):
    print(key, "=>", client.hgetall(key))
```

Result:

```
After updating Leonardo's grade:
student:1 => {'firstname': 'Leonardo', 'lastname': 'DiCaprio', 'age':
'7', 'grade': '3rd'}
student:2 => {'firstname': 'Tom', 'lastname': 'Cruise', 'age': '10',
'grade': '5th'}
student:3 => {'firstname': 'Harry', 'lastname': 'Potter', 'age':
'12', 'grade': '7th'}
```

g. **Updating the data**: Delete a specific record based on a condition (remove the students younger than 8 years of age):

```
for key in client.keys("school:student:*"):
    student = client.hgetall(key)
    if int(student['age']) < 8:
        client.delete(key)
print("\nAfter deleting students with age < 8:")
for key in client.keys("school:student:*"):
    print(key, "=>", client.hgetall(key))
```

Result:

```
After deleting students with age < 8:
student:2 => {'firstname': 'Tom', 'lastname': 'Cruise', 'age': '10',
'grade': '5th'}
student:3 => {'firstname': 'Harry', 'lastname': 'Potter', 'age':
'12', 'grade': '7th'}
```

h. **Delete table**:

```
# Delete all keys matching student:*
for key in client.keys("school:student:*"):
    client.delete(key)
print("\nAll student records deleted.")
# Optionally flush the entire DB
client.flushdb()
print("Database cleared (all keys deleted).")
```

Result:

- `All student records deleted.`
- `Database cleared (all keys deleted).`

i. **Close the connection**:

```
client.close()
```

Result: Redis connection closed.

Key features of Redis

Let us look at some important key features of Redis:

- **High performance**: Since all the data is stored in RAM, it has extremely low latency, which can easily handle millions of requests per second.
- **Multiple data structures**: Redis supports a variety of native data types as compared to simple key-value storage, such as strings, lists, sets, sorted sets, hashes, streams, and bitmaps.
- **Optional persistence**: Redis does not have a limitation to only be able to store data in-memory; rather, users get options to store it in secondary memory.
- **Scalability**: Redis cluster supports automatic sharding (data partitioning) across different nodes, enabling horizontal scaling with distributed data storage.
- **Pub/sub messaging**: It supports a publish/subscribe model for messaging between services, which is ideal for real-time notification, chat systems, and streaming apps.

Introduction to Amazon RDS

Amazon **Relational Database Service** (**RDS**) is a managed relational database service provided by AWS. This is an offering as a service, which means it is easy to configure, operate, and scale without needing to worry about the underlying hardware, operating system, backup, and database software installation.

This service is available with popular database engines like MySQL, PostgreSQL, MariaDB, Oracle, Microsoft SQL Server, etc.

Architecture

Amazon RDS is built on a distributed architecture that is designed to deliver scalability, high availability, and fault tolerance, making it suitable for a wide range of database workloads.

These DB instances from Amazon provide the required infrastructure for the database, including CPU, memory, storage, and input/output operations, which are all managed by Amazon. The user is only responsible for the configuration of the database, whereas hardware, maintenance, and backup will be taken care of by Amazon.

RDS replicates the primary database instance across different availability zones, e.g., the primary database instance in one availability zone and the standby in another availability zone. When the primary fails, the standby takes over to ensure there is minimal downtime.

There is another version of Amazon RDS, called Amazon RDS custom, which is a special version that facilitates us in creating database instances as per our requirements. This means it is resizable and can have a variety of database types, customization in the operating system, etc. Let us see the following figure to understand the AWS RDS custom architecture:

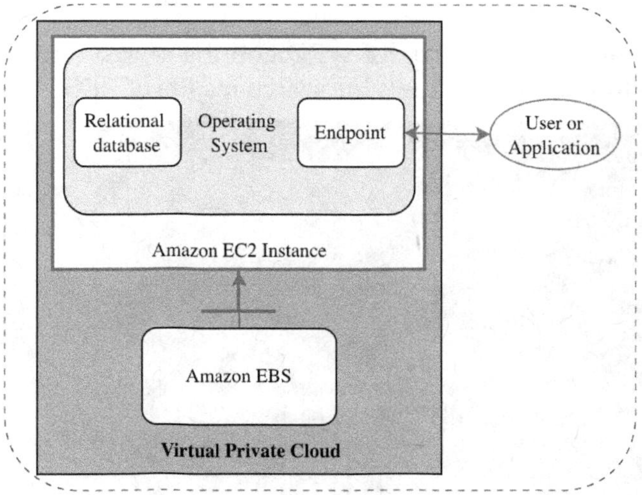

***Figure 8.31**: Amazon RDS custom architecture*

Figure 8.31 shows an RDS custom instance, where the RDS resides in a **Virtual Private Cloud (VPC)**. This custom DB instance consists of the following components:

- **Amazon EC2**: It is the virtual machine where the database runs. Access to this instance can be obtained using **Secure Shell (SSH)**, with which we can install additional software, change operating system settings, etc.
- **Instance endpoint**: This is the connection string or hostname using which any database client application or any downstream application can connect to and interact with the database.
- **Operating system**: This is the operating system image that is installed on the EC2 instance.
- **Amazon EBS storage**: This is called Elastic Block Store, which acts as a storage disk attached to the EC2 instance. This holds database files, logs, and the file system.

Configuration of Amazon RDS and hands-on with Python

Let us look at the following steps to understand the configuration of Amazon RDS:

1. Visit **https://aws.amazon.com/** and sign up with any email id by clicking **Create Account** and filling in the required details.

   Note: **The user may have to set up payment information, even for a free account, at the start.**

2. Go to the home page and search for RDS on the search screen, click on **Aurora and RDS**. The following figure shows the search results of RDS:

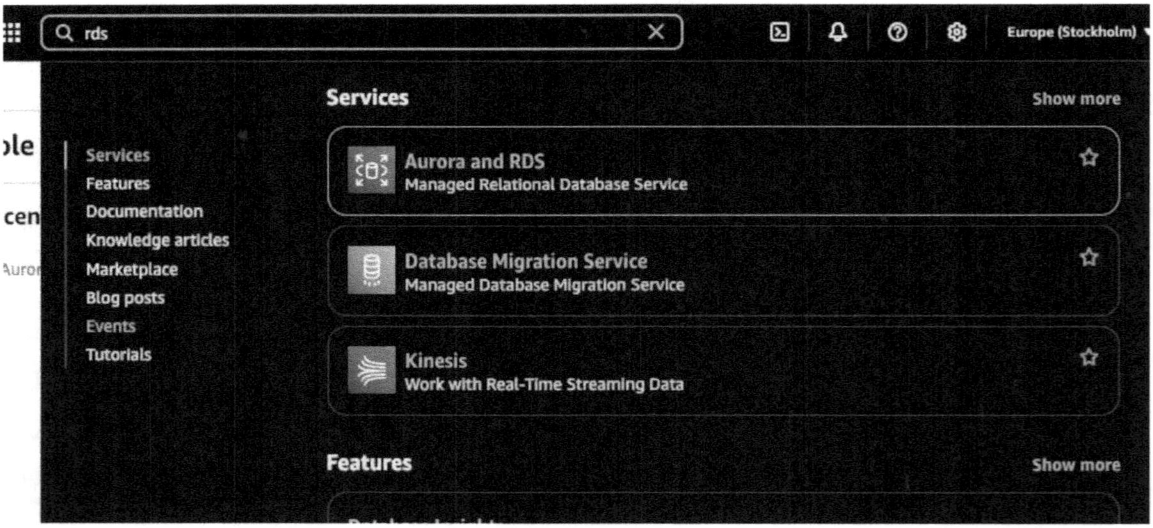

Figure 8.32: Search view in AWS console

3. Click on **DB Instances (0/40)** and click on **Create Database** and select **MySQL**; you may select any other database of your choice based on the requirements. Refer to the following figure:

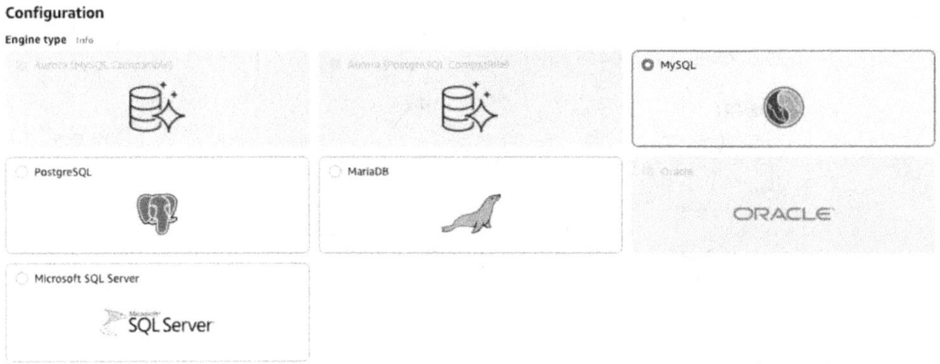

Figure 8.33: Database selection page in AWS console

4. Fill in the required details and click on **Create database**. The following figure shows how created database looks like after successful creation:

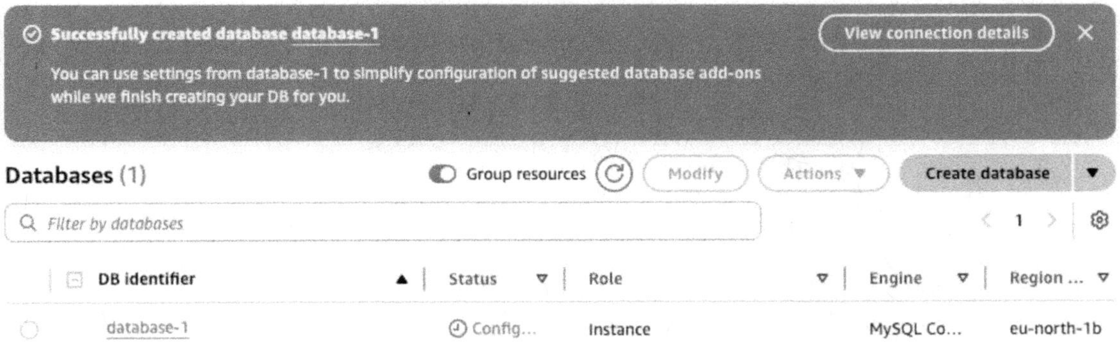

Figure 8.34: A successful database creation message and the database list view in AWS console

5. Click on **View connection details** and copy the **Endpoint**, username, and password.

6. Connectivity setup, make sure the database is **Publicly accessible** (if the need is to be used outside the AWS boundary) and has port 3306 allowed in the security groups **Inbound rules**. Refer to the following figure for the security settings:

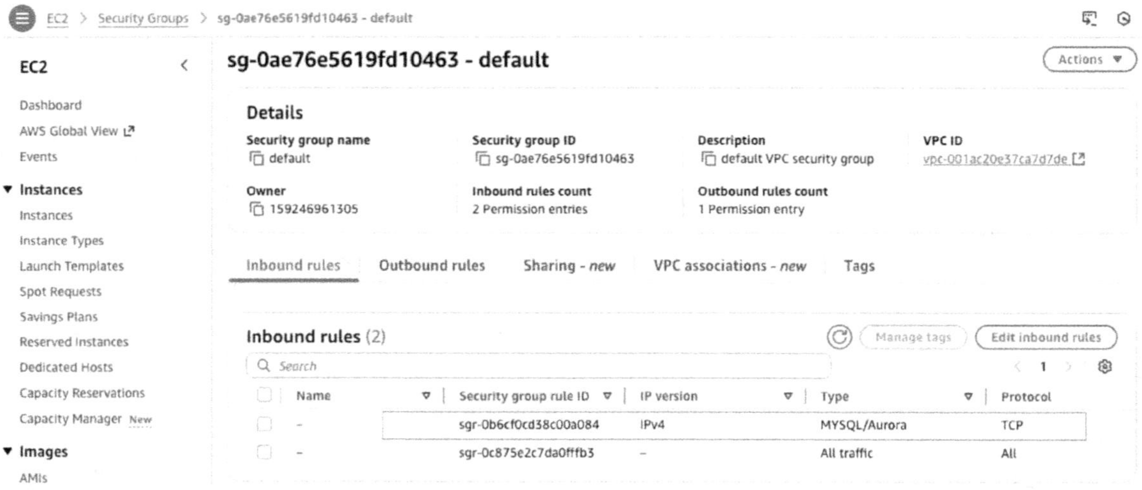

Figure 8.35: MySQL is allowed to be used from outside the AWS

7. Using the credentials, this MySQL can be accessed using Python, and the scripts listed in the following steps can be run:

   a. **Connect to AWS RDS (MySQL):**

```
import mysql.connector
from mysql.connector import Error
# Step 1: Connecting to AWS RDS MySQL
try:
    conn = mysql.connector.connect(
        host="database-1.cdicwgq66zfa.eu-north-1.rds.amazonaws.com",
        user="admin",                    # master username
        password="*****",                # RDS password
        database="mysql"        # Connect to default MySQL schema first
    )
    if conn.is_connected():
        print("Connected to AWS RDS MySQL successfully!")
except Error as e:
    print("Error while connecting to MySQL:", e)
```

   Result: Connection is successful.

   b. **Create a new database school and a table students:**

```
cursor = conn.cursor()
# Create database
```

```
cursor.execute("CREATE DATABASE IF NOT EXISTS school;")
print("Database 'school' created successfully!")
# Switch to new database
cursor.execute("USE school;")
# Create table
cursor.execute("""
CREATE TABLE IF NOT EXISTS students (
    rollnumber INT AUTO_INCREMENT PRIMARY KEY,
    firstname VARCHAR(50),
    lastname VARCHAR(50),
    age INT,
    grade VARCHAR(10)
);
""")
print("Table 'students' created successfully!")
```

Result: Database school and table students are created.

c. **Insert data into the table**:

```
# Insert multiple records
insert_query = """
INSERT INTO students (firstname, lastname, age, grade)
VALUES (%s, %s, %s, %s);
"""
data = [
    ("Leonardo", "DiCaprio", 7, "2nd"),
    ("Tom", "Cruise", 10, "5th"),
    ("Harry", "Potter", 12, "7th")
]
cursor.executemany(insert_query, data)
conn.commit()
print("Data inserted successfully!")
```

Result: Three student records were inserted into the students.

d. **Querying the data**: See the complete table:

```
cursor.execute("SELECT * FROM students;")
rows = cursor.fetchall()
for row in rows:
    print(row)
```

Result:

```
(1, 'Leonardo', 'DiCaprio', 7, '2nd')
(2, 'Tom', 'Cruise', 10, '5th')
(3, 'Harry', 'Potter', 12, '7th')
```

e. **Querying the data**: See the table with a conditional statement (getting the results of students older than 8 years of age):

```
cursor.execute("SELECT * FROM students WHERE age > 8;")
rows = cursor.fetchall()
for row in rows:
    print(row)
```

Result:

```
(2, 'Tom', 'Cruise', 10, '5th')
(3, 'Harry', 'Potter', 12, '7th')
```

f. **Querying the data**: See specific columns of the table (only first name and age):

```
cursor.execute("SELECT firstname, age FROM students;")
rows = cursor.fetchall()
for row in rows:
    print(row)
```

Result:

```
('Leonardo', 7)
('Tom', 10)
('Harry', 12)
```

g. **Updating the data**: Modify a specific record (change the grade of Leonardo to 3rd):

```
cursor.execute("UPDATE students SET grade = '3rd' WHERE firstname
= 'Leonardo';")
conn.commit()
print("\nAfter updating Leonardo's grade:")
cursor.execute("SELECT * FROM students;")
for row in cursor.fetchall():
    print(row)
```

Result:

```
(1, 'Leonardo', 'DiCaprio', 7, '3rd')
(2, 'Tom', 'Cruise', 10, '5th')
(3, 'Harry', 'Potter', 12, '7th')
```

h. **Updating the data**: Delete a specific record based on a condition (Remove the students younger than 8 years of age):

```
cursor.execute("DELETE FROM students WHERE age < 8;")
conn.commit()
print("\nAfter deleting students with age < 8:")
cursor.execute("SELECT * FROM students;")
for row in cursor.fetchall():
    print(row)
```

Result:

```
(2, 'Tom', 'Cruise', 10, '5th')
(3, 'Harry', 'Potter', 12, '7th')
```

i. **Delete the table and database**:

```
cursor.execute("DROP TABLE IF EXISTS students;")
print("Table 'students' dropped successfully!")
cursor.execute("DROP DATABASE IF EXISTS school;")
print("Database 'school' dropped successfully!")
```

Result: Both the table and the database were deleted.

j. **Close the connection**:

```
cursor.close()
conn.close()
print("Connection closed successfully!")
```

Result: Connection to AWS RDS MySQL closed properly.

Key features of AWS RDS

Let us look at the following key features of AWS RDS:

- **Fully managed service**: Since AWS handles database setup, patching, backups, and recovery automatically, it reduces administrative overhead, and developers can focus on application building, not maintenance.
- **Multi-engine support**: RDS is not limited to a single database engine but supports multiple well-known database engines such as MySQL, Maria, PostgreSQL, etc.
- **Scalability**: RDS supports both vertical and horizontal scaling. It can be vertically scaled by increasing the CPU, memory, storage, etc. And to scale horizontally, read replicas can be created to distribute read traffic across multiple instances.
- **Cross-region replication**: RDS supports cross-region replication, where data can be replicated across different regions, ensuring disaster recovery, data locality, and

compliance adherence. This feature is very useful to create applications that are needed to be globally available with low latency.

- **Monitoring and performance insights**: RDS provides monitoring through Amazon CloudWatch, which helps in tracking important metrics such as CPU usage, memory consumption, etc. This helps in understanding the behavior of the system, which supports taking scalability-related decisions or optimizations in required areas.

Introduction to Amazon Redshift

Amazon Redshift is a fully managed data warehouse offered by Amazon, which is scalable up to petabytes of data processing. This helps the data analysts to focus on their deliverables rather than worrying about the management of the entire data warehouse. It enables near-real-time analytics by easily integrating with streaming services, operational databases, and third-party applications without setting up a dedicated data pipeline.

Architecture

In this section, we will see what all the components of Redshift are and how they interact with each other to process the queries in an efficient manner. The following figure shows the architecture of AWS Redshift and its major components:

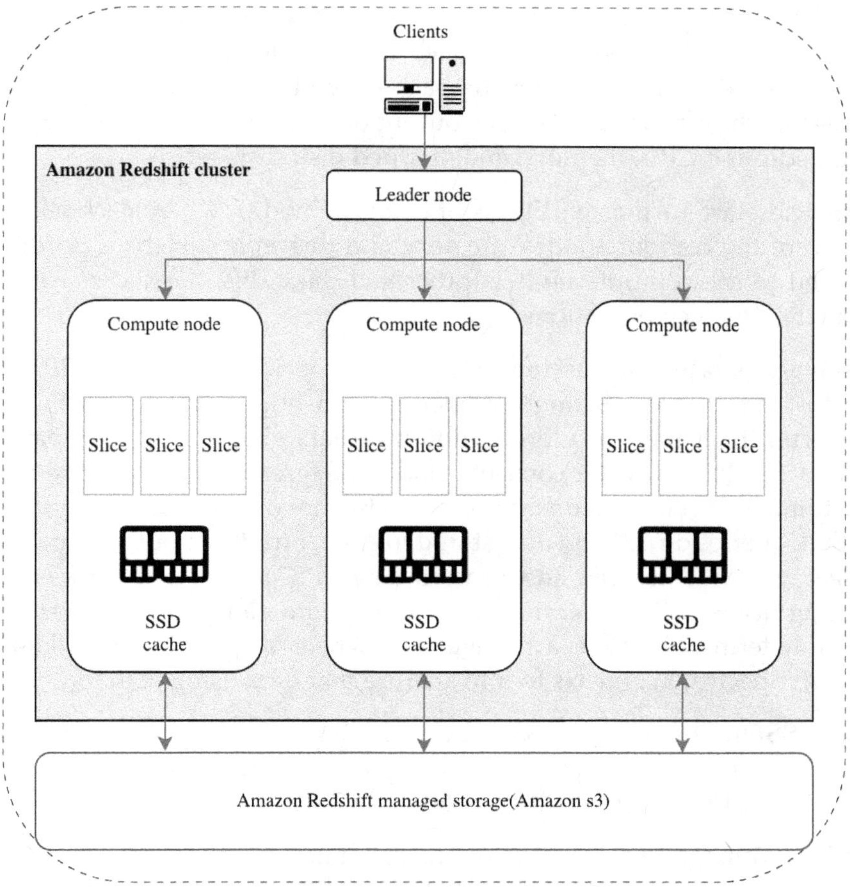

***Figure 8.36**: Architecture of Redshift*

As shown in *Figure 8.36*, these are the following major components:

- **Client applications**: These are the third-party applications that interact with Redshift for any data loading, ETL, any business intelligence reporting, or any other analytics needs. Amazon Redshift is based on the open standard PostgreSQL, so existing SQL-based applications will have minimal changes at their end. All these client applications will interact via the leader node only.

- **Clusters**: This is a core infrastructure component of Redshift data warehouse that consists of at least one compute node and a leader node.

- **Leader node**: A leader node manages the communication between client nodes and all compute nodes. For any query received, it plans the execution by distributing the compiled code to the compute node and then assigning slices of data to each compute node to process the query result.

- **Compute node**: This is a node where the query is executed. The compute node runs the compiled code (sent by the Leader node after planning and code compiling) and sends the intermediate results back to the leader node. The leader node finally aggregates the results based on the output of each compute node. Each compute node has a dedicated CPU, memory, and mapped disk storage.
- **Slice**: These are further partitions of compute nodes, where each slice is allocated a portion of the compute nodes' memory and disk space. Here, a portion of the work assigned to the compute node is processed. Like this, the slices work in parallel to complete the given operations.
- **Massively parallel processing (MPP)**: Amazon Redshift uses MPP architecture for speed of processing of complex queries with huge data, where multiple compute nodes run the same query on a portion of data given to them in parallel, and then the end result from each compute node is aggregated to generate the final result. Additionally, Amazon Redshift Spectrum feature of Amazon Redshift allows users to run SQL queries directly on data stored in Amazon S3 without moving it into Redshift. It leverages MPP to scan and process data in S3 in parallel across multiple nodes, enabling fast, scalable querying while reducing data movement, cost, and load time. In simple terms, S3 acts as a storage layer where large amounts of data are kept, and Redshift Spectrum connects to it to analyze that data using SQL.
- **Cache (SSD)**: These are the SSD caches in Redshift, which are used to speed up the query performance by keeping frequently accessed data close to compute nodes, so it doesn't have to fetch from slower storage.
- **Redshift Manage Storage (RMS)**: The full dataset in the Redshift data warehouse is stored in a separate storage called RMS. Using Amazon S3 storage provides the ability for this data warehouse storage to scale up to petabytes.

Configuration of Amazon Redshift and hands-on with Python

Let us look at the following steps to configure Redshift on AWS console:

1. Visit **https://aws.amazon.com/** and sign up with any email id by clicking **Create Account** and filling in the required details.

   Note: **The user may have to set up payment information, even for a free account, at the start.**

2. Go to the home page and search for **Redshift** on the search screen, and click on **Amazon Redshift**. The following figure shows the search results of Redshift:

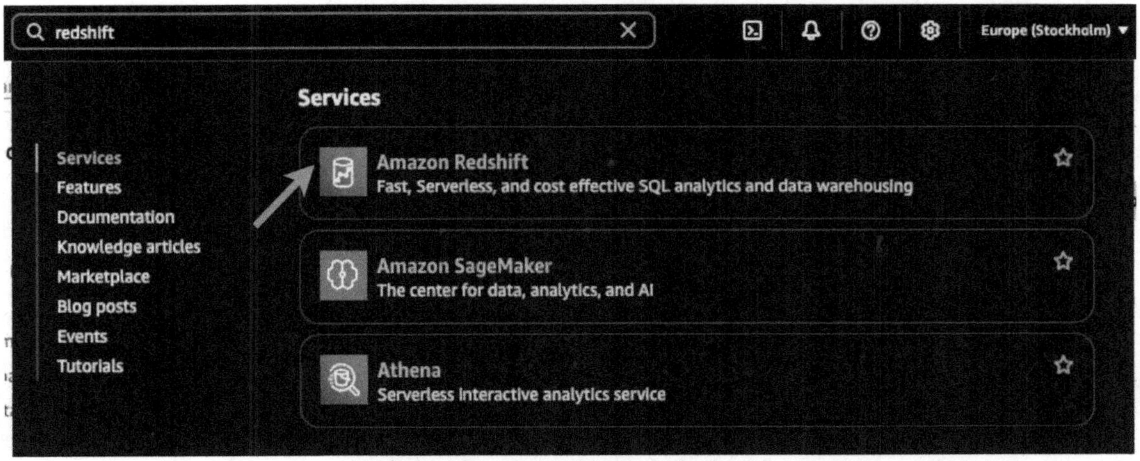

Figure 8.37: Search view in AWS console

3. On the landing page, click on **Try Redshift Serverless free trial**.

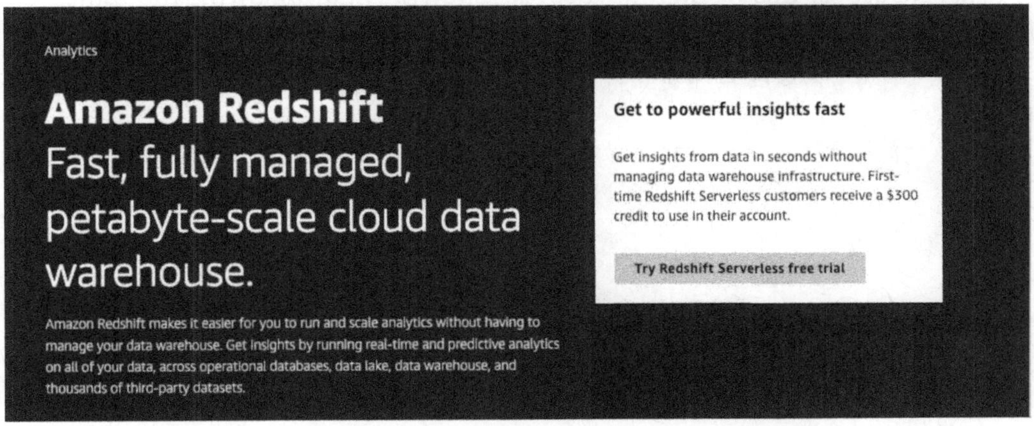

Figure 8.38: AWS page showing Redshift serverless free trial view

4. Fill in the required details and create a serverless instance. A dashboard can be seen, as shown in the following figure:

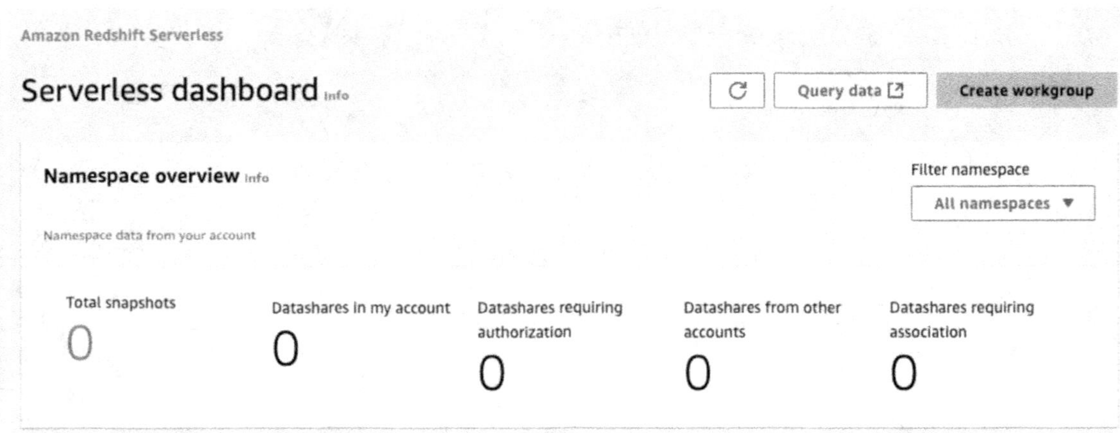

Figure 8.39: Default dashboard of AWS Redshift serverless

5. Click on **Create workgroup** and fill in the required details, and proceed. Also, create a namespace for this workgroup. See the following figure showing the namespace:

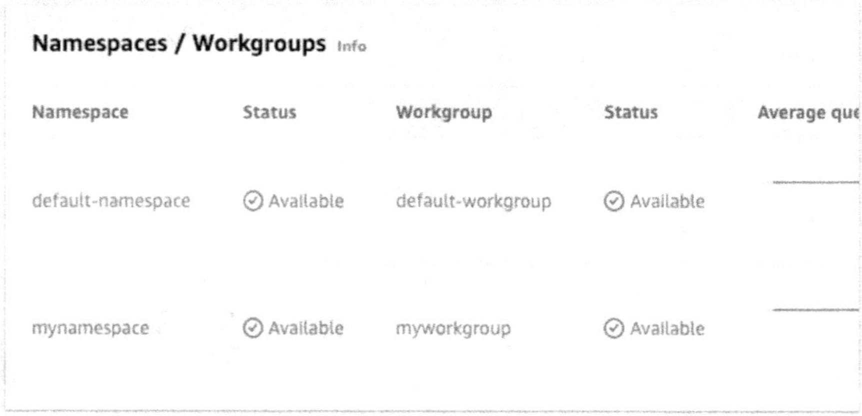

Figure 8.40: Namespaces view in AWS console

6. Go to the newly created workgroup and click on the **Data access** tab. Go to **Edit** and make **Publicly accessible** as **Turned On** and **Edit Inbound rules** to allow inbound connection on port 5439 with a specific IP or all IPs (not recommended). Refer to the following figure, which shows the network and security settings:

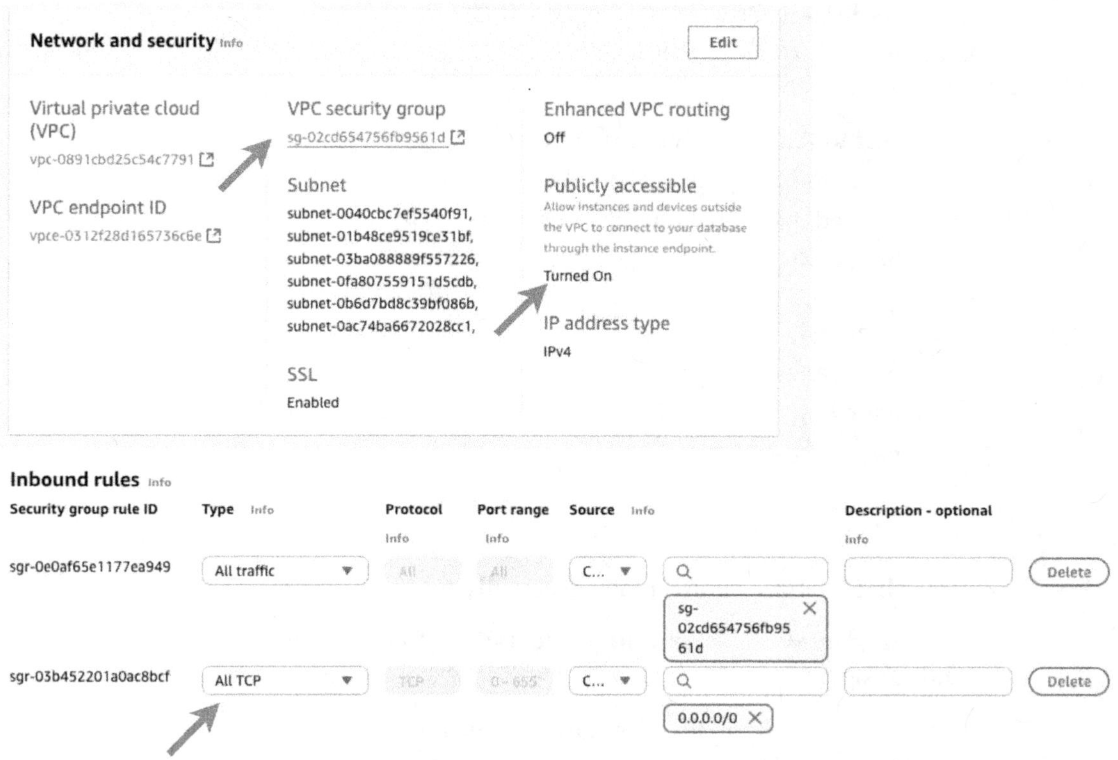

Figure 8.41: Inbound rules configuration view

7. Go to the created namespace and edit the admin credentials to create one for the connectivity. The following figure shows how to open **Edit admin credentials** page for configuring the connectivity:

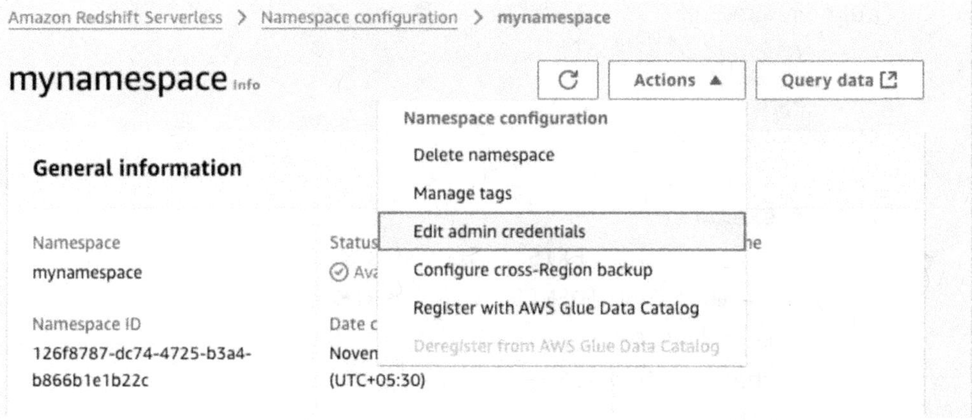

Figure 8.42: Figure showing the Edit admin credential option selection in AWS console

8. Using the credentials created above, this Redshift can be invoked using Python. The following steps show the Python command to connect with AWS Redshift and sample operation on the same:

   a. **Connect to Amazon Redshift Serverless**:

```
import redshift_connector
conn = redshift_connector.connect(
    host='myworkgroup.159246961305.us-east-1.redshift-serverless.
amazonaws.com',
    port=5439,
    database='dev',
    user='admin',                    # or your Redshift username
    password='*****'
)
print("Connected to Redshift Serverless successfully!")
```

   Result: Database connected successfully.

   b. **Create a new schema and table (since Redshift uses schemas instead of databases)**:

   Note: In AWS Redshift, the data is primarily organized using schemas within a database, rather than relying heavily on multiple databases as in systems like MySQL. A schema acts as a logical container for tables, views, and other database objects, allowing better organization and management of data within a single database.

```
cursor = conn.cursor()
# Create schema
cursor.execute("CREATE SCHEMA IF NOT EXISTS school;")
print("Schema 'school' created successfully!")
# Switch to the schema
cursor.execute("SET search_path TO school;")
# Create table
cursor.execute("""
CREATE TABLE IF NOT EXISTS students (
    rollnumber INT IDENTITY(1,1) PRIMARY KEY,
    firstname VARCHAR(50),
    lastname VARCHAR(50),
    age INT,
    grade VARCHAR(10)
);
```

```
""")
print("Table 'students' created successfully!")
```

Result: Both schema and table created successfully.

c. **Insert data into the table**:

```
insert_query = """
INSERT INTO school.students (firstname, lastname, age, grade)
VALUES (%s, %s, %s, %s);
"""
data = [
    ("Leonardo", "DiCaprio", 7, "2nd"),
    ("Tom", "Cruise", 10, "5th"),
    ("Harry", "Potter", 12, "7th")
]
cursor.executemany(insert_query, data)
conn.commit()
print("Data inserted successfully!")
```

Result: Records inserted successfully.

d. **Querying the data**: See the complete table:

```
cursor.execute("SELECT * FROM school.students;")
rows = cursor.fetchall()
for row in rows:
    print(row)
```

Result:

```
(1, 'Leonardo', 'DiCaprio', 7, '2nd')
(2, 'Tom', 'Cruise', 10, '5th')
(3, 'Harry', 'Potter', 12, '7th')
```

e. **Querying the data**: See the table with a conditional statement (getting the results of students older than 8 years of age):

```
cursor.execute("SELECT * FROM school.students WHERE age > 8;")
for row in cursor.fetchall():
    print(row)
```

Result:

```
(2, 'Tom', 'Cruise', 10, '5th')
(3, 'Harry', 'Potter', 12, '7th')
```

f. **Querying the data**: See specific columns of the table (only first name and age):

```
cursor.execute("SELECT firstname, age FROM school.students;")
for row in cursor.fetchall():
    print(row)
```

Result:

```
('Leonardo', 7)
('Tom', 10)
('Harry', 12)
```

g. **Updating the data**: Modify a specific record (change the grade of Leonardo to 3rd):

```
cursor.execute("""
UPDATE school.students
SET grade = '3rd'
WHERE firstname = 'Leonardo';
""")
conn.commit()
print("\nAfter updating Leonardo's grade:")
cursor.execute("SELECT * FROM school.students;")
for row in cursor.fetchall():
    print(row)
```

Result:

```
After updating Leonardo's grade:
[2, 'Tom', 'Cruise', 10, '5th']
[3, 'Harry', 'Potter', 12, '7th']
[1, 'Leonardo', 'DiCaprio', 7, '3rd']
```

h. **Updating the data**: Delete a specific record based on a condition (remove the students younger than 8 years of age):

```
cursor.execute("DELETE FROM school.students WHERE age < 8;")
conn.commit()
print("\nAfter deleting students with age < 8:")
cursor.execute("SELECT * FROM school.students;")
for row in cursor.fetchall():
    print(row)
```

Result:

```
(2, 'Tom', 'Cruise', 10, '5th')
(3, 'Harry', 'Potter', 12, '7th')
```

i. **Drop table and schema**:

```
cursor.execute("DROP TABLE IF EXISTS school.students;")
print("Table 'students' dropped successfully!")
cursor.execute("DROP SCHEMA IF EXISTS school CASCADE;")
print("Schema 'school' dropped successfully!")
```

Result: Table **students** and schema **school** dropped successfully!

j. **Close connection**:

```
cursor.close()
conn.close()
print("Connection closed successfully!")
```

Result: Connection closed

Key features of Amazon Redshift

Let us look at the following key features of AWS Redshift:

- **High parallel processing**: Redshift implements MPP, which enables fast running of complex queries on large amounts of data. Amazon Redshift distributes the rows of the table to the compute nodes so that data can be processed in parallel.
- **Columnar storage**: The data in the Redshift database is saved in a columnar approach by storing data in columns instead of rows, which improves the speed of processing analytical queries and reduces input/output operations.
- **Query optimizer**: The Amazon Redshift query run engine implements significant enhancements for processing complex queries by determining the most efficient ways to execute the queries, including operations like joins, aggregation, etc.
- **Result caching**: Amazon Redshift caches the results of certain types of queries in memory. If the user's query is already cached in the memory, then Redshift uses the cached result without having to re-run the query.
- **Data compression**: Since the data in Redshift is stored column-wise and each column contains the value of the same datatype, this allows very high compression ratios. This data compression reduces storage requirements, which leads to reducing the input output operations, improving overall query performance. When a user runs a query, Redshift reads compressed data from the disk to memory (which is faster because of its small size), and hence it takes less time moving the data from the storage disk to main memory. When the data is loaded in the memory, then Redshift uncompresses and works with it.

Conclusion

This chapter provided a comprehensive view of modern databases and their architectural differences, which include known names like Google BigQuery, MongoDB, Redis, etc. The information in these sections covers the basic technical understanding of each database in detail, with which the reader would be able to understand the fundamental working principles behind each database type and how they are able to achieve what they are meant to, be it huge storage, high availability, speed, etc.

This chapter also touched upon the basic commands, both SQL and NoSQL, that would be applicable to that specific database or data warehouse, and how these commands can be used in Python.

The next chapter will move to the application part of data, where different categories of data and their usage using various machine learning algorithms will be covered, along with the usage of these algorithms in real-world scenarios.

References

1. **https://cloud.google.com/bigquery/docs/introduction**
2. **https://cloud.google.com/bigtable/docs**
3. **https://sqlite.org/about.html**
4. **https://www.mongodb.com**
5. **https://www.geeksforgeeks.org/mongodb/mongodb-architecture/**
6. **https://cloud.redis.io**
7. **https://www.researchgate.net/publication/281629653_Performance_Comparison_of_NoSQL_Databases_in_Pseudo_Distributed_Mode_Cassandra_MongoDB_Redis**
8. **https://redis.io/technology/redis-enterprise-cluster-architecture/**
9. **https://aws.amazon.com/rds**
10. **https://aws.amazon.com/redshift/**
11. **https://docs.aws.amazon.com/prescriptive-guidance/latest/query-best-practices-redshift/data-warehouse-arch-components.html**

CHAPTER 9
Introduction to Machine Learning

Introduction

In previous chapters, this book has covered the in-depth details about the data generation, data processing, data storage, and how that storage affects the final business outcome.

However, all these activities are the roads to generate an outcome which helps customers take informed decisions, which will help them service their customers better or help their clients to serve their customers better. Another part of this road is **machine learning** (**ML**), which is often an integral part of these data-driven decisions. It helps computers to understand the power of data and learn patterns from data to support predictions and decisions.

ML is based on some statistical techniques and algorithms to find patterns in data and make predictions.

Unlike programming languages, where programs are written to generate results, ML learns a model (parameters) from input data instead of relying on hand-coded rules. It is essentially an automation of pattern recognition and decision-making without hand-coding every rule.

Structure

The chapter covers the following topics:

- Definition of machine learning
- Categories of data
- Algorithm selection framework
- Application of ML in the real-world
- Types of machine learning algorithms
- Introduction to MLOps

Objectives

At the end of this chapter, you will be able to understand the definition of ML and all the real-world applications of ML. This chapter will also cover different type of data that becomes the input for ML algorithms, and based on the data and business expectations, which algorithm to choose. This book will cover a high-level introduction to the different ML algorithms, which will give the reader an idea about the fundamental differences between these algorithms. These differences will provide a user with a framework to choose the type of algorithm, based on the known and unknown factors.

The chapter will also touch upon the concept of MLOps, which will provide an outlook on how an ML deployment merges with any existing or new application deployment at various automation junctures.

Definition of machine learning

A computer program is said to learn from experience E with respect to some class of tasks T and performance measure P, if its performance at tasks in T, as measured by P, improves with experience

– Tom Mitchell

In traditional programming, there is an input that goes through a fixed set of rules and produces some output. Any change in input will be processed by the same set of logic, and the result will remain determined based on the processing of the logic running behind. While in the case of ML, although the chosen algorithm remains the same, the model parameters change based on changes in the input data to reduce error, and hence the accuracy of the ML model improves.

Traditional programming: *Data + Code = Output*

Machine learning: *Data + Output = Code/Model*

So, to define, ML is a branch of AI that allows computers to learn from data and give predictions or results, and can improve as more data becomes available and the model is retrained or updated.

Application of ML in the real-world

Nowadays, ML-based solutions have become an integral part of our daily lives. Some of the examples are as follows:

- **Face recognition**: This is one of the best and most successful applications of ML, where face recognition has become a core part of our daily life. Right from unlocking our smartphones to clearing security in an airport has become easy. In fact, the CCTV-based image captures have been used to track suspicious people using face recognition technology.
- **Virtual assistants**: These are the 24/7 listeners that work on natural language processing. These devices understand our language and can work on our instructions. Some of the famous names in the industry are *Alexa*, *Siri*, *Google Assistant*, etc. In fact,

chatbots are being employed to resolve customer queries without needing a dedicated person, which saves huge costs and time of service and improves customer satisfaction.

- **Online fraud detection**: This is flagging the fraud in real-time, by looking at the pattern of the activity and finding out the suspicious activity. These are employed in financial institutions like banks, credit cards, other non-banking loan providers, etc.
- **Traffic prediction**: This is the application where the daily traffic data is collected and used for predicting the future traffic, based on the current flow of traffic. Some of the navigation apps like Google Maps, Apple Maps, and others, use these algorithms to provide users with traffic prediction and also help the application to find the fastest routes available in real-time.
- **Product recommendations**: Based on the history of the consumer's shopping behavior, visiting history on an e-commerce platform, the ML-based algorithms give the best suggestion of a product to the user, hence increasing the chances of purchasing the suggested product.

Categories of data

As we have discussed in the previous chapters, the data to be ingested in ML algorithms needs to have its categories identified first so that the appropriate actions can be taken. In real-life scenarios, data often comes with challenges such as missing values, class imbalance, data leakage, and noisy or incorrect labels. Identifying both the data type and these issues early helps in selecting the right preprocessing, validation, and modeling approach. Some of the categories are:

- **Labelled data**: This dataset contains the target variable/column/attribute for prediction. Using the label data, the ML algorithm is trained and tested.
- **Unlabelled data**: The dataset that does not have any target column or attribute; this is usually consumed in unsupervised learning algorithms.
- **Numeric data**: The dataset of the attributes that are represented by measurable values, e.g., weight, height.
- **Categorical data**: The attributes that represent the category, e.g., gender (male/female).
- **Ordinal data**: The attributes that are categorical with ordering, e.g., ratings (poor | average | good | best)

Types of machine learning algorithms

Although we know that ML is an automation of decision-making by using a data-driven approach. However, these automations are specific to use cases and employed algorithms.

The system learns from raw data to create a model, a function that maps **inputs to outputs**, or discovering **underlying structure** in the data etc., without explicitly writing a program.

For this, the machine needs to learn from the data, which can be done in fundamentally three ways, which are discussed in the following sections.

Supervised learning

This is a type of ML where the model is trained using labelled data, in which there is a relationship between input and output. The inputs are known as features or X variables, and the output is referred to as the target or Y variable, see *Table 9.1:*

Colour [X]	**Taste** [X]	**Fruit (Label)** [Y]
Red	Sweet	(Apple)
Yellow	Sweet	(Mango)
Orange	Tangy	(Orange)

***Table 9.1**: A sample dataset with labelled data*

In this modelling, a dataset is divided into multiple parts:

- **Training dataset**: This is the portion of the data (usually 80% of the dataset) on which the model is trained.
- **Validation dataset**: This is used to tune the model parameters and make decisions during training.
- **Test dataset**: This is the remaining data, which is used as a reference to check and validate how the model is behaving or predicting on unseen data. This data should remain untouched during training and tuning.

The labelled data has features, and the target, and supervised learning uses different algorithms to learn the relationship between the features and the target from the dataset.

Figure 9.1 shows the working of a supervised model where the input raw data is passed to the algorithm along with the labels, and the model is trained. After this model is trained, any dataset passed to this model will give the results based on the trained data. Later, this input data can be changed or updated, and the algorithm can be fine-tuned to get the results that are closer to reality.

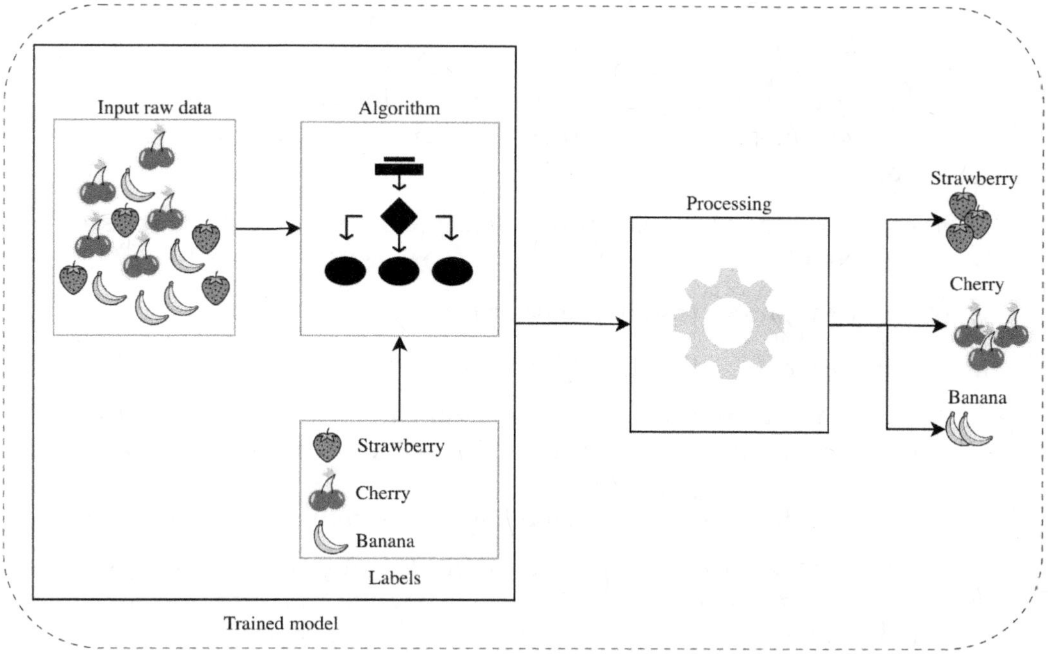

***Figure 9.1**: A visual representation of a supervised learning algorithm*

There are two types of supervised learning algorithms:

- **Classification**: These are the algorithms that have the output as categorical values. This means the output of the model has to be in one of the defined categories, e.g., classifying the email into the spam or non-spam category.

  Classification = categories (discrete output)

  In classifications, we may have multiple algorithms that can be used for classifying the output:

  - **Logistic regression**: This algorithm draws a straight line that separates two different groups, e.g., classifying the email as spam or not spam.
  - **Decision tree**: This algorithm makes the decision like a flowchart, e.g., if the speed is greater than 80 kmph, then the car is fast, else not fast.
  - **Random forest**: It takes many decision trees and checks the majority of votes based on individual outputs.
  - **K-nearest neighbors (KNN)**: This algorithm looks around to see the majority, to give the label, e.g., if the majority of people standing are male, then the target object will also be classified as male.
  - **Naïve Bayes**: This is a probabilistic model, which calculates the probability to generate the outcome, e.g., for a product review, if too many bad words are

used, then a negative review, or if many good words are used, then a positive review.

- **Support vector machine (SVM)**: This algorithm finds the widest boundary between the classes to categorize them clearly, e.g., separate red dots from green dots using the widest margin.

- **Regression**: These are the algorithms that predict the values, not classes, e.g., risk score for a credit card application.

  Regression = numbers (continuous output)

  In regression, we have different algorithms, such as:

  - **Linear regression**: It draws a straight line to find the relationship between independent variables and dependent variables to train the model, based on which it predicts the number, e.g., predicting the price of the house by taking inputs such as house size, number of rooms, bathrooms, etc.
  - **Polynomial regression**: It is an extension of linear regression, which draws a curved line instead of a straight line to find the non-linear relationship between independent and dependent variables while model training, and hence used to predict the output, e.g., predict the mileage of the car as the car gets older.
  - **Stepwise regression**: It is an algorithm that fine-tunes the model by adding or removing features. It has two steps of working:
    - **Forward selection**: It starts with no feature selection and keeps adding variables one by one, and checks the model's result. If the results are improving by adding the variable, it will keep the added feature; else, it will discard the features that are not adding any value. Once the model is ready, it can be used to predict a number based on the training.
    - **Backward elimination**: In this, the model starts by adding all the features by default and removes them one by one. If removing one feature does not affect the model's output and it is still predicting a good value, then that feature will be removed, and like this, the model is left with only the necessary variables that affect the model. This is how a model is trained with the bare minimum variables or features that can help the model predict the correct values.

    This model can be used to predict the price of any house, given the independent variables such as room, area, etc.
  - **Decision tree regression**: Predicting a number based on the flowchart, e.g., predict the salary based on experience.
  - **Random forest regression**: This algorithm uses many decision trees and calculates the average of the results, e.g., predicting the temperature of the next day.

- **Gradient Boosting regression (XG Boost)**: This builds multiple trees one after another to reduce the errors, e.g., flight fare prices with high accuracy.
- **K-nearest neighbour regression**: This algorithm finds the values of the neighbours and calculates the average to predict the final outcome, e.g., predict the weight of a person based on the nearest similar people.
- **Support vector regression**: This algorithm finds the best boundary line so that most of the points stay close to it and hence the model predicts the correct value, e.g., predicting the stock price in a smooth line.

Unsupervised learning

Unsupervised learning is a type of learning where the dataset does not have labels or predefined outputs. It is raw data, without any category, any tagging, or any correct answer. The algorithms just do pattern extraction from raw data and convert them into certain groups based on their similarity attributes and distance between them; the number of groups is typically not known upfront and may depend upon algorithm/parameters.

As shown in *Table 9.2*, there is no Y or labelled data but only the raw data. In this learning, the algorithm is left to do the autonomous identification of the innate structure of data that has not been labelled.

Color	Taste
Red	Sweet
Yellow	Sweet
Orange	Tangy

Table 9.2*: A sample dataset without labelled data*

Note: **This often requires human intervention to validate the output of the algorithm.**

There are several types of unsupervised algorithms:

- **Clustering**: It is the grouping of items based on common properties or identifying the structure or pattern in data. For example, identifying the customers with similar buying habits.

  As shown in *Figure 9.2*, the fundamental difference between classifications and clustering is that the number of clusters that will be created cannot be known, as opposed to classification, where the final outcome will be from the given set of categories only:

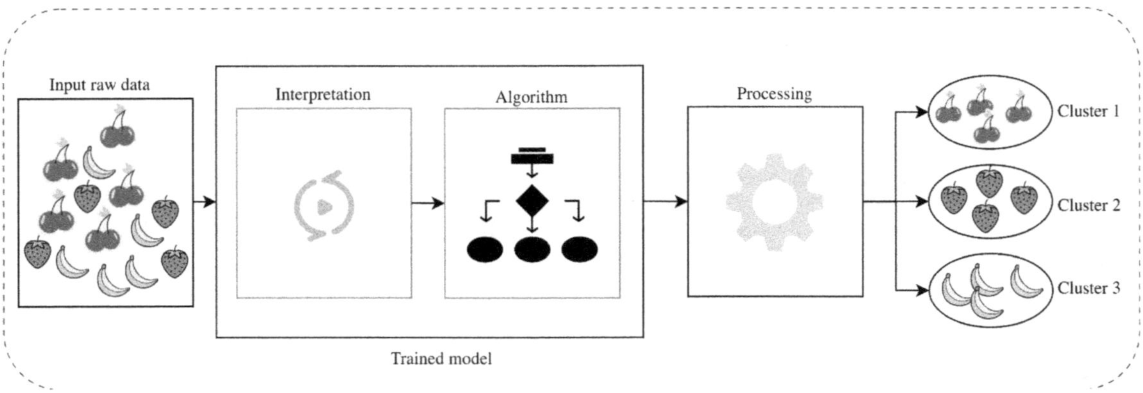

Figure 9.2: *A visual representation of an unsupervised learning algorithm (clustering)*

There are many clustering algorithms available, out of which k-means, **Density-Based Spatial Clustering of Applications with Noise** (**DBSCAN**), and **Gaussian Mixture Model** (**GMM**) are the ones that are majorly used.

- **Association rule mining**: This is an algorithm that works on raw data to find the general association between things and gives the output. Since the output is not fixed or identified, it comes in the category of unsupervised. For example, while shopping on Amazon, when a buyer selects a product, they also get the recommendation of the items that are generally bought along with the primary item. This is suggested by doing market basket analysis. This algorithm does not care about the similarity of the products but about the outcome of the historical transactions. For example, recommending the screen guard, back cover with a smartphone as frequently bought together, or recommending a mouse and backpack with any laptop purchase, etc.
- **Anomaly detection**: Finding the set of data that stands out as abnormal or outliers, e.g., this is used in finding the fraud in millions of transactions, where the algorithm predicts the unusual activity and flags it out as potential fraud activity.
- **Collaborative filtering**: This algorithm finds the similarities between the target objects and recommends the next best thing. For example, on several e-commerce websites, the ML algorithms find people who have common tastes and recommend the products based on their similar buying habits. On the other hand, there is an item-based similarity as well, which is, among the available items, which items are of possible interest to a user who has already bought something similar earlier. The item bought earlier is going to dictate the next item. For example, *Netflix* gives recommendations for movies of a similar taste that the user has already watched. It is independent of the user's taste but is similar to the earlier watched movie.
- **Principal component analysis (PCA)**: It is a popular technique to reduce the dimension of the data without using any labelled data or target variable. It reduces number of features by transforming the data into new uncorrelated components that retain most of the important information (variance).

For example, a weather station collects the following measurements:

Temperature, humidity, rain probability, cloud cover, and wind speed are the five features or dimensions. This data is to be used in an ML algorithm for the last ten years of each minute frequency, for the prediction of rain and wind. Since it will be a huge amount of data, it will require high computing and storage costs. We can now work on reducing the dimension so that only relevant features will go in the algorithm, and computation and storage costs can be saved.

To do that, let us assume the weather behavior as follows:

- o The humidity increases as the temperature decreases
- o Rain probability increases, and the cloud cover increases
- o Windspeed is an independent dimension

Using PCA, these five features can be transformed into a smaller set of components:

- o **Component 1** may combine humidity, cloud cover, rain probability, and temperature. This represents a general rainy weather pattern.
- o **Component 2** may mainly represent wind speed and is mostly independent of the other features.

This is all done using an unsupervised way. PCA is used in many critical areas, such as image compression to keep important features of an image with noise removal, stock market analysis by finding the important factors that affect the stock price, etc.

- **Feature extraction using deep learning**: It is a type of unsupervised feature extraction in which the features are extracted from raw data. This helps us avoid the laborious process of feature engineering, where we need to create features from raw data, which is time-consuming and not scalable. As a dataset grows with time, deep learning can quickly extract the pattern, making the entire feature engineering process fast and efficient.

Reinforcement learning

This is one of the most complex applications of ML. It starts without any background knowledge or labelled examples, and learns via interaction (trial and error) using rewards, rather than labelled training examples.

The algorithm in **reinforcement learning** (**RL**) focuses on how an agent learns to make decisions through several trials and errors. In this, the algorithm gets the output from the environment in terms of penalty and reward. The agent strives to accumulate as much reward as possible.

It has the following components:

- **Agent**: It is the core component of the algorithm that performs action and has been given a goal to achieve.
- **Environment**: The outside world, with which the agent interacts and which is responsible for giving the agent either a penalty or a reward.
- **State**: The current state of an agent.
- **Action**: The next logical move an agent takes.
- **Reward or penalty**: The feedback from the environment based on the agent's action.

There are many critical applications of RL, such as:

- **Self-driving car**: In which the car gets a reward for staying in the lane and gets penalties for a collision or a wrong move.
- **Netflix/YouTube/Amazon recommendation system**: In this, if the recommended movie/video/product has been liked by the user, then there is a reward, otherwise a penalty, etc. However, in real-world most recommender systems rely on supervised learning and ranking models, but reinforcement learning used only in limited or advanced settings.

Deep learning

Deep learning is another type of ML algorithm that uses multi-layer neural networks to learn patterns from data, especially for tasks like image and language processing. Deep learning is applied where decisions like classification and recognition are to be made, like humans. Areas like recognising the image of a dog out of all the animals or finding the next best pair of words after some input words, etc., are some of the examples of its application.

The structure of deep learning is based on the human brain, just as the human brain has millions of interconnected neurons to learn any information, identify patterns, and make decisions. Similarly, deep learning uses multi-layered processing nodes to work together.

A learning pattern of deep learning works on the same logic as a toddler, in which they are shown a dog and informed that the animal is a dog. If the child tries to say dog to another four-legged animal, let us say *cat*, then the parent says *no, this is not a dog*, and this is how the information is slowly registered in complex layers that the child creates in his brain to identify what is a dog and what is not. Similarly, the deep learning algorithms are given the data (images, text, etc.) and the labelled information around it, and it learns.

Deep learning has node layers, which are divided into three parts:

- **Input layer**: This layer is the one that is responsible for taking the input from the external world. This is where the data is fed to the model, and the number of nodes is dependent upon the size of the input, e.g., if the image of a dog is of 4x4 pixels, then there would be 16 input nodes.

- **Hidden layer**: These nodes may be called thinking nodes, which process the input data, layer by layer. They may have multiple layers inside, and each layer uncovers the pattern phase by phase. These are hidden, as nobody can access them and see what is happening within them. Each layer deepens the input data to classify the information given. For example, when an image of a human face is given, the first layer may find the edges or shapes; the second layer may be able to distinguish the eyes, nose, and mouth, and the third layer may be able to predict this as a human face.
- **Output layer**: This layer predicts the final outcome or takes the final decision.

Figure 9.3 represents how a handwritten text can be recognized using a deep learning method, in which each node or neuron in the algorithm works on **multiple inputs and multiple outputs** (**MIMO**) system, based on which a node or neuron can produce an output. This output is further input to the subsequent neurons, and hence, the final output is generated.

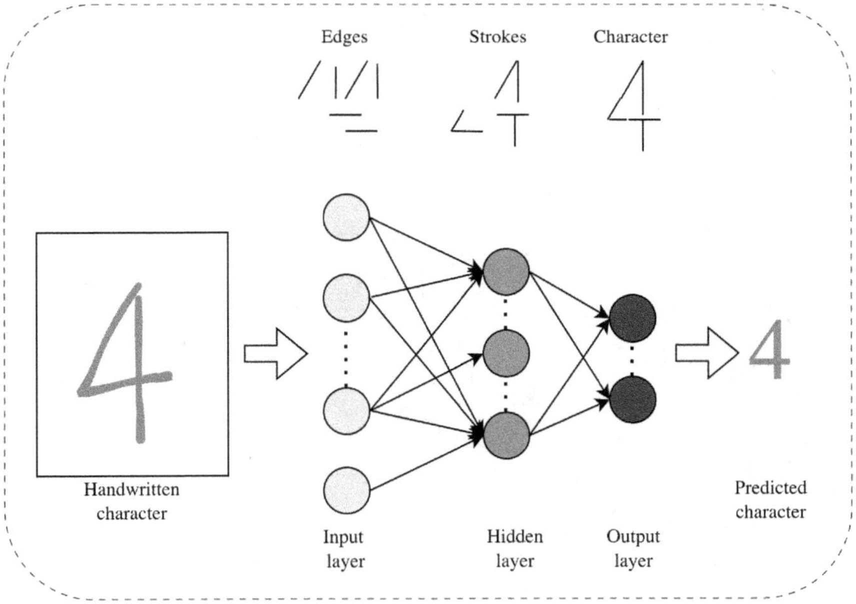

***Figure 9.3**: A visual representation of predicting a handwritten text in deep learning*

Deep learning has been instrumental in many real-world use cases, such as handwritten text prediction, image recognition, especially lane detection, traffic light detection, human detection in self-driving cars, face recognition for smartphones and security systems, and medical imaging, such as fracture detection, tumor detection, cancer detection, etc.

Algorithm selection framework

Although the selection of any ML algorithm primarily depends upon the use cases and the expected outcome, as a rule of thumb, a data engineer or data scientist can apply the following framework, which will help them to start with a strong foundation.

As shown in *Figure 9.4*, the first and foremost step to work is to collect and finalize the appropriate data:

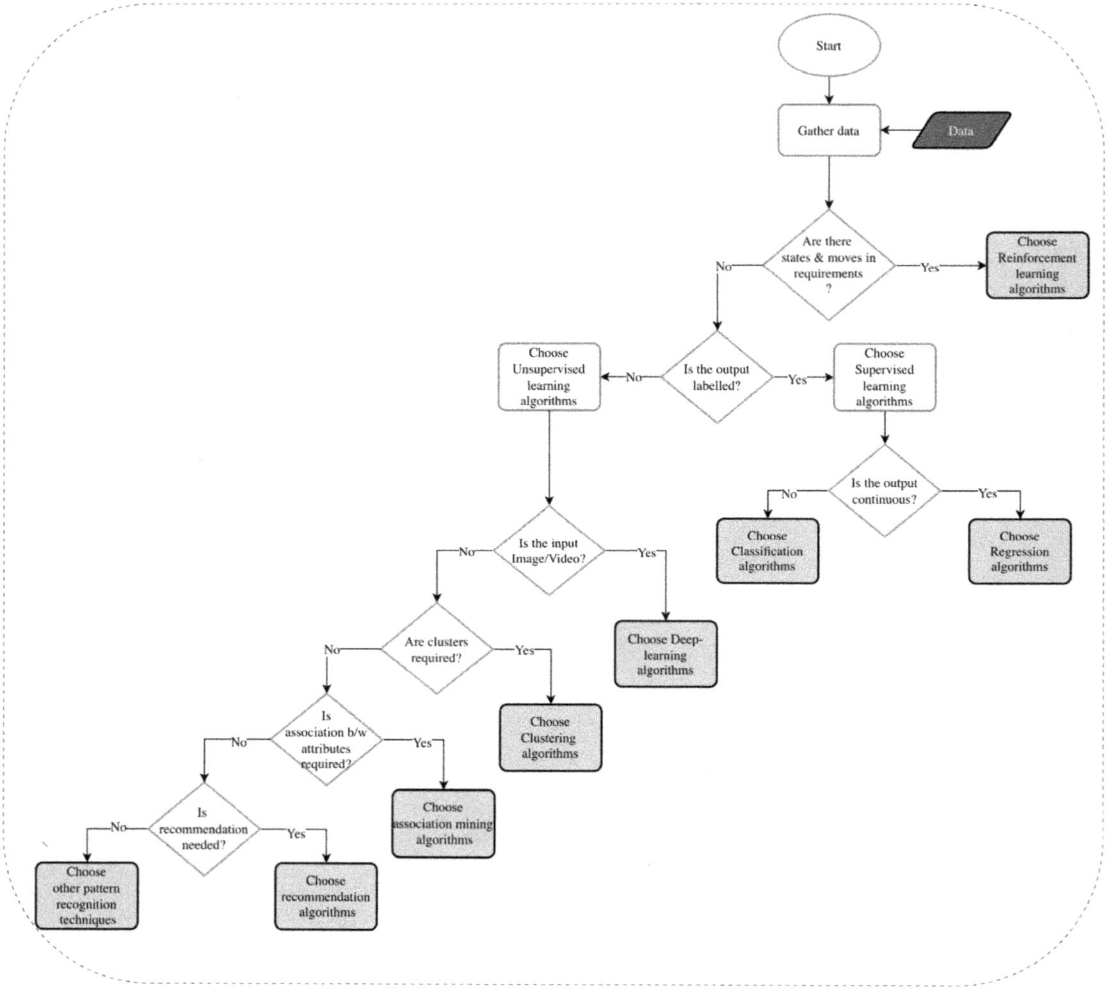

***Figure 9.4**: A flowchart to spot which type of algorithm to choose based on the data and business expectations*

Then, it should be checked if the requirement tells us about recording states and moves and achieving a goal, then reinforcement learning should be chosen so that the right algorithm can be selected to make it learn and improve. Otherwise, we should look at whether the data is labelled or not. If it is labelled, then check if the expected output is numeric or categorical. If it is numeric, then a regression algorithm is to be chosen; else, classification algorithms will be used.

As we discussed earlier, if the labelled data is not available, then we are left with an unsupervised way of working. Now, here, if the type of data is images or videos, then deep learning is often a good choice, though traditional methods may also work depending on the features, data size, and system constraints.; otherwise, we should revisit the requirements to understand the exact business expectations.

If it is asked to just find the available clusters, we can go with any clustering algorithm. As we know, we do not have any control over the number of clusters that the selected algorithm may be able to find; we may choose the limits of clusters, though. If the cluster is not required, then other outcomes like association identification, pattern recognition, or any other recommendation algorithm can be used based on the requirements.

In the data science world, there is no guarantee that the prediction done by the algorithm will be 100% correct, but still, the intention is to make the output as close as possible to the real-life output, based on which the required algorithm is chosen. For each category of algorithms explained above, there are multiple algorithms available that can be chosen and compared against each other to find the best-fitting algorithm to actual expectations.

Introduction to MLOps

MLOps can be defined as an approach to managing ML projects. It bridges the gap between the data scientists and the operations users, which helps them build a strong model that can be deployed reliably for the end use. In addition, a critical part of the operations phase is continuous monitoring and handling model drift, where model performance degrades over time due to changes in data patterns, requiring regular evaluation, alerts, and retraining to maintain accuracy and reliability. The following figure clearly illustrates the continuous and iterative nature of building AI systems. It breaks the process down into three main interconnected phases:

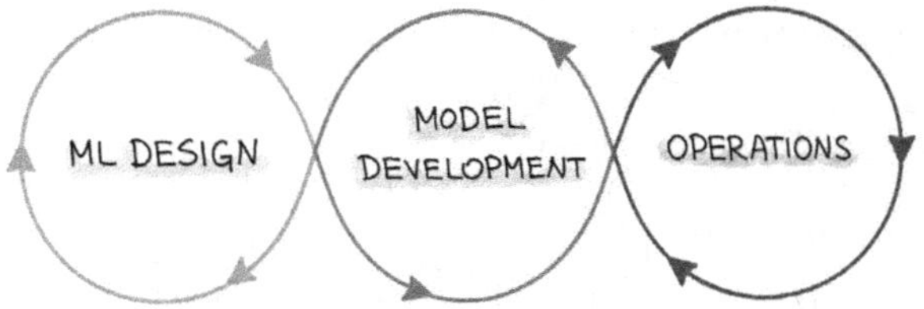

***Figure 9.5**: Shows a continuous flow, ML design to operations*

Figure 9.5 clearly articulates the fundamental cycle of ML in which the following phases are present:

1. **ML design**: This is a phase that is devoted to requirement understanding, data understanding, and design of ML algorithms. The objective of this step is to:
   a. Identify the potential user.
   b. Design an ML algorithm.
   c. Assess the potential development of the project, which focuses on increasing the productivity of users or increasing the interactivity of the existing application.

2. **Model development**: In this phase, the following things are covered:
   a. Data engineering.
   b. ML model engineering is completed, and the permutation and combination of the best hyper-tuning parameters are done to get the best score.
   c. Once the model is built, the testing and validation of the model are taken up, and various other optimization mechanisms are applied so that the expected result is closer to reality.
3. **Operations**: Focuses on delivering the developed model in production by using well-established DevOps practices that involve automatic model deployment, testing, versioning, continuous delivery. It also includes monitoring model performance and data drift, along with the governance practices like maintaining the model registry, ensuring reproducibility, and providing audit trails to track model changes over time.

The automation of the entire process plays a very important role here, and it shows the level of maturity of the ML project. The automation ensures the velocity of model deployment and also the retraining of the model.

This automation can be triggered manually, event-based, or at fixed schedules. They may also get triggered when a change in data is detected, which may, in turn, re-run the model for training for the new data, and hence the updated model will be redeployed automatically using this MLOps cycle.

The MLOps focuses on three key areas:

- **Manual process**: This is mostly the iterative process, which requires experimentation, such as data preparation, validation, model training, and testing, to be executed manually. They should be handled using **rapid application development** (**RAD**) using tools like Jupyter Notebooks.
- **ML pipeline automation**: This step is empowering the model to train itself automatically, which happens when there is a change in the data; the model should sense it and re-train itself with the newly added data (using strategies like incremental updates, sampling, curated versioned dataset). The next step, which is validating the model, should also be done automatically. Like **continuous integration** (**CI**) in software applications, **continuous training** (**CT**) can also be automated and be integrated with the target application. However, for production, it should include proper guardrails such as performance monitoring, approval gates and rollback mechanisms to ensure safe and controlled model updates.
- **CI/CD pipeline automation**: In this stage, the work is around deploying the model in a reliable manner, along with speed. The fundamental difference between the previous step and this step is that it automatically builds, tests, and deploys the data, ML model, and training pipeline components.

Key features

MLOps bridges the gap between building a model and actually running it reliably in business environment. The following are the core features that make it work:

- MLOps integrates the ML workflow into the traditional software application release cycle, which ensures faster, reliable, and automated deployments.
- MLOps enables the automated testing of ML artefacts that target data validation, ML model testing, and ML model integration testing.
- MLOps applies the agile principles to the ML output, which includes integrating them in a CI/CD approach. This reduces technical glitches, streamlines the delivery, reduces communication gaps, and hence smooth deployment and rollbacks.

Conclusion

This chapter explained briefly about ML and its various types of algorithms that are in use today. It also gave a clear perspective of how a data engineer should approach the problem statement and what the criteria are on which a particular algorithm is selected. It also covered the examples of ML-based products that are being used today as an integral part of human life. Finally, this chapter explained how ML models have integrated with the conventional software application delivery and how they can be merged together for quick and efficient deployments using MLOps.

The next chapter will cover the fundamentals of cloud computing, which will help the data engineer to think from the angle of an enterprise architect and decide which type of configuration is best for their business use-cases.

References

1. **https://cs229.stanford.edu/lectures-spring2022/main_notes.pdf**
2. **Master Machine Learning Algorithms - Discover how they work and Implement Them From Scratch by Jason Brownlee (z-lib.org).pdf**
3. **https://www.datacamp.com/blog/supervised-machine-learning**
4. **https://www.geeksforgeeks.org/machine-learning/types-of-regression-techniques/**
5. **https://www.geeksforgeeks.org/machine-learning/what-is-reinforcement-learning/**
6. **https://cloud.google.com/discover/what-is-deep-learning#**
7. **https://www.techtarget.com/searchenterpriseai/definition/deep-learning-deep-neural-network**

8. **https://www.newtownpartners.com/deep-learning-friends-for-handwritten-digit-prediction/**
9. **https://dlab.berkeley.edu/news/what-mlops-introduction-world-machine-learning-operations**
10. **https://bansalh944.medium.com/text-generation-using-lstm-b6ced8629b03**
11. **https://ml-ops.org/**
12. **https://ml-ops.org/content/mlops-principles**

CHAPTER 10
Understanding Cloud Computing

Introduction

For any data engineering project, as the data access, ingestion, processing, storing, and model creation are essential, at the same time, the deployment of the model that is created by this data is also important. The level of details, features that have been extracted from the data, will make the foundation of a machine learning algorithm or strong data analytics, but the availability, speed, and reliability of the data become imperative, especially when the organization has its teams, stakeholders, and clients spread across different geographies.

Since the end use of the developed application is the final objective, how and where they will be accessed will play a pivotal role, and when it comes to remote deployment or geographical level availability, the cloud is the concept that comes to mind first. However, given the hundreds of services in today's cloud ecosystems, teams need a clear understanding of core cloud concepts to choose the right components for the business objective and that brings the need of deep understanding of cloud components, how they are built, how cloud enables distributed access, faster deployment, elasticity for data/ML workloads and how they can be leveraged in order to help us achieve the final business objective of serving the customers even better than earlier.

Structure

The chapter covers the following topics:

- Definition of cloud computing
- Introduction to virtualization and hypervisor
- Containerization
- Operating system privileges
- Issues in cloud computing

Objectives

By the end of this chapter, this book aims to provide the reader with fundamental concepts of cloud computing, the core technology that backs the entire cloud computing industry, and what kind of business offerings or solutions are available in cloud computing. The reader would benefit from understanding the virtualization of the resources of the physical machines, including the network interfaces, and at what level the virtualization takes place. This chapter would also cover the basic difference between hardware-level virtualization and software-level virtualization. The readers will also understand how the privileges in operating systems work and how virtualization becomes part of the different privilege groups. Finally, the issues and challenges faced by the users when they opt for cloud computing will also be explained in this chapter.

Definition of cloud computing

According to the **National Institute of Standards and Technology** (**NIST**), cloud computing is a model for enabling ubiquitous, convenient, on-demand network access to a shared pool of configurable computing resources (e.g., networks, servers, storage, applications, and services) that can be rapidly provisioned and released with minimal management effort or service provider interaction. This cloud model is composed of five essential characteristics, three service models, and four deployment models.

Cloud computing is not a technology or framework but a model that defines the complete working capabilities of a cloud environment, which uses virtualization, distributed computing, networking, containerization, etc., technologies at its core to achieve the expected tasks.

Five essential characteristics

To better understand the cloud computing, it is important to examine the following essential characteristics:

- **On-demand self-service**: A user or consumer can provision the needed resources and capabilities based on their requirements, such as computing power, RAM, storage, and network connectivity, without any interaction needed with service providers.
- **Broad network access**: Cloud services are accessible over the network via standard mechanisms, supporting both public internet access and private connectivity models depending on application requirements. Which means, users can have their applications or solutions made available to the world without any geographical limitations or boundaries.
- **Resource pooling**: The resources are available to serve multiple consumers at once using a multi-tenant model. These resources are dynamically allocated and reassigned based on the demand, while maintaining strict isolation between the tenants. The resource allocation generally occurs within a selected region or availability zone, allowing customers to control data residency and compliance requirements.
- **Rapid elasticity**: This means the ability to scale based on the demand. It can scale horizontally by adding more instances when load on the application increases and reduce instances in case of a reduction of load. It can also scale vertically by increasing

resources such as CPU, RAM of a single instance, when the demand grows and scale them down as the demand reduces.

- **Measured services**: Most of the services of cloud are metered in order to monitor the usage and take the appropriate action to control and optimize the usage of the resources. These monitoring reports can be shared with the provider and consumer for billing, transparency, chargeback and cost optimization. E.g., storage space, network bandwidth can be measured to check how much of these resources have been used against the planned usage.

Service models in cloud computing

Based on the scope of responsibility, there are three types of service models in cloud computing:

- **Infrastructure as a service (IaaS)**: In this type of service model, the infrastructure is provided by the cloud provider that includes processing, storage capacity, network, and other basic requirements for the computing resources, where the consumer can deploy the underlying software, such as operating systems, dependencies, application software, patches, etc. They may have limited control over selected networking components such as network connections, firewall, URL restrictions, etc. Getting a virtual machine provisioned is an example of IaaS, such as **Amazon Web Services Elastic Compute Cloud** (**AWS EC2**), Google Cloud Engine, Azure virtual machine, etc. From the security perspective, the cloud provider secures the underlying infrastructure (such as hardware, networking etc.) and the customer is responsible for securing the operating system, applications, data, and configurations they deploy.

- **Platform as a service (PaaS)**: In this type of service, the cloud provider provides a ready-made platform to write the code on and run the application. Consumer does not need to manage the servers, networking, operating systems, patches, or any infrastructure as such, e.g., Google App Engine, AWS Elastic Beanstalk, Azure App Services.

- **Software as a service (SaaS)**: In this type of service model, the consumer is provided with the running application on a cloud infrastructure, where the consumer does not need to work on hardware, networking, or the application software at all, and just needs to consume the application for their usage. They can access the application using a web browser or an application that is installed on their machines or smartphones. However, there may be some configuration that may be possible with respect to accessibility, control, and user management of the application, but not from the programming or customization viewpoint, e.g., Salesforce, Google Workspace, Zoom, etc.

Note: **The application software may not necessarily be provided by the cloud provider; in fact, most of the service providers use cloud components (IaaS, PaaS) internally to create their SaaS products and provide them to consumers, e.g., Netflix uses AWS cloud infrastructure as its underlying infrastructure and has built the whole service model on top of it.**

Let us look at the following figure to understand the responsibility of work for different types of services:

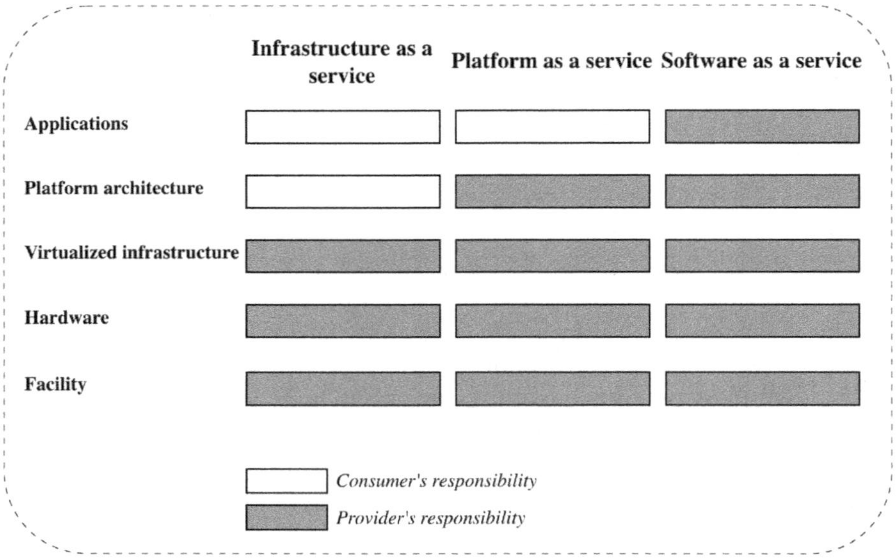

***Figure 10.1**: A representation of the scope of responsibility based on the type of service model*

As explained earlier, *Figure 10.1* clearly shows the scope of responsibility for each model and the type of services that are being offered in the respective model. For IaaS, the cloud provider takes care of the facility, hardware, and virtualization of the resources, but the operating system and the application running will be in the hands of the end user. On the other hand, in the case of PaaS, the end user focuses on developing their application on the existing platform without thinking of the infrastructure management. In the SaaS model, the end user is a consumer of the application that has been developed by an individual or an organization using IaaS or PaaS.

Deployment models

Based on the usage of the cloud components, there are four types of deployment models that are available:

- **Private cloud**: This is a cloud environment that is provided to a single organization only. This organization may have multiple business units and their respective users, but from an ownership point of view, it is dedicated to a single organization. This can be on-premises or located at the vendor facility, where full control is with the organization for high security and not shared with others.

In the case of an on-premises model, the cloud is extended to an on-premises environment where the physical servers are located at the customer's site, keeping all the cloud services operating within that ecosystem, e.g., AWS Outposts, Azure Stack, etc.

- **Public cloud**: The cloud infrastructure that has been provisioned to be used as a shared infrastructure amongst multiple consumers. It is situated in the cloud provider premises, e.g., AWS, Azure, Google Cloud, etc. The benefits of this kind of deployment are cost-effectiveness, scalability, and flexibility.
- **Hybrid cloud**: The type of deployment is a combination of both public and private clouds. It can also be the combination of the cloud provider's infrastructure and an on-premises data center at the customer's site. This allows the applications, services, and workload to be shared between the two in a smooth manner.

  This way of deployment offers great flexibility and control, in which customers can choose where to run their workload based on their specific security and performance requirements. This also helps them in optimizing the cost.
- **Community cloud**: The community cloud is provisioned for specific use by a specific community. This community may have several organizations that have similar requirements, security considerations, compliance, and similar community goals. This may exist in on-premises and vendor-provided environments as well.

  Government organizations may come in this category where they may have different sub-organizations using the community cloud, such as police, tax department, municipal organizations, etc., e.g., AWS GovCloud, Azure government cloud.

Introduction to virtualization and hypervisor

As we have understood earlier, cloud computing is not a technology or a framework, but a model, and it is dependent upon several technologies to make it possible to work, the way it is intended to be.

It is the virtualization and distributed computing that have made it possible to use the technologies as they are today. In fact, when the cloud is talked about, virtualization as a topic cannot be ignored.

Virtualization

Virtualization can be defined as the concept of creating a logical abstraction of the hardware entities. It abstracts physical resources by converting them into virtual resources that can be easily created, managed, and used.

On a high level, any physical machine has four components:

- CPU
- Memory (RAM)
- Storage (Hard disk)
- Network

There are other components also, such as memory bus, network bus, peripheral connection, etc., but on a high level, let us take the major constituents that are mostly talked about when describing any physical machine.

Each of the above physical components can be abstracted into a virtual entity and then managed as per the requirements.

As per *Figure 10.2*, we may have a physical machine with 32 GB RAM, 1 TB hard disk, and a 4-core CPU. This same physical machine can be logically separated into two virtual machines having same or different combinations of the components, such as a **virtual machine** (**VM**) may have 10 GB RAM, 256 GB hard disk and 2 core CPU and another VM may have 14 GB RAM, 512 GB hard disk and 1 core CPU and the remaining, 8 GB RAM, 256 GB hard disk and 1 core can be left with physical machine so that the host operating system can work properly for its general operations and allow both virtual machines to work, without any resource constraints.

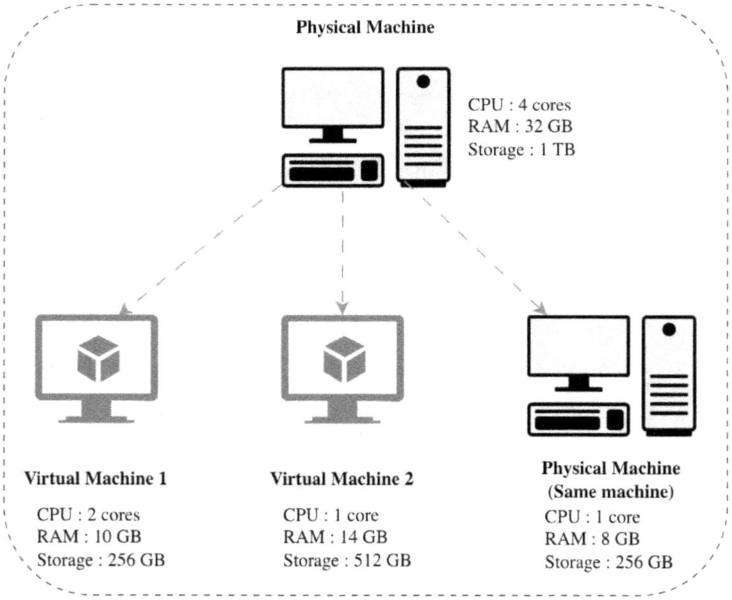

***Figure 10.2**: A representation of a physical machine converted into 3 partitions*

There are two types of virtualization possible today:

- **Operating system (OS) level virtualization**: In this virtualization, the host operating system creates a logical separation within the operating system so that different **guest processes** can run in parallel without interfering with each other. Although they do not interfere in terms of data access, networking, and users' management standpoint, all the guest processes share the resources of the same physical machine. This means that if one guest process needs more main memory and has been given memory, then the other may starve for memory. Since they are communicating directly with the host operating system and have fewer layers of communication, it is more efficient and has better performance.

As shown in *Figure 10.3*, it is evident that the host operating system isolates the guest processes without touching physical resources:

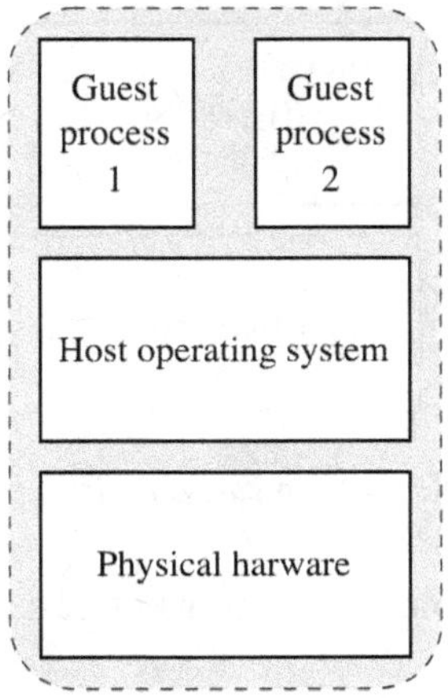

***Figure 10.3**: A representation of OS level virtualization*

Using containerized software, such as Docker or OS based user isolation, is one of the best techniques that is often used to achieve the OS level virtualization.

- **Hardware level virtualization**: In this virtualization, another layer of the operating system is created using hypervisors by distributing the components of the physical machines into virtual components such as virtual core, virtual memory, virtual network card, virtual storage, etc. The new operating systems sit on the new virtual machines created and allow the guest processes to execute with complete isolation from each other.

  The biggest advantage of this virtualization is that the physical resources are isolated, and once the virtual machines have been allocated the resources, there are no transactions of resources between the two virtual machines. This means that the load on one machine does not affect the performance of the other.

  As shown in *Figure 10.4*, the hypervisor is installed on the host operating system, which helps in allocating resources to the virtual machines. Once the virtual machines are configured, the respective guest operating systems are installed on those virtual machines. Eventually, the target applications can run on them in isolation.

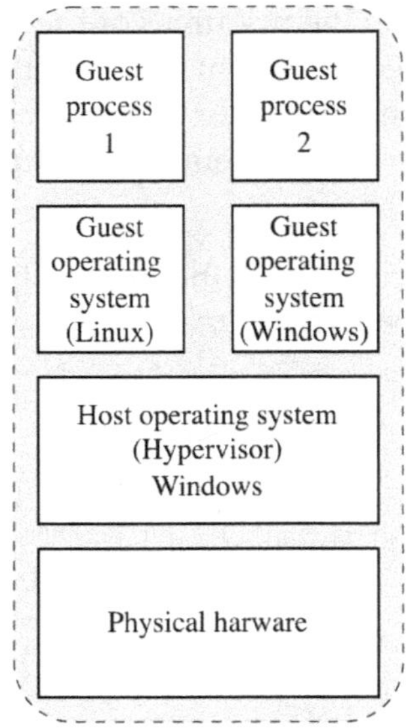

***Figure 10.4**: Showing hardware-level virtualization*

The virtualization software available in the market can be used for these purposes, such as VMware, Microsoft Hyper-V, etc.

In general, while creating the virtual machines, the engineer should take care of the resource requirements of the host operating systems too, which means the respective sum of all the resources of all virtual machines should be less than that of the physical machine resources.

If their sum is equal to or more than the resources of the physical machine, then it should be ensured that all the virtual machines are not run at the same time, else there would be resource starvation and the physical machine will hang, which will eventually make the VM also hang or crash.

Using the distributed computing technique, the resources from two or more VMs can also be combined and made into a single large virtual machine. In other words, workloads can scale horizontally across multiple VMs (clusters) and behave like one logical system. This type of scenario does not exist in real life, since the hardware is generally available in large sizes without the need to combine it in a distributed fashion, but conceptually, it is possible.

Hypervisors

The software tool that is used to create the virtualization is called a hypervisor. This divides one computer into multiple virtual machines. There are two types of hypervisors:

1. **Hosted**: These are the hypervisors that are installed over the top of an existing operating system (called host operating systems). These are generally used for personal use or testing of the functionality of the hypervisor. This is also called a Type

2 hypervisor. Some of the existing Type 2 hypervisors available in the market are VMware Workstation, VirtualBox, etc.

2. **Bare metal**: This is the type of hypervisors that run directly on the hardware without the need for any intermediate operating system layer. These hypervisors are fast and more secure since there is no layer between the hardware and the software. They are also known as Type 1 hypervisors, and all the cloud providers use Type 1 for the virtualization of their components. E.g., VMware ESXi, Microsoft Hyper-V, etc.

The following figure illustrates the architectural differences between Type 1 and Type 2 hypervisors:

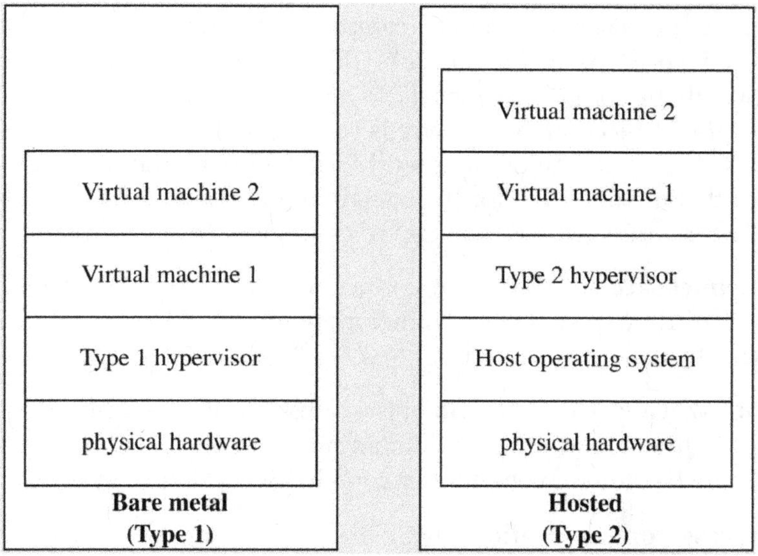

***Figure 10.5**: Figure showing the two types of hypervisors*

As it is clear in *Figure 10.5*, the Type 1 hypervisor can run directly on the physical hardware and has no layer in between, reducing the overall overhead of communication and thus increasing the efficiency. These require special skill and setup and are hard to manage manually. On the other hand, Type 2, which requires the host operating system as an intermediate layer between the physical hardware and hypervisor, is easy to install, test, and understand the functioning of virtualization techniques, but is slower, less secure, and not suitable for enterprise-level workloads.

Containerization

Containerization is an OS-level virtualization technique that creates a mini-isolated environment on top of the operating system. It is used to create an independent, isolated, and portable package for a software application or a model. This also creates the abstraction of the resources, but in a limited capacity.

Fundamentally, they are namespaces; in other words, they are separate, isolated worlds for a process. The processes inside the containers see their own version of resources and cannot see the other processes.

The following are the namespaces provided by a container, and all these entities are in the container and separate from the host operating system:

- **Process ID namespace**: Each container is a process in itself, but it can have multiple processes running inside it. Containers have their own process trees (Process control block), and only container processes specific to a container can be seen inside the container.
- **Network namespace**: Containers communicate over the network using a socket address, which is the combination of IP address and port number. External entity connects with the container via port forwarding, which is done from the host machine. For example, if the container service is running on port 5000 and the host machine is communicating with the outside world at 8000 port number, then all the incoming messages that are intended for the container will come via 8000 port and then will be internally forwarded to 5000 so that the container can act on them.
- **Mount namespace (MNT)**: Each container has its own dedicated file name space, which means they have their own hierarchy of file systems. There may be a different folder structure.
- **Unix time-sharing system (UTS)**: This namespace allows containers to have their own separate hostname and internal domain name. This way, each container can have its own identity without affecting other containers or the host system.
- **Inter-process communication (IPC)**: In a container, we can have more than one service running, such as a web server and MySQL, and these services can interact with each other using IPC namespaces just like an operating system. This communication may happen via shared memory, shared variables, shared filesystem, message passing, **remote procedure call** (**RPC**), and different methods are available for process communication within a container.
- **Users**: In containers, users are also isolated from the host operating system; containers can have their own set of users. Containers have their own user groups, control groups, and the user ID will define which user group a user belongs to, like the admin group, the concurrent user group, or the dedicated group. The level of authentication, isolation, and permission can be configured using a control group. We can have the same users in another container without any conflict
- **Control group (cgroups)**: This is the feature of controlling the resources like CPU, main memory, time, network allocation, and all the hardware resources. Limits can be applied to a particular control group. It keeps record logs of which user is assigned how many resources, controls the users, sets the priority for different uses, limits the

hardware usage, etc. The group is simply created, and then users are added to the user group, a name is given, and how much memory we want to allocate to that user group.

Note: **Containers do not create separate namespaces for CPU, memory, and storage; they share these from the host machine. Since the resource level separation is not there, the processing load on one container can affect the processing of the other container.**

Container creation is like creating a process, and we are configuring all the parameters (discussed above) on it; then this complete package becomes one atomic body.

Although other types of processes also provide separation, containers provide configurable separation. Like, we do not have the freedom to mount different configurations of the file system in generic processes such as Word, Paint, browser, etc.

Containerization versus virtualization

Both containerization and virtualization are means of achieving isolation among different processes or systems, but both have been developed to cater to specific use cases. Today, they are used in the industry actively and have become an integral part of any enterprise-level application.

Table 10.1 shows the differences and the use cases of both technologies:

Parameters	Container	Virtualization (Type 1)
Description	Running multiple lightweight packages (called containers) on a host operating system	Running multiple virtual machines on a single physical machine
Hosting	Works on a hosted operating system	Has its own operating system
Architecture	Hardware I Host OS I Container engine1 I Container 1; Container 2; Container 3	Hardware I Hypervisor I VM1; VM2; VM3
Size	Size in MBs	Size in GBs
Performance	Fast, lightweight	Slow and heavy
Isolation	Process-level isolation	Hardware level isolation (best suited for security)
Cost	Low cost	Expensive
Scalability	Very high	Limited
Use cases	Rapid deployments, Microservices, API services, Scalable Webapps, Data pipelines, Serverless functions	High secure isolation requirements, heavy monolith applications, Legacy applications, and different operating system requirements.

***Table 10.1**: A comparative study of containerization vs virtualization*

Operating system privileges

The common understanding of cloud computing is primarily around the hardware that is being shared and made remotely available to the end customer. However, it is also imperative to understand the software that interacts with the underlying hardware and makes this possible.

As we know, the operating system is the heart of processing and is responsible for managing the resources from the hardware. Different operating systems have different behaviors due to the differences in their architecture and the privileges assigned to them.

There are several layers of an operating system that can be seen and termed as protection rings.

As per *Figure 10.6*, we can have multiple layers, where the level of privileges starts from high to low, starting from the innermost layer to the outermost layer, depicting the lowest privileges at the outer layers:

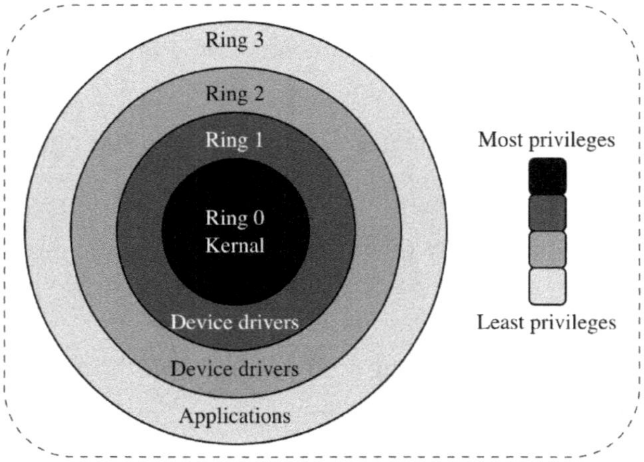

***Figure 10.6**: A depiction of a four-ring architecture*

For a typical x86 processor architecture, we can have 4 layers. The more the rings we have in the operating system, the more system checks and hence more performance overheads. Rings 0 and 3 (outer ring) are compulsory, with any number of other rings in between them as optional:

- **Ring 0**: This is the core of any operating system, also known as the kernel. It has the highest level of privileges, where the part of the code that runs here has direct access to the CPU and memory. Any problem in this part of the operating system may lead to complete system failure or system crash.
- **Ring 3**: User program, such as any user interface application like a browser, Word, etc., generally runs on this ring and cannot directly access the hardware. They cannot

interfere with the operating system scheduling algorithms. It is the least privileged mode ring.

Mostly, the applications that a user installs or works on stay in Ring 3, but in some special cases, they may go lower than that for more privileges. For example, installing VirtualBox or Hyper-V, which is used to create VMs, is installed by a user, but they definitely are not part of Ring 3, since they require more privileges than other generic applications.

- **Ring 1 and Ring 2**: These rings have more privileges than Ring 3 and allow the applications to access the hardware. The hardware peripherals software that needs computing resources can come in these rings, e.g., USB driver or camera drivers will fall in this category, where they need to interact with the hardware in order to save data to the memory or access the memory.

Operating system rings in virtualization

Due to this ring concept, the virtualization software was designed keeping in mind the level of hardware and privilege requirements from physical machines.

In *Figure 10.7*, it is shown that in the case of hosted virtualization, the **virtual machine manager** (**VMM**) sits inside the host operating system, which is in layer 0 and has the maximum privileges. The guest OS sits in layer 1 and will always have to communicate via the host operating system (in layer 0). This will always have a communication overhead in order to manage the computing resources.

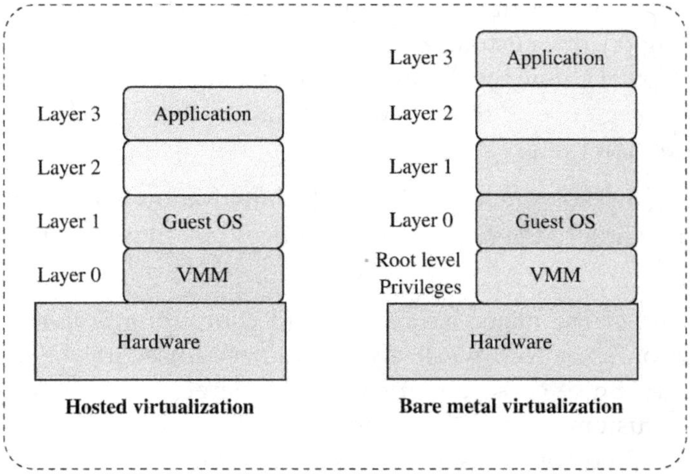

***Figure 10.7**: A visual representation of virtualization with respect to OS rings*

Whereas in the case of bare metal virtualization, the VMM is directly connected to hardware and has its own set of hardware drivers that can directly communicate with the hardware for the resources such as CPU, memory, etc., and the guest OS sits on layer 0 for the next level of required privileges. Due to the lower communication overhead, it is a better-performing architecture than the hosted one, and this is why it is used by most of the cloud solution providers for virtual machine provisioning.

Issues in cloud computing

As we know, cloud computing is the usage of computing resources coming from a cloud provider in a remote manner. Fundamentally, the customer or a user is not the owner of the platform; the platform has been lent, and customers must pay as per their usage. Due to the lack of ownership and less control, it brings its own set of issues, such as:

- **Privacy**: Customer's data is exposed to the cloud provider, which is accessible to them without many restrictions. Even if the data centers have always been set up by big and renowned organizations in the world, still there are possibilities of mishandling of data within these organizations too.

  However, these providers implement strong security and operational controls and follow a Zero Trust model where no implicit trust is assumed. Additionally, there are many enterprise-level agreements that are in place, which ensure data availability and isolation to build trust with customers.

  However, customers are still responsible for securing their data through: Encryption at rest and transit, strong **identity and access management** (**IAM**) policies and other key management practices because data privacy depends upon how effectively the customers implement these security controls within their shared responsibility.

- **Compliance**: There are many compliances that exist, which may belong to a particular country or region, that customers need to follow for data retention. Some of the regions, like the European Union region, expect the user data not to be stored anywhere outside the European region, or if that cannot be avoided, then it must be deleted at the end of the data retention cycle.

  Due to the complete remote setting and limited knowledge of the cloud, customers or clients may ignore the regional compliances that may lead to millions of dollars in penalties.

- **Security**: One of the major issues in cloud computing is the risk of data exposure due to misconfiguration, weak access controls, insecure APIs or untrusted third-party services. Since cloud environments are large and complex, organizations may expose their customers or clients sensitive data on the cloud. This data can be a health record of hundreds of thousands of people, which can be termed as super-sensitive information. For example, in recent times, a large language model company had its database compromised with users' private data. Therefore, strong IAM policies, encryption, monitoring and governance are essential to secure cloud-based data.

- **Sustainability**: Cloud infrastructure requires large data centers, that require significant amount of energy consumption to keep the servers running, computing, and cooled at the same time. Earlier, most of the data centers were heavily dependent upon coal-based energy generation, but now cloud providers are increasingly adopting renewable sources of energy (such as solar, wind etc.) and have implemented several efficiency innovations. Despite of significant improvements, energy to create and sustain these data centers is a big requirement. Some of the cold countries can be used for these purposes, which naturally provide the cooling due to their cold geography, but they may lack the amount of sunlight or power-generating sources. Other environmental impact related to, water usage, and land requirements remains a significant concern in cloud computing.

- **Abuse**: This is another big issue with cloud computing. Due to its very nature of availability to all, there may be some individuals or organizations that may engage in unethical deeds by hosting their attractive applications and tools and fooling people into taking their personal sensitive data, such as credit card information, which may be further used for financial fraud.
- **Confusion**: Although there are not many cloud providers in the market today, the ones that are available today have their own ways of configuring the components. This may be technical terminology used for their user interface or the placement of the settings and action buttons, which are changing continuously with time, too. This creates confusion in the system understanding and sometimes misconfiguration, unmanaged resource or lack of monitoring may lead to unexpected billing costs and operational issues. This leads to fear in customers when choosing any cloud services. Eventually, people who are skilled enough only become users of the cloud. Therefore, organizations need proper governance, automation, tagging, budget and alerts, and user trainings to effectively manage cloud infrastructure costs.
- **Cost**: The cloud providers often offer uninterrupted services that are chargeable at a cost. These services can become expensive due to the charges associated with more powerful machines, high bandwidth, and strong network. Additional costs may arise from data egress charges, idle resources, overprovisioned instances, or unmanaged services. For bigger customers, it is easy to have the budgets, but for smaller and budding organizations, the affordability becomes challenging. In fact, the return on investment on the infrastructure sometimes does not stack up and is solely dependent upon the price of the end application of their proprietary products. Therefore, effective cost management practices such as rightsizing resources, autoscaling, reserved capacity planning, monitoring, and budgeting are important to optimize cloud spending and improve return on investment.

Despite some of the challenges discussed above, cloud technology is being adopted by industries at a very fast rate, but a lot of times, these issues do intrude on quick decision-making and lead to delays in overall project execution.

Conclusion

This chapter covered the fundamental properties of cloud computing, the types of cloud infrastructure, and their offerings. This chapter also covered the technical foundation of cloud offerings that starts with the virtualization technology, which has been covered in detail. Different types of virtualization and how they all stand against each other were also shown in the chapter. The concept of operating system privileges and how they fit into the cloud infrastructure was also touched upon, along with the current issues that exist in cloud computing.

The next chapter will cover the key areas where organizations generally focus while working on data engineering or data science-related projects. There are several junctures or decision-making points that need to be taken care of to make the overall project a success, which are covered and will be seen in detail.

References

1. **https://nvlpubs.nist.gov/nistpubs/legacy/sp/nistspecialpublication800-145.pdf**
2. **https://www.gao.gov/assets/gao-14-753.pdf**
3. **https://aws.amazon.com/solutions/case-studies/netflix-case-study/**
4. **https://www.wiz.io/blog/wiz-research-uncovers-exposed-deepseek-database-leak**
5. **https://www.baeldung.com/cs/os-rings**

Chapter 11
Mapping Technologies in Data Engineering Lifecycle

Introduction

Today, it is a changing world where, earlier, we had different expertise available with specific people and organizations, which was unknown to most people around the world. People who were looking for a technology or a solution were able to reach out to these organizations to work with them, but now it is a fast-changing and connected world. Due to the abundance of knowledge available in the market, in terms of books, blogs, websites, and social media, and with dense connectivity, the knowledge is no longer an area to search for. In fact, whatever we are looking for comes in front of our eyes without even searching for it.

As it is a known fact that *necessity is the mother of invention*, but due to the abundance of almost everything today, the current mindset is distracted towards the things that are glittering, and we adopt the things that may not necessarily be required for business benefits. The energy that could have been used to make something beneficial is wasted on overdoing the research with different methods, technologies, and frameworks that are readily available.

This chapter covers the tactical aspects of what should be the factors that should be kept in mind in order to achieve the right balance between adoption and innovation.

Structure

The chapter covers the following topics:

- Team size and capabilities
- Speed to market
- Interoperability
- Cost vs. business value
- Location of deployment
- Build or buy
- Monolith or modular

- Serverless or servers
- Optimization in data engineering
- Performance in data engineering
- The undercurrents of the data engineering lifecycle

Objectives

By the end of this chapter, the reader will be able to understand the strategic and tactical concepts that exist in management. Most of the employees at the execution level do not work on these areas, but this section of the book will give the readers a hint of some of these critical decisions while working on any project. The readers would have a clear idea of what the criteria should be to choose the team size, what aspects would help them to limit their costs, so that ultimately the business is able to get maximum benefit at the lowest cost possible. This chapter will cover important key aspects, such as build vs. buy, serverless vs. server-based solutions, which are the starting point for any big product in development.

Team size and capabilities

To start with an analogy, when starting a long drive, it is important to check if everything that may be required is available, be it fuel, money, the health of tyres, clothes, etc. This planning does not ensure the availability of all things, but it definitely helps in minimizing the anticipated issues.

Similarly, before starting any project, it is important to assess the size and capabilities of the teams. *Are they a good fit for the size of the project? Is team size too small or too big?* We may have the right number of people working with us, but we may lack the technological requirements.

Team may be a combination of highly experienced and less experienced folks, and while planning the work for them, it is imperative to take their experience into consideration so that the right people fit the right purpose.

There may be several factors that should be kept in mind to align with the scope of work:

- **Learning speed**: Some people in the team can be very fast learners, and others can be moderate to slow. This does not necessarily mean that the person who can learn anything faster will be able to work on that area consistently, as compared to the one who is a slow learner. Since the project requires someone who is motivated enough to move ahead every day, even slowly. Accelerating at something is good, but consistency is what matters in the end.

- **Research capacity**: This is something that is not an area of strength for most people. Most people are comfortable adopting a technology if they know how it works and what it can achieve, but they may not be comfortable enough to go into an unknown territory and try to get the solution to the problem that is in their mind.

However, some are extremely good at research, and they will find the solution from anywhere around the world. They are ready to scrub a hundred thousand pages in search of the solution, but if they found one, they are least interested in the implementation because it is a slow process.

Some can be extremely good planners, start very well and slow down in the middle, others can start with messy visuals but with time start giving it a structured shape.

Team is basically a combination of heterogeneous backgrounds, interests, experiences, thought processes, personalities, temperaments, attitudes, and all have to work on a common goal. This is where the tactical aspect comes into play, where the best way is to plan according to the strength of the people. The project should not have undercapacity or overcapacity as well; the perfect balance or trying hard to achieve the balance is also enough to give the right energy to proceed with the development of any project. And leveraging what we have vs what we should learn should also give a critical view, this makes sure the team is spending the right time to crack the problem statement in an appropriate manner.

In modern data engineering practices, compact teams with strong ownership are equally important, where teams are responsible not only for building solutions but also for operating, monitoring, and supporting them through DevOps/DataOps practices.

Speed to market

In the current scenario, the speed to market is analogous to the agility of the team. The speed is key; the first entrant generally introduces the concept to the market and is remembered for the breakthrough.

Since perfection is nearly impossible to achieve, it is better to work to the best within the stipulated time and deliver. The project will not be considered complete until it is shipped, even if it is 99% completed. It is better to deliver the project at speed, get the feedback on the project, work on the improvements, and re-deliver.

Imagine if there were no milestones while going on a 200 KMs drive, how would one know if they are going anywhere, how many kilometres are remaining, should they speed up or relax?

Feedback brings acknowledgement and correction, until the client/customer/end-user sees what has been built, we as a team would not be able to gauge our own progress, quality of work, and areas of improvement.

So, the best practice is to develop at a decent speed, have an internal quality check, put it out there for the users, get the feedback, and improve upon it fast, have a quality check, and re-deliver, and this cycle must go on. In technical world, this approach is called *working backwards*, where teams build solutions based on user needs and feedback. To make changes quickly without affecting system stability, teams use automated testing, **continuous integration/continuous deployment** (**CI/CD**) pipelines, and regular quality checks before releasing updates to users.

Interoperability

Interoperability is the capability of being able to communicate or integrate with other applications with ease. It is one of the most important features of any application that we see in the market.

The more open the application is, the higher the chances of being adopted by customers and clients. Everyone in today's world demands a non-intrusive nature of integration where there should be minimal changes to their proprietary systems and applications, and these solutions should communicate via **application programming interfaces** (**APIs**).

Databases are the finest example of interoperability, where most of the databases can be connected via **Open Database Connectivity** (**ODBC**) or **Java Database Connectivity** (**JDBC**). The chances are very slim that someone would be worried about how a new database in the market will get integrated into their applications, since database connectivity has been standardized for many decades now.

In modern data engineering, interoperability is not just about connecting the system; it also about keeping the data format and meanings consistent across different tools and platforms using standards such as data contracts (*an agreement that defines the structure, format, and quality rules of data shared between systems*) and open table formats (*defines how large datasets are stored and managed reliably)* like Apache Iceberg and Apache Hudi.

Similarly, when working on any data science-related project, how the end user will actually use this product within their application should be well thought through. Will the model be deployed as a standalone, which can be called via API, or will it be embedded into the target application to provide the expected business outcome, or will it have a dedicated web portal or application where the user will interact for the results?

These are all to be well discussed, planned, and implemented in order to make the product easily acceptable and reusable for different customers.

Cost vs. business value

This is an important factor that needs to be taken care of while planning for any project. The cost of development of any project depends upon many factors, such as the number of people working on the project, the duration of the project, and the capital investment required for procuring the hardware (on-prem) or provisioning the servers (on cloud).

When a project is at the initial discussions, the **cost-benefit analysis** (**CBA**) should be done, where the advantage from the intended application is calculated in terms of money, and it is weighed against the cost that will be incurred during the development of the project. If the return on investment is positive, then the project can be assumed to give you the expected business value. The positive return should be around double or triple because at this stage, a lot of unknown factors are ignored in the planning, such as delays due to unavailability of people due to medical conditions, attrition and re-hires, integration challenges, design challenges, people conflicts, unclear expectations, etc.

Although the positive **return on investment** (**ROI**) is an ideal investment, in some cases, the negative ROI may also work where the cause of work is bigger than the outcome. Some of the examples can be the applications that have been developed to improve the brand value of the company by investing in improving customer satisfaction, capturing ratings, and improving society by means of their products, etc.

In general, as a thumb rule, the target benefit should be considered in the calculations for planning the number of team members and the time required to develop the application. Based on this, the exact scope of work that can be achieved within the specified time frame and selected number of resources can be frozen, and according to that, the respective return on investment can be calculated.

Once a proper background check and homework are completed, the project is commenced, and all the respective decisions are executed with confidence.

Location of deployment

This is another area that is crucial when it comes to the end usage, which talks about where the application should be deployed, and it has to be decided based on multiple parameters. There are three types of deployment: on-prem, cloud, or hybrid. The following are the parameters that are taken into consideration before adopting the technology for the deployment, and hence the location:

- **Focus**: This is the one area that is debatable and intangibly advantageous, but difficult to convince or prove at first. Generally, organizations that are building data science-based solutions or other applications are in the field because of their expertise in this area. Although they can work on the development of the complete solution locally, for deployment, they will have to host the application on servers that are accessible to the end users with minimum latency.

  For any on-prem implementation, the organizations have to set up a data center for themselves where they can host multiple server-grade hardware. The hardware has its own limitations, such as:

  - **Maintenance**: The hardware gets old, slows down, and stops working; these things need special vigilance and need to be replaced as soon as the issues occur.
  - **Inventory**: Each critical piece of hardware must have a backup inventory available so that it can be replaced with a new one almost instantly.
  - **Continuous monitoring**: There is a requirement for skilled manpower who needs to be aware of any mishap in the system from a hardware standpoint.
  - **Limitation**: The current hardware will have scalability limitations. It would be fine to be able to handle the load for a specific user base or transactions, but in

special cases, such as any calamity or seasonal sales that bring a spike in server access, it may not be able to handle the situation with the limited inventory.

These limitations may not exist in the organization at all times, but this is about focusing on important things for which the company exists. This is how different businesses are born and scaled. For example, *Apple Inc.*, one of the industry giants, has its iPhone's screen manufactured by *Samsung* or *LG*. That does not mean they are not doing it because they cannot; it is because they want to focus on their problems and outsource the rest to their vendors.

Similarly, choosing on-premise brings other cost too, in terms of cost of rent of data centers, inventory, labour and the headache of handling the situation of managing hardware. The other alternative to this is using cloud-based infrastructure, where the cloud providers are focused on providing the hardware, with unlimited capacity, and making sure that the platform remains up 99% of the time, or if it is down, then regular backups have been taken to avoid any data loss.

- **Latency**: This is another factor that needs to be taken care of, which is based on the location of the users. If the target users of the applications are situated in a specific location, then it is better to have the servers near the location of the users. If the location is global, then it makes sense to have the servers located in multiple regions so as to process the customers' requests locally and minimize the latency for processing the data and serving the customers. Cloud gives this flexibility of regional-level deployments, where we can have servers provisioned locally to serve the customer near their respective locations. For example, *Google* provides location-based customer service by combining the user's location, localizing content, and other automations. It takes care of local compliance by following company-specific policies, local language support, and fast and relevant responses.
- **Scaling**: This is another important requirement, as discussed earlier, in which, in peak hours or any uncertain situations when the number of users or transactions increases exponentially, the ever-ready cloud based solutions come in handy where the organization does not need to think about the limit of scalability but to focus on how their own application can be scalable with the current infrastructure provided by the cloud vendors. Earlier, at the start of cloud adoption, generally, **infrastructure as a service** (**IaaS**) was in place as a primary offering, which definitely helped their customers to pass on their infrastructure problems to cloud vendors, but kept the headache of high cost, maintaining the operating system, security, network, and patch management. Later, the **platform as a service** (**PaaS**) was introduced, which made the client organization focus only on the development of their solution, leaving the rest of it to the cloud providers. They would just pay for what they use and would not even think about the scalability. These components were scalable to nearly unlimited capacity with less overhead than other maintenance tasks.
- **Data sovereignty**: In organizations, it must be ensured that the data is stored, processed and managed according to the laws and regulations of the country or region

where the data belongs. This is called data sovereignty. Compliance requirements such as **General Data Protection Regulation** (GDPR), **Health Insurance Portability and Accountability Act** (HIPPA), or other industry-specific regulations need to be adhered to which may guide where data can reside, who can access it, and how it can be protected. Therefore, cloud architects need to follow region-specific deployments, access controls, auditing, and governance policies to meet legal and regulatory requirements.

As we have discussed earlier in this chapter, depending upon the requirements, a hybrid infrastructure can be adopted as well. In such an approach, sensitive data security and compliance can be maintained within localized data centers, while scalability and other aspects can be achieved through cloud components. These environments can work in tandem to meet both overall scalability and data security requirements.

Build or buy

This is a little sensitive and debatable topic when it comes to deciding whether to develop a software application ourselves or buy one that's already available in the market.

As the human race advanced, things or objects got integrated, but the industries got disintegrated. This disintegration led to bigger and more advanced products over time. For example, earlier, a person who was making a cloth would do everything on their own, be it the selection of textile, coloring, stitching, buttons, etc., but now, there are industries which are focused on textile production only, some others focus only upon coloring, others on converting the cloth into a shirt, and so on.

Both the approaches, build and buy, have their own set of advantages and disadvantages. Some of the attributes that can be seen are as follows:

- **Control**: Having everything built by ourselves, we have more control over the output than we would if it were coming from a third-party vendor or open-source community. If the requirement cannot compromise on the quality of the work, then teams can consider building on their own, at the cost of money and time.

- **Time**: Naturally, when something is already built, reinventing the wheel again does not make sense. When buying provides the expected decent quality of product that serves our purpose, then buying makes more sense in order to save time.

- **Customization**: When third-party products are used, they may not have been built keeping our requirements in mind. There is a high chance that we may not use all the features that have been built into the product. Also, mostly, since they are the products, they may have the configurability, but not the customizability, which may limit our capabilities. If the end requirement is fulfilled using minimum customization, then buying becomes the easy choice; otherwise, building makes true sense.

- **Focus**: This is the core intangible aspect that we have already covered in *Chapter 10, Understanding Cloud Computing,* too. It is often difficult to prove the power of focus, but certainly, the big organizations that have been built so far have been able to do so by rejecting all the things or ideas that are out of their scope of focus.

In 1997, when *Apple* was struggling to survive, *Steve Jobs* came in and cut down their current line of products by 70% and finalized only four products that the company would focus on. He said, *Deciding what not to do is as important as deciding what to do,* and that worked for Apple, and it reached a place where we see it today, having crossed trillions of dollars in valuation.

When the organizations focus on their expertise, they grow at a rapid rate compared to organizations that are spread everywhere.

So, if the requirement is to focus on developing a great product or solution, keeping the quality at the top, serving customers with the best possible efforts, and having as much control as possible, then building makes perfect sense. This will definitely affect their finances and time to market. Otherwise, buy the product that gives a satisfactory output.

Monolith or modular

Monolith is the type of architecture where multiple teams work together in building multiple services that are tightly coupled with each other and do not have any moving parts. This is a fast and easy way of implementation, but it is so connected with the other components that, if one component fails, then the entire piece breaks down.

For example, developing an e-commerce platform where a single code flow contains user login, product catalog, shopping cart, payment processing, order management, notification, etc. In this approach, everything is together and tightly coupled, but if the payment processing module fails, then the entire system stops working.

The entire suite is typically developed using a single programming language and technology stack. Once the stack is shortlisted and the application has matured, then changing the language and framework is extremely difficult and costly. This becomes a problem when a new component needs to be added, and the earlier programming language or technology has some technical limitations, then developers are forced to continue using it, ignoring the underlying limitations. A real-life non-technical example can be, a restaurant is designed for North Indian food, where the chefs, equipment, recipes, interiors and galleries are optimized for it and later the restaurant decides to move to South Indian food with almost negligible budget, the owner is now forced to utilize the current chefs, utensils etc. for the new requirement despite of their limitations and expertise.

On the contrary, the modular approach is nowadays preferred due to its multiple moving parts. The whole system to be developed is divided into small teams, which may work on their respective components, and each component communicates with the others via API. In this, different components teams are free to choose the technology stack they prefer based on their expertise, the strength of technology, and the cost of implementation. The major advantage of this approach is that the failure of one component affects that component only without touching the entire suite. For example, in an e-commerce platform, if the product recommendation module is not working, customers can still go to the website, see the products, and purchase them without being affected by the product recommendation feature.

This approach is also helpful when development teams are geographically spread, as they can concentrate on their implementation and do not have to worry about the communication between different components.

Some of the limitations of the modular approach can be the complexity of development, which requires careful planning and design efforts for communication with different modules. It may also have integration overhead where all the modules coming from different teams should seem like a single piece that also requires special efforts on user interface themes, collaboration, and selection, and extra efforts of testing and integration of all the components.

This system will have communication overhead, where API based communication may be slower than the monolith system. This requires proper version control, which may lead to compatibility problems between different versions of components.

Since it is a distributed approach, except for the architect (who is also limited), nobody has command over the complete product and cannot work in any module in case of any exigency.

Due to a modularized mindset, the risk of over-modularization occurs, which may result in communication overhead and make the system harder to understand.

This topic has also been covered in *Chapter 2, Designing a Data Architecture,* in the section, *Understanding the basics of data architecture,* where we have broadly seen the architectural difference between the monolith and microservices-based architecture.

Depending upon the business expectations, technological stack, and team's capability, the best-suited architecture can be zeroed down and implemented.

Serverless or servers

This is another area where any project needs to be thought through. The application can be designed using both server-based and serverless approaches. Let us look at these approaches in detail:

- **Server**: This is a type of implementation where the team owns the server and is responsible for the facility (server rooms) for placement of the server, power requirements, cooling requirements, software management, such as operating systems, applications, and dependencies installation, patch management, etc. The team ensures the maintenance of the hardware, redundancy management, and regular backup of the critical systems.

  In this, there are three types of management:

  - **Physical servers**: The organization is managing a small set of servers in its facilities completely, and the target application is hosted on them.
  - **On-prem data centers**: In this, the organizations can maintain their own data centers, managed by themselves, or can leverage the expertise of cloud providers to set up the physical servers on their own site, and all the connectivity and software layer will be managed by cloud vendors.
  - **Virtual machines**: In this approach, the organizations make use of the expertise of cloud vendors and get the virtual machines provisioned, which are managed by cloud providers from a hardware standpoint. The target organizations are only responsible for managing the application-level software layer, such as operating system, dependencies, antivirus or antimalware, and general patch management. This model can also be associated with IaaS, e.g., AWS EC2, Azure VM, etc.
- **Serverless**: This is the model provided by the cloud providers, where application teams can focus on writing their code and deploying their code on these components without even worrying about the management of the servers, operating systems, networking, facilities, and maintenance. Servers are available, but they are just abstracted for the user. They are associated with PaaS, e.g., AWS Lambda, Azure Functions, etc.

  There are many parameters that are to be considered before selecting any approach. Some of these parameters can be:

  - **Scalability**: This is the aspect that needs to be considered when the number of end users is known, and the kind of access to be given to the different user groups is planned. Some of the important factors, like peak time of the day, seasonality, etc., are also to be taken into consideration. In general, serverless are designed for instant auto-scalability, whereas server-based ones generally have to be manually configured for scaling purposes.
  - **Speed**: Speed is an area that is very important, since the end user's overall experience is dependent upon the speed of execution of the algorithm and providing the result faster for a better experience. Serverless components are generally event-driven, which means they start only when they are triggered, so they may experience the start latency, but once they are warmed up, the execution is very fast, and the performance varies with the load, whereas since servers are always running, there is no startup delay, and they have predictable and consistent performance.
  - **Cost model**: This is based on the expectation of the customers. If the requirement is something that must be paid for only when it is used or has variable usage, then the serverless components make sense, and if we want the servers to be running continuously irrespective of their usage, then the server approach makes sense, where the payment is done for the running time of the service.

- **Control**: This is the area that may be dependent upon the choice of the target organization. If the target organization expects to have more control over the servers for any operating system-related changes, hardening, policies, networking, or libraries, then server-based deployment becomes their preferred choice. On the other hand, if the target organizations want to focus on the deployment without bothering about the operating system and runtime, then serverless is preferred.
- **Operational overhead**: The organizations may choose serverless because it requires less burden of operations and maintenance, whereas the server-based implementation requires regular patching, monitoring, and maintenance, which is an operational overhead and will have a cost to it.

Optimization in data engineering

The fundamental meaning of optimization in data engineering is to get the correct results with the least amount of resources. These resources can be computational power, memory, input/output, storage, data, engineering efforts, cost, etc.

Delivering a product faster would only be seen as a secondary benefit and could not overshadow the quality of the output.

The optimization cannot happen at a particular place or at the end, but must be done at every stage. It should start with the mindset where the team that is working on a particular project has the tendency to be frugal and find the best solution with the least possible inputs.

Although it is difficult to standardize, let us try to look at it from a data engineering project point of view:

- **Data ingestion optimization**: If the choice is available, it is better to go for micro-batch processing than to ingest the data row by row.
- **Query optimization**: This is needed when the data needs to be accessed; it is mostly visible but often ignored. Avoid the `SELECT *` statement at all. If possible, the specific columns should be chosen, `WHERE` conditions should be applied, and the query should be optimized as much as possible to get the minimum required results. This is called funneling down to very specific results without any unneeded information. As it is said, *The best query optimization is not running the query at all.*
- **Execution optimization**: Although it depends on many factors such as tools, programming language, third-party input, etc., some of the optimization techniques should be kept in mind before implementation, such as parallel processing, usage of caching mechanisms, adaptive query execution, etc.
- **Cost optimization**: Most performance issues come from poorly managed costs. Some of the areas that take up most of the costs are full table scans, reprocessing history, over-retaining of data, and useless stream jobs.

The word optimization is linked to the word sacrifice; in fact, optimization cannot be had without sacrificing. And therefore, it is very important to know the area of optimization. Because optimizing one thing will lead to less of other related things, e.g., optimizing speed may take away flexibility, or optimizing safety may take away the speed, and so on.

Optimization is not only a part of the project execution but also takes part in the maintenance cycle. Some of the questions are always necessary to ask and check for the scope of optimization of the same. Some of the questions can be:

- Is the data model correct?
- Can we process less data for the same result?
- Can we save processing cost at the exchange of correct but delayed output?
- Can we delete the unused, old, irrelevant data?

Performance in data engineering

Like optimization in data engineering, performance is the ability to deliver the correct data at an acceptable cost. Performance is the combination of latency, throughput, reliability, and cost:

- **Latency**: It is defined by the time it takes for a system to respond to a particular query.
- **Throughput**: It is known by how many rows, events, or queries can be processed every second or unit time.
- **Reliability**: It is the ability of the system to consistently deliver complete and correct output without failure. It may not be confused with availability; the system may be up 24x7, but still be unreliable. On the other hand, a system can be unavailable for a couple of hours a day but always be reliable. A pipeline that is up but producing garbage data is worse than a pipeline that is down.
- **Cost**: This can be seen as cost per query, cost per dashboard view, or cost per transaction. Here, the target is not providing a result with minimum cost, but, on the contrary, at a given cost, the number of results, the quality of results, the correctness of results, and the availability of the system.

Undercurrents of the data engineering lifecycle

Although the data engineering looks straight or linear processing that includes:

Source | Ingest | Store | Transform | Serve | Consume

The undercurrents are the non-linear forces that are acting continuously beneath the flow and are usually unknown to people. Let us look at some of these aspects that cannot be ignored for any data engineering projects:

- **Gravitational power of data**: As discussed in one of the previous chapters of this book, the data becomes heavy over time and is difficult to move. Due to this, eventually, the compute needs to be moved near the data, and the tools need to be positioned around it. So, it becomes imperative to decide the ecosystem (on-prem, cloud, etc.), teams' skills, etc. They may not seem big at the start, but at later stages becomes critical.
- **Trust or freshness**: Generally, when the data pipeline is set up, the data engineering and other aspects are already taken care of. But still, the data needs to be continuously monitored for quality and respective transformation. Any change in the data, even after transformation, takes away a bit of trust and forces us to employ some more mechanisms of checks and reconciliation. The reconciliation builds trust but takes away the speed and freshness of the data. So, the organizational expectations of fresh and real-time data processing are catered to by either two pipelines, one with real-time streamed data without any audit, and the other is processed, audited, and reconciled, which is trusted.
- **Drifts**: This is referred to as the changes in the data or relationship between data and outcomes over time, causing the machine learning model to degrade. There are the following types of drifts:
    - **Data drift**: When the changes occur from a statistical standpoint, but underlying parameters remain the same, e.g., post-COVID-19, the retail sale of clothing sees a change from physical shops to online. The parameters to capture were the same, but the trend changed.
    - **Concept drift**: When the relationship between the input and output changes over time, e.g., Spam detectors in the email used to detect mass emails as spam, but now, due to changes in the trend and digital business marketing, they may not be considered as spam. Many big organizations, content creators, and other business individuals are reaching out to their customers via these mechanisms, and customers are used to it. So, the conventional spam detector will fail with the older logic.

  Assuming the stability of the schema/structure of the data and concept is a myth and cannot be guaranteed. This will result in continuous costs of governance, transformation work, and model retraining.

- **Human intervention**: As an ideal scenario, everything needs to be automated, but to build trust in the model and the system, the human in the loop is required to make sure there is continuous governance. Different roles have different demands of work and hence incoherent actions. For example, the analysts will always have as complex queries as possible to get the best combination of data from different dimensions, but the engineers will try to over-optimize the queries, which may result in the loss of flexibility.

  The pipelines get patched as more and more people (different roles) are involved in the loop, which results in a workaround-based architecture.

- **Illusions**: At the start of any data engineering project, the proof of concepts are developed, which are based on mostly static synthetic data, clean data, and have benchmarking created around a controlled environment. However, when the real project kicks in, things considered ideal earlier become realistic, and the environment grows out of control, data quality issues start to happen, failures of the systems happen, and misuse of human intervention is seen. The result is that, at a later stage, the unrealistic expectations from the product are not met, and the return on investment does not stack up against the cost at all or is achieved much later than expected. So, the benchmarking is based on ideal conditions and is good for sales, but real execution is complex and costly.

Conclusion

This chapter has covered the important aspects, which may not be directly technical but somehow make use of technical inputs and help the leadership to make decisions. The reader must have understood what the primary factors are that decision authorities are looking at when deciding on the size of the team working on a project, where and how the hardware will be managed, and what the risks and expectations are. This will help the reader to align themselves with the expectations of the leadership and eliminate confusion.

In the next chapter, some of the important tools needed in data engineering will be explored, which will help the reader to visualize how these different tools and technologies are making things possible in the data engineering world.

References

1. **Topics direction - Fundamentals of Data Engineering (Reis, JoeHousley, Matt)**
2. **https://timesofindia.indiatimes.com/technology/mobiles-tabs/apples-iphone-16-display-production-have-reportedly-begun/articleshow/112412136.cms**
3. **https://www.entrepreneur.com/growing-a-business/how-steve-jobs-saved-apple/220604**
4. **https://medium.com/@kiranvutukuri/performance-in-data-engineering-part-06-70683b125f8b**
5. **https://www.dataversity.net/articles/data-drift-vs-concept-drift-what-is-the-difference/**

Chapter 12
Key Tools Powering Modern Data Engineering

Introduction

So far, we have seen the end-to-end lifecycle of data and its processing, and how it is finally converted into a business outcome, which may be in the form of dashboards or feeding into machine learning models to predict a business outcome for informed decision making.

This provides us the right direction that is needed to take in order to achieve the business outcome, but when the actual projects are executed, they bring their own set of challenges and opportunities to solve. With time, there have been so many tools introduced to the market, which have individually and sometimes collectively solved these existing problems within organizations, and later they have standardized themselves to solve the problems of other people or organizations as well.

This chapter covers some of these key tools or areas that are essential to know when working on any data science-related projects.

Structure

The chapter covers the following topics:

- Basic SQL operations
- Introduction to Hadoop
- Introduction to Apache Hive
- Introduction to Apache Airflow
- Introduction to Dockers
- Python fundamentals
- Introduction to Apache Spark
- Introduction to Apache Kafka
- Introduction to Databricks
- Introduction to major cloud platforms

Objectives

At the end of this chapter, the readers will be familiar with basic SQL operations and have an understanding of Python. This chapter will also cover some of the very important frameworks, such as Hadoop, Spark, and data warehouses like Apache Hive. The readers will also learn about the available platform for real-time data processing using Kafka and get a basic understanding of Apache Airflow for end-to-end workflow management.

This chapter will also cover the basic information about the three major cloud providers, which will include the introductory details of the major solutions with respect to each cloud provider.

Basic SQL operations

The data is said to be so when it is stored and available for use whenever required. For this purpose, it is required to understand how it is stored using SQL and retrieved.

As covered in *Chapter 8, Practical Guide to Data Storage* since SQLite is a free and lightweight serverless database engine, it is a nice way to start learning SQL commands.

To start, you may use SQLite directly or use an online compiler; for this, we are using **https://sqliteonline.com/**

On a higher level, there are four different types of commands in SQL:

- **Data definition language (DDL)**: These commands are used to create and modify the database structure. This is like setting up the bricks for a building.
    - **Creating a table**: It is a command to create a table from scratch. It requires the table name, the columns to be created in the table, the data type, and the properties of the column.
      ```
      CREATE TABLE students (
      id INTEGER PRIMARY KEY,
      name TEXT NOT NULL,
      grade INTEGER
      );
      ```
      In the above command, the table name is `students` with three columns: `id`, which is an integer and a primary key (which is always unique and is an identifier for that row), name, which is textual in nature and cannot be null, and grade, which is an integer datatype.
    - **Altering a table**: This is the command used to make changes in the structure of the table that may include adding a column, removing a column, renaming a column, etc.

      Note: **Modifying the content of the table should not be confused with this command, as this command is meant for modifying the underlying structure.**

```
ALTER TABLE students
ADD COLUMN email TEXT;
```

In the above command, the **students** table has been modified by adding another column, email, of a textual type.

- **Drop table**: This is a command to delete a table from the database:

```
DROP TABLE students;
```

In the above command, the `students` table is deleted permanently along with its data. This process is irreversible, i.e., the information cannot be retrieved, unless the backup of the databases is taken.

- **Data manipulation language (DML)**: These are the commands that are used to work with the actual data (not the structure of the table).
  - **Insert**: This is the command used for inserting the values inside the existing table:

```
INSERT INTO students (name, grade) VALUES ('Peter', 90);
INSERT INTO students (name, grade) VALUES ('Sam', 85);
```

  - **Select**: This is the command used for fetching the records from the table.

```
SELECT * FROM students;
```

The above command is used to fetch all the rows of the table.

```
SELECT * FROM students WHERE name = 'Peter';
```

The above command is used to fetch the relevant rows. `WHERE` keyword is used as a filter to get the specific rows; this process is also called **slicing**.

```
SELECT name FROM students;
```

The above command is used to fetch the specific columns of the table. This processing is also called **dicing**.

  - **Update**: This command is used to update the data in a table.

```
UPDATE students SET grade = 95 WHERE name = 'Peter';
```

The above command is setting the grade value to 95 for a student named Peter.

  - **Delete**: This is the command used to delete the table.

```
DELETE FROM students WHERE name = 'Peter';
```

The above command is used to remove the row(s) where the name of the student is Peter.

- **Data control language (DCL)**: These are the commands used for access control and security. They manage database users and define who does what.

Since SQLite does not support DCL, the following example is for MySQL, which has some minor changes in the command.

```
CREATE USER 'teacher'@'localhost' IDENTIFIED BY 'mypassword';
```

The above command is used to create a user.

```
GRANT SELECT ON school.students TO 'teacher'@'localhost';
```

The above command is used to allow the `SELECT` command, but not the `INSERT` or `DELETE`.

```
GRANT INSERT, UPDATE ON school.students TO 'teacher'@'localhost';
```

The above command is used to allow `INSERT` and `UPDATE` as well.

```
REVOKE SELECT, INSERT, UPDATE ON school.students FROM 'teacher'@'localhost';
```

The above command is used to revoke the `SELECT`, `INSERT`, and `UPDATE` rights.

- **Transaction control language (TCL)**: These commands are used to manage transactions and ensure atomic and consistent changes. A transaction is a group of one or more SQL commands that are treated as a single unit of work. It ensures the ACID property, explained in *Chapter 3, Data Generation in Source System.*

  An example of following a transaction:

  ```
  "
  BEGIN TRANSACTION;
  INSERT INTO students (name, grade) VALUES ('Charlie', 88);
  UPDATE students SET grade = 92 WHERE name = 'Alice';
  COMMIT;
  "
  ```

  The following is the explanation of each command of the above transaction:

  - **BEGIN TRANSACTION**: This command shows the start of the transaction in which the database temporarily holds the changes without implementing them permanently.
  - **INSERT INTO students (name, grade) VALUES ('Charlie', 88)**: This command adds a student `Charlie`
  - **UPDATE students SET grade = 92 WHERE name = 'Alice'**: This command updates the grade of a student `Alice`
  - **COMMIT**: This command makes sure all the changes made after the `BEGIN` command are saved permanently. If there is a fatal error after the `BEGIN` statement, all the temporary changes made will be rolled back. The `ROLLBACK` command may not always be written.

Python fundamentals

Python is one of the most popular programming languages of today. It has been widely accepted because it is easy to read and write, which is beginner-friendly, it is very powerful, and it is used in various fields. It is free and open-source with a big community that keeps adding new features and improvements frequently.

Python can be used in fields like web development, data science, automation, **Internet of Things** (**IoT**), cybersecurity, finance, etc.

Integrated development environment

Integrated development environment (**IDE**) is software that helps write and run programs easily. Python IDEs have the following features:

- Code editor
- Auto-completion
- Error-highlighting
- Debugging tools
- Run code directly

Some of the most popular IDEs that can be used for Python are:

- **IDLE**: This comes built-in with Python, good for beginners, but has limited features.
- **PyCharm**: It is best for professionals and is considered very powerful in the industry.
- **VS Code**: It is a lightweight IDE with a lot of extensions. It is best suited for everyone.
- **Jupyter Notebook**: It is a development environment that allows cell-based execution. This is very advantageous when the piece-by-piece code needs to be executed, with its excellent visualization. This is usually used in data science and machine learning-related projects.

Code execution

Python is primarily an interpreted language, which means Python code is converted into intermediate bytecode, and this bytecode runs line by line inside the Python interpreter, which is nothing but the Python virtual machine.

There are various interpreters for Python; some of them are mentioned in the following:

- **CPython**: This is the official Python interpreter, which is the default and widely used across the globe. It has been implemented in the C programming language.
- **PyPy**: This interpreter is known for its speed and usage of **just-in-time** (**JIT**) compilation.
- **Jython**: This is a Java platform where Python code can use Java libraries.

Python syntax and semantics

Syntax and semantics are fundamental components of any programming language, defining both the structure and the meaning of the code. Let us understand them in depth:

- **Syntax**: Syntax is a defined set of rules that are the combination of symbols and letters to correctly structure programming languages.
- **Semantics**: Semantics refers to the meaning or interpretation of the symbols and commands written in a language.

As an analogy, *have to school go I to* is syntactically correct (spelling is fine, spacing is good, and each word can be read properly), but semantically it does not make sense. Whereas if we write *I have to go to school,* then it is syntactically and semantically correct.

Syntax mistakes can be caught while on interpretation or compilation of languages, but semantics issues come when the program runs and does not give the expected output.

Based on this, there are three types of issues:

- **Compile-time errors**: These are found before the program runs. It is detected by the compiler (or byte code generator). For example, syntax issues, incorrect variable types, missing parameters, etc.
- **Run-time errors**: these issues occur while the program is running. The program crashed under a certain condition. For example, division by zero, file not found, out of memory, etc.
- **Logical error**: These are the errors that are hardest to detect, as the program runs without any problem but does not give the expected result. For example, an incorrect formula or algorithm used, or wrong conditional statements, etc.

General rules in Python

The following are some fundamental rules that need to be followed while using Python:

- **Comments**: Comments are very important in any code since they give an opportunity to developers to express the details about the code in a simple and easy way without following programming syntax rules. In Python, we have two types of comments:
    - **Single line comment**: This comment is to write something in a single line only. It is created using a hash symbol.

      ```
      # This is a single line comment
      ```

    - **Multi-line comment**: This comment is to write something in multiple lines. It is created using triple quote symbols.

      ```
      """
      This is a multiple line comment,
      ```

```
which is used to explain something in detail
"""
```

- **Case sensitivity**: Python is a case-sensitive language, which means variables with different cases will be considered differently.

```
Greet = "Hello"
greet = "Hola"
print(Greet)
print(greet)
```

  In the example above, the variable **`Greet`** and **`greet`** will be treated differently, and they will have their respective values as output if they are printed.

- **Indentation**: Unlike other programming languages, Python does not need braces to limit the block of code; rather, it uses indentation to detect the group of respective statements. In fact, native programmers, when they use Python for a while, would find the braces unnecessary and time-consuming.

```
names = ["Ava", "Ben", "Mia"]
for n in names:
    msg = "Hello " + n
    print(msg)
```

  In this example, the statement inside will execute once the code is inside the for loop.

Variable and datatypes in Python

Let us look at the usage of variables and different datatypes used in Python:

- **Variable**: It is a named memory location that is used to store data. Unlike other programming languages, Python automatically assigns the type based on the value assigned to it.

```
name = "Vaishali"
age = 39
```

  In this example, the variable name is a string type, and the age is an integer type. So the variables do not need to be explicitly defined for the type of value.

- **Datatype**: Python has four categories of datatypes:
  - **Numeric**: This stores numeric type values:
    - **Integer**: Represents whole numbers without decimals, e.g., **`var = 10`**
    - **Float**: Represents the real values with decimals, e.g., **`var = 9.41`**
    - **Complex number**: Represents a number with real and imaginary parts, e.g., **`var = 2+3j`**

- **Boolean**: Represents a logical value of True or False and is used for conditions and comparisons, e.g., `is_var = True`
- **Sequence**: These store multiple values, but in an ordered manner:
  - **String**: Represents a text enclosed in quotes and it is immutable (cannot be changed after creation), once declared, e.g., `var = "python"`
  - **List**: They are an ordered and mutable collection of items like fruit, e.g., `= ["apple", "Banana", "Orange"]`
  - **Tuple**: They are an ordered but immutable collection of items, e.g., marks `= (10, 20, 30)`
- **Collection**: These store multiple values, which may not be in an ordered manner.
  - **Set**: It is an unordered collection of numbers, and duplicate values are automatically removed, e.g., `numbers = {1, 2, 3, 5, 11}`
  - **Dictionary**: Stores data in key-value pairs, which allows faster and structured access to data, e.g., `Student = {"name": "Kavish", "age": 41}`

Operators in Python

Operators allow us to perform the mathematical or logical operations in Python; these are building blocks for any conditional processing.

There are three types of operator:

- **Arithmetic operator**: These are the operators that are used for the mathematical operations. These operators and their examples are given in the following:

```
a = 7 #Assigning a variable 'a' with value as 10
b = 5  #Assigning a variable 'b' with value as 5
addition = a + b        #Adds a and b, the result will be 12
subtraction = a - b     #Subtracts b from a, the result will be 2
multiplication = a * b #Multiplies a and b, the result will be 35
division = a / b        #Divides a by b, the result will be 1.4
floor_divion = a // b  #Divides a by b and removes the decimal part, the result will be 1
modulus_result = a % b #Returns the remainder after division, the result will be 7 mod 5 = 2
exponential_result = a ** b #Raises a to the power of b, the result will be 7*7*7*7*7 = 16807
```

- **Comparison operator**: These are the operators that are used for any comparison-related operations:

- ==: This operator is to check whether two values or variable are equal e.g., **`10==5`** | False
- !=: This is to check if the two values/variables are not equal e.g., **`10!=5`** | True
- >: This is to check if the value in the left is greater than the value at the right, e.g., **`10>5`** | True.
- <: This is to check if the value on the right is less than the left, e.g., **`10<5`** | False
- >=: This is to check if the value on the left is greater than or equal to the value on the right, e.g., **`5>=5`** | True.
- <=: This is to check if the value in the right is less than or equal to the value in the left, e.g., **`5<=5`** | True

- **Logical operators**: These are the operators used to combine Boolean expressions. There are three types of Boolean expressions:
  - **and**: This condition returns true only if both conditions are True:

```
a = 10
b = 5
result = (a > 5) and (b < 10)
print(result)
```

The above Python statement will be True only if **`a > 5`** and **`b <10`**.

  - **or**: This returns true if at least one condition is true:

```
a = 10
b = 5
result = (a > 5) or (b < 10)
print(result)
```

The above Python statement will be true if either **`a > 5`** or **`b <10`**.

  - **not**: This operator reverses the result of the condition:

```
light_on = False
if not light_on:
 print("Light is OFF")
```

The above condition checks if the **`light_on`** variable is not on, then print that **`Light is OFF`**.

Conditional statements

Conditional statements are a part of the code that are used for conditional junctures in the code. There are three major components of it.

The **if** statement:

- **If**: This evaluates the statement and executes the block of code if the condition is satisfied:

```
marks = 75
if marks >= 90:
    print("Grade A")
```

  In the above example, the marks variable has 75 as a value, and it is checked if the value is greater than or equal to 90; if the condition is satisfied, then **Grade A** will be printed.

- **Elif**: It stands for else if. It allows us to check another condition if the first condition fails:

```
marks = 75
if marks >= 90:
    print("Grade A")
elif marks >= 60:
    print("Grade B")
```

  In the above example, the code first checks that the marks variable has a value greater than or equal to 90. If yes, then **Grade A** will be given as shown in the previous example. However, **elif** is allowing the marks to be checked against another condition where the marks are greater than or equal to 60; if that's the case, then the grade will be printed as **Grade B**.

- **Else**: This is the default condition, which executes when none of the earlier conditions are satisfied.

```
marks = 35
if marks >= 90:
    print("Grade A")
elif marks >= 60:
    print("Grade B")
else:
    print("Grade C")
```

  In the above example, if the marks of a student are greater than or equal to 90, then he will be given **Grade A**. If not Grade, then the student's marks will be compared against 60; if the marks are greater than or equal to 60, then he will be given **Grade B**. If both conditions match, then the code will execute the default statement, which is the else block, and will give the student a grade of **Grade C**. There may be any number of conditional blocks in the code.

Loops in Python

Loops in Python are used to execute the same piece of code again and again. There are two types of loops:

- **For loop**: This is the loop that is used to repeat a block of code for a fixed number of times, or it is used when the number of executions is already known.

  ```
  for i in range(1, 6):
      print(i)
  ```

  The above statement is used to generate a number from 1 to 5 and print that number.

  ```
  for i in range(1, 6, 2):
      print(i)
  ```

  The above statement is used to generate the number from 1 to 5, but the steps will be incremented by 2 each time.

  ```
  for i in range(10, 0, -1):
      print(i)
  ```

  The above statement is used to generate the number from 10 to 1 in reverse order.

- **While loop**: This is the loop, which repeats the block of code until a condition is met.

  ```
  Count = 0
  while count < 5:
     print(count)
     count +=1
  ```

  In the above statement, the loop starts from 0 and keeps on executing the print statement until the count statement is 4. Like this, there can be any other condition that can be used as a loop ender.

Functions in Python

Functions are defined as reusable blocks of code that can be defined once and reused again and again:

```
def check_result(marks):
    if marks >= 40:
        return "Pass"
    else:
        return "Fail"
```

The above block of code is used to declare the result. It is a **`check_result`** function, which is passed a value using the following code:

```
check_result(50)
```

If the mark is greater than or equal to 40, then the result is **PASS**; else it is **FAIL**.

Error handling in Python

Error handling is defined as a technique that is used to prevent the program from crashing if an error occurs. In the error handling, the block of code that has to be tested is kept under a **TRY** block, and any exceptions around the block will be handled in the **EXCEPT** block, and the final message that has to run every time will be executed.

```
try:
    file = open("data.txt", "r")
    print(file.read())
except FileNotFoundError:
    print("File not found")
finally:
    print("File operation completed")
```

In the above statement, in the **TRY** block, the code is trying to open and read the file. If the file does not exist, the **EXCEPT** block will be executed, and once it is finally executed, it will run every time and will be used to clean up or run as a final statement.

Example: Reading and inspecting CSV data using Python

The following example shows how Python can be used in data engineering to load and inspect structured data from a CSV file:

```
import pandas as pd
# Read CSV file
data = pd.read_csv("sales_data.csv")
# Display first 5 rows
print(data.head())
```

Output: This code displays the first five rows of the dataset so the user can quickly inspect the data.

Introduction to Hadoop

Hadoop is an open-source framework used to store and process very large amounts of data efficiently. It enables distributed storage using **Hadoop Distributed File System** (**HDFS**) and parallel data processing using models such as MapReduce, making it suitable for handling big data and large-scale analytics.

This topic is covered in detail in *Chapter 7, Introduction to Data Storage*, in the section *Understanding the architecture of Hadoop*.

Use case of Hadoop

Hadoop is used in areas like fraud detection where large amount of transactional data is analyzed in near real-time to identify the suspicious activities and fraudulent transactions.

Introduction to Apache Spark

Apache Spark is an open-source big data processing framework used to process large amounts of data very fast. This is a loosely coupled ecosystem and is compatible with **Yet Another Resource Negotiator** (**YARN**) and **Hadoop Distributed File System** (**HDFS**).

Some of the prerequisites for Spark:

- Python, using PySpark libraries
- SQL
- Big Data and Hadoop

The need for Spark is initiated due to the limitations of **MapReduce** (**MR**), which are:

- **Limited performance**: It is heavily dependent upon disk input output operations, where in the case of multiple operations, one operation is executed and stored onto the disk. Then the next operation takes place, and the same process continues. Due to this, the whole operation is highly input/output dependent, which is a latency-heavy operation.

- **Complexity**: It is a very complex syntax that has lots of verbose or boilerplate code and is hard to remember.

- **Only batch processing**: MR processes only batch data, which is good when we have slow data available, but in the case of real-time data, there is no processing on real-time or streaming data.

- **Rigid structure**: Every operation in MapReduce needs to follow the map | shuffle | reduce operation. In fact, every simple operation has to move to these three operations, be it a simple filter or group by, etc.

- **No interactive interface to monitor**: MR does not have any interactive, live way to monitor the progress of the processing.

Apache Spark is a distributed computing system designed to process large-scale datasets quickly because the process happens in-memory rather than storage systems.

Characteristics

The following are some of the important characteristics of Apache spark:

- **In-memory processing**: Everything in Apache Spark is processed in-memory and does not use secondary memory.

As shown in *Figure 12.1*, on the left, the map reduces execution by processing each map reduce process by reading from the disk and then writing back before any other map reduce operation. Whereas in the case of Spark, the memory is read once, and all the operations happen in-memory without the need to read and write to the disk.

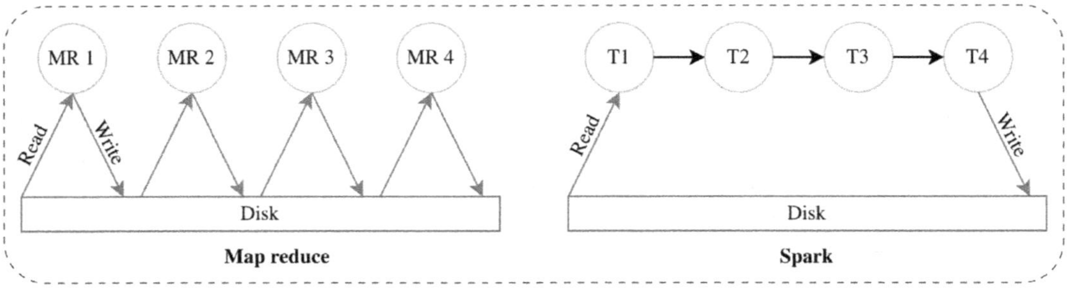

***Figure 12.1**: A representation of operations in MapReduce and Spark*

- **Ease of use**: Spark provides an API for all languages and makes it easy to write code. Even SQL can be written on it.
- **Unified framework**: Spark can handle multiple type of processing that includes batch processing, real-time processing, machine learning and graph processing can also be done on Spark.

Features

Let us look at the features of Apache Spark:

- **Speed**: Since every processing is in-memory, it is very fast. Also, it supports caching, which adds additional speed to the overall Spark processing speed.
- **Scalability**: Spark is easily scalable. The code written for a single machine can be scaled to multiple machines, and the user does not need to do any specific settings for that, but that is automatically handled by the framework.
- **Fault-tolerant**: In Spark, there is no data loss, and data loss can be recovered easily.
- **Polyglot**: It supports multiple languages such as Python, Java, Scala, etc.

Spark ecosystem

Spark consists of multiple layers with a core engine and multiple integrated libraries, all running on the same execution network. The following figure shows which layers in the Spark ecosystem:

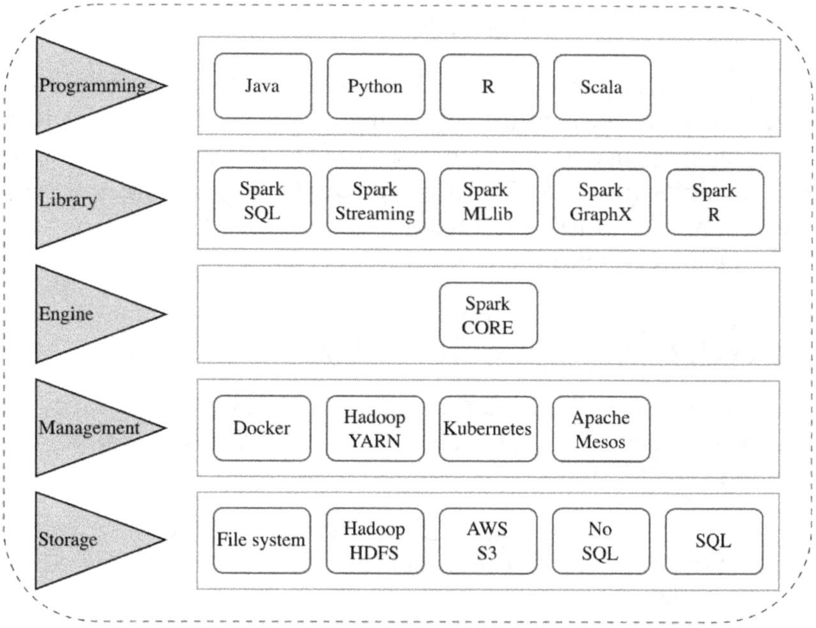

Figure 12.2: *A representation of the Spark layers*

As shown in *Figure 12.2*, there are the following layers in Spark:

- **Storage layer**: In this layer, the data needs to be stored; it supports different types of storage systems, including file systems, Hadoop distributed file systems, Amazon S3 buckets, and any NoSQL or SQL databases.
- **Management layer**: Spark runs on a cluster, which requires a resource manager that will use Hadoop YARN, Docker, Kubernetes, etc.
- **Engine**: This is where everything in Spark works; it is also called Spark core, which consists of low-level APIs. It is difficult to implement, but due to the ability to be inside the core system, it also provides the flexibility to control a lot of things. This handles scheduling, memory management, and fault tolerance.
- **Library**: They are high-level abstracted API which are easier to implement but have less flexibility. Some of the components here are SparkSQL which processes the structured data and allows the big data to be accessed using SQL commands. Spark streaming processes the real-time data, and it works well with Kafka, Flume, etc. Spark MLib is a machine learning library that is used for applying various machine learning algorithms, such as classification, regression, and clustering. Spark GraphX is a component used for graph processing, which is used for network analysis.
- **Programming**: This layer is to handle different programming languages such as Python, R, Scala, Java, etc.

Use case of Apache Spark

Apache Spark is used in cases where huge amounts of data are being generated that require big data analytics, or informed decision-making using machine learning algorithms, or in places where real-time streaming needs to be processed. For example, in the banking and finance domain, where thousands of transactions are happening every second, there are systems at the backend that need to analyze these transactions in real-time to detect any fraud or suspicious activity, like blocking a credit card if any unusual spending is detected.

Introduction to Apache Hive

Apache Hive is a distributed, fault-tolerant data warehouse that is built on top of Apache Hadoop. This is used for querying and analyzing the large dataset stored in HDFS using SQL-like language called **HiveQL** (**HQL**). This makes data analytics easy for people who know SQL well.

This makes sure that the data, which is available in HDFS, can be processed in a fast and easy way, unlike the MR complex way.

Need for Hive

With Hive, there is no need to write Java-based complex map-reduce programs. Hive provides HQL, which is an abstraction of MR under the hood, and gives users a simple interface to interact with the huge database. It was developed at *Facebook*, with the idea of saving time for writing code for MR, which later became open-source with the Apache Software Foundation, with the name Apache Hive.

Hive is not a relational database where we have primary keys, constraints, etc., rather it is a schema for a read operation for big data analysis that works on the files stored in Hadoop. Unlike SQL, it is not meant for row-level updates, small and fast transactions; rather, it has been built for batch processing, where queries may take some seconds to minutes.

Architecture of Hive

As shown in *Figure 12.3*, the following are the components of Hive:

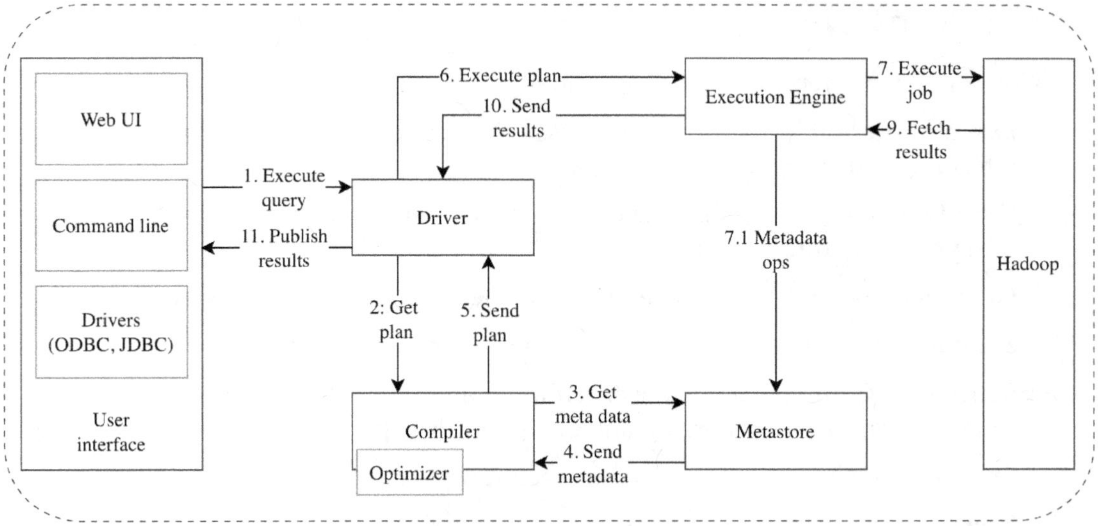

Figure 12.3: An overview of Apache Hive architecture

- **User interface**: This is the part where a user interacts with HDFS. This can be directly accessed by the user or can be integrated with an application, they can be Hive web interface or command line interface, and connectivity using **Open Database Connectivity** (**ODBC**), **Java Database Connectivity** (**JDBC**), etc. This accepts the queries and passes them to driver processing.
- **Hive driver**: This is used to control the query execution from start to finish. It will receive the HiveQL statement, and it will create the session to process the query.
- **Compiler**: Parse and translate HiveQL into an execution plan and break down the query into a **directed acyclic graph** (**DAG**) of MapReduce/Tez/Spark jobs.
- **Optimizer**: This component works on execution efficiency by making the input command optimized or transforming the command for faster results.
- **Meta store**: It is a central repository that stores the metadata about the tables, databases, columns of the table, their datatypes, and HDFS mapping is stored. This is stored in a relational database such as Derby DB or MySQL.
- **Execution engine**: Executes the optimized query and generates the results using MapReduce(default), Apache Tez (faster than MapReduce), or Apache Spark (Fastest due to its in-memory processing). It interfaces with Hadoop to fetch and process the data from HDFS.
- **HDFS**: This is the layer where the actual data resides in textual, file, or other formats.

Working of the Hive

The following are the steps for executing a query:

1. **Execute query**: Hive's interface accepts the command from the command line, web interface, or drivers (ODBC, JDBC, etc.).
2. **Get plan**: The driver takes the help of a query compiler that parses the query to check the syntax and query plan.
3. **Get metadata**: The compiler requests the metadata from the metadata store.
4. **Send metadata**: The meta store sends the metadata to the compiler.
5. **Send plan**: Compiler sends the execution plan to the driver to execute the query. This is the end of the query parsing and compilation step.
6. **Execute plan**: The driver sends the execution plan to the execution engine.
7. **Execute job**: This is a MapReduce job internally.
8. **Metadata Ops**: While the execution of the query is in place, the execution engine can execute the metadata operations.
9. **Fetch results**: The execution engine receives the results from HDFS.
10. **Send results**: The execution engine sends the result to the driver.
11. **Publish results**: The driver then publishes or sends results to the Hive user interfaces.

Use case of Apache Hive

Now, since it is clearly understood that the Hive is all about doing the analysis on big data in an efficient manner, it is used in places where a lot of data is being generated every minute and requires quick processing of data. For example, in an e-commerce world where thousands of orders are being placed in seconds or minutes, Hive is used to understand the monthly or yearly sales, find top-selling products, understand customer buying trends, seasonality-based products, etc.

Another example can be, in telecom world, the data they have is about call details, internet usage logs and network data using Hive on this data, they can quicky and efficiently analyse the network trend, find the peak usage hours in terms of calls or internet and based on that they can take informed actions such as planning the expansion of infra or driving some marketing roadmaps etc.

Similarly, Hive is being used where there is a huge historical data accumulation happening, where batch processing is required, and has cost-effective storage like HDFS, where the data analysts need to understand the data in easy language like SQL for specific business outcomes. Some of the other industries where this works are social media, healthcare organizations, advertising and marketing companies, government and public sector bodies, etc.

Introduction to Apache Kafka

Apache Kafka is a distributed event-streaming platform used to collect, store, and process real-time data. In other words, it is a distributed messaging system for real-time data streaming between the systems.

Working of Kafka is very simple, the producer sends data, which is also called an event, the data is stored in Kafka topics, and the consumer reads the data from the topic:

Producer ǀ Kafka topics ǀ Consumer

A real-life example can be, on a food delivery application, the order is placed ǀ Producer. This event is stored in Kafka; now, this event will be consumed by multiple consumers, such as billing services, notification services, analytics services, etc.

Features of Kafka

Let us look at some important features of Apache Kafka:

- **Real-time**: Kafka is designed to handle a high volume of real-time data with low latency. Due to its architecture, it can handle millions of real-time events per second.
- **Scalable**: The architecture of Kafka supports horizontal scaling, which means the user does not need to worry about the increasing number of events in real-time.
- **Fault-tolerant**: Kafka supports no data loss in case of any server failure due to the data partitioning, which copies are in multiple brokers.
- **Decoupled**: Kafka architecture is completely decoupled, which means consumers and producers of data can have their own level of abstraction and be independent of each other.

Traditional messaging queue platform vs Kafka

There are many traditional message queues available in the market that work on a producer and consumer philosophy. They receive messages from one system and deliver them to another. They act as a middleman between systems, so they do not talk to each other directly, e.g., RabbitMQ.

On the other hand, Kafka brings some features that are not available or available in limited capacities in these traditional messaging Queues. Some of those features are listed in the following table:

Features	Traditional messaging queues	Kafka
Message retention	Messages are removed from the queue after the consumer has consumed the message	Messages can be persisted for a configurable period

Scalability	Limited due to a broker-based approach	It is horizontally scalable, which means the streaming data can be scaled to potentially unlimited capacity
Data throughput	Lower	High
Fault tolerance	In cases of any system failure, the messages can be lost	Kafka's architecture supports the replication of data across multiple brokers, which ensures durability
Data processing	Data is processed in batches or intervals	Data is processed in real-time.
Real-life analogy	It is like a courier delivery; once delivered, it is gone	It is like a video recording that can be rewound again
Best for	Low-latency message delivery	High-throughput real-time streaming

***Table 12.1**: A comparison between the traditional message queue and Kafka*

Architecture of Kafka

As we know, Kafka is a distributed real-time stream processing system where publishers and subscribers are decoupled, and it is a fault-tolerant system that is designed to achieve no data loss. The following figure represents the Apache Kafka architecture:

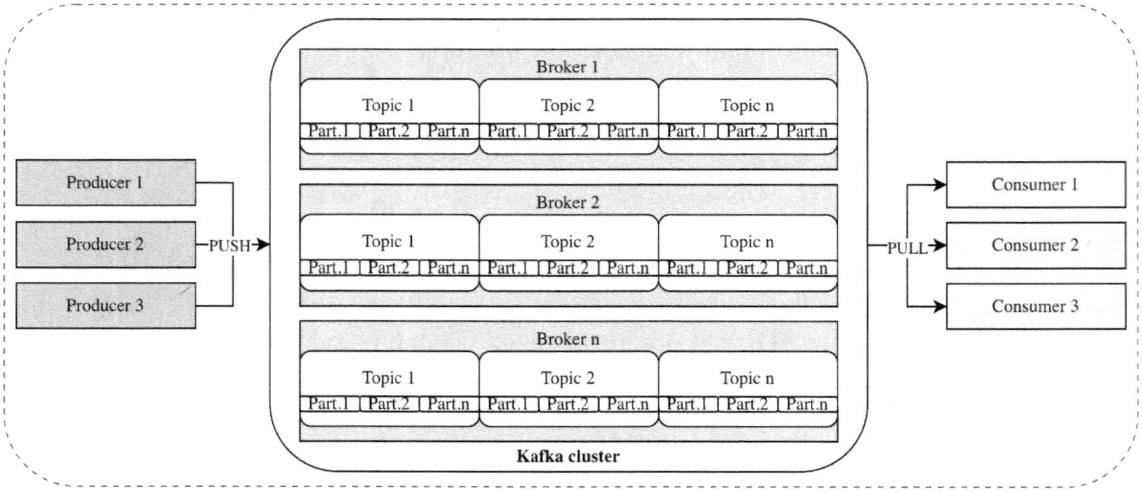

***Figure 12.4**: A visual representation of Apache Kafka architecture*

As per *Figure 12.4*, Kafka has the following components:

- **Brokers**: These are the servers that are responsible for storing the data, performing read/write operations, and copying the data among different brokers for data reliability.

- **Kafka clusters**: This is the complete distributed system that contains multiple brokers to ensure the data replication, fault-tolerance, and high availability of data, e.g., a Kafka cluster may have ten servers, each acting as an individual broker and replicating data amongst them.
- **Topics**: It may be defined as a category or logical grouping or channel where specific messages are published or stored, e.g., on *WhatsApp*, we may have different groups for different purposes, there may be a dedicated group about the stock market information, and there may be a family group where all the relatives feed personal posts.
- **Partition**: This is the methodology to divide the data within the groups/topics so that the data access can be done in parallel to improve parallelism and scalability, e.g., in a bank, there may be multiple ATM machines so that people can get the cash in parallel rather than having a single long line on a single ATM machine.
- **Producers**: These may be the client applications that are producing the data and pushing it onto the Kafka Topics, e.g., web applications, mobile apps, microservices, databases, IoT devices, sensors, etc.
- **Consumers**: These are the consumers of data who have subscribed to a topic and get the required messages only related to those topics.
- **Offset**: The unique message IDs that are used by consumers to track their read history, e.g., it is like milestones on the road that tell us how far we have covered.

Use cases of Apache Kafka

Kafka is extensively used in many businesses, such as e-commerce, where when an order is placed on the application, it creates an event on Kafka and is stored on it. Now there are multiple services which are subscribed to this event will start consuming the data e.g., Inventory service to reduce the stock count from the database, payment service which will be responsible to charge the customer for the order, email services that will send the order confirmation to the user and analytics services which will track the sales and executes the existing algorithms for any predictive and prescriptive analysis.

Another example for an online ride booking application, when user searches for a ride from place A to place B, the event is generated and stored in Kafka, now the next consumer services will get activated to do their respective steps such as checking the active rides in the area, finding the driver who is closet and available for this request, a pricing service which will calculate the price for the trip, a special price service that will check if any specific charge needs to be applied like surge price, night charges etc.

Introduction to Apache Airflow

Apache Airflow is an open-source platform that is used to create an end-to-end workflow. It is used to programmatically author, schedule, and monitor the workflows.

In simple language, it helps us define what tasks to run, in which order, and when.

It is used in scenarios where the execution of one task is dependent upon the other one. It may also be useful to automatically retry if the defined task has failed.

Apache Airflow is best when the workflow becomes complex and is heavy when implemented using only code.

A workflow in Apache Airflow is represented as a DAG, which contains individual tasks that are arranged in a sequenced fashion.

It is because every task is defined one after another based on the dependencies; it is called a **directed** graph. Since there is no loop back to any task, which will rerun in a cycle, this is why it is called an acyclic graph; this makes sure there is no infinite loop, and the graph has a definite end point.

Components of Apache Airflow

A minimal airflow has some components that are required to run a workflow completely without breaking. It should have all the dependencies for each task and retry mechanisms for failure cases. The following figure explains Apache Airflow visually:

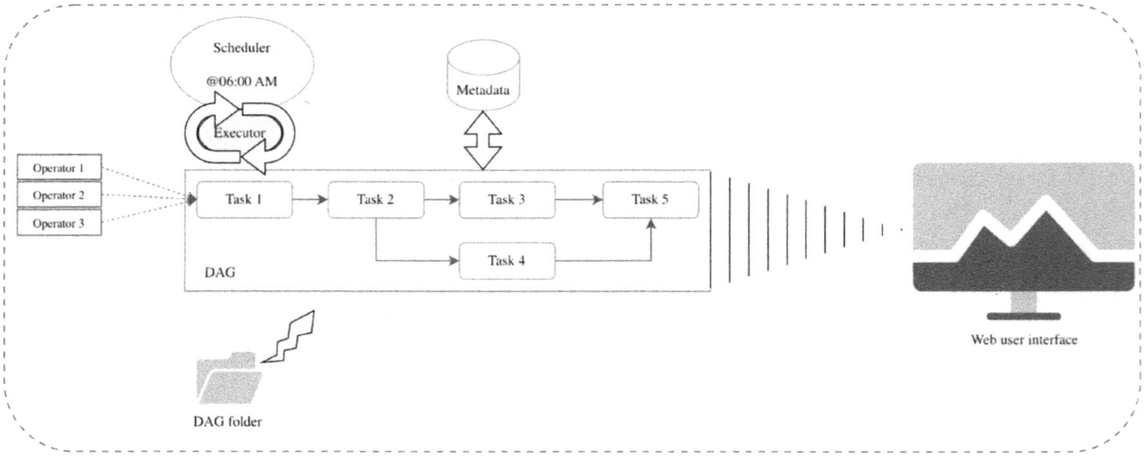

***Figure 12.5**: Components of Apache Airflow*

As shown in *Figure 12.5*, there are eight components of Apache Airflow:

- **DAG**: This represents a workflow in the system that shows the collection of tasks with the dependencies amongst them without any loops.

  For example: Start | fetch data | process data | store data | train model | deploy model | end.

The DAG is written in Python code.

- **Tasks**: These are the individual, single units of work. It can be individual Python code execution, executing the SQL query, or triggering any other command.
- **Operators**: Operators define what a task does, e.g., **`PythonOperator`** executes the Python code, or **`BashOperator`** executes bash commands, or **`EmailOperator`** sends emails.
- **Scheduler**: This keeps track of execution time for all the tasks and decides which task runs when. It triggers the task on its scheduled time, e.g., at 6 AM or after finishing one task, etc.
- **Executor**: It is an entity inside the scheduler that decides how the tasks are executed, e.g., sequential execution, parallel execution, or distributed execution.
- **Webserver**: A web UI that presents an intuitive user interface to inspect, trigger, and debug the behavior of DAGs and tasks.
- **Metadata database**: This is a database that stores the current state of DAGs and tasks so that their current status can be shown on the user interface and stored for logging purposes. They are generally PostgreSQL or MySQL.
- **A DAG folder**: This is a folder containing DAG files, which a scheduler accesses to plan which task to run and when.

There may be some optional components as well, based on the business requirements, which may enhance the capabilities of the complete workflow, but the above components are the bare minimum that are must-haves.

Features of Apache Airflow

The following are the important features of Apache Airflow:

- **Pure Python**: Apache Airflow supports standard Python to create workflows, scheduling, and monitoring. Understanding the acceptability of Python in the world of software development and machine learning is an advantage in itself.
- **Web UI**: Apache Airflow supports a user-friendly web interface that provides important information about the end-to-end flow, important logs, current status of the tasks, retries, and failed tasks. This makes governance of the complete system unified and convenient, which also helps in quick debugging.
- **Integration**: It provides the ready connectors for various third-party applications, which makes the overall working of a system easy and single-blocked, especially when the system consists of various heterogeneous subsystems or different cloud providers such as Google Cloud Platform, Microsoft Azure, or **Amazon Web Services** (**AWS**).

Benefits of Apache Airflow

Apache Airflow has several benefits, some of which are:

- **Python**: Since configuring and customization require learning Python, which is very easy to learn, it increases the adoptability of the system.
- **Highly scalable**: Apache Airflow works as a containerized application, which is highly scalable with minimal effort.
- **Strong community support**: The open-source community of Apache provides the mechanisms for developers or contributors to share their improvements without any barriers or complex procedures, which helps people to improve the collective system as a whole, ask questions, and share their experience, which ultimately makes the community grow.
- **Easy monitoring and debugging**: Using Apache Airflow's user interface, it is very easy to see the progress of the workflow, get information about the issues that occurred in the pipeline, and quickly debug and fix the problem as early as possible.
- **Suitability of complex workflows**: Although the sequencing of workflow can also be achieved in only Python, there are some limitations that have been overcome by complete orchestrators like Apache Airflow, such as:
    - **No built-in dependency management**: Using a Python script, the developers need to make sure Task B runs only after Task A, and failure of Task A does not break the system as a whole.
    - **Requirement to create a user interface**: In Python, there is no easy way to see the current status of the workflow, and logs may be scattered across multiple files, unlike Airflow, where everything is available in one place.
    - **No automatic retry and alerts**: Python natively does not have any mechanism to retry; developers need to write logic to do that. Similarly, the alert mechanism has to be set up manually.
    - **Lack of scalability**: Using Python, running tasks in parallel is difficult, and it is complex to have a distributed configuration of execution, which makes overall management of resources hard. Apache Airflow brings scalability and distributed configuration with ease.

Airflow is not a replacement for Python; rather, it is one layer on top of it to ensure the management of the complete lifecycle with durability.

Use case of Apache Airflow

Apache Airflow is used where the tasks need to run in a specific order, on a schedule, with monitoring and reliability.

A simple use case or the most common use case is ETL. In this, the pipeline needs to extract the data from sources, which can be databases, APIs, IoT, or sensors, etc. Once the data is received, it needs to be processed for cleansing, transformation, and error detection. Post that, the data will be stored in the data warehouse. For example:

Fetch data from SQL | clean the missing values | load the data into BigQuery.

Airflow ensures that the tasks execute in the correct order, and they are triggered at the correct schedule, and if there is any failure, then the retry mechanism is there to make sure it is not missed.

Other use cases can be machine learning workflows:

Data collection | feature engineering | model training | model evaluation | model deployment

Another use case can be report generation with the following sequential steps:

Generate daily report | Create PDF or Excel | Email report to stakeholders

Introduction to Databricks

Databricks is a cloud-based managed data analytics platform that has been built on top of Apache Spark. It provides an interactive workspace for data engineers, data analysts, and scientists to process large amounts of data very easily.

Databricks has been developed by the creator of Apache Spark to overcome the issues of the open-source product, such as Apache Spark.

Databricks versus Apache Spark

Although Databricks is built on Spark, it has some fundamental differences from it. The following table represents the comparison between Databricks and Apache Spark:

Parameter	Databricks	Apache Spark
Infrastructure	Cloud managed	User-managed
Open-source	Uses open-source and proprietary features	Yes
Scalability	Automatic	Manual cluster scaling
Setup	Complex and manual configuration	Fully managed
Storage	HDFS/S3 etc.	Delta Lake
Cost	Free and Infra cost	Pay as you go

***Table 12.2**: Difference between Databricks and Apache Spark*

Usage of Databricks

The following are the areas where Databricks can be used:

- Databricks is used to process huge datasets in terabytes and petabytes.
- Used to build data pipelines.
- It is used to process real-time streaming data.
- It is meant to do advanced analytics at scale.
- It also supports advanced machine learning and machine learning flows.

Architecture of Databricks

In the architecture of Databricks, there are two layers:

- **Control plane**: This part is responsible for handling user management, cluster management, workspace management, job scheduling, and metadata storage. This is managed by Databricks.
- **Data/compute plane**: This runs Spark computation, **Databricks File System** (**DBFS**), and data processing, and is managed by cloud providers such as Azure, **Google Cloud Platform** (**GCP**), and AWS.

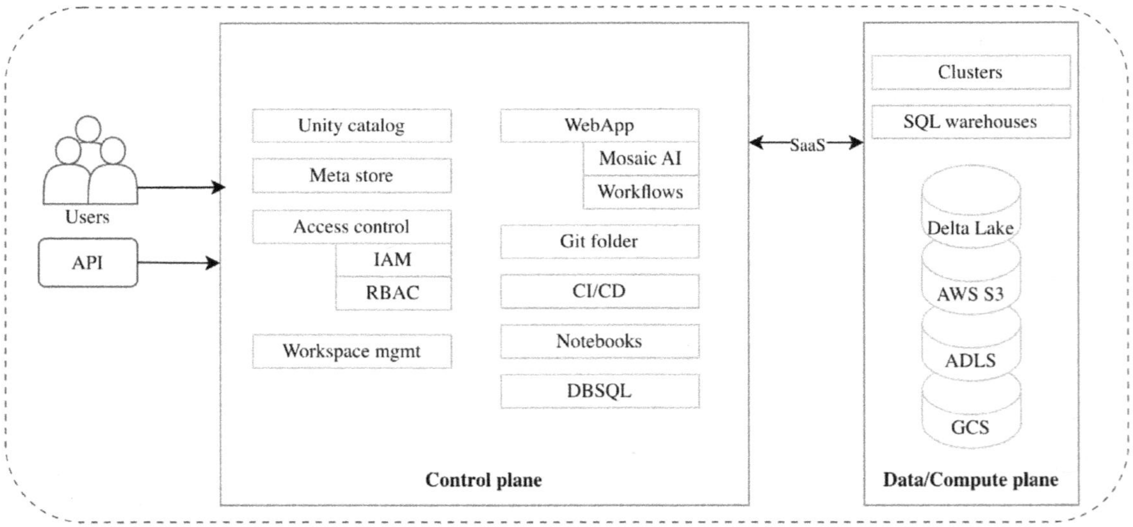

***Figure 12.6**: Components of Databricks*

As shown in *Figure 12.6*, there are several key components in Databricks:

- **Control plane**:
  - **Unity catalog**:

        - **Data governance**: Controls who can see and access the data.
        - **Lineage tracking**: Tracks where the data is coming from and how it is used.

    For example, only the finance team has access to the salary data.

    This stores the data about the data but not the data itself. The information can be in table structures, schemas, and partitions.

    - **Access control and security**: This takes care of who will be allowed to use the platform; it further has two components:
    - **Identity and access management (IAM)**: Manages users, groups, and service accounts.
    - **Role-based access control (RBAC)**: This makes sure which role is allowed to do which operation; these roles can be viewer, admin, etc. For example, an analyst can read the data but cannot delete it.
    - **Workspace management**: This is the main working area, which provides the interface to manage notebooks, clusters, jobs, and dashboards. It helps organize the project and teams and control who can access it. For example, each team has its own folder with restricted access.
    - **Web application and AI tools**: It further has two components:
        - **Mosaic AI**: This helps teams build and manage AI models easily. It is used for machine learning models and AI applications, and supports model training, testing, and deployment.
        - **Workflows**: This is used to automate tasks, such as running the tasks in sequence, scheduling the data pipeline (hourly, daily, etc.), and handling failures automatically.
    - **Git**: Support version control using Git and support team collaboration.
    - **CI/CD**: Usage of CI/CD to automate the deployment, including automated testing and a deployment pipeline without manual intervention.
    - **Notebooks**: Notebooks are interactive coding documents that support various programming languages such as Python, R, Scala, and SQL. This is supported by Databricks, where multiple users can work together in the same notebook.
    - **Databricks SQL (DBSQL)**: It is a fast SQL engine specially designed for analytics and optimized for large storage. It is serverless and can be used for reporting and dashboarding.

- **Data/compute plane**: It is the place where the actual data processing is happening in Databricks. This part runs the code, processes the data, and reads/writes the data to storage.

Some key components in the planes are:

- **Compute cluster**: These are the group of machines(nodes) that work together to process a large amount of data. These run the notebook, jobs, and queries, and process huge datasets with speed. They are powered by Apache Spark. E.g., a cluster divides the big file into parts and processes them in parallel.

  These clusters are auto-scalable, i.e., will add more machines when the workload increases and remove the extra machines when the workload decreases.

  It supports Apache Spark and SQL warehouses for execution.

- **Storage and Data Lake**: Databricks integrates with multiple cloud storage solutions, such as:
  - **Delta Lake**: An open-source storage layer for ACID transactions (explained in *Delta Lake* topic, later in the chapter).
  - **AWS S3**: A cloud storage from Amazon for structured and unstructured data.
  - **Azure Azure Data Lake Storage (ADLS)**: It is a Data Lake from Microsoft Azure.
  - **Google Cloud Storage**: It is a storage provided by Google for analytics.

In the market, we have two types of products available: community edition and cloud-based Databricks, and the following table explains the fundamental differences between them:

Features	Community edition	Cloud-based Databricks
Cluster type	Single-node cluster (only driver)	Multi-node cluster with worker nodes
Data processing	Limited datasets only	Scalable to big data processing
Storage	Using DBFS (local file system)	Can be integrated with cloud data storage
Cloud connectivity	No	Yes, with GCP, AWS, Azure
Usage	Learning and small-scale projects	Enterprise-grade application

***Table 12.3**: Difference between Databricks community edition and cloud edition*

Databricks File System

It is a distributed file system provided by Databricks that allows users to store data easily within the Databricks ecosystem. It may also be understood as an abstraction layer in Databricks, which lets users access cloud storage as if it were a local file storage system; in other words, the data is stored in the cloud, but DBFS simplifies it, avoiding complex cloud processes for data storage.

Delta Lake

Delta Lake is an open-source storage mechanism that is designed to be used with the Apache Spark ecosystem. It is known that data lakes are preferred to store raw data, structured, and unstructured data at a very fast speed, but this often struggles to address data inconsistencies, schema validation, and performance issues.

Delta Lake solves these challenges by introducing schema enforcement, scalable data processing, and the ACID property to big data transactions.

Use case of Databricks

Due to its huge data processing capability, it is used in e-commerce platforms to analyze customer interaction datasets that involve their click history, view history, purchase history, and search history, to deliver personalized shopping experiences. Databricks can easily consolidate data from web portals and mobile apps and run machine learning models to generate these personalized recommendations.

Companies like *DoorDash* rely on Databricks to build a unified customer 360 data store based on customers' profiles and tastes, with an objective to improve the personalized customer experience.

Introduction to Dockers

Docker is a containerization platform that allows us to package an application with all its dependencies, such as libraries, runtime environment, and configuration, into a single unit called a container.

This container can simply run on any system, laptop, server, or a cloud virtual machine or container instances as well.

The containerization topic can be referred to from *Chapter 10, Understanding Cloud Computing*, where how containerization works has been explained in depth.

Introduction to major cloud platforms

Till now, this book has explained in detail about the cloud and its components, where if the customer wants to utilize the high-end servers for their projects, they do not need to set up the infrastructure themselves, but can opt for any of the available cloud platforms and pay for what they use. The complete headache of maintaining the space, the appropriate temperature of servers, and replacing the fault components goes away, keeping only the business outcome and cost of the platform as focus areas.

There are many cloud providers in the market today, but today we will cover the three major cloud providers, *the big three*, which are Azure, GCP, and AWS.

Amazon Web Service

AWS is the largest and oldest cloud computing platform (launched in 2006) that provides on-demand computing services and storage space over the internet. It is the product of Amazon Inc., which offers a wide range of cloud services such as compute (virtual machine), storage space, databases, various analytics tools, machine learning, etc.

It offers **software as a service** (**SaaS**), **platform as a service** (**PaaS**), and **infrastructure as a service** (**IaaS**) as standard offerings.

The following are some services provided by AWS:

- **Compute**:
    - **Amazon EC2**: Resizable virtual machines/servers to run applications on them.
    - **AWS Lambda**: A serverless compute engine that runs code without the need to manage servers.
    - **AWS Fargate**: A serverless compute engine that runs containers without managing the servers.
- **Storage**:
    - **Amazon S3**: An object storage for storing and retrieving any data.
    - **Amazon Elastic Block Store (EBS)**: This is a block storage service designed to work with EC2 virtual servers.
    - **AWS Backup**: A centralized service that is meant to automatically manage data backups.
- **Database or data management**:
    - **Amazon RDS**: A managed relational database service supporting multiple database engines.
    - **Amazon DynamoDB**: A managed NoSQL database for fast and scalable applications.
    - **Amazon Redshift**: A managed data warehouse for large-scale data storage and reporting.
    - **AWS Glue**: A serverless ETL service for data integration and preparation.
- **Networking and content delivery**:
    - **Amazon Virtual Private Cloud (VPC)**: This creates isolated network layers in the AWS cloud.
    - **AWS Direct Connect**: This creates a dedicated private connection from on-premises to the AWS cloud.

  - **Amazon CloudFront**: This is a content delivery network for fast and global content distribution.

Some other services are:

- **AWS IAM**: This manages user identity and access permissions.
- **AWS Web Application Firewall (WAF)**: This protects the web applications from common security threats.
- **AWS Shield**: This service provides protection against **distributed denial-of-service (DDoS)** attacks.
- **Amazon SageMaker**: This helps in building, training, and deploying the machine learning models at scale.
- **AWS CodePipelines**: This automates CI/CD pipelines.
- **AWS CodeDeploy**: Automates application deployment to various compute services.
- **AWS Step Functions**: Orchestrate the workflow by coordinating across multiple AWS apps and services.

There are many more services that exist in AWS.

Microsoft Azure

Microsoft Azure, formerly known as *Windows Azure*, was publicly available in 2010 and is mainly used in sophisticated enterprise settings. It offers all the required services right from servers, storage, networking, database, etc., as a pay-as-you-go model or a fixed reserve instance model as well.

The following are some offerings from Microsoft Azure:

- **Compute**:
  - **Azure Virtual Machines**: Provide scalable virtual machines to run applications in the cloud.
  - **Azure Kubernetes Services (AKS)**: It is a managed Kubernetes service for deploying and managing containerized applications.
  - **Azure Functions**: These are the serverless compute engines that run the code without managing the virtual machines or servers.
- **Storage and databases**:
  - **Azure Blob Storage**: Object storage service for structured and unstructured data such as audio, video, and images.

- **Azure Files**: Fully managed file sharing services that are accessible via standard file transfer protocols.
- **Azure Cosmos DB**: Globally distributed NoSQL database for highly scalable applications.
- **Azure SQL Database**: A fully managed relational database service based on SQL Server.

- **Networking**:
  - **Azure Virtual Network**: Creates a private, isolated network within the Azure environment.
  - **Azure Load Balancer**: A managed service that distributes the traffic across multiple servers for high availability.
  - **Azure Express Route**: It creates a private, dedicated, and high-speed connection between the on-premise network and Azure.

Some other important services are:

- **Azure Active Directory**: Manages user identities and access to Azure resources.
- **Azure Monitor**: It collects and analyzes the performance of Azure resources for health checks.
- **Azure Security Center**: Monitors security and provides threat protection recommendations.
- **Azure DevOps**: It provides managed tools for CI/CD and source control.
- **Azure Logic Apps**: Automates the workflow by connecting apps and services.
- **Azure Site Recovery**: Provides disaster recovery by replicating data and workloads across regions.
- **Azure Machine Learning**: Helps in building, deploying, and scaling the machine learning model.

There are many more managed services available in Microsoft Azure.

Google Cloud Platform

GCP is a cloud service suite that offers various cloud services that help organizations build, deploy, and scale their applications to offer services to their respective customers or clients. This is the same infrastructure that powers giants like YouTube, Google Search, and Gmail. It was launched in 2008 to provide high-performance cloud solutions.

Some of the services provided by GCP are:

- **Compute**:

  - **Google Compute Engine (GCE)**: These are scalable virtual machines for running applications or workloads on Google infrastructure.
  - **Google App Engine**: It is a serverless, PaaS used to build and deploy applications without any need to manage servers.
  - **Google Cloud Run**: A managed serverless platform that is used to run containerized applications.
  - **Google Kubernetes Services**: A fully managed Kubernetes service that is used to deploy and manage containers.
- **Storage and database**:
  - **Google Cloud Storage**: It is an object storage used to store structured and unstructured data.
  - **CloudSQL**: It is a managed relational database service from Google for MySQL, PostgreSQL, and SQL Server.
  - **Google Bigtable**: It is a high-performance NoSQL database for large-scale operational workloads.
  - **Google Firestore**: A Serverless NoSQL document database for mobile and web applications.
  - **Google BigQuery**: A serverless data warehouse for fast, large-scale analytics.
- **Networking and content delivery**:
  - **Google VPC**: It is a private and isolated network to connect various Google Cloud resources.
  - **Cloud CDN**: It is a content delivery network for faster global content access.
  - **Cloud Interconnect**: This provides high-speed, dedicated private connectivity between on-premises and Google Cloud resources.

Some other important services are:

- **Google Dataflow**: Managed services for stream and batch data processing.
- **Dataproc**: Managed Apache Spark and Hadoop service.
- **VertexAI**: A managed service for building, training, and deploying a machine learning model.
- **AutoML**: This managed service helps the creation of machine learning models with minimum machine learning expertise.
- **TensorFlow Enterprise**: An enterprise-ready machine learning framework optimized for GCP.
- **Security Command Center**: Centralized security and risk management platform.

- **Identity-Aware Proxy**: This is a user identity-based control access platform for applications.
- **Cloud Build**: A managed service for continuous integration and building for applications and containers.
- **Firebase**: It is a managed platform for building and scaling mobile and web applications.
- **Bare metal solution**: Runs a GCP service on on-premise hardware.

There are many more services that exist in GCP.

Market and business comparison of AWS, Azure, and GCP

The *big three* combined share the 60% of worldwide cloud architectures. A quick summary of their individual market share is covered in the following table:

Criteria	AWS	Azure	GCP
Launched	2006	2010	2008
Market Share (Q3 2025)	29%	20%	13%
Total revenue (billions)	$33	$26.7	$15.2

***Table 12.4**: Market share information for AWS vs Azure vs GCP in Q3 2025*
*(**Source**: https://www.emma.ms/blog/cloud-market-share-trends)*

There are other cloud providers that are also quite prominent in the industry and growing at a rapid rate. Some of these names are *Alibaba Cloud, Oracle, Salesforce, IBM Cloud, and Tencent Cloud.*

Conclusion

This chapter begins with the fundamentals of SQL and covers generic SQL commands for a high-level understanding of some of these SQL operations. It then provides in-depth information about Python, including the development environment setup, various IDEs available in the market, and different types of variables, datatypes, operators, conditional statements, etc., which are considered essentials in Python. This chapter also covered various open-source frameworks and tools, such as Apache Spark, Hadoop, Hive, Kafka, etc., which cannot be ignored in today's modern world for quick data processing, having a reliable data pipeline, and durability across the complete end-to-end lifecycle.

In the next chapter, this book will introduce stream analytics, in which the reader will understand the fundamental differences between traditional data processing and stream processing, and why traditional machine learning algorithms cannot be directly applied to streaming data.

References

1. **https://sqliteonline.com/**
2. **https://www.geeksforgeeks.org/python/what-is-python-interpreter/**
3. **https://www.altexsoft.com/blog/apache-spark-pros-cons/**
4. **https://hive.apache.org/**
5. **https://www.tutorialspoint.com/hive/hive_introduction.htm**
6. **https://www.geeksforgeeks.org/devops/architecture-and-working-of-hive/**
7. **https://www.udemy.com/course/big-data-engineering-bootcamp-with-gcp-and-azure-cloud**
8. **https://aws.amazon.com/what-is/apache-kafka/**
9. **https://www.geeksforgeeks.org/apache-kafka/kafka-architecture/**
10. **https://airflow.apache.org/**
11. **https://www.databricks.com/blog/data-intelligence-action-100-data-and-ai-use-cases-databricks-customers**
12. **https://www.geeksforgeeks.org/devops/what-is-microsoft-azure/**
13. **http://azure.microsoft.com/en-us/get-started**
14. **https://medium.com/@accentfuture/databricks-architecture-overview-components-workflow-ee00c965a445**
15. **https://www.datacamp.com/blog/aws-vs-azure-vs-gcp**
16. **https://www.geeksforgeeks.org/devops/aws-vs-google-cloud-platform-vs-azure/**
17. **https://www.theknowledgeacademy.com/blog/microsoft-azure-vs-aws-vs-google-cloud**
18. **https://www.emma.ms/blog/cloud-market-share-trends**
19. **https://www.cargoson.com/en/blog/global-cloud-infrastructure-market-share-aws-azure-google**

CHAPTER 13
Understanding Stream Analytics

Introduction

Being data processing, the core of data engineering, we have already covered some of its aspects earlier in the book.

Due to the advancement of hardware nowadays, our capability to work with big data has improved significantly. Today, in many applications, it is still very difficult to store data on the disk, and even if it is to be stored on the disk, it cannot be processed more than once due to its humongous size. Therefore, it makes more sense to process and analyse the data online without storing it first. Storing such data may be more costly than the return on investment it provides.

Once the analysis is done on the live or stream data, the results can be stored, which may be the final inference for business advantage.

Structure

The chapter covers the following topics:

- Introduction to stream analytics
- Clustering techniques for stream data
- Classification techniques for stream data
- Data outlier and anomaly detection in stream data
- Use cases of stream analytics

Objectives

This chapter will clarify the fundamental differences between conventional data processing and stream data processing. The readers will be able to understand how the stream data is processed and what the inline algorithms are behind processing the streaming data.

Some of the techniques that are used for data mining and database operations, such as classification, clustering, and other pattern detection, will be touched upon in this chapter.

Introduction to stream analytics

In the current modern world, technology has advanced enough to ensure that the data that is being generated continuously can be captured continuously and stored. This has been possible due to innovation in hardware, better connectors and integrators available in the market, and the new frameworks that have been defined for optimized ways to access the data with minimum computational power.

Capturing continuous data was one challenge; another challenge was to collect data from several computing devices at the same time and bring all of them together to process, and try to figure out some meaningful information. This data can be the dataset coming from various sensors, IoT devices, banking transactions, web browsing data, social media, etc., that is being continuously fed 24/7, around the world.

Current challenges

With the increase in the volume of data, we may see some of the computational and storage challenges:

- **Impossibility of processing data in multiple passes**: Since the data is so huge that it is nearly impossible to have it processed more than once. The simple possibility to pass the data only once and get the expected outcome.

  In the traditional data mining system, the algorithm would use the data a couple of times. For example, in clustering, there would be three steps to be followed:

  1. **First pass**: Compute the average of the data.
  2. **Second pass**: Compute the distance of a datapoint from the average.
  3. **Third pass**: Refine the clusters based on the distance from the average.

  From the above example, it is clearly seen that the data is being accessed a couple of times to conclude on the final outcome.

  If the data is huge and continuously being filled, then it is a storage and compute-heavy operation to do the data processing, and that too, if it is to be done continuously.

  Whereas in the case of streaming data, when the data arrives, it is to be processed immediately, summary statistics are updated, and then finally, the data is discarded.

  In conclusion, the reason multiple passes are not possible is that:

  - Data arrives continuously and rapidly
  - Total data size is unbounded
  - Storing all the data is impractical
  - Real-time decisioning is required

- **Temporal state of data**: In stream mining, data arrives continuously over time, and the order in which it arrives plays a very important role. This is a temporal component that represents the current state of the system more accurately than the old data.

  As time progresses, the statistical behaviour of the data may change due to changing users' behaviour, system conditions, and other external unknown factors. This is because the older data become irrelevant and may be misleading to the expected outcome.

  For example, see *Figure 13.1*, processing the stock market data for more than a specific time may start giving wrong results because the circumstances in the market may change, and people may have an interest in a current stock due to some influencing news in the market:

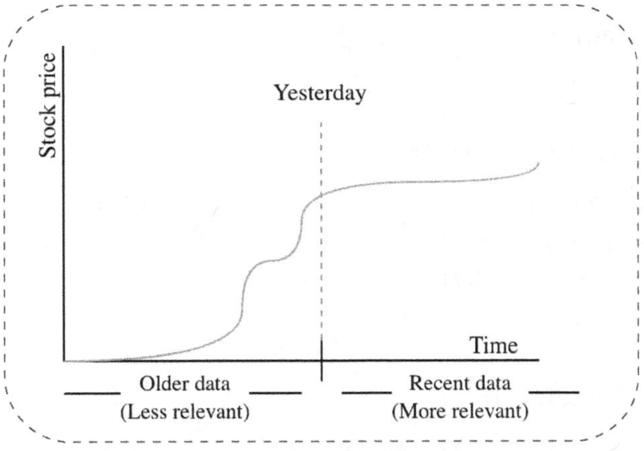

***Figure 13.1**: A visual representation of a stock price*

  Now the data, which is being captured every second, minute, or hour, may be beneficial for quick analysis, but including six-month-old data for processing may make the overall inference incorrect.

- **Backpressure**: In stream data, the backpressure situation occurs when the rate of data ingestion becomes higher than the rate of data processing. The high velocity of incoming data may create memory pressure, increase latency, cause buffering issues, or even sometimes lead to data loss, if not handled carefully.

Apart from the above, there are other challenges as well, which are; the stream data may be heterogeneous, which may include structured, unstructured, diverse data types that may require pre-processing before analyzing in real-time. Stream data is often noisy and incomplete and may require outlier and error detection early before feeding into the main algorithm. Time criticality is the key in stream analysis, and latency in processing may reduce the usefulness of the same, e.g., for any banking transaction, fraud detection is the key; if the processing is not done at the instant, the fraudulent transaction can take place. The count of stream sources may increase over time, which may require horizontal scaling of processing.

Stream mining algorithms

As we have seen, there may be many challenges in processing the stream data, which is the fundamental reason why the conventional algorithm will not work and requires the modification of the same or rebuilding of the new algorithms from scratch. Some of the algorithms that are used for stream data mining or data processing are discussed in the following sections.

Data stream clustering

As we now know, due to the limitations in processing the stream data, the conventional clustering algorithm may not work due to single-pass requirements. To work on this, it may require modifications to the existing algorithms, which may work on limited dimensions of data rather than the complete dataset. The clustering on stream data must be incremental, memory-efficient, and adaptive. The clustering techniques used in stream data are explained in the next topic.

Data stream classification

Classification is one of the most widely studied problems for streaming data. Similar to clustering, this algorithm should work online, adapt to the changing data, and be able to operate in a single-pass constraint. Elaboration of these algorithms is discussed in the forthcoming topic.

Frequent pattern mining

Frequent pattern mining is used to determine the patterns or sequences that occur frequently in the streaming data. It has the same challenge of getting determined in a single pass; the data may be unbound, and we may have limited memory and computational power.

Now, to work on this kind of problem statement, users need to define a window in which the algorithm can be applied to make sure that the data fits in existing memory and can be processed in a single pass.

The following figure illustrates the different types of models that may be applicable for pattern mining:

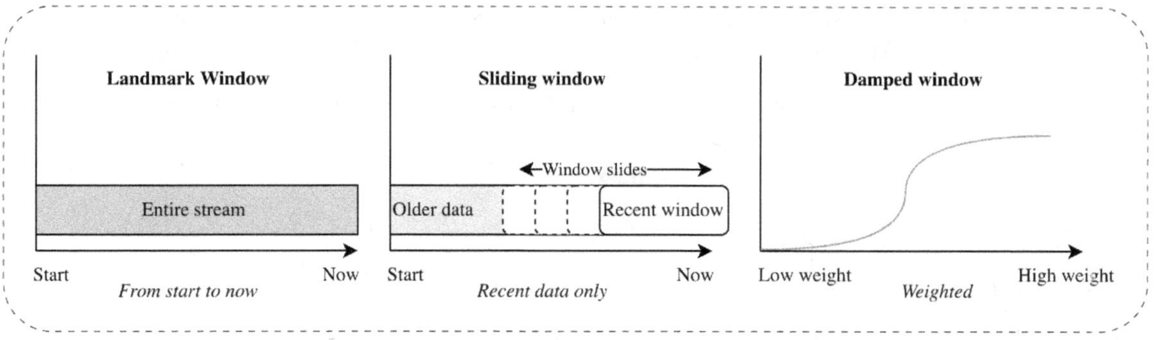

***Figure 13.2**: Figure showing the different types of windows*

As shown in *Figure 13.2*, the pattern mining can be done on three types of models:

- **Landmark window**: In this model, the analysis is done on the data, starting from one point to the current time point. In other words, the window size has the starting time = 1 to the current time t. Pattern recognition is fine for the cases in the initial period of analysis, but as the data and time increase, it becomes similar to the conventional algorithm and requires good computational power for a single pass analysis to provide the inference.

  An important point to note here is that data at each point is treated equally, which may not be relevant if there is a change in pattern in recent data. For example, as a retail company, it is finding which products have been frequently purchased since the store opened.

- **Damped window model**: This works on the entire stream, but it assigns more weight to the recent transactions while still considering the older ones. The picture on the right in *Figure 13.2* shows how this model is prioritizing the recent data by giving it more weight compared to the older one. For example, in cases of the stock market, the recent price movement matters more than the older ones.

- **Sliding window**: Sliding windows are one of the best techniques that are used in stream processing to analyse only the recent portion of the data. All the calculations are done only on the current window, forgetting the older window. The middle picture in *Figure 13.2* shows how window slides are processing the recent data. This window can be time-based (used when data arrives regularly), e.g., the last 10 minutes of data, or it can be count-based (used when data arrives irregularly), e.g., the last 100 transactions.

  Since the window is not very large, the entire processing can fit in the main memory for quick processing. The data can be processed incrementally. One of the known algorithms proposed is MOMENT. This algorithm is the first one for mining closed frequent itemsets in a data stream using an in-memory data structure called the **closed enumeration tree** (**CET**).

This is developed to efficiently monitor closed frequent itemsets as well as itemsets that form the boundary between closed frequent itemsets and the rest of the itemsets.

The following figure represents a sliding window concept with a simple example:

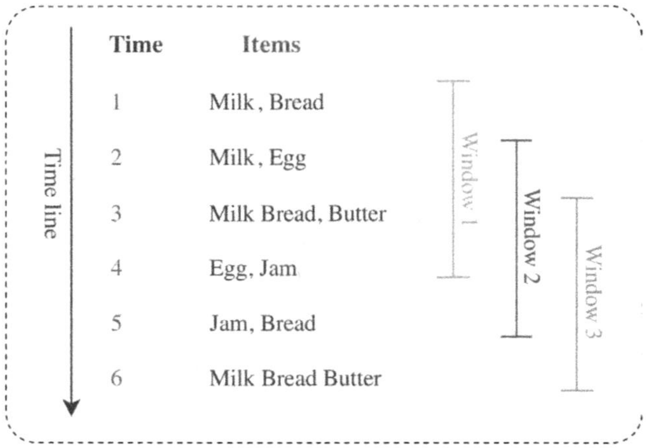

***Figure 13.3**: A representation of a sliding window*

As shown in *Figure 13.3*, taking the above algorithm in a real-life example of an e-commerce platform with a window of recent 10000 transactions (assuming this much can fit in the main memory). The CET can give something like the following:

- **{Bread, Milk}**: Closed frequently, i.e., it is a frequent pattern and stable (unlikely to change)
- **{Milk}**: Frequent but not closed, i.e., appear frequent but give no extra information
- **{Bread, Milk, Butter}**: Boundary itemset, i.e., these itemsets have frequency close to the minimum support threshold, which could be frequent (if appear again) or infrequent (if old transactions leave the window)

Now, when the new transactions come, old transactions leave the window, and MOMENT only updates the boundary, and stable items remain unchanged:

- **{Bread, Milk}**: Remain closed frequent
- **{Butter, Jam}**: May drop
- **{Milk, Egg}**: May move to the frequent zone if they repeat

MOMENT tracks the boundary items, which are frequent enough or just about to become infrequent, and items that are closed.

Important note: **In production grade streaming systems, the time used in these algorithms may refer to either processing time or event time. Processing time represents when the system processes the event, while event time represents when the event actually occurred. This distinction becomes important when delayed or out-of-order events are present in the data stream.**

Change detection in data streams

This is an important problem statement in data stream analysis because the data stream may change over time, which can be due to some underlying phenomenon change in the system, which may be called data evolution with time. However, in some cases, these changes are sudden, which need to be captured so that the cause of the same can be analysed.

The method that can be used for detecting changes is called the velocity density method. This method can detect the change (may be a concept drift) by jointly analyzing the velocity and density of the data points in real-time.

Let us understand both with simple examples:

- **High density**: This means that many data points are close together.
- **Low-density**: This is defined by a region with a very sparse area. For example, in analyzing an e-commerce stream, it is found that the purchase amounts between $50 to $100 is very high, so this is a high-density data, as compared to rare purchases of $5000 and above, which will come under low density.
- **Velocity**: This denotes how fast the density changes over time. *How quickly are the data points moving from one cluster to another?* For example, due to a natural calamity, the purchase of food items increases suddenly, to stock up the required supplies in each household.

The reason the density and velocity are combined is that the rate of change of density will capture slow drift that may go unnoticed (if only density is analyzed). In some cases, the sudden spikes may look like noise, so they separate noise from concept drift.

To compute the velocity density, a temporal window is used to perform calculations. Temporal windows are associated with the time horizon over which the rate of change is measured. If is chosen to be large, then velocity density estimation will provide a long-term trend, whereas if If it is chosen to be small, then the trends are for the short term. This provides a user with the flexibility of analysing the changing trend with different kinds of time horizons.

A real-life application of change detection is network intrusion detection, which may show sudden data packets from new IP addresses, where the density increases rapidly, and velocity crosses the threshold limit.

This method works in a single pass, handles evolving data by detecting both sudden and gradual change, detects noise, and is very suitable for real-time analysis.

Dimensionality reduction and forecasting in data streams

This is another important aspect that is important to analyse a data stream, especially when data is coming from multiple sources, and they are interrelated and have a correlation between them. This technique intends to capture the correlation and find the hidden variables corresponding to the time series data, being collected for a data stream.

A hidden variable refers to an unobserved factor that influences multiple observed variables and creates correlation between them. It is not directly measured, not explicitly present in the dataset, but affects several observed variables. In a simple world example, if we are getting data for ice-cream sales and sunglasses sales for the entire year. Then it will look like both ice-cream and sunglasses sales increase in summer and are correlated. This somehow represents that one is increasing the sales of another. However, the underlying hidden variable is the temperature, which is not explicitly present in the story. So the correlation between ice cream and sunglasses exists, but because of temperature, we can reduce these two correlated variables into a single dimension, temperature.

Generally, data coming from multiple sources in a single place or unit is mostly correlated, e.g., traffic in a particular network, temperature readings coming from various sensors in the same building, which can be reduced to a limited set of hidden variables, and the analysis can be done only on these reduced and compact dimensions.

Dimensionality reduction in stream data aims to represent high-dimensional streaming data using a small number of variables while preserving the essential structure and patterns of the data.

Since the data arrives, is continuous and rapid, and its size is unbounded, only pass processing is possible. Dimensionality reduction helps in reducing computation and memory cost, removes the redundant and noisy dimensions, and supports the scalability for a large number of streams.

There is a method called **streaming pattern discovery in multiple time series** (**SPIRIT**), which is used to discover the correlations that effectively and efficiently summarize large collections of streams. SPIRIT satisfies the following:

- It is streaming, i.e., it is incremental, scalable, and any-time.
- It scales linearly with the number of streams, which makes it highly suitable for large-scale sensor networks and real-time monitoring systems.
- It automatically detects the changes in the input streams and finds the related hidden variables.

Instead of tracking hundreds or thousands of streams separately, SPIRIT finds a small number of hidden patterns that explain the major behaviour of all the streams by following these steps:

1. **Receiving the data**: SPIRIT receives one value for each stream, e.g., temperature from multiple sensors at a time.

2. **Check the hidden pattern**: In this, it checks how the new data matches with the hidden pattern, which produces a small set of hidden variables that summarize the existing system at a time. Instead of many numbers I few meaningful values.
3. **Rebuild**: SPIRIT tries to rebuild the original data from the hidden patterns (created in the earlier step). This checks how good the reconstruction is and how much information is lost. This makes sure that the current pattern is sufficient and has a meaningful definition to the collective streams.
4. **Correction**: If the reconstruction is erroneous, then adjust the weight and find the streams that affect the pattern most. The objective is that the found pattern should be closest to the behaviour of the original stream.
5. **Decision**: SPIRIT automatically adds new hidden variables if too much information is lost or removes the hidden variables if they are not needed. Not too few patterns to avoid poor accuracy and not too many parameters to avoid the computation wastage.
6. **Adapt**: As SPIRIT gives more weightage to recent data, it helps it to track gradual and sudden changes, and old behaviour slowly fades away.
7. **Usage**: Once the patterns are tracked, SPIRIT is enabled:
    a. **Forecasting**: Predicting the future values using hidden patterns faster
    b. **Missing value estimation**: If at any point a stream fails, SPIRIT estimates it using correlation.
    c. **Correlation discovery**: Identifies which streams behave similarly.
    d. **Anomaly detection**: Any unusual activity will be detected.

SPIRIT is very powerful because it can work on infinite streams with one-pass processing, can work with very low memory as it does not need to store the past data, scales linearly as the stream count increases, and is adaptive as it handles concept drift as well.

Clustering techniques for stream data

As we already know, there are many classification and clustering problems that have been studied in the data mining world, but these methods will not be applicable for the data stream processing due to not only the size and velocity of the data but also the temporal relationship between them. These temporal correlations can help us determine hidden characteristics of the data, but that requires online and continuous mining of data. Also, the system should have the capacity to do offline data analysis based on the business expectations.

The stream mining framework adopts a tilted time window framework (recent data in great detail and older data in progressively lower detail) that takes micro-clustering as a pre-processing process and integrates the pre-processing with an incremental, dynamic mining process. This pre-processing compresses the data, preserves the temporal correlations between them, and allows both online and offline processing.

Micro clustering framework

The micro clustering framework is designed to analyse massive data coming as a fast stream by summarizing the data and storing it, instead of storing everything. The summary information is defined by two core structures:

- **Micro-clusters**: A micro-cluster is a compact summary of many data points. Instead of storing the complete data, only the summary of the data is stored. These summaries can be the sum of values, the sum of squared values, the sum of timestamps, the sum of squared timestamps, the number of points, etc.

  These summaries are additive, i.e., multiple micro-clusters can be easily combined. Since micro-clusters preserve detailed statistics, the changes in the clusters (cluster splitting or merging) can be easily detected.

  Let us look at the following figure to see how the cluster evolves with time:

  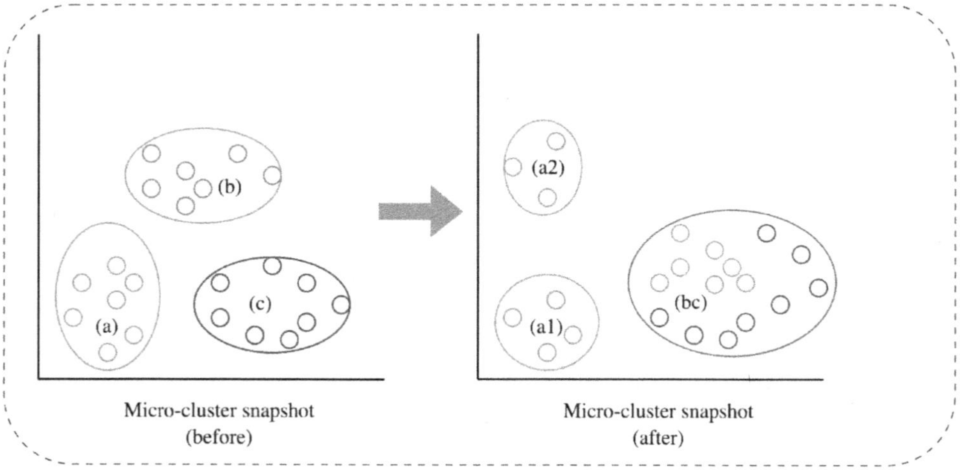

  ***Figure 13.4**: Showing the micro-cluster snapshots at two different times*

  As shown in *Figure 13.4*, the left figure shows that there are three clusters formed: a, b, and c. On the right, at a later stage, the clusters were updated, in which cluster a was divided into a1 and a2, and cluster b and c were merged into a single cluster, bc.

  If we keep the micro-clusters preserved, the evolution as discussed above can be easily captured, but if we only preserve the cluster centers (a, b, c), then the relationship between the evolutions of the clusters cannot be derived.

- **Pyramidal timeframe**: Since the storage of micro-cluster snapshots (micro-clusters at a particular moment called snapshots) cannot be stored every second, the snapshots are stored at a time interval that follows a pyramidal-like pattern, such as very frequent snapshots of recent data and a few, more spaced-out snapshots of older data. This helps in low-cost storage and the ability to generate summary information for any time window for later analysis (e.g., 5 minutes, last 10 days, or last 6 months).

For this, the equation has α as spacing multiplier and l as maximum depth of pyramidal time frame and i as time granularity.

If we assume, $\alpha=2, l=2$ and clock time = 55 unit time

Taking the formula (α^l+1) to capture the number of snapshots = 2^2+1 = 5, i.e., total snapshots to capture for a particular order.

Snapshots of frame number i are stored at clocked times, which are divisible by 2^i that means:

- For order 0 | $2^0 = 1$ unit time
- For order 1 | $2^1 = 2$ unit time
- For order 2 | $2^2 = 4$ unit time
- For order 3 | $2^3 = 8$ unit time
- For order 4 | $2^4 = 16$ unit time
- For order 5 | $2^5 = 32$ unit time

So the pyramid time frame becomes visible in the following table:

Order of snapshot	Clock time (last 5 snapshots)
0	55 54 53 52 51
1	54 52 50 48 46
2	52 48 44 40 26
3	48 40 32 24 16
4	48 32 16
5	32

Table 13.1: *Table showing the snapshot stored for*

The advantages of snapshot storage are:

- Users can see the clusters from a specific historical window (e.g., last 24 hours).
- No need to store data, but only micro-cluster snapshots.
- By subtracting the older snapshots from the current ones, the clusters of the past can be approximated.

A good example can be stock market data, where recent data needs great details for intraday analysis, volatility detection, and sudden anomaly or trend detection, so this data has to be frequent (tick by tick or second-level data). However, when the data gets older, analysts care about long-term trends, moving averages, basically less frequent and more summarized data.

Clustering in data stream using a micro-clustering approach

Clustering in a data stream is the online part of the algorithm that continuously processes incoming data from a data stream. It maintains a fixed number q of micro-clusters in the memory. Each micro-cluster represents a group of nearby data points, and every micro-cluster will have a unique ID.

At the very start of the stream, a fixed number of data points are collected, and a standard k-means clustering algorithm is applied, which creates the initial q clusters.

When the new datapoint arrives, the nearest distance to available clusters' centroids is calculated. The datapoint is checked if it fits within the boundary of that cluster:

- If it fits, the datapoint is absorbed into the micro-cluster.
- If it does not fit, it may be an outlier, or a new micro-cluster may be created.

Since this has to be worked on with limited memory in real-time, we cannot have new clusters created without affecting the memory. This means creating a new cluster will be done only after freeing up some space. Memory is freed in two ways:

- Deleting an outdated micro-cluster, there may be a cluster that was important in the past but is not important anymore. So, a cluster is checked with how recently the points have arrived in this cluster; if that time is older than the threshold limit, the cluster is deleted.
- If no clusters are old enough to delete, the two closest micro-clusters are merged with each other.

At a regular interval, this set of clusters is saved to disk to do high-level clustering and analyze how clusters evolve over time.

Classification techniques for stream data

As we know, the classification is a supervised technique where the dependent variables are predicted by the analysis of the independent input variables. Most of the available algorithms today work on multiple passes and are good contenders for conventional processing using static datasets. In the case of stream analysis, it is nearly impossible to process the entire stream dataset in one pass, and it needs to be designed for the high-speed nature of data, unbounded memory requirements, and concept drift.

There are several classification techniques that have been proposed so far:

- **Ensemble-based classification**: This framework is designed to handle concept drift in evolving data streams and uses an ensemble of classifiers (C4.5, RIPPER, Naïve Bayes, etc.) to improve prediction. It addressed the following challenges:

- **Concept drift**: Classifiers accuracy drops when the underlying data changes. It requires a selected portion of data to be consumed for better accuracy, and to also make sure there is not too much data being ignored when there is no existing drift.
- **Efficiency**: Updating the data model for concept drift is expensive, as it needs to operate on high-stream data without a delay.
- **Robustness**: It ensures the ensembles avoid overfitting of the model and how to effectively manage the ensembles for high-velocity streams.

The following figure figure illustrates the working model of ensemble learning approach for data streams:

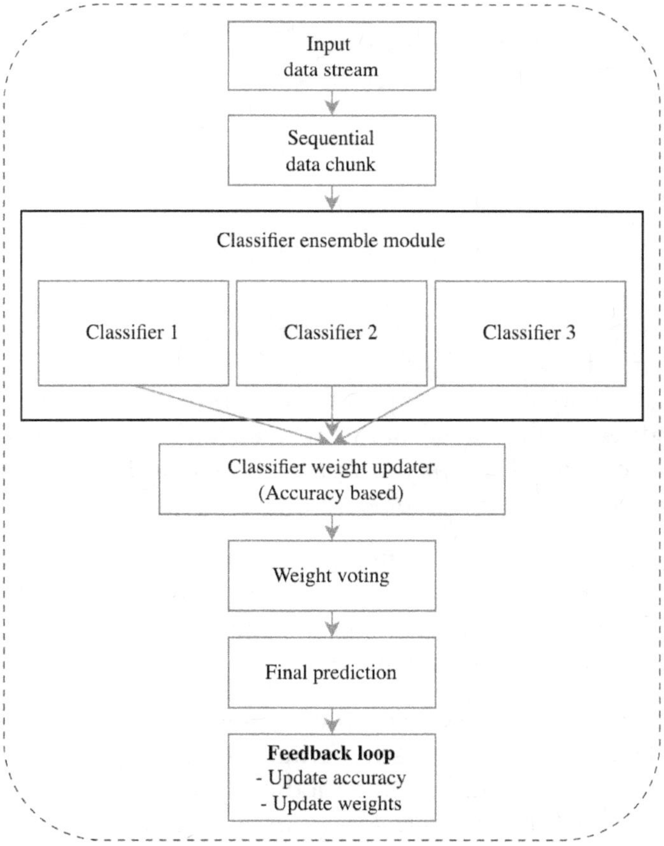

***Figure 13.5**: Ensemble-based classification flow*

As shown in *Figure 13.5*, there are multiple classifiers at work, where each classifier is assigned a dynamic weight based on its current accuracy. These weights change as the stream evolves and the classifiers become more or less important, depending upon the recent performance.

Final weight prediction will be done, based on the weight vote of all classifiers.

- **Very fast decision trees (VFDT)**: *Domingos and Hulten* introduced the VFDT, a decision tree system that is built on Hoeffding trees to support high-speed data streams. Refer to the figure to understand the VFDT learning system:

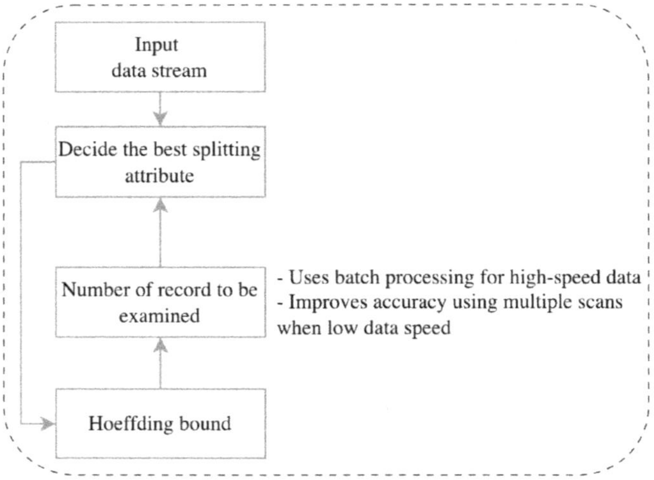

***Figure 13.6**: Very fast decision tree learning system*

As shown in *Figure 13.6*, in this stream-based classification, the decision tree is built over time incrementally by splitting the nodes into two, using a small amount of incoming data stream. The number of samples to be seen by the learning model to expand the node depends upon the statistical method called the Hoeffding bound. This bound is required to decide on how many samples are statistically required before each node is split. As the data arrives, the tree is evaluated, and its tree nodes are expanded.

The best split identified by VFDT using the Hoeffding bound ensures that the decisions made from the partial data are statistically closer to the standard decision tree algorithm. This processing is very efficient because the splitting criteria are computed in batches without re-scanning data.

In long-running streaming systems, the accuracy of VFDT may reduce over time due to concept drift, where the underlying data patterns gradually change. To maintain model accuracy, the tree may need periodic pruning, adaptation, or rebuilding based on updated data streams. Modern stream mining systems often use drift detection and continuous learning mechanisms to handle model decay effectively.

To handle concept drift, VFDT was later extended to the **concept-adapting very fast decision tree** (**CVFDT**), which uses a sliding window approach to continuously update and rebuild parts of the tree when the underlying attribute statistics change.

- **On-demand classification**: This uses micro-clusters based on summarized statistics to classify the data efficiently. This method divides the classification approach into two components: one component continuously stores summarized statistics about the data stream, and the second component continuously uses these summary statistics to perform classification.

These summary statistics are represented in the form of class-label-specific micro-clusters, which means each micro-cluster is associated with a class-label that defines the class-label of the data points in it.

Both components of this classification can be used in online mode. This means test data can come anytime and be classified on demand. At the same time, the summary statistics can be efficiently updated in case of the arrival of new data, and therefore, learning continues.

The key property (also known as subtractive property) of micro-clusters is to ensure the compute can be horizon-specific. This enables classification to be done over multiple time horizons, based on the rate of concept drift, i.e., for smaller concept drift, it processes a larger time horizon to ensure robustness, and on the contrary, in case of greater concept drift, a smaller time horizon will be sufficient.

- **Online information network (OLIN)**: This is an online classification method that rebuilds its model using the most recent data and adjusts dynamically to the concept drift. The following figure illustrates the simple flow chart of the OLIN process:

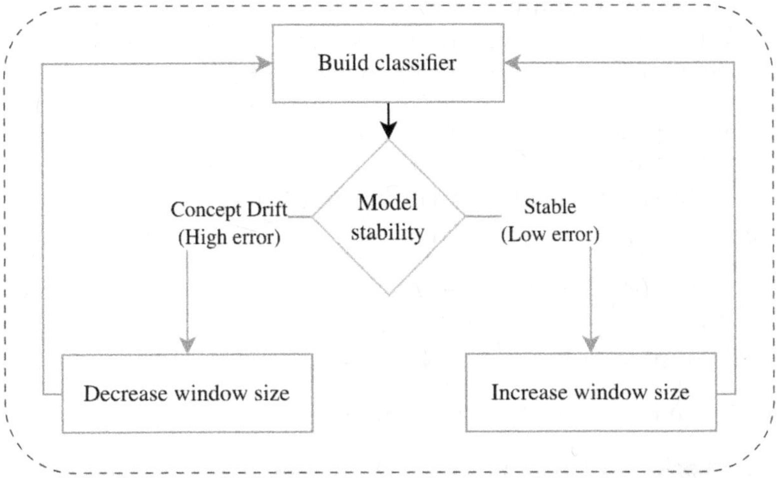

***Figure 13.7**: Online information network system*

As shown in *Figure 13.7*, the system monitors the classification error rates to detect the drift; when the model is stable, the sliding window increases, and the model rebuilding happens less frequently, whereas in the case of an increased error rate, the sliding window shrinks, and the model rebuilds itself frequently to reduce the errors.

Data outlier and anomaly detection in stream data

As we have already covered in this book, the goal of outlier detection is to identify the data points that are far from the normal definition or behaviour of the data, e.g., Salary to be -$1000 or body temperature to be 100 degrees Celsius.

This may be due to faulty sensors, attacks, or intentional intrusion into the system.

In the traditional machine learning world, this is detected using the calculation of the distance between every pair of data points. The points that are far from others will be called outliers. This is already covered in *Chapter 5, Data Transformation,* in the *Data cleaning* section in detail.

The problem with the existing approach is that they work well with static datasets and have an O superscript base, open paren n, end base, squared close paren (can be pronounced as *Big-O of n squared i.e.*) complexity, which means computation grows proportional to the square of the input size. In simple words, if the input size doubles, then the computation increases by four times. This is not suitable for stream data where the data arrives continuously.

In the case of distributed data streams, data arrives at multiple locations, and these nodes may have limited memory and computing capabilities. In addition, the cost of communication may be very expensive. In today's continuously changing world, the anomalies need to be detected in real-time, which may require incremental, approximations, and heuristic (trial and error) approaches as alternate options that are fast and more efficient.

One of the techniques used to detect outliers using distributed computing is by maintaining the summary at each node. These nodes will exchange the local outlier (not full summaries to save the communication cost). A point will be considered a global outlier if all the nodes agree or have the same outlier at their local point.

Moving from global processing to local, edge-based detection is an effective architectural pattern for modern IoT systems. It helps reduce data gravity by processing data closer to the source and minimizes unnecessary network bandwidth usage and egress costs.

Let us try to see the method in the following examples:

- **Sensor network anomaly detection**: In this, each sensor maintains a local model of normal behaviour. The following figure illustrates a real-world scenario in which multiple sensors are connected to a centralized server, showing how alerts are generated and transmitted to the server after processing:

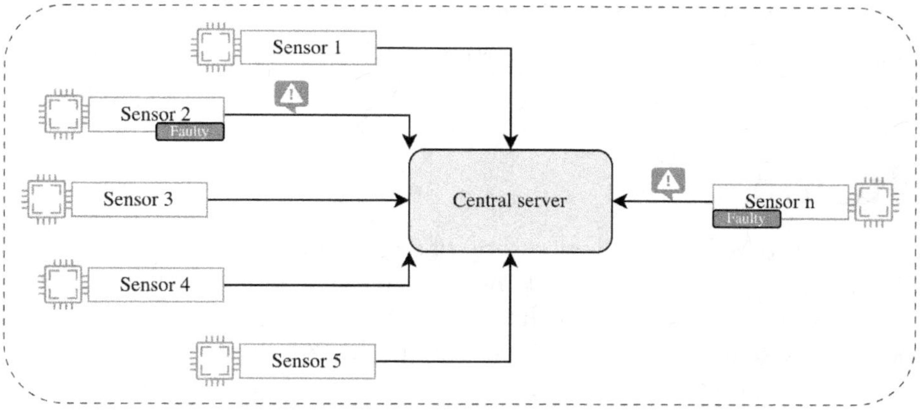

Figure 13.8: *A representation of a sensor network*

As shown in *Figure 13.8*, each sensor has its own local processing unit. If a sensor's reading deviates significantly (due to a fault), it will be flagged as faulty. This processing is taking place close to the sensor, and only alerts will be shared with the central server. This saves huge traffic costs.

Thus, anomaly or fault detection is happening at the local level and incremental processing at each node to identify outliers or faults in real-time. However, the global faults or outliers are concluded based on a lightweight coordination between different nodes.

- **Network intrusion detection**: This is a major application area, as today, there are a large number of hosts available in any network, and attacks can originate from any host or many hosts at the same time. At a single node level, it is difficult to detect the suspicious activity, but when multiple nodes share the summary, alert, or suspicious activity at the centralized server, it is much easier to detect the attack, this way, global threats can be detected and addressed, and these messages can be passed to the unaffected nodes for their proactive actions to prevent the attacks.

Use cases of stream analytics

Due to the very nature of real-time data processing, the real-world application of stream analytics can be:

- Real-time stock market analysis.
- Fraud detection in credit card or debit card transactions.
- Faulty sensor detection.
- Detecting early signs of machine failure in supercritical applications such as airlines, power industries, etc.
- Intrusion detection in the network to identify the abnormal traffic patterns.

- Detection of distributed **denial of services** (**DoS**).
- Detecting rapidly growing or trending topics in social media and web analytics.
- In healthcare, real-time patient health monitoring and detecting medical emergencies.

Conclusion

This chapter covered the basic understanding of stream analytics, in which the fundamentals of streams were explained, including current challenges we have in analyzing stream data and why conventional machine learning techniques do not work on this kind of continuous data. Some of the most used operations, like classification, clustering, pattern mining, etc., were also covered, which gave an idea of how some of the existing algorithms are tweaked for single-pass processing, and in some cases, new algorithms have been developed altogether to reach speed, cost effectiveness, and efficiency of processing.

In the next chapter, we will cover the data safety and security aspects and see why data is considered so precious that the complete governance cycle needs to be maintained around its usage. What are the various regional or country-level governance that are applicable will also be seen. These aspects may not be technical, but they play a crucial role in any data-sensitive project.

References

1. **https://charuaggarwal.net/streambook.pdf**
2. **https://link.springer.com/article/10.1007/s10115-006-0003-0**
3. **https://quix.io/blog/windowing-stream-processing-guide**

CHAPTER 14
Data Governance and Security

Introduction

Data governance and security are often under-prioritized in data projects, a data engineer's mindset focuses first and foremost on the problem statement that is to be solved from the business expectation perspective. Data security may sound like a low priority, but they are critical to regulatory compliance, operational resilience, and stakeholder trust. Any negligence or lack of awareness in this area may severely impact the organization.

This is the topic that has to be continuously monitored to ensure that the data coming from the client is in safe hands. The organizations are handling tons of users' personal data, such as salary, passwords, credit card numbers, investments, medical reports, and other highly sensitive data, which people do not want anyone to see until it is very important. The companies that are using this data need to make sure that they keep the data secure and govern the entire lifecycle so that it is only accessed on a need-to-know basis and when only required.

The threat is not only the attackers or cyber threats that can take this highly sensitive data, but also the intended or unintended misuse by internal staff who are working in operations, support, and development of the project. So data governance and security have to be an integral part of the data engineering journey so that proper mechanisms of data access control, anonymization, least privileges, and safety measures can be taken.

Structure

The chapter covers the following topics:

- Introduction to data governance
- Typical data governance organization structure
- Requirements for a data governance program
- Benefits of data governance
- Data governance activities

- Logging, monitoring, and alerting
- Security for low-level data engineering
- Introduction to data protection in the European Union under GDPR
- Introduction to data protection in the USA
- Introduction to data protection in India under DPDP
- Cross-framework comparison

Objectives

By the end of this chapter, the readers will be able to understand the importance of data safety and security. They will see the different types of compliance that have been applicable for different countries and regions, and what these compliances intend to protect. This chapter will also cover the typical data governance structure that entails the requirement of data governance, benefits, and all activities involved in a complete data cycle, which is properly governed.

This chapter will also touch upon the **General Data Protection Regulation** (**GDPR**), what its requirements are, and how it operates in the European region. In addition, data governance in the United States of America and India will also be covered in this chapter.

Introduction to data governance

As we know, data is considered to be the new oil in the information technology world. This is not because an individual datapoint has high value, but because valuable insights and inferences can be generated when large amount of data are analysed collectively. While individual records may contain sensitive information, aggregated and properly governed data can provide significant strategic and revenue-generating value for organizations.

Example 1: An **online travel agent** (**OTA**) company ABC has 10000 customers, out of which 5000 customers do their transactions with their credit cards. Now, if the information of any customer can be fetched by the wrong person, his credit card information can be compromised, and misuse of it may happen, so it is sensitive information that should be used only by trusted people and when required. However, from the abstract level it can be seen that around 50% of the travellers use credit cards, which means banks of these credit cards can have a tie-ups with these OTAs and they can have a bank and OTA specific offers to the customers, this will serve the customers better, and have banks churn more revenue and at later stages people may get attracted to go for more credit cards. This way, the abstracted and collective data becomes a revenue generator.

Example 2: Online pharmacy companies may have hundreds of orders placed in minutes. Now, taking a particular customer's order history is a very sensitive data because this is how you can track their entire family's health history which is not ethical and is very sensitive to people but if the collective data of a particular area is taken, then the pharmacy will get to know the demand of some specific products and they can get them at better rates for that area or can introduce better products at lower rates, this will not only satisfy the customers but also will have chances to improve the revenue for the company.

So, data creates value when it is accurate, trusted, accessible, and responsibly used, and governance is what makes that possible.

Data governance can be defined as a set of processes and procedures aimed at managing the data within an organization to focus on data availability, integrity, and compliance with regulations.

Data governance leads to the correct data access policies by measuring the risks and taking security exposures into account. It also provides a mandate for dealing with data issues. It is a function that not only has to be worked on by the IT department alone, but also has to be worked on in collaboration with business teams.

Taking data seriously is a cultural shift that cannot come from the bottom but has to be driven by the upper management, so that the correct guidelines and direction are taken and is considered a serious and sensitive act in itself.

Typical data governance organization structure

A typical data governance organizational structure has four key pillars:

- **Steering committee**: This is the **senior leadership** that is responsible for setting up the strategy and direction of all the data products. They work on the adoption of enterprise-level data capabilities. They are responsible for the funding of these activities and aligning the resources from the business units.
- **Data governance council**: These are the business **data owners** who are accountable for the data, access policies, and governance decisions. They have the authority over the data they own. This team is in charge of defining the data, usage policy, and cost of maintaining the data. This team works on deriving the cost and investment strategies and presents them to senior leadership for their approval.
- **Data standard group**: These are the **data stewards** who are responsible for data quality, consistency, and business definitions. They are responsible for ensuring that the data-related work follows proper, defined procedures. These are the ones who give permission and usage rights to the required team members. Since they have access to both business teams and technology teams, they get involved with both to resolve the data-related issues.
- **Delivery group or execution group**: These are the **custodians** of data, who implement technical controls, storage, security, and operational management of data. They are responsible for understanding the data modeling, access, and implementation. They

are also involved in tracking the usage of data. Their primary objective is to ensure that the data is available, accessible, optimized, and, if required, recoverable.

Figure 14.1 shows how all the roles in an organization play their crucial roles and help the company to set up the entire governance cycle. These teams define how the data is managed, protected, and used across the organization.

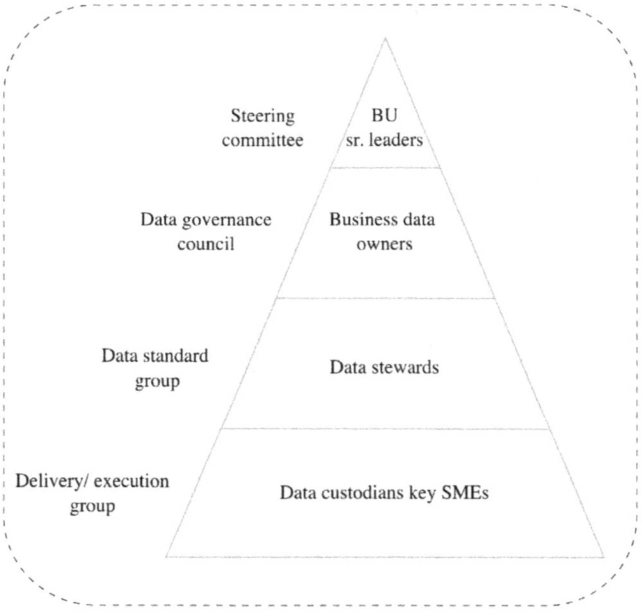

***Figure 14.1**: A typical governance organization structure*

Requirements for a data governance program

To make any data governance program successful, the following things are needed:

- This program must be sponsored by the senior leadership of the organization and business units.
- A data steward manager is required who would train, support, and coordinate with the data stewards. Data stewards are not a job but a role that actually does not own any data but has a duty to administer it.
- The core objective of data governance is to provide transparency for internal users and regulators while enhancing the overall value and trustworthiness of the data.
- A governance committee must be headed by one person and should have data steward managers, executives, senior leadership, IT leadership (e.g., data administrators), and business unit leaders. This committee would set strategic goals, coordinate activities, and provide guidelines and standards for managing the enterprise data:

- o Determines the targets for data quality and availability.
- o They measure the data quality and availability.
- o Determine the efforts required for work on mitigating the risk for bad and unsecured data.
- o They periodically review the audit process.

Benefits of data governance

By now, it is understood that data governance provides a structured framework to manage data as a strategic organizational asset. The outcome of this standardization is as follows:

- **Reliability**: This means the degree to which data is considered accurate, consistent, and trustworthy. Data reliability is achieved through well-defined data governance policies, standards, and procedures. These policies ensure that the data is created, maintained, and used consistently across the systems, teams, and departments.

  From the business perspective, clear data ownership and accountability improve confidence in reports and analytics, as it is known who/which team is responsible for maintaining the data quality.

- **Authenticity**: This ensures that the data is genuine, authoritative, and trusted. This means the data is consumed from only approved (may be certified in some cases) data sources. The governance frameworks define authoritative datasets, such as master data or golden records, to prevent the use of inconsistent and manipulative data. Strong authentication and validation rules and quality checks ensure that the data remains accurate throughout its lifecycle. This prevents multiple versions of data and ensures the coherency of the data source.

- **Traceability**: Traceability can also be known as data lineage, which refers to the ability to track the data from its origin throughout the cycle until its usage. This helps the organization to know where it has come from, how it has been processed, and how it is being used. This is essential from the audit and compliance perspective.

- **Accountability**: This is defined by the roles, such as who owns the data and who is responsible for its quality, security, and compliance. Data governance clearly defines roles as data owners, data stewards, and custodians. These roles ensure that the issues related to data are addressed and worked upon promptly, and proper policies are enforced.

- **Better compliance**: The compliance ensures adherence to the legal, regulatory, and industry standards. Data governance provides the policies for data privacy, security, retention, and auditability. By enforcing standardization, data governance reduces regulatory risks and audit failures.

- **Agility**: Agility refers to the organization's ability to respond to market and operational changes swiftly using the data or business documents. With properly governed, reliable, and well-documented data, business teams can quickly analyze the trend, launch new products, and adjust strategies without delays caused by data inconsistencies and validation issues.

  From an IT perspective, with properly defined data architectures, standardized data models, and reusable data assets, IT teams can implement the changes without breaking the downstream systems. Data governance reduces technical debt and supports scalable, modular architectures such as data lakes, lakehouses, etc.

  Data governance enables self-serving analytics that help in faster decision-making.

- **Stronger insights**: Stronger insights are the result of high-quality, trusted, and meaningful data. When the data is reliable, traceable, authentic, and well-governed, there is an increase in the probability that the analytics and machine learning algorithms will produce more accurate and meaningful results. Proper data governance ensures consistent metrics, correct data engineering and feature engineering practices, and reduces biases, which leads to better strategic and operational insights.

Data governance activities

As we have seen earlier, the data governance activities define how data is managed, controlled, protected, and used across an organization to ensure trust and compliance. The following are examples of some high-level activities done in data governance:

- **Data quality management**: This is defined by the steps that are taken to improve the overall quality of data. The objective is to make the data fit for the target analytics. This is all about improving the health of data by utilizing certain processes and technological aspects.

  Some of the dimensions the governance teams work on:

  - **Accuracy**: The data must conform to the actual real-world scenario and reflect real-world events and objects. This is how the final outcome will be aligned with the real-world business expectations.

  - **Completeness**: For complete data analytics, it is important that none of the dimensions of the data are missed from the analysis and that it has all the features as inputs.

  - **Consistency**: This ensures that the data is uniformly transferred from one system to another system when it is being generated from multiple sources.

  - **Timeliness**: This makes sure that the required data is always available and is up to date at all times.

- **Uniqueness**: This is a very important aspect where the analytics and machine learning output will be affected if the data is not unique. So it is imperative to have the data engineering techniques applied so that the data is clean for any processing on it.
- **Validity**: Validity plays a very important role here, as it means that the analysis we are doing has the data that is valid. Validity depends on the business problem, model design, and decision horizon. For example, while predicting stock prices for the next week, recent market data may often be more relevant than very old historical data. However, the appropriate time range depends on the specific use case, market conditions, and modeling approach being used.

- **Metadata management**: This involves establishing the policies and processes to ensure that the information can be integrated, accessed, shared, linked, analyzed, and maintained to the best across the organization. This is more of an administrative work of data that describes the other data. Metadata can include:
  - **Business metadata**: Business definition, data owners, policies and business rules.
  - **Technical metadata**: Table names, schemas, datatypes, **application programming interfaces** (**APIs**) etc.
  - **Operational metadata**: Data pipeline logs, job execution details, refresh frequency, system performance information etc.

  Effective metadata management enables important governance capabilities such as data lineage tracking, data cataloging, impact analysis, discoverability, and better understanding of how the data moves and changes across the systems.

- **Master data management (MDM)**: It is the practice of creating and maintaining a single trusted master record for every key business entity, such as a customer, product, employee, supplier, location, etc., by integrating data coming from multiple systems. This is done because in an organization, the same entity may appear in different systems, which leads to duplicate records, conflicting information, and inconsistent reporting. MDM solves this problem by establishing a single authoritative source of truth.

- **Data protection**: It refers to the set of policies, procedures, and technologies used to ensure that the data is secure, private, accurate, and used lawfully throughout its lifecycle, right from generation to processing to storage to sharing to deletion. Its primary objective is to protect sensitive information and personal information from any unauthorized access, misuse, loss, or any breaches, etc., and to ensure compliance with legal and regulatory requirements.

Logging, monitoring, and alerting

Till now, we have seen all the policies and procedures that are defined to ensure data is complete and secure from any unauthorized access. However, as part of data governance, real-time tracking plays a very important role in making sure that people know what has been implemented. The threat may not only be outside but inside the organization as well. There may be some employees, vendors, or contractors who may have access to the data and may be planning for the breach.

As in the real-world, a thief can be caught only while stealing, similarly, organizations should have mechanisms to log security-relevant and audit-relevant events across identity, access, data movement, and privileged actions, with retention and alerting policies aligned to risk and compliance requirements. For this, a complete audit trail should be implemented in the system where every single move in the system can be captured, starting from the login activity to any activity done on the system to logging out. This will ensure that anyone touching the system will leave their footprints on the system. This approach deters hackers and bad actors from pursuing the wrong intentions. This is how the logging and monitoring can be done. Moving on to one step further, since there can be role-based accesses in place, which would monitor which operation is taking place on which system, and in case of any suspicious activity, the alert can be generated on the systems, and instant emails or messages can be sent to the required authorities for their quick action.

Some of the areas that could be monitored are:

- **Access**: This is to check who is accessing what in the system, what access rights are given, and what operations are being performed. *Are the operations legitimate? Are they done within the expected time frame?* This is to ensure that the operations being done are legitimate and do not compromise the system.
- **Resources**: Continuous monitoring of the computational resources, such as CPU, memory, and I/O usage, is also an important aspect to be captured. If the daily pattern is the same or similar, then it may be concluded as a legitimate activity, whereas sudden spikes in the resource consumption seen on the system can be concluded as a suspicious activity or an attack, and then it must be checked and acted on with priority.
- **Billing**: This is another dimension of monitoring the usage, especially in cases of cloud components. As we know in cloud computing, most things are monitored, and every usage has a cost associated with it. It also gives us the facility to track the spend based on usage. Based on the daily usage, the billing can be given a limit. If at any time this billing threshold is crossed, the alert is generated, and if it is due to suspicious activity, it can be caught before it does the damage. E.g., tool like AWS Cost Anomaly Detection automatically detects unusual spending patterns and generates alerts for unexpected cloud usage and costs.

- **Time-bound access**: All the permissions given to people accessing the system should have some validity associated with them. This makes sure that at regular intervals, the permissions are re-evaluated and can be modified based on the actual usage as compared to the initial decision. Also, these permissions should be automatically revoked if there is inactivity for a defined period of time, e.g., if there is no activity from a vendor for more than 30 days, then the access to the system should be revoked, which can be restored after following all the required procedures. This also closes the potential security threat to the system.

There are many other areas where the close monitoring of the usage, alerting whenever necessary, can be setup along with the continuous logging, which also helps to analyze the usage of the system, not only to catch the suspicious activity but also to track who uses the system for how long and what all activities are performed. It also helps in verifying whether the activities are intended and compliant with the expected usage.

Security for low-level data engineering

Low-level security focuses on infrastructure-level data security as compared to the above-discussed security aspects, which were more about application-level protection. In this, the focus area can be the places where data is ingested, processed, moved, and stored. This layer is highly technical and implementation-driven.

Normally, it is the information security teams in an organization that set up the guidelines based on compliance and regulatory-related aspects.

Some of the areas that need to be looked at are:

- **Data ingestion security**: This is the part where the data enters first, and the following are the places where the ingestion security is applied:
    - **API security**: The APIs should be well tested for attacks, and proper authentication mechanisms using authentication tokens should be used for any transaction.

      Data transit across the network is secured using **Transport Layer Security** (**TLS**) or **Secure Sockets Layer** (**SSL**) encryption. SSL protocols are now deprecated due to security risks, and modern applications should use TLS 1.2 or TLS 1.3 for secure communication. Additional security controls such as **mutual TLS** (**mTLS**), certificate management, and API gateway enforcement can further strengthen authentication, trust, and secure service-to-service communication.
    - **Data sources authentication**: The devices, which are the data sources, need to be authenticated.
    - **Throttling**: Proper rate limits and throttling limits should be applied to prevent any abuse and attacks.
- **Storage level security**: All the security aspects that are applied at the storage level are applicable in this section. The data stored in file or object storage is encrypted. All

the databases have security configured for access control. File systems should have permission-enabled access only.

- **Compute and execution security**: This is the security that is applicable at the processing engine or job level. The cluster access can have **Secure Shell** (**SSH**) or **identity and access management** (**IAM**) based access only. Codes are deployed in containers or Kubernetes with secrets. Job-level authorization control, which will clearly guide *who will do what*, is implemented. Clear isolation of platforms, such as development, testing, and production platforms, where the client data should be allowed to be processed only in the production environment, which is more secure and has tight data access guidelines.
- **Pipeline and orchestration security**: This is the security layer that ensures the controlled data movement and scheduling. It involves using secure workflow tools and using credentials in security vaults (that should get rotated on a regular basis). No hardcoded passwords or secret keys should be available in the code. Secure retries and failure handling should be implemented. Complete traceability of each step should be in the pipeline.
- **Access control and identity management**: This deals with who can access the data and systems. Some of the access can be as follows:
    - **Role-based access control (RBAC)**: The privileges can be defined based on the roles, and the people who are provided with that particular role will have all the applicable privileges, e.g., anyone given admin access will have most of the important privileges. RBAC is a foundational security mechanism but, modern sensitive data platforms often extend RBAC with **attribute-based access control** (**ABAC**), policy-based controls, and just-in-time privileged access to provide finer-grained, context-aware, and temporary access to critical resources.
    - **Principle of least privileges**: In this type of access, user will be granted only the minimum access permission that is necessary to perform their legitimate tasks and not more.
    - **Multi-factor authentication**: In this, a user needs to enter the **one-time password** (**OTP**), which may be received on their email or phone number, and then only they will be allowed to enter the system.
    - **Service-to-service authentication**: In this, instead of a person, a service tries to interact with the system and uses the authentication for identity verification, and then only the subsequent operation can take place.
- **Network security**: This is the security of the path through which the data movement takes place. This involves the use of firewalls and security groups, which will allow very specific traffic to enter. Networks are isolated by creating their private subnets, **Virtual Private Networks** (**VPN**), so that no outside system or person can be part of this private group.

- **Data masking and minimization**: This is an application-level security technique that is used to protect sensitive information from early access to data. These can involve detecting the **personally identifiable information** (**PII**) and **sensitive personal information** (**SPI**) data while ingestion and storing it after the masking of the same. If the actual data is required but the visualization needs to be controlled, then PII or SPI data can be stored as is, but can be masked while displaying the data on the user interface to avoid any misuse of data, e.g., only the last 4 digits of credit card information can be shown.

- **Data hashing and sensitive data protection**: This is another important aspect of application security for protecting sensitive data. Password storage typically uses salted one-way hashing techniques, which is done by applying mathematical, cryptographic functions to transform it into a fixed-length string of characters, known as a hash value, e.g., if someone has saved his password as `mypassword`, then the hash value stored in the database can be `89e01536ac207279409d4de1e5253e01f4a1769e696db0d6062ca9b8f56767c8`. When a user logs in, the entered password is converted using the same hashing technique. For authentication, the hashes (stored and the newly entered) are compared; if the hashes match, then the login is allowed, else, it is not.

  Sensitive personal identifiers such as social security numbers and phone numbers are more commonly protected using encryption, tokenization, or format-preserving protection techniques, depending on the business and compliance requirements.

Introduction to data protection in the European Union under GDPR

GDPR is one of the strict regulations about data privacy, which came into effect on 25 May 2018, when it was passed by the **European Union** (**EU**). It obligates the organizations or individuals (freelancers, consultants, sole traders, etc.) to manage the data collected, related to people, to ensure that there is no breach of the same.

Under GDPR, organizations are expected to follow several core principles:

- **Lawfulness, fairness, and transparency**: Personal data must be processed legally, fairly and, in a transparent manner.

- **Purpose limitation**: Data should be collected for specific, explicit and legitimate purposes only.

- **Data minimization**: Only the minimum amount of data that is required for a particular task must be collected and processed.

- **Storage limitation**: Data should not be retained longer than necessary for the intended purposes.

- **Accuracy**: The collect data must be accurate and up to date wherever necessary.
- **Integrity and confidentiality**: Appropriate security measures must be taken to protect personal data from any unauthorized access, loss or misuse.
- **Accountability**: Organizations are responsible for demonstrating compliance with all GDPR principles.

The GDPR levies huge fines against the defaulters who violate its privacy and security standards. The penalties can reach up to €20 million or 4% of global annual turnover, whichever is higher.

With GDPR and its strict regulations and harsh fines, Europe is sharing the message across the world that personal data collected from people should be taken seriously, and every single bit of information needs to have a known destination. Since more and more people are trusting big organizations and using their services and inputting their personal sensitive data, it becomes the organization's responsibility to make use of their data appropriately, and data management should be at their highest priority to avoid huge penalties due to breaches and data theft.

History of GDPR

The right to privacy is a part of the European Convention on Human Rights, adopted by the Council of Europe in 1950 (can be found in **https://www.echr.coe.int/documents/d/echr/Convention_ENG**). That states that *Everyone has the right to respect for their private and family life, their home, and their correspondence.*

Some of the articles that were covered in this treaty are:

- **Right to life**: This is covered in *Article 2* under the section, *Convention for the Protection of Human Rights and Fundamental Freedoms*. This law protects everyone's right to life. A person may be lawfully deprived of life only if a court has sentenced them for a serious crime where the law allows such a punishment. Death caused by force is not considered unlawful if the force is strictly necessary to protect others, or make a lawful arrest, or prevent escape, or control a riot, etc.
- **Prohibition of torture**: It is covered in *Article 3* under the section, *Convention for the Protection of Human Rights and Fundamental Freedoms*, which states that *No one shall be subjected to torture or inhuman or degrading treatment or punishment.*
- **Right to respect for private and family life**: It is covered in *Article 8* under the section, *Convention for the Protection of Human Rights and Fundamental Freedoms*. This states that everyone has the right to privacy in their personal and family life, home, and communications. Public authorities may interfere with this right only when permitted by the law and when it is necessary in a democratic society for a reason that may be national security, public safety, preventing crime, protecting health or morals, and safeguarding the rights of others.

- **Protection of property**: This is covered in *Article 1* under the protocol to the *Convention for the Protection of Human Rights and Fundamental Freedoms*. This states that everyone has the right to peacefully enjoy their possessions and property. These possessions can be taken away only in the public interest and according to the law. The state may regulate the use of property and enforce laws, including taxation and penalties, when required in the general interest.
- **Right to education**: This is covered in *Article* 2 under the protocol to the *Convention for the Protection of Human Rights and Fundamental Freedoms*. This states that every person has the right to education, and no one should be denied the right to it. The state must respect parents' rights to ensure that education is provided in accordance with their religious and philosophical beliefs.

Similarly, there are several articles and protocols that are clearly defined, which protect human rights.

As innovation and technology evolved, the EU realized that existing privacy laws were not sufficient to protect personal data. So in 1995, the EU introduced the European Data Protection Directives, which set some benchmarking for data privacy and security. However, the developments showed that personal data was being collected, processed, and shared at a rapid rate. As a result, in 2011, the EU's data protection authority called for *a comprehensive and modern approach to personal data protection*, which began updating the 1995 directive, which led to the creation of GDPR. This was approved by the *European Parliament* in 2016 and became fully enforceable on *25 May 2018*, making the compliance mandatory for all organizations and individuals that process data of EU residents.

Scope, penalties, and key definitions

The following provides clear information on the scope, penalties, and key definitions:

- **Scope**: If an organization or individual processes the personal data of any EU citizens for offering any goods and services to these people, then GDPR is applicable to these organizations or individuals, even if those organizations or individuals do not belong to the EU.
- **Penalties**: There are two tiers of penalties: either a maximum of 20 million euros or 4% of the global revenue of the organization (whichever is higher). In addition to this, the affected data subjects have the right to ask for compensation for the damages.
- **Definitions**: The following are some important definitions that are used for understanding the GDPR clearly:
    - **Personal data**: Personal data can be defined as the data or information that is related to any individual. This contains name, email address, location, gender, ethnicity, age, political opinion, religious beliefs, etc. If the data is pseudonymized and still it is able to identify the person, it will also be considered as personal data.

- **Data processing**: Any action performed on data will be considered data processing. It may be collecting, organizing, cleaning, removing, etc. This processing can be manual and automatic.
- **Data subject**: The person whose data is being processed.
- **Data controller**: This is the person who is responsible for deciding why and how the personal data will be used.
- **Data processor**: This may be defined as a third party who processes the data on behalf of the data controller. These could also be the cloud service providers that may be storing the data on behalf of an organization.

Data protection principles

GDPR clearly defines the seven principles that are to be followed for processing personal information:

- **Lawfulness, fairness, and transparency**: Data processing should be lawful, fair, and transparent to the data subject. Data subjects should know how their data will be used.
- **Purpose limitation**: The data collected should be used for legitimate purposes for which the data subject is explicitly informed. No further processing, such as archiving for public interest, scientific or historic research, or any other purposes, is allowed.
- **Data minimization**: The data to be collected is absolutely necessary for the purpose specified, while collecting the data, and no extra personal data is to be collected for any purposes.
- **Accuracy**: The personal data is to be kept accurate and up to date.
- **Storage limitations**: The PII data is to be stored for the duration, until it is needed in the system for a specified purpose.
- **Integrity and confidentiality**: Data processing to be done in such a way that the data is secure, protected against unauthorized access or unlawful processing, and against accidental loss, destruction, or damage using appropriate technical and organizational measures.
- **Accountability**: The data controller should be able to demonstrate GDPR compliance with all of the above principles.

Conditions to process data

As per GDPR, any individual or organization is not allowed to touch the personal data unless the following justification is present:

- The data subject has given specific, unambiguous consent to process data, e.g., they have opted to be part of the marketing email list.

- Processing is necessary to execute or prepare a contract to which the data subject is a party, e.g., a background check is required before leasing the property to a potential tenant.
- Data needs to be processed in order to comply with legal obligations, e.g., receive an order from the court.
- Data is needed to process to save someone's life. This applies to any emergency situation when the data subject is not in a position to give consent, such as a medical emergency, accident, or natural disaster.
- Data processing is necessary to perform a task in the public interest or an official function. This may not only be applicable to government bodies but also to private organizations performing public services such as waste collection, public transport, or utility management.
- The organization may process the personal data if it has a legitimate business or operational reason to do so, provided this interest does not override the fundamental rights and freedoms of the data subject. The individual's privacy rights always take priority if there is a conflict.

Consent from data subjects

The following are some rules that constitute the consent of data subjects:

- The consent must be freely given, specific, informed, and unambiguous.
- The request for consent must be clearly distinguishable from the other matters and must be presented in plain and simple language.
- Data subjects can withdraw their previously given consent whenever they want, and the organization or individual must respect their decision.
- Under GDPR, the default age of consent for children is 16 years. However, member states are allowed to lower this limit to a minimum of 13 years, below which parental or guardian consent is required.
- The documentary evidence of consent needs to be preserved for any reference.

Rights of data subjects

As per GDPR, a person using the internet becomes a data subject. Any organization that collects and processes data must know the following rights that data subjects have, in order to be GDPR compliant:

- **The right to be informed**: The data subject has a right to know what data has been collected from them, how it will be used, and who it will be shared with.

- **The right of access**: The data subject has a right to ask an organization *What data do you have about me, and how are you using it?*.
- **The right of rectification**: The data subject has a right to ask for data correction if it is wrong, incomplete, or outdated.
- **The right to erasure**: The data subject has a right to ask an organization to delete the data if it is no longer needed, or if they want to withdraw the consent, or if it was used unlawfully.
- **The right to restrict processing**: The data subject has a right to ask an organization to temporarily stop processing the data for accuracy or legality review.
- **The right to data portability**: The data subject has a right to transfer the data to any other service provider.
- **The right to object**: The data subject has a right to say *No* to data processing for any of the specific purposes that they are not comfortable with.
- **Rights in relation to automated decision making and profiling**: The data subject has a right to not be judged only by an algorithm and can ask for human review for important decisions, e.g., loan approval, credit scoring, etc.

Introduction to data protection in the USA

The United States privacy law is a complex patchwork of national, state, and local privacy laws and regulations, as opposed to the sophisticated GDPR regulation in the European Union, which means there is no single principal data protection law in the USA. This makes US privacy law complex and harder to manage for businesses.

At the **federal level**, privacy laws are sector-specific, which means different rules will apply to different industries. E.g., there would be separate laws for healthcare data, financial data, children's data, email marketing, credit reporting, etc.

At the **state level**, privacy protection has grown rapidly. Starting with California in 2018, many states have introduced their own comprehensive privacy laws. These laws give rights to individuals over their personal data. Today, more than 20 states have passed their laws, which have come into effect in 2025 and 2026.

California's privacy law, the **California Consumer Privacy Act (CCPA)** is the most detailed and strict. It applies not only to consumers, but also to employees and business-to-business data. Californians have the right to know what data is collected, accessed, and deleted, and to opt out of data selling and sharing. It also has a dedicated privacy enforcement authority.

Other states' privacy laws are broadly similar to each other, but differ slightly in areas such as:

- Which businesses are covered?
- Whether the consent is required?
- What counts as sensitive data?
- Enforcement mechanisms

Most states do not apply to employee or B2B data, unlike California.

SPI receives extra protection, which includes healthcare data, financial details, passwords, biometric data, precise location, children's data, and government IDs.

In some cases, individuals can file lawsuits or class actions, especially for data breaches, biometric and data misuse, children's data violations, etc.

All US states have data breach notification laws, requiring companies to inform affected individuals and authorities when sensitive data is compromised.

To summarize, the US data protection is strong but fragmented, and businesses must comply with multiple overlapping laws, making privacy compliance a major ongoing challenge.

Introduction to data protection in India under DPDP

In India, the right to privacy is an extension of the right to *Life and Liberty*, as per *Article 21* of the *Indian Constitution*.

The **Digital Personal Data Protection** (**DPDP**) Act was passed on 11 August 2023, which identifies itself as *An Act to provide for the processing of digital personal data in a manner that recognizes both the right of individuals to protect their personal data and the need to process such personal data for lawful purposes and for matters connected therewith or incidental thereto.*

The following are the key definitions:

- **Data Fiduciary**: Any person who alone or in conjunction with other persons determines the purpose and means of processing the personal data.
- **Data Principal**: The person to whom the personal data belongs. If a child, then it includes the parents or lawful guardian; or in cases of a disabled person, the lawful guardian, acting on their behalf.
- **Data Processor**: Any person who processes the personal data on behalf of a Data Fiduciary.
- **Data Protection Officer**: An individual appointed by a significant Data Fiduciary under the provisions of this act.

DPDP Act, 2023

The act applies to the processing of digital personal data within India, where such data is collected online or collected offline and is digitized. It will also apply to such processing outside India, if it is for offering goods or services or profiling individuals in India.

It states that the personal data should be processed for lawful purposes for which an individual has given consent. Consent may be deemed in some cases.

Data fiduciaries are obligated to maintain the accuracy of data, keep the data secure, and delete the data once its purposes have been met.

Requirements for deemed consent

Deemed consent means that a person's consent is assumed by law, even if they do not explicitly say *Yes*, because their actions, situation, or context clearly indicate agreement. The following are the cases where deemed consent can be assumed:

- In a situation where the Data Principal voluntarily provides her personal data to the Data Fiduciary, and she has not indicated to the Data Fiduciary that she does not consent to the use of her personal data. For example, an individual makes a purchase at a pharmacy and provides the pharmacy with her personal details, such as name, mobile number, email, etc., so that the pharmacy can send the receipt to her mobile phone or email.
- For the performance of any function under any law, or the provision of any service or benefit to the Data Principal, or the issuance of any certificate, license, or permit for any action or activity of the Data Principal, by the state or any instrumentality of the State. For example:
    - An individual buys an insurance policy using a mobile application or the website of an insurer. She gives the insurer consent for processing her personal data by the insurance company, for the purpose of issuing the policy, and waiving her right to complain to the *Data Protection Board of India*.
    - A pregnant woman enrolls herself on an application or website to avail herself of the government's maternity benefits program, while consenting to provide her personal data for availing such benefits. The government may process her personal data to determine her eligibility to receive any other prescribed benefit from the government.
- For compliance with any judgment or order issued under any law.
- For responding to a medical emergency involving a threat to the life or immediate threat to the health of the Data Principal or any other individual.
- For taking measures to provide medical treatment or health services to any individual during an epidemic, outbreak of disease, or any other threat to public health.
- For taking measures to ensure the safety of, or provide assistance or services to any individual during any disaster, or any breakdown of public order.
- For the purposes related to employment.

- In the public interest, including for
    - Detection and prevention of fraud
    - Mergers, acquisitions, or any corporate restructuring
    - Network and information security
    - Credit score calculations
    - Operations of a search engine for processing the publicly available personal data
    - Recovery of debt
- For any fair and legitimate purpose.

The Data Fiduciary may continue to process the personal data until and unless the Data Principal withdraws her consent.

Data Protection Board of India

The central government established the **Data Protection Board of India** (**DPBI**) on 13 November 2025, to adjudicate non-compliance with the provisions of the bill:

- DPBI will determine non-compliance and impose respective penalties.
- It will direct the individuals, as defined by the act, to act in accordance with the act and withdraw/modify/suspend such directions as it fits.
- Direct the Data Fiduciaries to adopt measures to mitigate harm to Data Principals, and act to address a data breach.

Rights of a Data Principal

The Data Principal shall have the right to obtain from the Data Fiduciary to whom she has previously given consent, some of the rights mentioned in the following:

- Right to information about personal data which is being processed.
- Right to correction and erasure of personal data.
- Right of access to the grievance redressal mechanism provided by the Data Fiduciary or consent manager.
- Right to nominate, who shall, in the event of death or incapacity of the Data Principal, exercise the right of the Data Principal in accordance with the provisions of this act.

Duties of a Data Principal

Along with the rights, the Data Principal also has some duties. A Data Principal shall:

- Comply with the provisions of all applicable laws while exercising rights under the provisions of this act.

- Ensure not to register a false or frivolous grievance or complaint with a Data Fiduciary or the board.
- Under no circumstances, including while applying for any document, service, unique identifier, proof of identity, or proof of address, furnish false particulars or suppress any material information or impersonate another individual.
- Furnish only such information as is verifiably authentic while exercising the rights to correction or erasure under the provisions of this act.

Special provisions

The central government may, after an assessment of such factors as it may consider necessary, notify such countries or territories outside India to which a Data Fiduciary may transfer personal data, in accordance with such terms and conditions as may be specified.

The central government may exempt government agencies from the application of provisions of the bill in the interest of specified grounds, such as security of the state, public order, and prevention of offenses.

Cross-framework comparison

Let us look at comparative Analysis of DPDP Act, GDPR, and CCPA:

Aspect	GDPR	CCPA	DPDP
Region	EU	California, USA	India
Objective	Protect personal data and privacy rights	Give consumers control over personal data	Regulate processing of digital personal data
Applies to	Organizations processing EU residents' data	Businesses handling California residents' data	Entities process digital personal data in India
User rights	Access, correction, deletion, portability and objection	Access, correction and opt-out of sale/share	Access, correction, erasure (right to be forgotten), grievance redressal
Children's data	Default consent age 16 (can be lowered to 13)	Special protection for users under 16	Verifiable parent consent for children
Consent requirement	Strong and explicit consent	Opt-out model for many cases	Consent based processing
Penalties	Very high fines based on global turnover	Civil penalties and statutory damages	Financial penalties under the Act
Focus area	Privacy and individual rights	Consumer data privacy	Digital data governance and consent

Table 14.1: *Comparison of the GDPR, CCPA, and DPDP Act across key aspects*

Conclusion

This chapter covered the fundamental concepts of data governance, its working steps, and the organizational structure that supports governance within an organization. The chapter introduced security consideration in data engineering including application-level and infrastructure-level controls and measures, that help in keeping the sensitive data safe. In addition, it provided a foundational overview of major data protection regulations, such as GDPR, data privacy practices in United States and India's DPDP Act. Overall, the key takeaway is that the data governance and security are not merely support functions but core enablers of trusted, compliant, and scalable data engineering systems.

In the next chapter, we will cover the basic understanding of business analytics and the processes, principles, and tools that are used for the same.

References

1. **https://www.infosys.com/services/data-analytics/insights/documents/effective-data-governance.pdf**
2. **https://gdpr.eu/what-is-gdpr/**
3. **https://eur-lex.europa.eu/legal-content/EN/TXT/PDF/?uri=CELEX:32016R0679**
4. **https://www.echr.coe.int/documents/d/echr/Convention_ENG**
5. **https://gdpr.eu/article-5-how-to-process-personal-data/**
6. **https://www.dlapiperdataprotection.com/?c=US**
7. **https://www.meity.gov.in/static/uploads/2024/06/2bf1f0e9f04e6fb4f8fef35e82c42aa5.pdf**
8. **https://www.mea.gov.in/images/pdf1/part3.pdf**
9. **https://www.delhilawacademy.com/art-21-right-to-privacy/**
10. **https://www.meity.gov.in/static/uploads/2025/11/cc217843dc3bcb37b2b05bcc3b4e031f.pdf**
11. **https://www.neostra.io/blog/a-comparative-analysis-of-dpdp-act-gdpr-and-ccpa-understanding-global-data-privacy-regulations**
12. **https://technoplanetenterprise.com/post?id=blog_6950a2f9b3a16**

CHAPTER 15
Core Concepts of Business Analytics

Introduction

Overall, this book focuses on various steps and stages in data engineering, which is a subject in itself, but fundamentally, data engineering is a foundational enabler of **business analytics** (**BA**) because it supports the collection, processing, and availability of data used for analysis. BA is a requirement that arises from the business problem that is seen in any operational or functional process. These problem statements can be, dropping sales of a product or services of a company, an increase in the cost of resources in the operations, accruing losses due to inefficient actions or compliance issues, etc. These business problems are translated into analytical questions, which guide data collection, analysis, or finding hidden patterns and decision-making that may solve or improve the overall business. These analytics may help organizations increase their revenue and/or profit, cut down the cost, or improve their customer satisfaction score.

This chapter covers the detailed understanding of what goes behind any BA project and the stages that are applicable to these businesses and their analysis.

Structure

The chapter covers the following topics:

- Definition and scope of business analytics
- Business analytics process
- Tools in business analytics
- Python programming for data analytics
- Maturity stages in analytics
- Application of business analytics
- Principles in business analytics
- R programming for data analytics
- SQL for data analytics

Objectives

At the end of this chapter, the reader will be able to define and understand the theory behind BA and the key components that work for any good BA.

The readers will get the high-level clarity of where BA can be applicable and what steps need to be executed for any successful BA process. The chapter will also touch upon the core principles behind BA and the tools that are available in the market, without which BA cannot be a possibility.

Definition and scope of business analytics

BA may be defined as the process of utilizing data and statistical analysis to find useful insights and make informed decisions for any business.

It involves collecting, sorting, and analyzing the data to identify the patterns, trends, and hidden correlations that can help the organization in maximizing the results by optimizing their operations, making their processes efficient, and able to serve the customer better than ever before.

BA primarily focuses on decision support and improving business outcomes through data-driven insights. While **business intelligence** (**BI**) mainly emphasizes reporting, dashboards, and performance monitoring, BA extends further into predictive and prescriptive analysis for strategic decision-making. In comparison, data science often includes broader experimentation, machine learning model development, and advanced statistical techniques to solve complex business and technical problems.

As shown in *Figure 15.1*, this chapter focuses on various processes, tools, and principles applied in a business setting for any BA project:

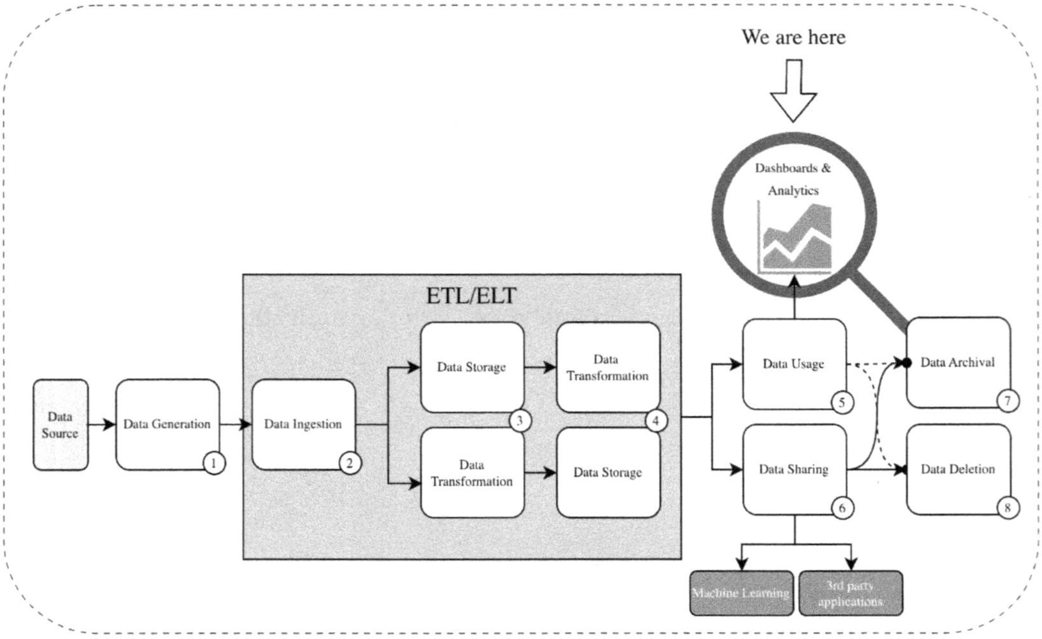

***Figure 15.1**: Current phase covered in the chapter*

Key components of business analytics

Although most of the components for BA have been covered in this book in some shape or form, to specifically point out the components for a BA project, it can have seven key components (refer to *Figure 15.2*):

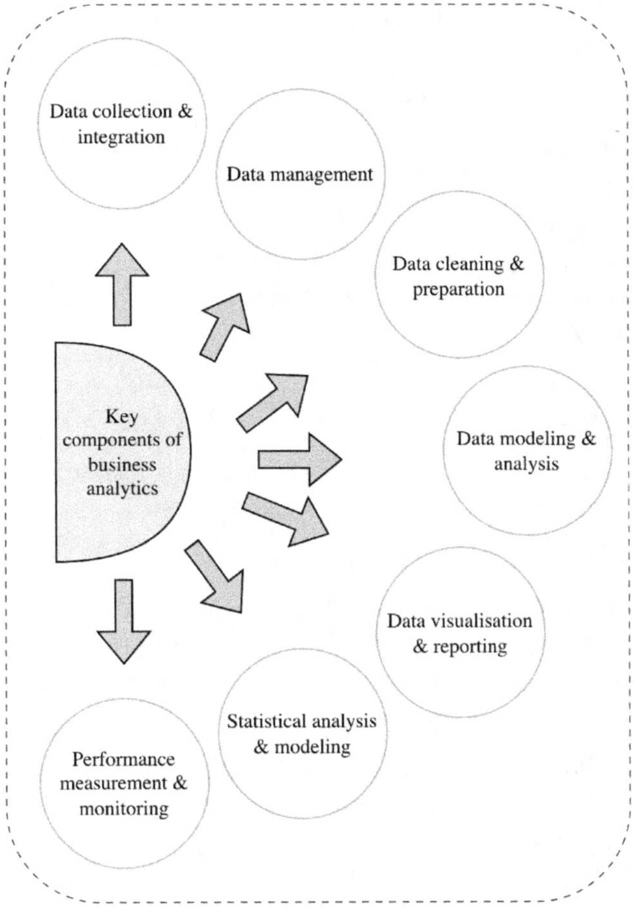

Figure 15.2*: Key components of BA*

- **Data collection and integration**: This involves gathering and integrating the data from various data sources, including internal historical data, internal databases, external sources, and real-time streaming data.
- **Data management**: This involves storing, organizing, and maintaining the data in an accessible manner (mostly structured) so that accessibility, accuracy, and reliability of the data are ensured.
- **Data cleaning and preparation**: This involves making the data ready for analysis by ensuring the quality, consistency, and suitability for analysis.

- **Data modeling and analysis**: This is the process of structuring and organizing the data into well-defined models and then applying various analytical techniques to analyze the data, uncover patterns, trends, relationships amongst them, and derive valuable insights.
- **Data visualization and reporting**: This is the process of converting the analysis into a human-readable or understandable format so that the interpretation of the complete analysis is easy. This is generally pictorial, which involves charts, graphs, dashboards, and reports to help in informed decision-making.
- **Statistical analysis and modeling**: This is the method of applying statistical techniques, algorithms, and mathematical models to the data to uncover deeper insights, perform predictive and diagnostic analysis, and develop analytical models.
- **Performance measurement and monitoring**: This is the process of establishing **key performance indicators** (**KPIs**) and metrics to assess the effectiveness and impact of analytics initiatives.

Scope of business analytics

BA can be broad and cross-functional, covering how data is used to support decision-making, strategy, and performance improvement in an organization.

The following are the areas where BA can be applied:

- **Descriptive analysis**: This finds *what has happened* from the data. It summarizes the current and historical data, identifies trends and patterns in the dataset. Generally, reports, dashboards, and KPIs are the output of this analysis. E.g., monthly sales reports, operations dashboards, etc.
- **Diagnostic analytics**: This analytics figures out *why it has happened* from the data. It examines the root cause, compares performance across dimensions, and users can drill down and do correlation analysis. E.g., identify the reason for the drop in sales for a commodity on an e-commerce platform
- **Predictive analytics**: This analytics shows *what is likely to happen* by looking at the data. It forecasts the future outcomes by using statistical models and machine learning. It estimates probabilities and risks. E.g., predicting future sales of a product in a company.
- **Prescriptive analytics**: This helps to figure out *what should be done* by identifying recommended actions by evaluating multiple scenarios and optimizing the decisions. E.g., suggesting a maintenance period for a machine.

Application of business analytics

The following are the areas of application of BA:

- **Financial analytics**: This is one of the key areas where the financial data is analyzed to assess performance, profitability, cash flow, and overall financial health of an organization. It also involves budgeting, forecasting, and financial modeling.
- **Marketing analytics**: This involves understanding customers' behavior, market trends, marketing campaign effectiveness, and optimizing marketing strategies. It includes customer segmentation, campaign analysis, and return on investment measurement.
- **Banking analytics**: This involves analyzing banking data to check customers' behavior, fraud detection, managing credit risk, and optimizing loan portfolios. This also involves customer segmentation, credit scoring models, and profitability analysis.
- **Internet of Things (IoT) analytics**: This is done by utilizing data coming from various IoT devices and sensors to gain insights into machine performance, predictive maintenance, energy consumption, and process optimization. It involves real-time analytics, anomaly detection, and predictive modeling to improve operational efficiency.
- **Operations analytics**: This means analyzing operational data to improve efficiency, optimizing the process, and reducing operational costs. It involves supply chain management, inventory optimization, production planning, and resource allocation.

Similar to these, there are other areas such as risk analytics, sales analytics, Inventory management analysis, etc., where BA can be applied and utilized.

From descriptive to prescriptive analytics: A retail example

A retail company notices a sudden decline in monthly sales across several stores. Using **descriptive analytics**, the company analyzes the sales dashboard and reports to identify when and where the decline started. The analysis reveals that the sales dropped significantly in urban location during last quarter. After this, **diagnostic analytics** was done to find the root cause of the sales decline. By examining customer feedback, inventory records and competitor pricing trends, the company discovered that frequent stock shortage and high prices of products compared to competitors contributed to the sales decline. The company then uses **predictive analytics** to build forecasting models to estimate future sales trends and predict which products are likely to face stock shortage during peak demand. Finally, **prescriptive analytics** recommends specific actions to improve business outcomes such as increasing inventory level for high-demand products, introducing targeted discount in affected stores, and optimizing supply chain schedules to avoid stockouts. By implementing these recommendations, the company improves product availability, customer satisfaction and overall sales performance.

Business analytics process

Firstly, the BA process begins with identifying a business problem and framing the right analytical questions. These questions may not necessarily come from a technical standpoint but from a functional one as well. For a successful business analysis, the following seven-step process needs to be executed:

1. **Defining business requirements**: This is the starting point of any BA project, and the success of the project is highly dependent on this step. In this, the expected outcome of the activity needs to be understood and defined clearly without any ambiguity. It should have minimal assumptions at this point, but only a clear outcome that a business expects. In this, we must define key questions, success criteria, and challenges. E.g., a customer support department wants to increase the customer satisfaction score by 10%.

2. **Collect, prepare, and explore data**: This is the stage where the data is gathered for the analysis. At this stage, data is cleaned, refined, missing values are handled, and outliers are removed. This way, the data quality is improved, and the final relevant structure of the data is given. In this step, some visualization is also done using visual tools so that the understanding of the data becomes easy. E.g., the data for historical customer satisfaction score is collected, which involves agent behavior, customer's sentiment, time to solve the query, number of holds while on the call, duration of the call, number of calls for the same query, and customer's feedback, etc., and this data is processed and made visually understandable for the next step.

3. **Analyze data**: This is the step where the analysts will apply various statistical methods, such as correlation analysis, hypothesis testing, etc., that will help them find the relationships between input variables and the target variables. The analyst may perform a simple regression analysis to see whether a simple prediction can be made. E.g., the analysis is done to check which factors are affecting the customer's satisfaction score. This will help them find the majorly affecting parameters that can be worked upon or improved. An agent's rude behavior may affect the customer's satisfaction inversely.

4. **Make a prediction**: One important goal of BA is to predict future outcomes, but it also includes understanding past performance, diagnosing causes, and recommending actions. At this stage, the analysts use various machine learning algorithms to estimate the probabilities and future trends. Some of these techniques can be decision trees, neural networks, and logistic regression. These algorithms unveil the hidden insights and patterns that may exist and influence the outcome. Then the predictions are compared with actual outcomes, and hence the model is improved for accurate prediction. E.g., predict which agents are going to bring positive customer feedback and who are struggling to get the same and need to be trained more.

5. **Optimize**: At this stage, the analysts run the *what if* scenarios and try to apply them to the current models to analyze the outcome against the real-world. These scenarios

may come from their seniors or operations, which will bring all the possibilities that are to be tested on the model. Finally, the solution that best satisfies business requirements such as profit, service level, budget, or operational capacity is selected for implementation. E.g., all the possible ranges of input variables for the machine learning model are tested, and the set of values that gives the most effective and accurate business results compared to the real-world scenarios is selected.

6. **Measure**: This step ensures continuous improvements. It tracks the performance of the analysis from the KPIs and metrics that were defined in the first step. It compares the actual results with the expected output and refines models or redefines strategies based on the feedback. E.g., checking if the action taken based on model predictions has resulted in an increase in positive feedback, if not, then the model will be re-analyzed, and the other factors that may be hidden will be worked upon after a defined duration.

7. **Reporting, retention and reusability**: Finally, all the results, decisions, actions, and outcomes are recorded for future reference and kept in the database. These results help the business to track the number of iterations, duration of the projects, and insights around these steps. This will help them to know what has been covered and how it can be planned better in the future. Also, this data will help the business to plan the other projects based on the learnings that have taken place in the current project. E.g., all the strategies that have been applied can be stored in the DB, and similar strategies can be applied in some other customer support department of other business units.

Principles in business analytics

Before commencing any project for analytics, the following principles are imperative to be kept in mind:

- **Problem formulation**: The problem formulation is the most important of all the principles. It involves clearly identifying the problem statement or the objective of the BA. This ensures the team is focused on generating the relevant insights that are aligned with the organizational goals. E.g., a credit card company wants to increase the credit card transactions of its existing customers by 10%.

- **Data-driven decision making**: This principle emphasizes using data to inform and strengthen decision-making, alongside business context and managerial judgment, rather than relying solely on intuition. This helps organizations to justify their actions and make accurate and informed decisions. E.g., an e-commerce firm wants to increase its profit by analyzing the data of the products on sale and checking which products are sold in good quantities and which are not. Out of that, which products have more margins, which products are in high demand, so that appropriate planning can be done.

- **Data quality**: The success of any data-driven project is highly dependent upon the quality of the data used. If the quality of the data is not good, the probabilities of getting accurate results will be lower. This requires appropriate data cleaning and pre-processing, and it should be free from any errors and inconsistencies. E.g., a company wants to do research on standard salaries across the market. Before they commence the work, they must make sure that there is no duplication of the records, that the data is free from outliers (e.g., -$1000), and that it does not have any missing salary details.

- **Continuous process**: BA is not a fixed-duration project but a continuous one. It may take dedicated time and cost for initial setup, creating the statistical analysis and model development, but it needs iterations for refining on a continuous basis due to continuously changing business conditions. E.g., a retail company continuously analyzes the customer's feedback on old and newly launched products and adjusts its offerings accordingly by analyzing the sales continuously.
- **Data safety and privacy**: This is a non-negotiable principle when it is thought from the customer's perspective. The data that is being processed may be confidential and may have PII or SPI. For this, organizations must follow all the data security and compliance requirements in order to safeguard the data and avoid huge penalties. E.g., a travel company masks the PII and SPI data while working in the operations so that nobody can see their names, contact information, credit card information, etc., until necessary.

Tools in business analytics

The fundamental difference between business analysis and analytics is that business analysis focuses on identifying business problems and requirements, while BA focuses on analyzing the data to derive data-driven insights for informed decision-making.

This means that without tools, good BA may not be possible. So there are some tools that are available in the market for BA, listed in the following sections.

Data visualization tools

These are the tools that are used for quick visualization of the data for easy understanding by the analysts and the business people. They present the insights through interactive charts and dashboards. Some of the known tools available in the market are:

- **Tableau**: A powerful data visualization tool used to create interactive dashboards and reports.
- **QlikView**: A **business intelligence** (**BI**) tool that enables quick associative data exploration and analysis.
- **FusionChart**: A JavaScript-based charting library used for building interactive and animated charts.
- **Sisense**: An end-to-end analytics platform for embedding analytics and dashboards into the customer's applications

- **Highcharts**: A JavaScript library used for creating responsive and interactive charts for web applications.
- **Datawrapper**: An easy-to-use online tool for creating charts, maps, and tables for reporting.
- **Plotly**: A data visualization library that can be used in Python for creating interactive charts and graphs.

Statistical analysis system

These tools are used to collect, analyze, interpret, and visualize the data using statistical methods to support decision-making. Some of the well-known tools in the market are:

- **Python**: A versatile programming language widely used for data analysis, machine learning, and automations.
- **Statistical analysis system (SAS)**: A statistical analytics software that is used for advanced data analysis and business intelligence.
- **Matrix Laboratory (MATLAB)**: A numerical computing tool used for mathematical modeling, simulation, and data analysis.
- **Waikato environment for knowledge analysis (WEKA)**: A machine learning software suite used for data mining and predictive analytics.
- **Konstanz information miner (KNIME)**: An open-source analytics platform for data integration, analysis, and reporting.
- **RapidMiner**: A data science platform for predictive analytics and machine learning workflows.
- **International Business Machines Statistical Package for the Social Sciences (IBM SPSS)**: A statistical software package from IBM, used for data analysis in research and business.
- **R**: A programming language specially built for statistical analysis and data visualization.
- **Apache Hadoop**: A big data framework used for storing and processing large datasets in a distributed environment.
- **Minitab**: A statistical tool used for quality improvements and process analysis.
- **SAP**: An enterprise software platform used for data management and BA.
- **TIBCO Statistica**: An advanced analytics software used for data mining and predictive modeling.

Machine learning tools

These are the software libraries that help in building, training, testing, and deploying machine learning models by automating learning from data. Some of the well-known names in the industry are:

- **TensorFlow**: An open-source framework used for building and training deep learning and machine learning models.
- **Keras**: A high-level deep learning API that simplifies building neural networks on top of TensorFlow.
- **Scikit-learn**: A Python library used for classical machine learning tasks such as classification, regression, and clustering.
- **Caffe**: A deep learning framework optimized for image processing and computer vision tasks.
- **H2O.ai**: An open-source machine learning platform for scalable predictive analytics
- **Amazon SageMaker**: A cloud-based service for building, training, and deploying machine learning models.
- **Apache Spark MLib**: A scalable machine learning library built on Apache Spark for big data analytics.
- **BigML**: A cloud-based machine learning platform for creating and deploying predictive models.

Cloud computing platforms

These are the online service environments that provide computing resources such as servers, storage, databases, networking, and analytics over the internet on a pay-as-you-use basis. This is already covered in detail in *Chapter 10, Understanding Cloud Computing*. Some of the well-known names in the market today are as follows:

- **Amazon Web Services (AWS)**: A comprehensive cloud platform offering computing, storage, analytics, and machine learning services.
- **Microsoft Azure**: A cloud computing service for building, deploying, and managing applications through Microsoft-managed data centers.
- **Google Cloud**: A cloud platform providing data analytics, machine learning, and scalable infrastructure services.
- **Alibaba Cloud**: A cloud computing platform offering enterprise-level cloud services, mainly popular in Asia.
- **Oracle Cloud Infrastructure**: A cloud platform providing high-performance computing and enterprise database services.

- **IBM Cloud**: A cloud platform combining AI, analytics, and enterprise cloud solutions.
- **Tencent Cloud**: A cloud service provider offering computing and AI services, widely in China.
- **OVHcloud**: A European cloud provider offering public and private cloud infrastructure.
- **Linode**: A cloud platform providing simple and cost-effective hosting solutions.
- **DigitalOcean**: A cloud service provider offering simple, developer-friendly infrastructure for deploying and scaling applications.

R programming for data analytics

R is an open-source programming language that is used in BA due to its powerful statistical analysis, data visualization, and modeling capabilities that help analysts turn data into business insights. It was developed by *Ross Ihaka* and *Robert Gentleman* in the early 1990s. It provides the flexibility of working with structured and unstructured data.

Reasons to choose R programming

R is a language that provides ample features for data analysis that make it unique in many senses. R is particularly strong for statistics-heavy analysis, academic research, and specialized data visualization workflows, whereas Python is more widely used for general-purpose programming, machine learning, and production-oriented AI applications. Some of the important features are as follows:

- **Open-source**: R has been developed as an open-source, which means people around the world modify or add essential features and distribute their work freely.
- **Large packages repository**: R has the **Comprehensive R Archive Network** (**CRAN**), which hosts thousands of packages that users can download and install as an extended functionality of the R programming language.
- **Compatibility**: R programming is platform-independent or cross-platform compatible, which means it can work on Windows, Linux, and Mac operating systems.
- **Designed for data**: The whole idea behind R is data analysis, so it has all the required tools that are essential for statistical computing and graphics.
- **Excellent visualization**: R creates high-quality charts and graphs for clear business insights.

Limitations of R

Although R is used in a variety of fields, including data science, finance, healthcare, etc., it has its own set of disadvantages as well:

- It may be slow for large-scale computation.
- Consumes high memory, making it unsuitable for very large datasets.
- Syntax is not easy to understand in the beginning.
- Error handling is less structured.

Python programming for data analytics

Although Python has been covered in *Chapter 12, Key Tools Powering Modern Data Engineering,* as a programming language, it is one of the most popular languages for building websites using its various web frameworks. However, in this part, we are looking at Python as a data analytics language, which has become one of the most important languages for data science, machine learning, and general software development.

For data analysis, interactive computing, and data visualization, Python is often compared with other widely used open-source and commercial tools such as R, SAS, MATLAB, Stata, etc. The development of open-source libraries like pandas and scikit-learn has increased Python's popularity for data analysis and made it an excellent primary language for building data-driven and analytics applications.

Reason to choose Python programming

Python is often preferred for broader end-to-end workflows, application integration, automation, and machine learning production use cases, whereas tools such as R are more focused on statistical computing and research-oriented analysis. The following are the reasons why Python should be the go-to language for any data analytics projects:

- **Easy to learn and use**: Simple, readable syntax helps beginners to understand the language faster and scale its use.
- **Rich library ecosystem**: Like R, Python also comes with libraries like NumPy, Pandas, Matplotlib, and Scikit-learn that support a complete data science workflow.
- **Strong data handling**: Python is efficient in data cleaning, transformation, and analysis.
- **Excellent visualization**: Easy creation of charts and dashboards is possible in Python.
- **Open-source and free**: Python requires no licensing cost and is free to use.
- **Scalable**: Python can easily handle small as well as large, complex data pipelines.
- **Machine learning and AI support**: Python is one of the most popular languages for building predictive and intelligent models.

Limitations of Python

Due to its very nature, the following are the limitations that can be seen for Python:

- **Slower execution speed**: Python is an interpreted language, so it is slower than compiled languages for large computations.
- **High memory consumption**: Handling a large dataset may require significant memory, and may struggle with real-time processing requirements.
- **Global Interpreter Lock (GIL)**: This is the mechanism that prevents the interpreter from executing more than one Python instruction at a time. This limits true multi-threaded CPU execution, affecting performance in CPU-bound tasks.
- **Less specialized**: Python is less specialized for statistics, unlike R, and it is complicated for advanced statistical techniques.

SQL for data analytics

SQL is one of the most important languages for data analytics because it is used to store, retrieve, clean, and analyze data directly from the databases. It enables analysts to efficiently retrieve, filter and manipulate large datasets using queries. It also supports operation such as data aggregation, joining multiple tables and performing calculations, which are sometimes essential in extracting meaningful insights.

Reasons to choose SQL

Because of the single platform, it is easy to do the following:

- It works directly on the large dataset stored in the databases, which reduces the work of data movement.
- Fast and efficient for filtering, aggregation, and summarization.
- Easy to learn and widely supported around the world.
- It is essential to extract data before analysis in other tools like Python, R, etc.
- It can handle large data efficiently and works with almost all the major databases.

Limitations of SQL

Although it is widely accepted around the world, still it has the following limitations,

- **Limited advanced analytics**: SQL is not suitable for complex statistical analysis or machine learning.
- **No data visualization**: SQL cannot create charts or dashboards on its own.

- **Database dependent**: Syntax and functions vary across databases (MySQL, Oracle, PostgreSQL, etc.)
- **Complex queries become hard to read**: Advanced joins and subqueries reduce readability and maintainability.
- **Not suitable for unstructured data**: Works best with structured and tabular data only.
- **Scalability limitation**: Complex analytical workloads may require additional tools or engines.

Maturity stages in analytics

The maturity stages in BA refer to the gradual development of an organization's analytical capability over time. These stages represent an increasing level of sophistication, analysis capability, and actions in using data and analytics to generate business value.

As these stages are already covered in the above topic scope of BA, one needs to understand that they are not independent but incremental and connected. Moving from one stage to another requires investments in technology, skills, thought process, business understanding, maturity of expectation, etc.

Figure 15.3 illustrates how different stages are connected and move gradually up as the organization's maturity as a whole improves:

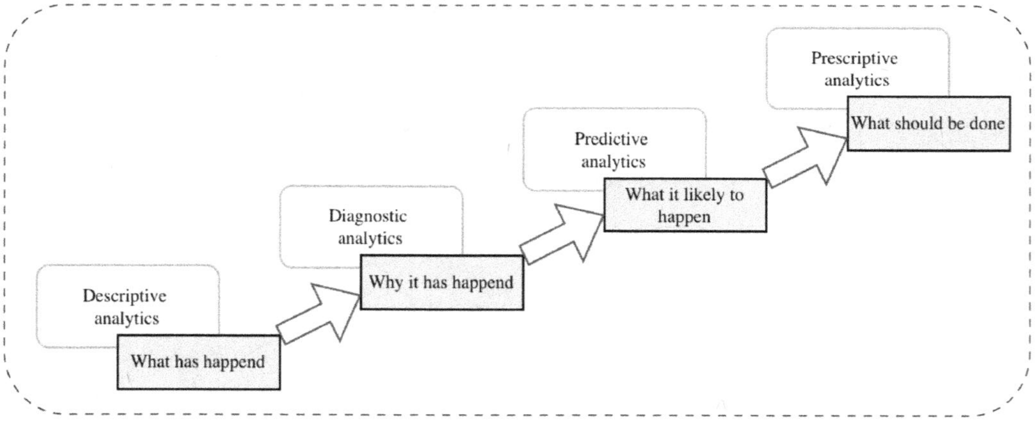

***Figure 15.3**: Maturity stages of BA*

In the initial stage of **descriptive analytics**, organizations focus on understanding, summarizing, and reporting the data. This is just to show what has happened by reporting and visualization. This helps businesses see and compare the trends from the past data and draw inferences from their own experiences.

Once the organization stays with the descriptive analysis for some time and does back and forth on the issues identified, the next logical question that comes to mind is, why it has happened, or in other words, what is the root cause of it, that is causing a particular behavior. This process is called **diagnostic analytics**. Although analytics maturity is often presented sequentially, organizations may operate across multiple analytics stages simultaneously across different teams or business functions and gradually mature with time and experience. This stage involves researching certain behaviors or patterns to unveil the underlying root cause of the same. These analytics involve some advanced techniques such as data mining, correlation analysis, and statistical modeling to get there.

When organizations get well-versed in finding the right reasons and causes for certain behavior, it becomes like seeing the behavior and knowing the root cause of it. This expertise will also work in the reverse direction, i.e., get the root cause and predict the behavior. Using this, organizations reach the stage where, by identifying certain patterns and trends in data, they can expect a specific result; this is called **predictive analytics**. This is done by developing statistical and machine learning models to identify patterns and trends in historical data and apply them to make informed forecasts. The target is to estimate the probabilities and make data-driven predictions.

Once the organization reaches the stage where they are able to do the prediction well close to the real-world outcome and have achieved substantial success in that, then the next logical step is to make use of the overall experience and find the best course of action for a specific behavior. This is called **prescriptive analytics**. It uses optimization techniques in algorithms and simulations to provide recommendations and prescribe actions. It takes certain assumptions, constraints, trade-offs, and optimizations to provide actionable recommendations.

Some real-life examples

The following are some very simple daily life examples that we follow without consciously noticing them, and get mature over time to handle the situations:

- **Daily commute to office**:
  - **Descriptive**: Traffic is heavy on Monday.
  - **Diagnostic**: Office timings and school buses cause this congestion.
  - **Predictive**: Next Monday will be congested.
  - **Prescriptive**: Leave 30 mins early.
- **Mobile phone battery**:
  - **Descriptive**: Battery drains very fast, and the phone heats up.
  - **Diagnostic**: Many apps are running in the background, and the screen brightness is always high.
  - **Predictive**: If this continues, the phone will start shutting down in ~3 hours.
  - **Prescriptive**: Close background apps, reduce brightness, and turn on battery saver.

- **Customer churn in a telecom company**:
  - **Descriptive**: Customer cancellations increased by 12% this quarter.
  - **Diagnostic**: Customers are dissatisfied due to frequent network issues and slow support response times.
  - **Predictive**: Customers with repeated complaints are more likely to cancel their subscriptions next month.
  - **Prescriptive**: Improve network quality in affected regions, provide proactive support, and offer retention discounts to high-risk customers.

Conclusion

This chapter covered the key concepts and the essential components of a BA project including scope, principles and applications, supported by some real-life scenarios. Some of the renowned tools were also mentioned in this section that would help the readers to learn about some popular tools and perform hands-on practice with them to improve their understanding. It has also covered, the incremental approach of how the maturity of an organization improves for any BA project by connecting the dots together, and as a result, readers can visualize how all the stages are linked to each other.

The next chapter will cover some practical techniques in BA and see how they can be used to solve real-world problems in detail.

References

1. **https://www.tutorialspoint.com/business-analytics/index.htm**
2. **https://www.iss.nus.edu.sg/community/newsroom/news-detail/2016/06/24/the-7-step-business-analytics-process**
3. **https://www.geeksforgeeks.org/r-language/r-programming-language-introduction/**
4. **https://www.lkhibra.ma/books/Python-for-Data-Analysis.pdf**
5. **https://www.geeksforgeeks.org/data-analysis/data-analysis-with-python/**

CHAPTER 16
Business Analytics Implementation and Problem Solving

Introduction

Till now, this book has covered the end-to-end lifecycle of analytics problem solving enabled by data engineering which starts with understanding a business problem statement, conceptualizing the approach of solving for it, selecting a right team, finding the data sources, pre-processing and processing of data, storing the data appropriately and making use of the data against the business problem with the intention to solve the same.

Now, we will look at these concepts from a broader perspective. This chapter will demonstrate how the earlier theoretical concepts are applied in the real-world analytics problems and how these techniques help in decision making and achieving the specific business goals.

Structure

The chapter covers the following topics:

- Practical techniques in business analytics
- Process of business problem solving in data science

Objectives

By the end of this chapter, the reader will be able to understand and apply the practical techniques, explain the process of solving business problems using data science approaches, and understand the lifecycle of BA from problem identification to decision making and continuous improvement.

Practical techniques in business analytics

Business analytics involves several practical techniques that help organizations analyze data and make better decisions. However, before looking at these techniques, let us see the importance of understanding them.

Importance of practical techniques in decision-making

Practical techniques in business analytics play an important role in improving the quality of decision-making in an organization. These techniques help convert the raw data into meaningful insights that help managers and business leaders in making informed decisions. Some of the other important aspects are:

- **Real-world relevance**: Practical techniques are designed to address real-world problems. They focus on understanding the actual data and apply the learnings to improve the existing process.
- **Savings**: Practical techniques help the business to focus on what is truly important rather than investing time, effort and money on broad or less relevant activities. This focus helps the operations become more efficient and optimized, and saves time, effort, and money.
- **Actionable insights**: Practical techniques not only focus on understanding the data and getting the inference out of it, but also believe in getting the actionable insights too, along with the inference, so that these actions can help organizations to improve their current process and serve their customers better.
- **Competitive advantage**: Leveraging the practical techniques in BA helps the organization analyze its data to identify trends, patterns, and opportunities that the competitors might miss out on. This will help organizations to take a leap and grow much faster than the other players.

Types of practical techniques in business analytics

There are various dimensions in BA that should be looked at. These are very important as a starting point that provides a direction to approach a problem and broadens the horizon of the analytics. Some of the most important areas are discussed in the following sections.

Seasonality analysis

Seasonality analysis is defined as a practical technique that is used to detect the pattern or trend that repeats itself over the course of time, again and again at fixed and known intervals. That may be daily, weekly, monthly, or yearly. It may also occur due to seasonal factors such as holidays, weather changes, or cultural events. Let us look at the following chart (*Figure 16.1*) to see the seasonal pattern of sales data of an e-commerce company in the festival season:

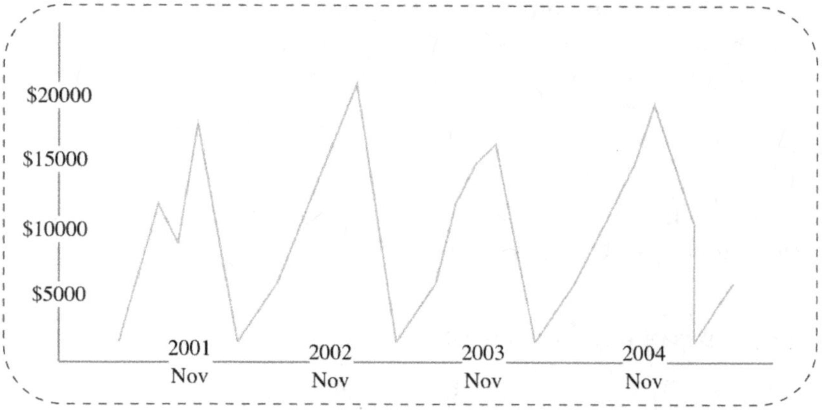

***Figure 16.1**: A chart showing illustrative sales data of an e-commerce company in India during the Diwali festival*

This differs from a **trend**, which represents a long-term upward or downward movement in the data over time, such as steadily increasing online sales over several years. It is also different from **cyclic** variation, where patterns rise and fall over irregular time periods due to broader economic or business cycles, and the duration of these cycles is not fixed or predictable like seasonality.

Key steps to take for seasonality analysis:

1. **Data collection and exploration**: This is the step in which the data is collected and explored for any initial analysis on the same to detect any pattern. This is to initially understand its characteristics.
2. **Decomposition**: In this step, the available decomposition techniques are applied, such as seasonal trend decomposition using LOESS, to separate the data into its constituents, such as trends or seasonality, etc.
    - **Locally Estimated Scatterplot Smoothing (LOESS)**: It is a statistical technique used to smooth the data and identify trends in time series or scatter plots. Instead of fitting one global model, it fits small regression models to different subsets of data.
3. **Seasonal analysis**: Analyzing the seasonal component obtained from the decomposition step to identify the nature, strength, and duration of the seasonal patterns.
4. **Modeling**: Develop a seasonal model that incorporates the seasonal data and patterns.
5. **Evaluation**: This is the process of evaluating the model for accuracy and improving wherever gaps are identified.
6. **Forecasting**: This is utilizing the developed model for future predictions and forecasting using techniques such as **Autoregressive Integrated Moving Average (ARIMA)**. ARIMA is a widely used time series forecasting model that predicts future values based on the past observations and historical patterns in data.

7. **Continuous monitoring and tuning**: This is a non-negotiable step, which is keeping an eye on the results of the model, identifying the changing trends, and improving or tuning the model according to the new patterns.

Trend analysis

A trend is the general direction of change in data over time. The process of understanding these trends and figuring out a significant strategy to operate in a business is called trend analysis.

There are different types of trends, such as:

- **Market trend**: These are trends that show how the market is behaving around a certain product or service. This focuses on checking how customers' demand changes or industry patterns change over time. E.g., during festive seasons, there is a rapid increase in spending on clothes and electronics. This repeated increase in sales indicates a market trend during festivals.
- **Operational trend**: These are the trends that focus on the organization's internal performance and efficiencies of business operations. E.g., a tire manufacturing company notices the average time to produce a tire has decreased from 30 minutes to 25 minutes due to automation and improved processes. This pattern represents an operational trend showing increased efficiency.
- **Financial trend**: Financial trend shows a pattern in financial metrics such as revenue, profit, or expenses. E.g., a company's annual revenue has increased from $5 million in 2022 to $6.5 million in 2023 and $7.5 million in 2024. This consistent growth indicates the positive financial trend of a company.
- **Predictive trend**: A predictive trend uses historical data and analytics to forecast future outcomes. E.g., based on the 5-year sales data and seasonal patterns, an e-commerce company predicts that the sales of the company will increase by 20% during the Christmas week.

Key steps to take for trend analysis

Trend analysis requires the historical data to determine patterns or trends over the course of time. The following are the steps to follow for the same:

1. **Data collection**: This is the step in which the data is collected from various sources. These sources can be the company's historical data, market data (available on the internet), research data, surveys, or any other data sources.
2. **Data preparation**: These steps involve cleaning the data for any anomalies, outliers, and missing values, and making it suitable for analytics.
3. **Visualization**: This is the process of converting the data into visual charts, plots, etc.

This helps in understanding the patterns quickly and more easily. Some initial trends can be easily identified in this step.

4. **Trend identification**: These are the statistical techniques that are used on the data to identify the trends that may not be obviously visible. These techniques can be moving averages, exponential smoothing, and regression analysis. These algorithms or techniques help in identifying the direction and strength of the trends.

    a. **Simple moving averages**: It calculates the average of a fixed number of past observations to smooth the short-term fluctuation and identify the overall trend. E.g., a small grocery store records daily sales of milk packets as Monday 100, Tuesday 120, Wednesday 110. The 3-day moving average would be *(100+120+110) /3= 110*. This helps in understanding the general trend without being affected by daily fluctuations.

    b. **Exponential smoothing**: This smoothing gives more importance to recent data while considering the past observations. E.g., an e-commerce company forecasts tomorrow's sales by giving more weightage to today's sales than older sales data; this way, the prediction reflects the most recent market conditions.

    c. **Regression analysis**: Regression identifies the relationship between the variables and predicts the future. E.g., sales of ice cream increase when the temperature rises.

5. **Root-cause analysis**: The trends identified are analyzed from the business angle to find the factors affecting it and understand the stability of the trends. This may help the organizations to detect the unknown factors that went unnoticed over the period of time.

6. **Forecasting**: This is the process of predicting the future trend or outcome based on the analysis done. These can be achieved by employing various forecasting techniques such as time series analysis, predictive modeling, etc.

7. **Decisioning**: This is the process of understanding the result of trend analysis and taking the critical business decisions that may help businesses generate more revenue, increase customer satisfaction, etc. These may involve developing new strategies, changes in resource allocation, modifications in market positioning, etc.

Comparative analysis

Comparative analysis is the process of examining two or more items, datasets, or situations to identify their similarities and differences. This is done with the intent of drawing meaningful insights or making better decisions. E.g., a company compares its monthly sales of 2025 with the sales of 2026 to understand whether the business performance has improved or declined. Similarly, an online retailer compares the sales performance of two products to determine which product performs better in the market.

Figure 16.2 illustrates the comparison of sales of an XYZ model of scooter across four years. This way it is easy to compare the sales of any product and analyze how it is overall doing in the market over a year's timeframe.

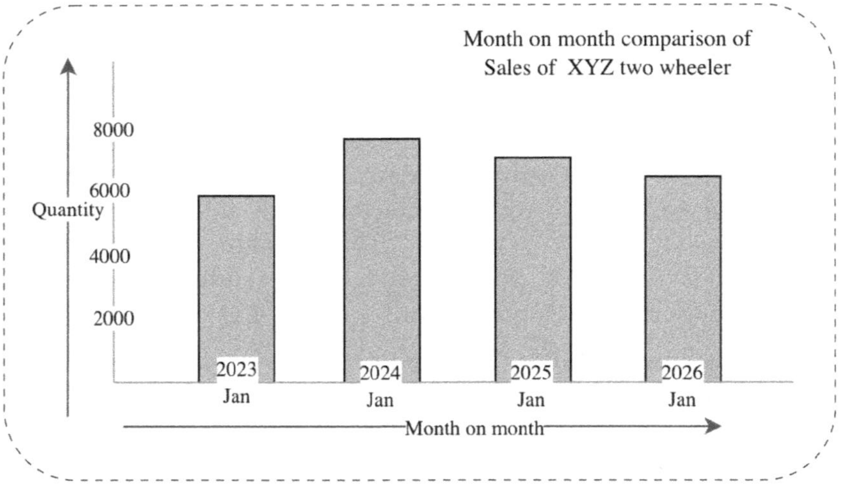

Figure 16.2*: A bar chart representing the yearly sales of a two-wheeler company*

Some of the common areas where comparative analytics is used are:

- **Business analytics**: Comparing sales, profits, or customer trends.
- **Market research**: Comparing products and different services.
- **Finance**: Comparing financial statements across the years.
- **Policy analysis**: Comparing outcomes of different policies.

Key steps to take for comparative analysis

The following are the steps that need to be followed for comparative analytics:

1. **Understand the problem**: In this step, what needs to be compared and what is the final objective of this analysis should be defined.
2. **Define scope and data availability**: The comparisons can span many business dimensions, so the specific scope of the analysis should be finalized, and the relevant data should be checked against it.
3. **Identify analytics techniques**: Select the appropriate analytical methods or models that can address the problem effectively.
4. **Consider data processing**: Examine the nature and quality of data; if inappropriate, consider the transformation to make it viable for analytics.
5. **Insights generation**: This is the step where the insights are generated and checked for the results. The result must be easy to understand and have a meaningful outcome for decision-making.

6. **Validation and testing**: Verify the accuracy and reliability using various testing and validation techniques.
7. **Scalability**: Ensure the chosen approach can handle large datasets and complex scenarios.
8. **Iterate and refine**: Continuously improve the analytical model based on the feedback, results, and new/updated data.

Value-based analysis

Value-based analysis is a fundamental concept in which any organization evaluates the value of the investment made. The cost of any implementation is compared against the benefit reaped, for that cost, and hence the decision is concluded as right or wrong.

There are some key aspects that can be seen in value-based analysis:

- **Financial value**: This is evaluating the financial impact of any investment or decision. The financial impact can be changes in revenue, profit, cost of operations, or return on investment. By understanding the financial values, businesses can make decisions on whether their previous investments or decisions have brought advantage to the business or not. If it has been beneficial, then businesses can make strategies to invest more time and money in that area; if not then, they should stop making the investment for the same. E.g., a company evaluates whether its digital marketing campaign increased revenue enough to justify the advertising cost.
- **Strategic value**: This involves the evaluation of the strategic impact of any investment or decision. This is considered positive if the outcome of the investment has been aligned with the company's overall strategies, long-term goals, and competitive advantages. Unlike financial values, the financial return in the business impacts may be ignored, keeping other tangible and intangible outcomes in focus. E.g., a technology company invests in research and development work to strengthen its future market position, even if the profits are not immediate.
- **Risk assessment**: This requires evaluating the risks associated with a decision or investment. It involves important factors like market volatility, regulatory changes, and other unknown uncertainties that may impact the business. By incorporating the risk assessment, businesses can make more informed decisions by evaluating both potential rewards and potential risks. E.g., before expanding its business to a new country, a company evaluates regulatory policies, currency fluctuations, and market stability.
- **Trade-off analysis**: This is a type of value-based analysis in which different strategies and options are compared, and the best strategy is chosen by comparing all the advantages and disadvantages of each strategy. This way, the business gets prepared with what they are going to gain and lose for the chosen strategy. This analysis helps

businesses to be comfortable with the outcome and avoid any panic situation by knowing the adverse impact in advance. E.g., a company evaluates and compares building its own data centers versus using cloud services to decide which option is more cost-effective and scalable.

Similar to other analyses, value-based analysis should be revisited continuously as outcomes are measured against expectations and strategies are adjusted.

Correlation analysis

Correlation analysis can be defined as a statistical technique that is used to determine the relationship between two or more variables. It shows the strength and direction of the relationship and helps to determine if changes in one variable are associated with changes in another variable.

There are three types of correlation:

- **Positive correlation**: When both variables move in the same direction, e.g., temperature increases, and eventually the sales of ice cream increase.
- **Negative correlation**: When one variable increases, the other decreases and vice versa, e.g., when the product price decreases, the sales increase.
- **Zero correlation**: When there is no relationship between the variables, e.g., height and intelligence.

Types of correlation analysis

There are various types of correlation analysis that can be done on the data. Based on their very nature, these analyses target specific behavior. The following are some of the types of correlation analysis:

- **Pearson correlation**: This analysis focuses on understanding the linear relationship between two continuous variables, e.g., more hours studied leads to higher exam marks.
- **Spearman rank correlation**: This analysis measures the relationship of the variables using their ranked values, e.g., finding the relationship between a student's rank in mathematics and rank in science, in other words, a student who is first in math is also first in science.
- **Kendall's Tau**: In this analysis, the measurement is done on the strength of association between two ranked variables based on agreed ranking, e.g., finding the relationship between two judges' rankings of contestants in a competition.
- **Point-biserial correlation**: This measures the relationship between a continuous variable and a binary variable, e.g., finding a relationship between exam scores (continuous) and gender (male/female).

- **Phi coefficient**: This analysis measures the association between two binary variables, e.g., the relationship between smoking (yes/no) and the presence of lung cancer (yes/no).
- **Canonical relationship**: In this analysis, the focus is to measure the association between two sets of variables, e.g., finding the relationship between student characteristics (IQ, study hours, extra tuition) and academic performances (math score, science score).
- **Partial correlation**: This measures the relationship between two variables while ignoring the effect of third variable from both the variables, e.g., measuring the relationship between study hours and exam marks after removing or controlling the effect of IQ from both the variables i.e., to see whether studying more really improves marks when IQ difference is ignored or every student is assumed to have same IQ.
- **Semi-partial correlation**: This measures the relationship between the two variables after removing the effect of a third variable in only one variable, e.g., finding the relationship between study hours and exam marks after removing the IQ effect only from study hours, i.e., the teacher adjusts study hours based on the IQ, then checks how these adjusted study hours affect the marks.
- **Cross-correlation**: This analysis finds the correlation between two time series variables at different time lags, e.g., advertising this month and sales next month.

Time series analysis

Time series analysis is a statistical technique used to analyze data collected over time in order to identify patterns, trends, and make future predictions.

Key components of time series are as follows:

- **Trend**: Long-term upward or downward movement in the data, e.g., a company's sales is increasing every year.
- **Seasonality**: Regular pattern or behavior that repeats over a fixed duration, e.g., higher retail sales in the Diwali or Christmas season.
- **Cyclic variation**: The fluctuations that occur over the longer period due to economic cycles, e.g., businesses grow during economic expansion and decline during recession.
- **Irregular variation**: Random or unexpected change in the data or trend, e.g., sudden drop in tourism during COVID-19.

Time series analysis helps businesses to make predictions of the future based on the historical data, detect anomalies or abrupt behaviors, and provide valuable insights for critical and informed decision-making.

Regression analysis

Regression analysis is a technique used to study the relationship between a dependent variable and one or more independent variables, and to predict the value of the dependent variable. Some of the regression analyses that are often used in the industry,

- **Simple linear regression**: This is a type of regression analysis that is employed to examine the relationship between one dependent and one independent variable only, e.g., study hours | exam marks.
- **Multiple regression**: This is used to analyze the relationship between one dependent and two or more independent variables, e.g., predicting the price of the house based on the number of rooms, balconies, toilets, amenities, room size, kitchen, sunlight, etc.
- **Logistic regression**: This is a statistical technique that is used to predict the probability of a binary outcome (two possible categories) based on one or more independent variables, e.g., predicting whether the student will pass or fail based on study hours, attendance, IQ, and previous grades.

Process of business problem solving in data science

As we have seen so far, any business problem starts with an idea or a problem statement that needs to be solved. Depending upon the problem statement, there are certain steps that need to be taken in order to make sure that no critical item is missed that should be part of our analysis.

Let us understand a real-life problem as an example and see all the steps that may be necessary to take, ensuring complete end-to-end steps.

Use case on predicting liver disease

This use case demonstrates not only a machine learning classification problem but also an important business and healthcare decision-making scenario. Predicting liver disease can help hospitals and healthcare providers prioritize patient triage, support early-stage screening, and allocate medical resources more efficiently. By identifying high-risk patients earlier, healthcare organizations can reduce diagnostic delays, improve treatment planning, optimize specialist availability, and lower overall healthcare costs while improving patient outcomes.

The liver is the largest internal organ in the body, with the capability to regenerate itself. It plays an important role in filtering blood, storing energy, and producing bile for digestion. When the liver is damaged due to conditions such as alcohol consumption, infections, fatty liver diseases, or medical toxicity, its ability to function properly declines.

To diagnose liver problems, doctors usually perform **Liver Function Tests** (**LFT**), which measure different substances and enzymes in the blood.

For this use case, we have a dataset that has the details about the patients and their vitals, so that we can use this data in our algorithms to check if the liver disease exists or not.

As learned in *Chapter 15, Core Concepts of Business Analytics*, we will follow the BA process so that each and every step will be very clear on how any business problem needs to be approached.

Step 1: Defining business requirements

The objective of the problem statement is clear, i.e., predicting liver disease by feeding the patient data to a machine learning model. This solution intends to help doctors, diagnostic teams and hospital administrators in improving screening efficiency and prioritizing high-risk patients for further medical evaluation.

The success criteria for the project may include achieving acceptable accuracy, minimize false negatives (missing actual liver disease cases), improving early detection rates, and reducing delay in treatment.

Step 2: Explore the data or information

In this step, the data needs to be checked and validated to determine if the data is complete and sufficient for us to be able to predict the liver disease or not. In our current dataset, we have 583 records with 11 features or columns.

This dataset can be downloaded from the link :**http://archive.ics.uci.edu/dataset/225/ilpd+indian+liver+patient+dataset**

Explanation of each column is as follows

Feature name	Python column name	Description
Age	Age	Shows the age of the patient in years.
Gender	Gender	Gender of the patient (Male/Female).
Total Bilirubin	Total_Bilirubin	Total amount of bilirubin in the blood; high values may indicate liver problems.
Direct Bilirubin	Direct_Bilirubin	Processed bilirubin level in the blood; elevated values may suggest liver dysfunction.
Alkaline Phosphatase	Alkaline_Phosphotase	An enzyme related to the liver and bones; elevated levels may indicate liver or bile duct disease.

Alanine Aminotransferase (ALT/SGPT)	Alamine_ Aminotransferase	A liver enzyme; higher values may indicate liver damage. Also known as **Serum Glutamic Pyruvic Transaminase** (**SGPT**).
Aspartate Aminotransferase (AST/SGOT)	Aspartate_ Aminotransferase	An enzyme found in the liver and heart; high levels may indicate liver damage. Also known as **Serum Glutamic Oxaloacetic Transaminase** (**SGOT**).
Total Proteins	Total_Protiens	Total amount of protein in the blood.
Albumin	Albumin	A major protein produced by the liver that helps maintain fluid balance in the body.
Albumin/Globulin Ratio	Albumin_and_ Globulin_Ratio	Ratio of two major blood proteins; abnormal values may indicate liver problems.
Liver Disease Status	Has_liver_ disease(Yes_1, No_2)	Target variable indicating whether the patient has liver disease or not.

Table 16.1: *Shows all the columns and their descriptions in the dataset*

Data access

Reading the **`.csv`** file for the patient data:

- **Python command**:

```
df = pd.read_csv('/content/Indian Liver Patient Dataset (ILPD).
csv', header=None)
```

- **Output**:

  This will store the entire dataset inside the **`df`** data frame.

Dataset structure modification

Since the data received does not have the column headers, add them:

- **Python command**:

```
df.columns = ["Age", "Gender", "Total_Bilirubin", "Direct_Bilirubin",
              "Alkaline_Phosphotase", "Alamine_Aminotransferase",
              "Aspartate_Aminotransferase", "Total_Protiens",
              "Albumin", "Albumin_and_Globulin_Ratio",
              "Has_liver_disease(Yes_1, No_2)"]
```

- **Output**:

  This command adds column headers to the existing dataset.

Explore the structure of the dataset

This is to ensure that the number of rows and columns is complete before using them for data analysis:

- **Python command**:
```
print('Total number of rows are',df.shape[0])
print('Total number of columns are',df.shape[1])
```
- **Output**:

  Total number of rows is 583, Total number of columns is 11

Exploring the high-level structure of the dataset

To see what the dataset looks like:

- **Python command**:
```
df.head()
```
- **Output**:

Age	Gender	Total_Bilirubin	Direct_Bilirubin	Alkaline_Phosphotase	Alamine_Aminotransferase	Aspartate_Aminotransferase
65	Female	0.7	0.1	187	16	18
62	Male	10.9	5.5	699	64	100
62	Male	7.3	4.1	490	60	68
58	Male	1.0	0.4	182	14	20
72	Male	3.9	2.0	195	27	59

***Figure 16.3**: Showing the high-level structure of the dataset with rows and columns*

Step 3: Analyzing data

There are various levels of analysis to be done; some are shown in the following for reference:

a. **Analyzing the datatypes of columns**: This is used to understand the datatypes of columns so that appropriate action can be taken. E.g., some values which look numeric may be of string type and require transformation at later stages.

   - **Python command**:
```
print(df.info())
```
   - **Output**:
```
RangeIndex: 583 entries, 0 to 582
Data columns (total 11 columns):
 #   Column                                    Non-Null Count  Dtype
```

```
---  ------                          --------------  -----
 0   Age                             583 non-null    int64
 1   Gender                          583 non-null    object
 2   Total_Bilirubin                 583 non-null    float64
 3   Direct_Bilirubin                583 non-null    float64
 4   Alkaline_Phosphotase            583 non-null    int64
 5   Alamine_Aminotransferase        583 non-null    int64
 6   Aspartate_Aminotransferase      583 non-null    int64
 7   Total_Protiens                  583 non-null    float64
 8   Albumin                         583 non-null    float64
 9   Albumin_and_Globulin_Ratio      579 non-null    float64
 10  Has_liver_disease(Yes_1, No_2)  583 non-null    int64
```

The above table shows that most of the columns are integer and float types, which means they can be used in a machine learning algorithm; however, the gender column may require a data type change.

b. **Descriptive analysis of each column**: This is done to understand and summarize data in a meaningful way before making decisions on applying advanced analytics.

- **Python command**:

```
for features in df.columns:
  print('----***Describing',features,'***----','\n')
  print(df[features].describe())
  print('-------------------')
```

- **Output**:

```
----***Describing Age ***----
count    583.000000
mean      44.746141
std       16.189833
min        4.000000
25%       33.000000
50%       45.000000
75%       58.000000
max       90.000000
Name: Age, dtype: float64
-------------------
----***Describing Total_Bilirubin ***----
```

```
count     583.000000
mean        3.298799
std         6.209522
min         0.400000
25%         0.800000
50%         1.000000
75%         2.600000
max        75.000000
Name: Total_Bilirubin, dtype: float64
------------------------------------------------------------
```

Also, so on for all the other columns or features.

This step helps us see the details about each column/feature. E.g., for **Age** column, the data shows:

- **count** **583.000000**: Total number of patients is 583
- **mean** **44.74614**: The average age of patients is 44.74
- **std** **16.189833**: It tells how much ages differ from the average, i.e., 44.74
- **min** **4.000000**: The youngest patient in the dataset has an age 4
- 25% **33.000000**: 25% of patients are below age 33
- 50% **45.000000**: Half of the patient count is below 45
- 75% **58.000000**: 75% of the patients are below 58
- **max** **90.000000**: Oldest patient's age is 90

Descriptive analysis can also help identify important data characteristics and issues such as skewed distributions, outliers, missing values, inconsistencies, and potential data quality problems before further analysis or model building.

c. **Visual analysis of some key features**: This is done to represent the data graphically so that patterns, trends, and insights can be understood quickly and clearly.

- **Python command**: To see the age distribution of the patients:

  ```
  ageplot = sns.distplot(df['Age'])
  ```

- **Output**:

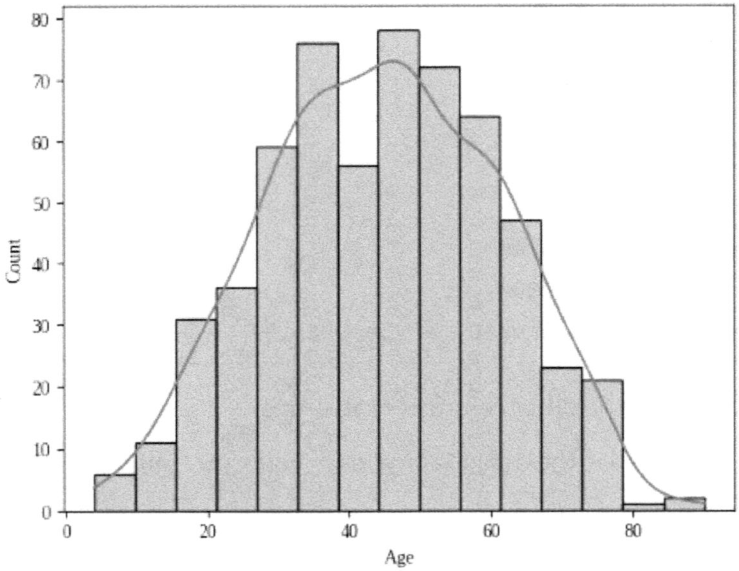

***Figure 16.4**: Distribution of age, showing most of the individual are between 30 and 60 years*

- **Python command**: To see the gender wise distribution of liver disease:

```
gender_dist = df['Gender'].value_counts().plot(kind='bar')
```

- **Output**:

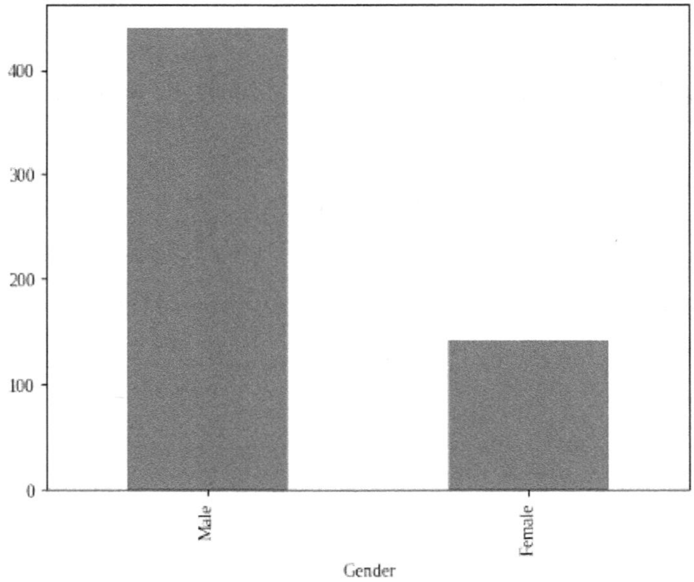

***Figure 16.5**: Gender wise distribution, showing males are more in quantity than female in the dataset*

- **Python command**: To show the distribution of patients with liver disease or not:

```
#As per data, how many patients have liver problem or not
lp = df['Has_liver_disease(Yes_1, No_2)'].value_counts().sort_
index().plot(kind='bar', color=['green', 'red'])
lp.set_xticks([0, 1])
lp.set_xticklabels(['Have Liver Problem','No Liver Problem'])
# Set the labels
# Add labels and title
lp.set_xlabel('Liver Condition')
lp.set_ylabel('Count')
lp.set_title('Liver Patient Distribution')
for p in lp.patches:
    lp.annotate(str(int(p.get_height())),
                (p.get_x() + p.get_width() / 2, p.get_height()),
                ha='center', va='bottom')
plt.show()
```

- **Output**:

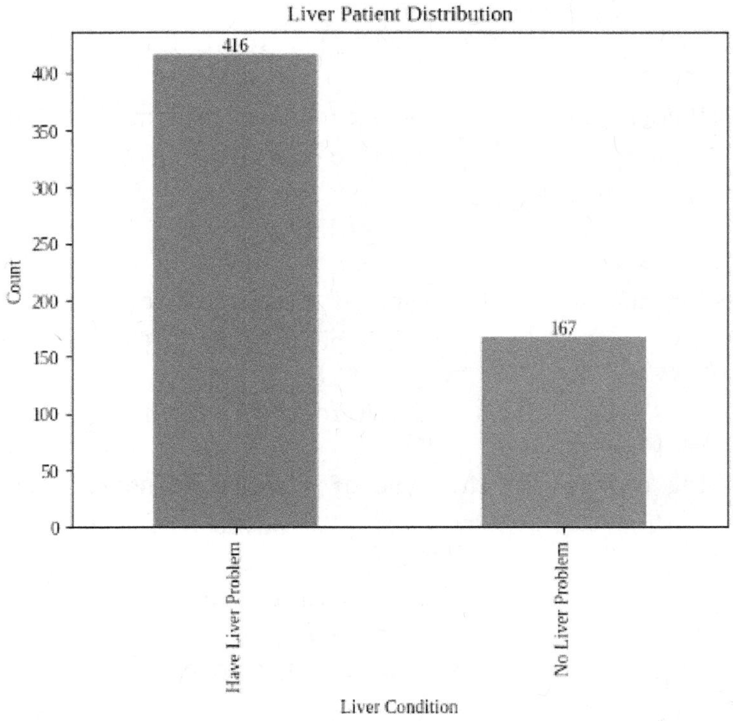

***Figure 16.6**: Figure representing the Liver problem distribution*

d. **Handling string-type columns**: This is cleaning the spaces from all string data type columns.

   - **Python command**:

```
for i in df.columns:
  if df[i].dtypes == 'object':
    df[i] = df[i].replace(' ','')
    print(i)
```

   - **Output**: All the string columns will have unnecessary space removed. In this case, the **Gender** column is the object type that will be corrected.

e. **Data preparation**: Changing the type and handling missing values wherever applicable.

   - **Python command**:

```
#Making changes in the Gender column without any Ordinal dependency
df['Gender']= df['Gender'].replace({'Male': 1, 'Female': 0})
#Making changes in the type of Total_biliribin columns
df['Total_Bilirubin'] = pd.to_numeric(df['Total_
Bilirubin'], errors='coerce')
df['Total_Bilirubin'].fillna(df['Total_Bilirubin'].mode()
[0],inplace=True)
#Making changes in the type of Direct_biliribin columns
df['Direct_Bilirubin'] = pd.to_numeric(df['Direct_
Bilirubin'], errors='coerce')
df['Direct_Bilirubin'].fillna(df['Direct_Bilirubin'].mode()
[0],inplace=True)
#Making changes in the type of Alkaline_Phosphotase columns
df['Alkaline_Phosphotase'] = pd.to_numeric(df['Alkaline_
Phosphotase'], errors='coerce')
df['Alkaline_Phosphotase'].fillna(df['Alkaline_Phosphotase'].mode()
[0],inplace=True)
#Making changes in the type of Alamine_Aminotransferase columns
df['Alamine_Aminotransferase'] = pd.to_numeric(df['Alamine_
Aminotransferase'], errors='coerce')
df['Alamine_Aminotransferase'].fillna(df['Alamine_
Aminotransferase'].mode()[0],inplace=True)
#Making changes in the type of Aspartate_Aminotransferase columns
df['Aspartate_Aminotransferase'] = pd.to_numeric(df['Aspartate_
Aminotransferase'], errors='coerce')
df['Aspartate_Aminotransferase'].fillna(df['Aspartate_
```

```
Aminotransferase'].mode()[0],inplace=True)
#Making changes in the type of Total_Protiens columns
df['Total_Protiens'] = pd.to_numeric(df['Total_
Protiens'], errors='coerce')
df['Total_Protiens'].fillna(df['Total_Protiens'].mode()
[0],inplace=True)
#Filling null values in Albumin_and_Globulin_Ratio column
df['Albumin_and_Globulin_Ratio'].fillna(df['Albumin_and_Globulin_
Ratio'].mode()[0],inplace=True)
```

- **Output**: All the columns have been converted to numeric format for better calculations, and missing values have been imputed by their mean, mode, etc.

f. **Validation**: Validating that there are no null values in the dataset now.

- **Python command**:

```
df.isnull().sum().sort_values(ascending=False)
```

- **Output**:

Age	0
Gender	0
Total_Bilirubin	0
Direct_Bilirubin	0
Alkaline_Phosphotase	0
Alamine_Aminotransferase	0
Aspartate_Aminotransferase	0
Total_Protiens	0
Albumin	0
Albumin_and_Globulin_Ratio	0
Has_liver_disease(Yes_1, No_2)	0

***Figure 16.7**: None of the columns has any null values after data processing*

Shows that no column has missing values.

g. **Re-analyzing the dataset after transformation**: This is a repetition of *Step b* above to validate the summarization of the data after the transformation.

h. **Data analysis for feature extraction**: In this step, the correlation between different features is calculated. When two or more features are correlated, then one of them can be removed.

- **Python command**:

```
corr = df.corr()
ax = sns.heatmap(corr,
                 cmap="Greys",
                 annot=True,
                 fmt=".1f",
                 annot_kws={"size": 8})
# Set proper tick labels
ax.set_xticklabels(corr.
columns, rotation=45, ha='right', fontsize=8)
ax.set_yticklabels(corr.columns, rotation=0, fontsize=8)
plt.show()
```

- **Output**:

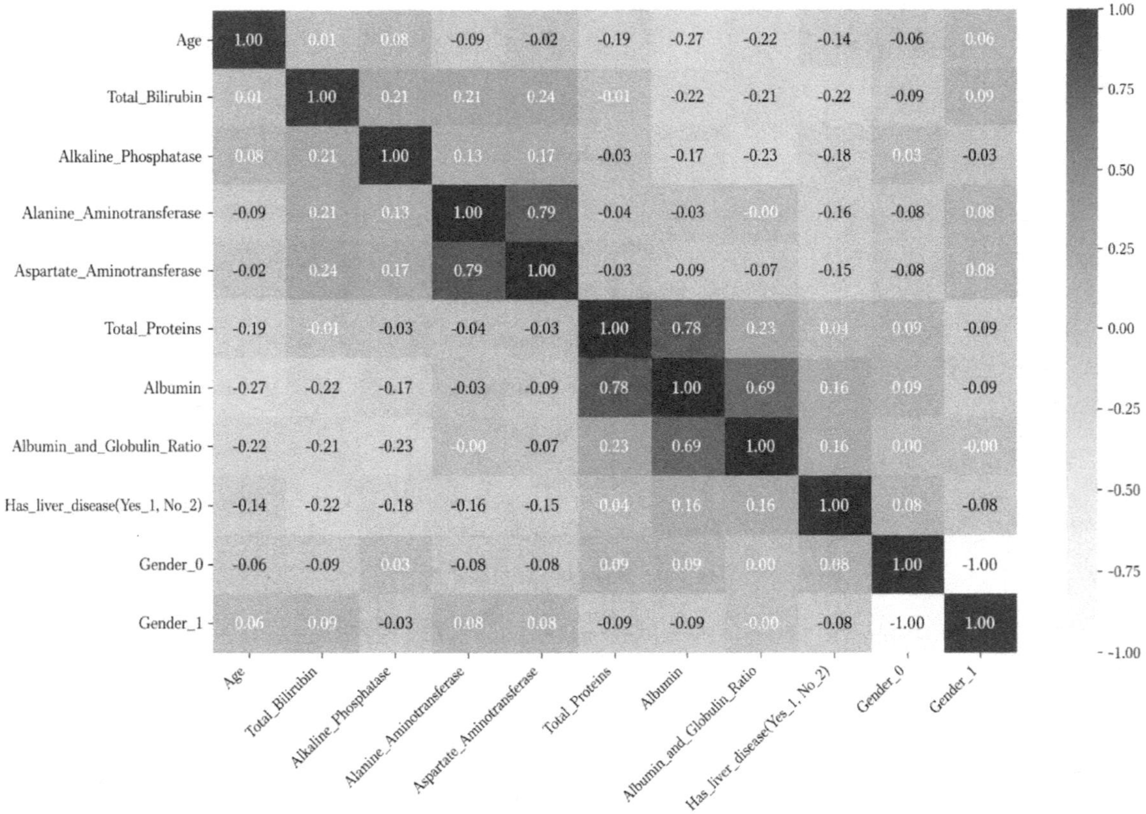

__Figure 16.8__: Heatmap showing the correlation between all the features

From bivariate analysis, we can conclude that **Total_Bilirubin** and **Direct_Bilirubin** are quite correlated with 87%, and one of them can be removed.

i. **Removing the unnecessary columns**:

  - **Python command**:

```
#Dropping the Direct_bilirubin column
df.drop(['Direct_Bilirubin'],axis=1,inplace=True)
```

  - **Output**: The column **Direct_Bilirubin** was removed successfully.

j. **Data transformation**: Applying 1-hot encoding to relevant columns, since most machine learning algorithms work with numbers.

  - **Python command**:

```
#Applying 1 hot encoding on the Gender column so that there is no
Ordinal dependency
df['Gender']= df['Gender'].replace({'Male': 1, 'Female': 0})
df = pd.concat([df, pd.get_
dummies(df['Gender'], prefix='Gender')], axis=1)
df = df.drop(columns=['Gender'])
```

  - **Output**: Converts the gender column into two columns (**Gender_0** and **Gender_1**) using one-hot encoding and then removes the original column. And converts the categories to numbers.

Step 4: Make a prediction

In this section, the cleansed data will be used in a machine learning algorithm for advanced analytics.

a. **Selecting the right data**: Deciding on the data for the training and test set.

  - **Python command**:

```
training_features= ['Age', 'Total_Bilirubin', 'Alkaline_
Phosphotase',
       'Alamine_Aminotransferase', 'Aspartate_Aminotransferase',
       'Total_Protiens', 'Albumin', 'Albumin_and_Globulin_
Ratio', 'Gender_0', 'Gender_1']
target = ['Has_liver_disease(Yes_1, No_2)']
X_train, X_test, Y_train, Y_test = train_test_split(df[training_
features],
                                                    df[target],
                                                    test_size=0.2,
```

```
random_state=12,

stratify=df[target],

shuffle=True)
```

- **Output**: Splitting the dataset into training (80%) and testing (20%) sets while preserving the class distribution of the target variable.

b. **Data normalization**: Normalizing the data using the standard scalar.

- **Python command**:

```
from sklearn.preprocessing import StandardScaler #Z = (X-mu)/sigma
# Assuming X_train and X_test are your training and testing data
scaler = StandardScaler()
# Fit the scaler on the training data
X_train = scaler.fit_transform(X_train)
# Transform the testing data using the same scaler
X_test = scaler.transform(X_test)
```

- **Output**: Features are standardized so they have a mean of 0 and a standard deviation of 1.

c. **Selecting a machine learning algorithm**: Using a decision tree.

- **Python command**:

```
from sklearn import tree
dt = tree.DecisionTreeClassifier(
  max_depth=5,
  min_samples_split=2,
  min_samples_leaf=2,
  max_features=10,
  random_state=42,
  criterion='entropy',
  )
dt.fit(X_train, Y_train)
predicted=dt.predict(X_test)
# Model Accuracy, how often is the classifier correct?
print("Accuracy:",metrics.accuracy_score(Y_test, predicted))
```

Output:

```
Accuracy: 0.6923076923076923
```

It shows the percentage of the prediction that is correct, i.e., 69.23% of the predictions are correct.

d. **Prediction**: Predicting the liver disease using the manual input data

- **Python command**:

```
patient_data = np.array([[17,0.9,202,22,19,7.4, 4.1, 1.20,0,1]])
# Prediction
prediction = dt.predict(patient_data)
# Output result
if prediction[0] == 1:
    print("Result: Patient HAS Liver Disease")
else:
    print("Result: Patient DOES NOT have Liver Disease")
```

- **Output**:

```
Result: Patient HAS Liver Disease
```

Step 5: Optimize

In this step, various optimization techniques are applied to improve the model's predictive performance, efficiency, and reliability. The model is evaluated and fine-tuned using performance metrics such as accuracy, precision, recall, F1-score, and confusion matrix analysis.

For medical classification problems such as liver disease prediction, relying only on accuracy may not be sufficient because false negatives and false positives can have serious consequences. In this use case, recall (sensitivity) is particularly important because missing an actual liver disease patient (false negative) may delay diagnosis and treatment. Optimization techniques such as hyperparameter tuning, feature selection, cross-validation, and threshold adjustment can be used to improve the model's overall effectiveness and balance between different evaluation metrics.

Step 6: Measure

Testing the model accuracy after the optimization:

- **Python command**:

```
#checking the suggested optimized parameters from Optuna
predicted=dt_opt.predict(X_test)
print("Accuracy:",metrics.accuracy_score(Y_test, predicted))
```

- **Output**:

```
Accuracy: 0.7094017094017094
```

The optimization actually generalizes better or improves important metrics. Here, in this case, we can see the accuracy increased from 69.23% to 70.94%. However, as discussed earlier, for a medical classification use cases, additional metrics such as precision, recall, F1-score, and confusion matrix analysis are equally important and should not be ignored.

Step 7: Reporting

The model output report can be published, and a comparative study of multiple algorithms can be conducted to evaluate and identify the most effective model.

The above process is just an example that shows how we approach a problem and take valuable steps in order to understand the requirements, select the right dataset, apply the data transformations, and make it ready for advanced analytics. Multiple machine learning algorithms can be used, and their accuracy can be checked against the real-world output. The algorithms must be tuned to accommodate the changes in trends or user behavior with time as a continuous activity.

Conclusion

This chapter covered the practical aspects of BA, where several practical ways of BA can be applied. The importance of the practical techniques was deliberated in this chapter along with the different types of techniques that could be applied based on specific business scenarios, such as seasonality analysis, trend analysis, comparative analysis, etc. These analyses are core but could be missed in the initial phases of BA, and the cost of implementation of these at later stages is much higher. Finally, a real use case was also covered, which shows how the processes mentioned in the book can be applied in practice to support business-decision making. In real-world implementations, such analytical solutions should also include continuous validation, monitoring, and iterative improvements over time to maintain reliability and effectiveness under changing business conditions.

References

1. *Course provided by Futurense for IIT Jodhpur for PG diploma in data engineering*
2. **https://medium.com/@shwedoshi/business-problem-solving-with-data-science-a76cf3f0fc7**
3. **https://my.clevelandclinic.org/health/body/21481-liver**
4. **https://www.mayoclinic.org/tests-procedures/liver-function-tests/about/pac-20394595**
5. **https://medlineplus.gov/lab-tests/globulin-test/**
6. **https://www.maxhealthcare.in/blogs/bilirunbin-test-normal-range-and-benefits**
7. **http://archive.ics.uci.edu/dataset/225/ilpd+indian+liver+patient+dataset**

Index

A

B

C

D

www.ingramcontent.com/pod-product-compliance
Lightning Source LLC
LaVergne TN
LVHW060542061126
851857LV00017B/1869